BYE BYE
BIG BANG

D0967394

Bye Bye Big Bang – The Song

Throw out all that phony stuff;
It can't be good enough.
Bye Bye, Big Bang.

Truth and science is for you;
Cosmic nonsense just won't do
Bye Bye, Big Bang.

None of them can know
Or understand it.
Oh, what awful garbage
They all hand out.

Use your head and think it through;
You'll arrive at the truth.
Bye Bye, Big Bang.

BYE BYE BIG BANG
Hello Reality

William C. Mitchell

COSMIC SENSE BOOKS

**Post Office Box 3472
Carson City, Nevada 89702
U S A**

– To Holly –

Hello Reality

© Copyright, 2002 by William C. Mitchell. All Rights Reserved.

COSMIC SENSE BOOKS
Post Office Box 3472,
Carson City, Nevada 89702, U S A

Library of Congress Catalog Card Number: 2001119358
ISBN: 0-9643188-1-4

THIRD PRINTING
- M M V -

Book Design & Prepress:
Paul Cirac
WHITE SAGE STUDIOS
Virginia City, Nevada
whitesage@gbis.com

Printed by Sheridan Books, Chelsea Michigan

CONTENTS

APPENDICES

FIGURES

PREFACE

I am driven to try to right a terrible error that pervades the world of science. That wrong is the almost total acceptance of the Big Bang cosmological theory.

Virtually the whole world has accepted that erroneous theory on the authority of those they believe to be experts in that field. It has been taught for decades. Not only is it taught as absolute truth in class rooms and text books, but it is also disseminated to the public throughout the world in journals, magazines, books, and newspapers, and on radio, television and the internet.

I've been reading, studying, calculating, thinking, talking and writing about cosmology full-time for over a dozen years. At the start of that time I, like most others, had accepted the Big Bang, but as time went on, I found more and more flaws in it—both scientific and logical. After about a half a dozen years of that I wrote a book that was primarily devoted to exposing the flaws that I had found.

In discussions of those flaws with others, I would frequently be asked, "If you don't believe in the Big Bang, what do you believe in?" Therefore, I presented in that book a variation of the old steady state cosmology that incorporated relativity and quantum theory, that was intended to avoid the flaws of Big Bang Theory or old Steady State Theory. I believed that scheme might provide explanations for expansion based on cosmic repulsion, and for the creation of new matter in space based on quantum theory's postulated creation of new matter out of the energy of the vacuum, not in one huge vacuum fluctuation, but particle by particle in intergalactic space.

However, as my studies continued for a few more years, I abandoned that idea, and, about three years ago, a sudden insight provided me with the basis for a recycling universe cosmological theory that truly avoids the problems of those previous theories.

Since then I have been writing this book, not only to present all the old problems of Big Bang Theory and a number of new problems I have since discovered, but primarily to present a rational replacement for the Big Bang.

That new cosmology is not based on complex nonsense, such as the curved four-dimensional space-time of relativity, or the instantaneous creation of the universe out of nothing or a quantum fluctuation of the energy of empty space, but on astronomical observations, science and logic.

I am so appalled that a theory so flawed as that of the Big Bang has been accepted by virtually all the world, that I have been driven all these years to try and correct that error. Now, after years of night-and-day preoccupation with this subject, I am thrilled to be able to present a new cosmological theory that is far superior to the illogical Big Bang.

I am grateful to several friends, especially Vincent Sauvé and Professor Roger Rydin, who have taken their time to provide valuable suggestions for improvements to the manuscript of this book, and I would like to thank John Chappell, director of the Natural Philosophy Alliance, who has encouraged me in this work for several years.

I would also also would like to thank science writer Helge Kragh for writing his invaluable book *Cosmology and Controversy*, from which I learned (and quoted) much regarding the history of cosmology, and I will always be grateful to plasma physicist Tony Peratt, astronomer Chip Arp and cosmologist Professor Jayant Narlikar for their past encouragement in my struggle to expose the fallacies of Big Bang Theory.

I am especially grateful to my wife for having tolerated my involvement in this activity for long hours, day after day, for all these years, meanwhile ever continuing to encourage my efforts.

W. C. M.

INTRODUCTION

Virtually every media article or program that touches on the subjects of astronomy or cosmology presents the Big Bang cosmological theory (BBT) as scientific fact, and a Big Bang (BB) has been almost universally accepted by the literate populace of the world as the origin of the universe.

Education establishments involved in the fields of astronomy, astrophysics, theoretical physics and cosmology are dominated by those who have accepted BBT as the theory to be pursued, and those who seriously question it are generally considered disruptive, ridiculed and derogatorily referred to as big bang bashers. As the result of those attitudes, and other considerations, alternate cosmological possibilities are left uninvestigated. While other possibilities are ignored, untold man-hours and vast sums of money are spent in pursuit of data in support of the prevailing theory that has little basis in science, logic or fact.

Such endeavors are not in keeping with the ideals of impartial scientific investigation, and it is all but forgotten that BBT is not fact, but an unproven theory. However, due to the efforts of fighters for evenhanded cosmological investigation, and despite the powerful influence of mainstream BB cosmologists, evidence against the BB has been building to the point where the world may soon begin to question it.

• • •

The purpose of this book is not only to present evidence against BBT, but, more importantly, to present a new recycling universe cosmology (RUC) that, unlike BBT, is in agreement with astronomical observations, accepted science and logic, and to demonstrate the superiority of that theory to BBT. But, in order for the reader to evaluate or appreciate that new cosmology, he or she should have some background on the prevailing theory and its many problems. So this book is organized in the following manner.

The first two chapters present an abbreviated history of cosmology and a short description of the some of the attributes of the BB universe, such as its creation, its smoothness and its age.

The next three chapters (3, 4 and 5) discuss its chronology, its various "cases", and galaxy formation according to BBT.

The sixth chapter presents items that are thought to provide proof of BBT.

In the next six chapters (7 through 12) some of the better known problems of BBT are discussed. Those include singularity problems, smoothness and horizon problems, flatness and missing mass problems, and problems related to the Hubble constant, distance and velocity measurements, the so-called age paradox, and galaxy formation in the BB universe.

In the seven chapters following that (13 through 19) some lesser known problems are discussed. Those include problems related to the microwave background radiation (MBR), MBR photons, neutrinos from the BB, redshift, quasars, chronology, and elements from the BB.

Three chapters (20 through 22) are then presented on BB problems related to relativity and the expansion of the universe, on which it is based, and those related to quantum theory, on which the inflationary variety of BBT is based.

In chapters (23 and 24) inflation theory is briefly described, and some of its faults are presented.

Chapter 25 and 26 present a review of some logical problems regarding BBT, and some violations of scientific method by BB cosmologists.

Before getting into the recycling universe cosmology, Chapter 27 provides a short discussion of some of the alternatives to BBT that have been presented in the past.

Then, in a very long, and perhaps tedious, chapter (28), a new alternative recycling universe cosmology is described, which is followed by a concluding chapter.

Before the essential bibliography, name and subject indexes, there are five appendixes. Four of those (A through D) provide background information regarding relativity, particle physics, quantum theory and some of the wild ideas of "modern" theorists. A fifth appendix (E) presents some of the calculations that support the work presented in the main text of the book.

• • •

In this book, for the sake of simplicity, the words "smoothness" or "uniformity" (of the universe) are used in place of several other commonly, and somewhat redundantly, used words by BB cosmologists to convey a similar concept. Those words are isotropy, homogeneity, Copernican Principle and Cosmological Principle.

Isotropy is defined as indicating the universe is the same in all directions, but not necessarily the same everywhere. Homogeneity is defined as indicating the universe to be the same everywhere, but not necessarily the same in all directions. (If the universe is isotropic everywhere it is also homogeneous.)

The Copernican Principle states that we occupy no special place in that universe, and the Cosmological Principle, in addition, says that is true for any other observers there might be in the universe.

For economy of ink and space, the letters "BB" are used for Big Bang, "BBT" for Big Bang Theory, "SS" for Steady State, "SST" for Steady State Theory, and "RUC" for Recycling Universe Cosmology.

Also, MYRs is used for million years, BYRs for billion years, MLYs for million light years, BLYs for billion light years, Pc for parsec, and Mpc for million parsecs.

EMR is used for electromagnetic radiation, and MBR for microwave background radiation, CDM for cold dark matter, IGS for intergalactic space, GUT for Grand Unified Theory, and TOE for Theory of Everything.

Also for economy of words, "establishment" or "astronomical/cosmological community" is used to mean those mainstream cosmologists, astronomers, astrophysicists and theoretical physicists who have accepted BB, inflation theory, or both, as true science.

The terms "cosmic repulsion" and "cosmological constant" refer to the same phenomena.

The terms "Schwarzschild radius" and "event horizon" refer to the same phenomena.

• • •

The reader is asked to remember that the BBT described in the early chapters of this book is not scientific fact, but merely a widely accepted, unproven theory.

ONE

Some History of Big Bang Cosmology

This chapter presents a very abbreviated sketch of some of the more important events in the history of BB cosmology.

Early Ideas.

For a number of years astronomers had noted that the spectrum of radiation from some stars was slightly shifted toward the red. It was guessed that it might be due to their receding velocity. In 1924 German astronomer Carl Wirtz correlated the available star data to their faintness, suggesting that their distance correlated to their velocity.

Belgian cleric, physicist and astronomer Georges Lemaitre, who had studied under British astronomer Sir Arthur Eddington, associated those ideas with General Relativity and was able to postulate an expanding universe. As the matter of the universe expanded, it thinned out, cooled down and aggregated into stars and galaxies.

It is interesting to note that in 1848 the American author Edgar Allen Poe had presented a cosmological scheme that was similar to that postulated by Lemaitre three quarters of a century later, and the German philosopher Friedrich Nietzsche also had suggested a similar universe. Also of possible interest, Swedish physicist Hannes Alfvén and others have suggested that Catholic priest Lemaitre's work was an attempt to reconcile his scientific knowledge with church doctrine.

While at Harvard in 1924 and 1925 Lemaitre heard from Edwin Hubble of the relationship of the redshift and distance. Following that, he spent two years developing his cosmological theory based on Albert Einstein's equations of General Relativity, which was published in 1927, two years before Hubble published data that was believed to confirm the expansion of the universe.

Lemaitre's paper, which appeared in a little known publication, was hardly noticed until 1929, when its value was recognized by Eddington; and within a couple of years his work became widely known. In 1931 he published an expanded version of his theory which incorporated the idea that the universe started from a highly compressed and extremely hot state. Because the Second Law of Thermodynamics indicated that the entropy of the universe was ever increasing, he suggested that it might have originated at a very low entropy, that of a "primeval atom".

In 1928 an American theorist, Howard Percy Robertson, independently presented a theory similar to Lemaitre's.

Although the term "Big Bang" wasn't coined until much later (in 1950 by Fred Hoyle, one of the originators of the rival Steady State cosmology), Lemaitre is considered to be the father of the Big Bang. But perhaps that honor should have gone to multi-talented and adventurous Russian meteorologist and mathematician Alexander Friedmann.

Einstein's General Relativity.

Albert Einstein, and others of his time, thought that the universe was static; that is, except for the planets of the solar system, all the heavenly bodies were fixed in space. Therefore, Einstein's interpretation of his own theory didn't include consideration of an expanding universe. However, Friedmann's solution to Einstein's General Relativity equations resulted in a family of expanding universe possibilities. His work clearly included consideration of an expanding universe of finite time since its creation which, at one point, he guessed to be "tens of billions of our ordinary years."

That occurred in about 1922, when Friedmann was in his early 30s. Unfortunately, as a result of one of his adventures in 1925, he became ill and died of typhus fever at the age of 37. Possibly because of his absence, neither he, or any one else, contested the acceptance of Lemaitre as the father of what later became known as BBT. (It seems unclear whether Lemaitre had been aware of Friedmann's work prior to publication of his ideas.)

Standard BBT.

The astronomical observations of Edwin Hubble and Milton Humason in the late 1920s provided data that appeared to confirm an expanding universe. Over 20 years later, Russian-American physicist and MIT professor, George Gamow, who was born in Odessa, Russia and studied under Friedmann at the University of Petrograd, utilized Friedmann's solutions to Einstein's General Relativity field equations, and in 1948 presented what became accepted as the basis for the standard BB cosmology that has followed.

Einstein's equations contained a term of undetermined magnitude, now known as the "cosmological constant," that he assumed represented a cosmic repulsive force that opposed the force of gravity and provided the balancing force required for a static universe. But following Friedmann's work, later supported by the work of mathematicians Howard Robertson and Arthur Walker, and after it became accepted that the universe was expanding in accordance with Hubble's law, most physicists, including Einstein, accepted the BB cosmology.

That cosmological model was also called the "FWR cosmology" after Friedmann, Walker, and , Robertson; and sometimes this was expanded to "FLWR cosmology", to include Lemaitre. It is also sometimes referred to as the Friedmann-Lemaitre model, but I will call it "Standard BBT."

Upon the general acceptance of an expanding universe, Einstein abandoned his cosmic repulsion term (by merely setting it equal to zero), calling it the greatest mistake of his career and, after some hesitation, accepted Friedmann's work. (His initial reaction to Friedmann's solution to his equations had been that it was merely an exercise in mathematics.)

Unfortunately, if he had not interpreted his cosmological constant term as representing a gravity balancing force, he might very well have crowned his achievements by showing his equations to predict the expansion of the universe. Instead, that prediction was made by Friedmann.

Over the intervening years, Gamow's basic theory has evolved.

BB scenarios based on General Relativity have been elaborated, and Gamow's original age of the BB universe of less than two billion years (and Friedmann's guess of tens of BYRs), has been gradually adjusted to 10 to 15 billion. In general, three alternate scenarios for closed, open or flat universes, resulted from the FWR solutions.

Competing Ideas.

BBT suffered from several technical problems and, as a result, a competing theory, the Steady State Cosmological Theory (SST), proposed in the late 1940s by scientists who questioned BBT, gained some credence. Major contributors to that theory included British mathematicians Herman Bondi, Thomas Gold and British astronomer Fred Hoyle.

In addition to SST, other cosmological schemes, such as Plasma Theory, each appearing to have some merit, have been proposed, but none of those have received wide acceptance.

A number of factors were felt to provide proof of BBT; and in 1965, when microwave background radiation (MBR) was found to be received equally from all directions of space, in accordance with predictions by some BB proponents—including Gamow and his students, Ralph Alpher and Robert Herman—it was accepted as virtual positive proof of BBT.

As a result, SST, was almost totally abandoned.

Inflation.

As time progressed, questions regarding details of BBT have arisen.

Through the years many modifications to that theory have been proposed, and some have been incorporated. Most innovative among them is the idea of inflation; an enormously rapid "inflationary" expansion of the minutely tiny universe before the start of the traditional hot BB expansion that had gained acceptance over the past 20 years. Quantum theory, which had been developed and became accepted years after BBT had originated, was put to work by theorists to solve some BB problems.

In 1981 MIT professor Alan Guth published his theory of inflation that was designed to solve those problems. He postulated a vast superluminal expansion that occurred very shortly after the BB. That occurrence, which, based on some aspects of quantum theory, was claimed to overcome the most serious problems of Standard BBT. As a result, an inflationary BB model was readily accepted by much of the establishment.

It's of interest to note that Einstein's cosmic repulsion was resurrected in support of inflation theory.

New Inflation.

Unfortunately, Guth's inflation introduced some problems of its own.

Among other problems, it resulted in unacceptable "bubbles" in the universe. In the mid-1980s Russian physicist Andrei Linde invented a modified inflation theory, called "new inflation." Its vastly greater rate of expansion was said to solve Guth's bubble problem while solving several other problems of Standard BBT.

The Appeal of BBT.

BB Cosmological theory seems to have been the natural outcome of Einstein's General Theory of Relativity and the later discovery of the expansion of the universe. In hindsight, the idea of tracing back the rate of expansion of the universe in accordance with solutions to Einstein's gravitational field equations to a time of zero size, infinite density and infinite pressure seems inevitable.

That concept has had immense appeal. Stories of the origin of the universe abound in the various religions of the world, but none of those are acceptable as literal truth to modern scientific minds. To those minds the BB filled a void by providing a reasonably credible evolution of the universe and at least a stopgap concept of its origin.

Man's intense desire for knowledge of the origin of his world and himself, as evidenced by the myths of all the tribes of the world, seems to have been at least partially and tentatively answered.

BBT has been well received by the more liberal minded of the Judeo-Christian community who have found it to be an acceptable interpretation of the Bible's story of creation.

Difficulties Remain.

Although inflation schemes have been accepted by some as providing solutions to the major problems of BBT, many of those problems remain; and inflation has introduced some additional problems of its own.

Because some hopes for the verification of that theory have failed to materialize, it has been abandoned by some who have now turned their attention to finding other means of support for BBT.

Several serious problems, such as a violation of the conservation of mass/energy and problems concerning the age of the universe, continue to plague BBT.

TWO

Standard
Big Bang
Theory

This chapter is intended to provide a short general introduction to Standard BBT, and some of its attributes.

BB Cases Based on General Relativity.

The Friedmann solutions to Einstein's General relativity equations are said to result in three possible "cases" of the more-or-less Standard BB universe that has continued to expand since the BB.

Those include the "closed," "open" and "flat" universe cases. In each of those the expansion of the universe would have started at the time of the BB at a velocity that is said to be somewhere between the speed of light and 1,000 times that rate. The BB cases introduced here are discussed in more detail in the next chapter.

The Closed BB Universe.

Some BBers believe the average density of the universe is greater than a critical amount. Therefore its space is positively curved. Its rate of expansion is decreasing and will someday cease. It will then begin to collapse at an ever increasing rate until it ends up in what has been called the "Big Crunch."

Of those who accept the collapsing universe case, some think that it has done so in the past, and some that it will continue to do so in the future.

The Open BB Universe.

Many BB cosmologists believe in an open universe whose average density is less than a critical amount, and its space is negatively curved. It is expanding and will continue to expand in the future, but at an ever decreasing rate.

The Flat BB Universe.

Many BBers subscribe to the flat universe case wherein the average density of its uncurved space is at a critical value. It is a borderline case between the open and the closed universe case. Its rate of expansion is decreasing and will also eventually cease.

A Fixed-Rate BB Universe.

A fixed-rate BB universe, one in which the rate of expansion has remained the same since the BB, is not included as a possible Standard BB case.

BB Happened Everywhere.

The idea of expanding curved space-time of General Relativity incorporates the concept that the BB didn't happen at a single point within the present universe; it happened at a single point that has expanded to be everywhere within the present universe.

As one group of astronomers (Gott, Gunn, Schramm and Tinsley) have put it, "it is not sensible to ask where the big bang took place. The point-universe was not an object isolated in space; it was the entire universe, and so the only answer is that the big bang happened everywhere."

A single site of the BB cannot be found. It is everywhere in the universe.

The Centerless BB Universe.

In keeping with the above, our galaxy may be thought of as being at at the center of the universe, but so is every other galaxy. We are no more in the center than any other "observer" in another part of the BB universe might be.

In accordance with Einstein's work, and that of mathematicians who followed him, the concept of curved space-time that has no edge and no center has been incorporated into BBT.

The Expanding BB Universe.

Also in accordance with General Relativity and BBT, rather than the matter of the universe expanding in space, it is the space of the universe that is expanding.

As British astrophysicist and BB cosmologist W. B. Bonnor once said, "This is not merely a difference of words, the active role of space in dynamics is one of the main ideas which Einstein brought to physics when he created general relativity." And Einstein eventually wrote (in 1961) "that theory [general relativity] demands the expansion of space."

Nothing Before the BB.

Regardless of whether it is closed , open or flat, the BB universe is said to have come out of nothing. That is, before the BB there was no time, no space, no matter, and no energy; just an inconceivable nothing.

Among the many prominent BB cosmologist who have endorsed that idea are Heinz R. Pagels, who, in *Perfect Symmetry,* (in 1985) explained how, "the very origin of the universe—how the fabric of space, time and matter can be created out of nothing," and Paul Davies in *Physics and Our View of the World* (also in 1985) confirmed that, "the appearance of the Universe from nothing need not violate the laws of physics."

The BB Singularity.

At the start of the BB the universe was minutely tiny, and it had infinite temperature (energy), density, pressure and gravity. In accordance with General Relativity, rather than infinite gravity, it would be more proper to say that its space had infinite curvature.

That situation describes a "singularity;" something that can't be coped with by science or mathematics.

BB Smoothness.

Standard BBT also postulates that the BB explosion was perfectly isotropic and homogeneous, and that the present universe continues to be "smooth" or "uniform."

Since the discovery of gigantic galactic formations in the universe, that feature has been modified to, smoothness of the present universe prevails "on the very large scale."

Hubble Expansion and the Age of the BB Universe.

The expansion of the universe is presently believed to be that of the Hubble rate, as expressed by the Hubble constant, which is thought to be on the order of 50 to 80 kilometers per second per megaparsec (km/sec/Mpc), equivalent to about 15 to 25 kilometers per second per million light years (km/sec/MLYs).

According to those figures, if there had been a fixed rate of expansion, the age of the universe would be 12 to 20 billion years (BYRs). That time is called the "Hubble time" or "Hubble age", which is often presented as the age of the BB universe. [Hubble time equals the velocity of light divided by the Hubble constant, $T_H = c/H_0$.]

However, most BBers have accepted a flat or nearly flat universe. It turns out that, in accordance with those numbers, the age of the flat universe would be two thirds of the Hubble time, or about 8 to 13 BYRs. The age of the closed universe would be somewhat less, and the age of the open universe would somewhat more.

Particle Creation.

Following the BB, the universe continued to expand from an infinitesimally small point, its temperature cooled, and its density decreased. At various intervals of fractions of seconds following the BB the fundamental particles, out of which all the elements of the universe would later form, came into existence.

BB Nucleosynthesis.

During a short period, starting at about one second after the BB, the fusion of particles into some of the light elements of the universe occurred.

At the end of that process of "nucleosynthesis" the matter of the universe is said to have consisted of about 75 percent hydrogen, almost 25 percent of helium, a tiny percentage of lithium and deuterium.

Photon Decoupling.

At about 100,000 to 1,000,000 years after the BB the universe is said to have cooled enough for electrons to combine with the nuclei to form complete atoms, and photons were freed to travel through the universe.

Since that era, called the "decoupling," those photons, in their travel through the expanding universe, are said to have cooled to a present temperature of 2.7, and thus lost energy equivalent to a redshift of about 1,000, and filled the entire universe at an average density of about 400 per cubic centimeter. They are said to have come to us directly from the BB, and now are observed as microwave background radiation (MBR).

Neutrino Decoupling.

Considerably earlier than that, it is said that there also was a "decoupling" of neutrinos, and that about 100 of them per cubic centimeter "flood" the entire universe at the present time.

They have similarly lost energy due to cooling, but by a much greater factor than the MBR photons, to the point where they are presently undetectable.

The Formation of Stars and Galaxies.

Following the period of fusion of light elements, their accretion is said to have started and, perhaps some hundreds of millions of years later, the accumulations of matter became sufficiently dense for the nuclear processes of stars to commence, and for galaxies to form.

The Evolving BB Universe.

As supported by astronomical observation, and the *accepted interpretation of redshift data,* BBers believe that, in some manner, the rate of formation of quasars was considerably greater in the early ages of the universe. Because that provided an important point in overcoming the upstart rival SST decades ago, "evolution" has become an important element of BBT.

Cosmological Redshift.

According to BBT, the redshift that is observed in the spectrum of radiation from distant bodies in space is not Doppler redshift, but is "cosmological redshift".

Although it is sometimes loosely referred to as Doppler, that is not proper BBT terminology. Because it is the space of the universe that is expanding, redshifts of distant bodies can't be due to the velocity of matter. Therefore, it must be due to the "cosmological expansion" of space.

Lorentz Transformation Applied to Space.

It should be noted that the velocity and distance of bodies in remote space, as judged by their redshift in the accustomed manner, is not a linear function.

Although cosmological redshift is the result of the expansion of space, rather than that of the matter of space, the Lorentz transformation that is applicable to "relativistic" velocity of matter, is believed to apply to expanding space as well.

Density of the BB Universe.

Although the directly observed density of the universe is only one to two percent of the critical level, from observations of galactic rotation it can be inferred to be about ten times that amount, or 10 to 20 percent of critical. However, many BBers believe the actual average density to be much greater.

Because BBers believe that the BB universe is flat or nearly flat, they also believe that the average density is at or very near to the critical level that is postulated for the flat universe case (and inflation theory insists on that).

Missing Mass.

That critical level of density results in the belief that up to 99 percent of the mass of the universe might be of invisible missing mass. That matter is perhaps in the form of unseen cold dark matter (CDM), hot dark matter (HDM), or some combination of the two, and those might be of some exotic forms having no known characteristics other than gravitational attraction.

The presence of that missing matter is also important to BBT because it is thought to be necessary for the accretion of matter as required for the formation of galaxies, clusters and larger galactic structures.

THREE

Big Bang
Chronology

BBcosmologists have worked out a detailed chronology of the evolution of the universe that is described here and illustrated in Figure 1. In it a series of events based on The Standard Model of Particle Physics and Quantum Theory (see Appendices B and C) have been placed at various points in time in the history of the BB universe. Not all BB cosmologists agree on the details of this description, but it is representative of what exists in the literature.

10^{-43} Second.

Prior to the invention of inflation theory, other than the singularity that occurred at zero time, BBT provides no details of what might have happened before 10^{-43} second (Planck time) after the BB. At that time the temperature of the minutely small and unbelievably dense universe had cooled from infinity to about 10^{32} degrees K, and the size of the universe is said to have been 10^{-14} centimeters.

At about that energy level, equivalent to about 10^{19} GeV (billions of electron volts), a Higgs-type scalar field caused gravitons to acquire mass, lose their symmetry, and form the "quantum soup" of the early universe. Until then, the universe contained no particles with mass; just a "symmetrical gas" of energetic stuff that had no recognizable form, that is said to have been in "perfect equilibrium."

Following that, as the universe cooled and expanded, symmetry would be broken again and again to produce the other fundamental particles of the universe, that is, they would acquire mass from the hypothetical Higgs field (or fields—there may be more than one) and come into existence as unique particles.

10^{-33} Second.

According the BBT, the next postulated symmetry breaking occurred at about 10^{-33} second, when the temperature cooled to about 10^{27} K, equivalent to about 10^{15} GeV.

According to presently popular hypothetical grand unified theories the symmetry of the still tiny, dense universe was broken, this time to produce quarks and gluons, the mediators of the strong force that bind quarks to form hadrons. However, because the energy level of the universe was too great, hadrons couldn't be held together. Quarks, antiquarks and gluons that "fell out of equilibrium" remained uncombined until the temperature dropped to about 10^{14} K, at about 10^{-8} second.

10^{-10} Second.

At 10^{-10} second, when the temperature of the universe was about 10^{15} degrees K, which corresponds to about 100 GeV, weak force bosons (W minus, W plus and Z zero), and leptons (electrons, muons, neutrinos and photons) started to form.

Until then they were just part of the massless and formless energy of the symmetrical gas of the universe. They were then given mass by the Higgs scalar field, and they too "fell out of the quantum soup."

10^{-8} second after the BB, at a temperature of about 10^{14} K, electroweak symmetry breaking was complete, and the hot dense gas of the universe included leptons, quarks, gluons, antiparticles and photons. At that time the energy level of the universe became low enough to allow the coupling strength of gluons to bind quarks together, and hadrons (and antihadrons) started to form.

That continued until about 10^{-4} second (one ten-thousandth second), at a temperature of 10^{12} K, at which time no individual quarks remained.

10^{-4} Second.

Prior to 10^{-4} second continual quark/antiquark and gluon creation and annihilation had occurred.

Until then quarks were "free," but ever since then, because of the great strength of the strong force bosons, quarks have never existed singly. Scientists have seen evidence of their presence in hadrons, but never as individual particles.

At the end of the period of hadron formation the temperature of the universe had cooled to about 10^{12} K (one trillion degrees), and the density of the universe is said to have decreased to the still enormous value of about 1,000 tons per cubic centimeter. The universe then consisted of the leptons, their antiparticles, mesons, their antiparticles, some neutrons and protons. It is said that Grand Unified Theory (GUT) processes had resulted in the elimination of antineutrons and antiprotons from the universe.

One Second.

At about one second after the BB, tau neutrinos, mu neutrinos and electron neutrinos were formed due to symmetry breaking. Neutrons decayed into protons and antielectron neutrinos, and muons and antimuons annihilated into electrons, positrons, muon neutrinos and electron neutrinos. Some tau neutrinos also remained, but tau particles were annihilated. It is believed that all positrons had been annihilated. But because of an initial excess of electrons, they remained.

Photons (electromagnetic radiation) then dominated the universe, and they continued to do so until about 300,000 years after the BB. The ratio of electrons and protons to photons was only about one in hundreds of millions, and there was only about one neutron for each five protons.

Neutrinos, like photons, are believed to have survived to this day, and they "flood" the universe.

At that time the temperature of the universe had dropped to about 10^{10} K (10 billion degrees absolute), and its density to a couple of hundred pounds per cubic centimeter, but it was still a hot, dense, opaque fluid. If the universe had expanded at a constant rate its size would then have been on the order of 300,000 kilometers, as compared to its present size (according to BBT) of about 10^{23} kilometers. (Expansion is linear; temperature and density are inversely proportional to time. The volume of the BB universe, of course, increases as the cube of its size.)

Quarks became bound into neutrons and protons, and electrons joined with protons to form nuclei of the first and the simplest of atoms, those of hydrogen. It is supposed that at that time thermonuclear reactions started.

In the period of one second to a couple of minutes after the BB, this process (nucleosynthesis) is said to be responsible for the production of the nuclei of a number of light elements, including about 25 percent of helium and small amounts of deuterium and lithium. Because of the high energy level of photons their reactions with electrons wouldn't allow the formation of complete stable atoms.

100 Seconds.

At about 100 seconds after the BB the period of nucleosynthesis ended.

Expansion and cooling then continued until about 300,000 years (estimates vary between 100,000 and 1,000,000 years) after the BB when the temperature dropped to on the order of 3,000 K.

In the meantime, nothing else of great significance occurred. Radiation continued to dominate the universe, i.e., photons continued to react with electrons which were absorbed and reradiated at a furious pace throughout the universe.

300,000 Years.

At about 300,000 years, photon decoupling occurred, when, as professors of astronomy Martin Rees (of Cambridge), and Joseph Silk (of the University of California at Berkeley) said, "the fireball ceased to be a plasma of electrons and particles."

The temperature had cooled and the density decreased to the point where photon interactions with electrons largely ceased. Electrons then combined with nuclei to form complete atoms of the light elements. Photons were freed to travel through the universe.

The universe, which until that time was opaque, now became transparent, and thereafter, matter is said to dominate the universe rather than radiation.

(Princeton University cosmologist P. J. E. Peebles tells us that, "Black holes that collapsed near the end of this radiation dominated epoch," at a redshift of about 10,000, "are not uncommon." However, there is no reason to believe in the formation of an abundance of black holes at that time—or at any other time—in this postulated BB chronology.)

A Few Hundred Million Years.

After the photon decoupling it is said that small irregularities of distribution of matter in the expanding universe resulted in the eventual accumulation of matter into galaxies and clusters of galaxies. This process is thought to have started in earnest at a few hundred million years after the BB, and the evolution of the universe has proceeded since then, producing the universe as we see it today, about 3 to 5 times 10^{17} seconds (10 to 15 billion years) after the BB.

The reconciliation of the "creation" of fundamental particles with quantum theory that is described above is believed to lend support to BBT.

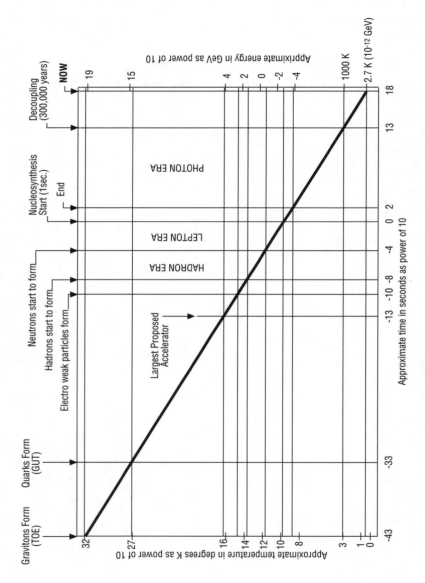

FIGURE 1. BIG BANG CHRONOLOGY – Temperature/Energy/Time Relationships

FOUR

Big Bang Cases

BB theory tells us that the universe is closed, flat or open, with its space positively curved, uncurved or negatively curved, but it is impossible to directly determine which, if any, of those choices might be correct.

Some BBers favor the closed case, some the open case, and some the flat case. Among those who favor the closed case, some believe in a repeating BB, a closed universe that will "bounce." Those Standard BB cases, all of which have decelerating expansion, are discussed below.

Two additional possibilities that are not decelerating, and not considered part of Standard BBT, are also discussed. All of those cases are based on Friedmann's solution to Einstein's General Relativity equations.

It should be understood that only the present rate of expansion of the universe might be determined. Therefore, as illustrated in Figure 2, for each of the BB cases the present rate (at "NOW") is the presently accepted value of the Hubble constant. What the rate of expansion might have been in the past, and what it might be in the future, is a function of the average density of the universe and possibly of other factors that are not well known.

A summary of the characteristics of BB universe cases is presented in Figure 3.

The reader is again cautioned not to lose sight of the fact that this material is not scientific fact, but merely discussion of an unproven cosmological theory.

Density Parameter and Deceleration Parameter.

Before proceeding, a couple of technical items should be reviewed.

Astronomers and cosmologists refer to average density of the universe by means of a "density parameter," the symbol for which is Ω, (omega, the Greek letter Z). Its value is proportional to average density, with Ω equal to 1 for the BB critical density (a flat universe).

It is said that, at that critical density the ratio of the gravitational energy of the universe equals its kinetic energy.

A similar, but more confusing scheme, that is still sometimes used, involves a "deceleration parameter," q_0. In that scheme, for critical density (a flat universe), q_0 equals 1/2; and for zero density, q_0 equals 0. For q_0 between 0 and 1/2 the average density would be less than the critical amount (an open universe), and for q_0 greater than 1/2, the density would be greater than the critical amount (a closed universe).

The Closed BB Universe.

This universe, represented by the area below Curve 2 in Figure 2, has the highest deceleration rate of the three standard cases.

Its average density exceeds the critical value (Ω is greater than 1), its space is positively curved (said to be closed, that is, spherical or ellipsoidal), and its rate of expansion is below its escape velocity. Its rate of expansion in the past would have been considerably greater than the present Hubble rate; perhaps several times the Hubble rate. Its age is less than two thirds of the Hubble time. Its rate of expansion will continue to decrease until, at some point in the future, it will cease. The closed BB universe will then start to collapse.

At that time its density will have reached a minimum, after which it will start to increase. Its density and its rate of collapse will continue to increase until it eventually collapses into the Big Crunch. The greater its density is beyond the critical level, the sooner that will occur.

Of course, Curve 1 of Figure 2 represents only one of many possible closed universe variations that could be shown below Curve 2, and that could span various lengths of time. In each of those the rate of expansion would decrease until it ceases, then they would begin to contract, and eventually collapse.

Regarding one such closed universe case, theoretical physicist and BB advocate Stephen Weinberg (in 1977) estimated that, if Ω were to equal 2, that is, be at twice the critical density, the universe would continue to expand for another 50 billion years and, at that time, when its size becomes twice its present size and its temperature one half its present temperature, it will start to collapse. (However, Weinberg believed the average density of the universe to be only a few percent of critical, and therefore, did not believe that to be its fate.)

The Closed Cycling BB Universe.

Some BB cosmologists have believed that, upon its collapse, the universe may again re-explode or bounce, resulting in a new universe, that it may have done this one or more times in the past— not shown in Figure 2—and may continue to do so in the future, as represented by Curve 1a.

Among those who have favored a closed cycling universe are astronomer Joseph Silk, physicist John Archibald Wheeler, who is now professor emeritus at Princeton University, and W. H. Bonner. George Gamow thought there was at least one previous collapse of the universe but that it wouldn't happen again, and Silk calculated that the number of past cycles of the universe is limited to less than 100.

Some BB cosmologists have suggested that the universe would lose energy with each cycle, and others have suggested that it might gain energy with each cycle. The appeal of a universe that has cycled in the past may be that it avoids the problem of its creation out of nothing, "ex nihilo," as in other BB cases.

(Strangely, in an essay called *Heureka*, Poe's previously mentioned early cosmological speculation was of a universe that arose from an initial explosion that was followed by cycles of expansion and contraction.)

The Open BB Universe.

The BB open universe case, represented by the area between Curves 2 and 3 of Figure 2 , has the lowest rate of deceleration of the Standard BB cases. (Actually, all curves in the area above Curve 2 would be "open.")

Its average density is less than the critical amount, that is, Ω is between zero and one. Its space is negatively curved (said to be "saddle shaped"), and its present rate of expansion is greater than its escape velocity. Its rate of expansion in the past would have been greater than the flat case, putting its age at more than two thirds of the Hubble time. Its rate of expansion would continue to decrease at an ever diminishing rate, and its average density would eventually approach zero. It will not collapse.

As with closed universe cases, curves of a variety of open cases might be drawn; this time in the area between Curve 2 and 3. In each of those the rate of expansion would be also ever decreasing. The average density would approach zero, but those represented by curves closer to Curve 3 would take longer to each zero.

Proponents of the BB open universe case in the past have included astrophysicists Richard Gott and James E. Gunn, and physicists George Gamow and George Ellis.

The Flat BB Universe.

This universe, illustrated by Curve 2 is at the boundary between that of the open and closed cases, wherein expansion is opposed by the equal and opposite force of gravity.

It has flat, uncurved, "Euclidean" space, which means that its space is just like the three dimensional space of our everyday experience. Its expansion in the past would have been about twice the Hubble rate, and puts its age at two thirds of the Hubble time.

As an example, if the Hubble constant (H_0) is about 65 km per second per megaparsec (Mpc) or about 20 km per second per MLYs, the Hubble time (T_H) would be about 15 BYRs, and the BB of the flat universe would have occurred about 10 BYRs ago. (It has been shown that the age of the flat universe equals 2/3 of the Hubble time—the time of the BB if it had expanded at a fixed rate.)

Its average density, although ever decreasing, has remained at the critical level, that is, at Ω equal to 1, and will continue to do so in the future. Also, its rate of expansion has ever been at escape velocity and will ever remain so. Eventually both its rate of expansion and its average density will approach zero. It also will not collapse.

Flat BB universe proponents believe sufficient missing mass exists in space for the average density of the universe to be at the critical level. However, the flat universe has a very special requirement; some rationale as to how nature might have provided the necessary precise balance of forces.

Several prominent BB cosmologists, including B. J. Carr, Paul Davies and Andrei Linde, support the flat universe case. Although formerly indicating a preference for a closed universe, Stephen Hawking, Cambridge professor of theoretical mathematics, famous for his work in quantum cosmology and theory of black holes has been quoted as saying that his "best guess" is that the universe is flat.

A Fixed-Rate Universe.

There are at least two additional possibilities that are not usually considered by BBers, one of which is a fixed-rate Universe, illustrated by Curve 3 of Figure 2.

Under BBT this universe would be "very open". Its space would be more negatively curved and its expansion rate lower than the usual BB open case. It would expand at the Hubble rate, putting its age at the Hubble time; and its density would approach zero at some time in the distant future, but sooner than an open universe case.

Only in this case would the Hubble constant really be "constant," that is, the rate of expansion of the universe would not have changed since the BB. Its density would have decreased at a fixed rate, and it would never collapse.

Two possible rationales can be imagined for a fixed-rate universe.

One of these is that the negative curvature of space is just the amount needed to cause the expansion of the BB universe to have a fixed rate of expansion. The equivalent of that might be that an unknown or unproven expansive force—such as cosmic repulsion—of a magnitude that compensates for curvature of the space of a BB universe and holds its expansion near to a fixed rate.

To BBers that suggestion is not as "far out" as it might seem. Since the introduction of inflation theory has incorporated such an expansive force, the idea of cosmic repulsion has received new acceptance. As in the flat universe case, this fixed-rate BB universe would require nature to have provided just the right balance of forces.

Another suggestion for a fixed-rate universe is simply that the density of the universe is quite low.

If the universe were expanding, but space is uncurved, the universe could be close to flat and Euclidean. If its average density were very low, the result would be a universe very close to that state; but, of course, that would not be in accordance with BBT or with the Friedmann solution to the General Relativity equations on which it is based.

Data presented by Hale Observatory astronomer Allan Sandage, who started as an assistant to Hubble in the early 1950s, indicates the recessional velocity of galaxies is very close to a linear function, i.e., increasing at a fixed rate, out to a distance of over 3 billion light years. However, in Standard BBT, there is no rationale for a fixed-rate universe or one of increasing expansion.

A Universe of Increasing Expansion.

That sort of BB universe, represented by Curve 4 of Figure 2, which also is not included in Standard BBT, would require an unknown force, such as cosmic repulsion as mentioned above, for its existence.

Its space, according to BBT, would be more open and more negatively curved than the previously described cases. Its rate of expansion—its Hubble constant—was lower in the past and is ever increasing. Its density, which is far below escape velocity, is ever decreasing, and will approach zero sooner than the fixed-rate case. This type of BB universe has been postulated in the distant past, and a similar scheme has been given renewed consideration in the past few years.

If the rate of expansion of the universe were slower in the past— a lower Hubble constant in the past—the age of the universe would be greater than in the other BB cases. Thus it is thought that it might solve a serious problem—known as the BB "age paradox"—which arises because some stars are known to be older than the age of any universe of the Standard BB cases.

As with with other BB universe cases mentioned above, curves of other possible cases of accelerating expansion might be drawn, this time in the area above Curve 3. In each of these variations the rate of expansion would be accelerating, and the average density would be diminishing.

The higher the curve of a universe of accelerating expansion is drawn above Curve 3, the faster its rate of acceleration would be, the sooner it density would approach zero, and the older that BB universe might have been.

Purposeful Obfuscation.

Although the plots of the various BB cases shown in Figure 2 are perfectly straightforward, and undoubtedly well understood by many BBers, when they have attempted to show them, it never is done properly or completely. I suspect that is quite intentional; an attempt to support the contention that others of us are ill-equipped to understand their advanced science. Such "purposeful obfuscation" is frequently found in material published by BBers.

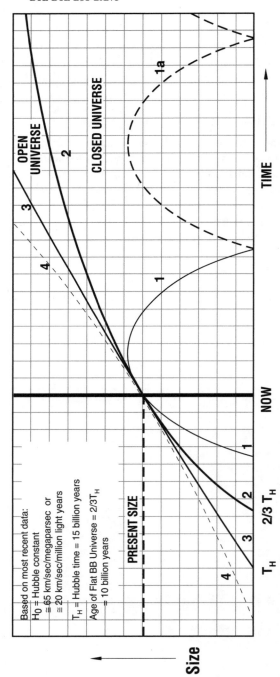

Based on most recent data:

H_0 = Hubble constant
$\cong$ 65 km/sec/megaparsec or
$\cong$ 20 km/sec/million light years

T_H = Hubble time = 15 billion years

Age of Flat BB Universe = $2/3 T_H$
= 10 billion years

PRESENT SIZE

OPEN UNIVERSE

CLOSED UNIVERSE

Size

TIME

T_H 2/3 T_H NOW

FIGURE 2: BIG BANG COSMOLOGICAL CASES Size of the Big Bang Universe vs. Time

1.   Closed Universe. All cases below Curve 2 will close.
1a. Additional cycles of closed cycling universe.
2.   Flat Universe, border between open and closed universe.
     All cases above Curve 2 are open.
3.   Fixed Rate Universe. Constant expansion.
4.   Universe of Increasing Expansion. Not a standard BB case.

~ 38 ~

	Acceleration or Deceleration	Velocity (VE = Escape Velocity)	Space Curvature	Ave. Rate of Expansion Since the BB (H0 = Hubble Constant)	Age of the BB Universe (HT = Hubble Time)	Ave. Density of the BB Universe	Density Parameter Ω	Deceleration Parameter q_0	Possible Future Rate of Expansion	Possible Final Density
Accelerating*	Accelerating Expansion	>>> VE	Most Negatively Curved	Less than Ho (< HO)	> HT	Negative	Negative	Negative	Increases to some high value	Decreases to zero earlier than fixed rate case
Fixed Rate**	No Exceleration No Deceleration	>> VE	More Negatively Curved	HO	HT	Zero	0	0	Unchanged	Linear decrease to zero
Open	Decrasing Deceleration	Greater than VE (> VE)	Negatively Curved ("Saddle-shaped")	More than Ho (> HO)	Between HT & 2/3 HT	Between Zero & Critical	Between 0 and 1	Between 0 and 1/2	Continues to decelerate slower than fixed rate case	Decreases to zero later than fixed rate case
Flat	Fixed Rate of Deceleration	At Escape Velocity	Uncurved (Euclidean)	>> HO	2/3 HT	Critical	1	1/2	Continues to decelerate faster than open case	Decreases to zero later than open case
Closed	Increasing Deceleration	Less than VE (< VE)	Positively Curved	>>> HO	> 2/3 HT	Greater than Critical	> 1	> 1/2	Expansion stops Contraction starts, ends in "Big Crunch"	Slow decrease to minimum, then increases to infinity

FIGURE 3. CHARACTERISTICS OF THE BIG BANG CASES - Comparative Characteristics

* A universe of accelerating expansion presently is, and occasionally in the past, has been, given consideration by big bang theorists in the hope of solving their "age paradox" problem.

** A Fixed rate universe in not usually given consideration in Big Bang theory.

FIVE

Galaxy Formation in a Big Bang Universe

This chapter provides a short discussion of the formation of galaxies in accordance with BBT, which is based on the opinions and assumptions of a number of BB cosmologists.

Smooth BB.

BB cosmologists believe that the universe was initially very smooth, that is, homogeneous and isotropic.

Therefore, questions arise as to how the galaxies and clusters of galaxies could have formed as a result of gravitational attraction if there weren't relatively large irregularities in the density of the early BB universe. But many BB cosmologists have decided that tiny imperfections in the smoothness of the matter of the BB explosion would have been sufficient to provide the "seeds" for the formation of galaxies and clusters.

Seeds.

As an example, University of Chicago cosmologist David Schramm is quoted (in *SCIENCE* in 1991) as saying, "To get the whole process started, theorists envisioned seeds: tiny wrinkles in the fabric of the universe, which would have originated during the first fraction of a second after the Big Bang." Those must be the "seeds" that University of California cosmologists Barrow and Silk had in mind in (in 1980) when they wrote, "We think of the universe as [having] only an infinitesimal degree of irregularity at the time of its creation."

More recently, X-ray astromomers J. Patrick Henry, Ulrich G. Briel and Hans Bohringer (in *SCIENTIFIC AMERICAN* in 1998) have stated, "The radiation [MBR], a snapshot of the universe after the BB and before the formation of galaxies, is almost perfectly smooth. Its tiny imperfections somehow grew to the structures that exist today, but the process is still not clear," and Martin Rees wrote (in *SCIENTIFIC AMERICAN*, in 1999) that, "Ever since the beginning, gravity has been amplifying inhomogeneity, building up structures."

BB Nucleosynthesis.

As has been described, during the period of BB nucleosynthesis that started at about a second after the BB, and lasted for a couple of minutes, the nuclei of hydrogen, helium and a small amount of light elements were produced, which are said to be the elements from which galaxies began to form.

The Decoupling.

That period of nuclei fusion was followed within a few hundred thousand years by a period of photon decoupling. Prior to that the universe is said to have been "dominated by radiation," but following the decoupling of photons, the universe is said to be "dominated by matter." As mentioned in Chapter 3, those photons zoomed off into space, and the formerly opaque BB universe became transparent.

Dark Matter.

There are some concerns regarding the period that followed the decoupling. According to *ASTRONOMY* magazine managing editor David J. Eicher, "the key question is how the universe went from smooth to lumpy with galaxies," and Space Telescope Science Institute astronomer Anne L. Kinney asked, "How did the universe go from gentle smoothness to chaotic clumpiness?"

The answer to that question, that has become widely accepted, is that the presence of dark matter in the space of the universe provided the gravitational force to overcome its rate of expansion to start the accretion of matter.

Although the directly observed density of the universe is only 1 or 2 percent of its critical density, there is evidence of dark matter supporting a density of perhaps 10 times that amount. Because many BB cosmologists believe that the universe is flat, and that it will ultimately be shown that the density of the universe is at the critical level, they have had no problem with that answer.

As stated by astronomer David Eicher, "because of its [dark matter's] huge gravitational influence subatomic particles formed quickly, which condensed into atoms a few minutes after the BB," and astronomy professor Peebles, (in 1994) has assured us that, "Gravity causes the growth of density fluctuations in the distribution of matter, because it more strongly slows the expansion of denser regions, making them grow still denser."

Although the BB universe is said to be expanding at a tremendous rate at those times, it is generally accepted that gravitational forces were sufficient to overcome that expansion velocity to provide for the formation of stars and galaxies.

Energy of Expansion.

Gamow, who estimated (in 1954) that the kinetic energy of the galaxies fleeing each other was about 50 times that of gravity, recognized there could be difficulties regarding the accretion of matter, and postulated that there would have been sufficient turbulence, in a still very smooth universe, to solve that potential serious problem.

Barrow & Silk (in 1980) reported that, "The work of Barry Collins and Stephen Hawking of the University of Cambridge shows that a highly but not perfectly regular universe is unstable. The slightest deviation from regularity would tend to grow in time as the universe expanded." They explained that after the decoupling, when "atoms can travel through the radiation, so that the gravitational growth and collapse can proceed....Density fluctuations start to collapse when they acquire a mass of more than 100,000 suns." However, that ignores the impossibility of the accretion of matter in a universe that, at that time, would still have been expanding faster than the speed of light.

Gravitational Attraction.

Physics professor James Trefil has written in *The Moment of Creation* that, "In order for galaxies to form by the process of gravitational accretion...the clumping of matter need not have been very large. In fact for galaxies to form, it was only necessary that there were regions of space where the density is 0.01 percent higher than normal," and University of Arizona astronomer Chris Impey is quoted as saying, "About 100,000 years after the big bang the universe had few features larger than ripples on a lake. Over hundreds of millions of years, gravity sculpted the ripples into features large enough to collapse into galaxies."

In explanation of globular clusters that are found around galaxies, Princeton University professors Peebles and Robert H. Dicke have suggested (in *SCIENTIFIC AMERICAN* in 1985) that, "the pregalactic clouds, which formed in great numbers, are most likely to have been the size of globular clusters. The clouds drifted together under their mutual gravitational attraction. Although most of them coalesced into the larger agglomerations that formed galaxies, some of them escaped collision while remaining gravitationally bound to the larger structures. Such clouds went on to form the globular clusters of the galactic halo."

Stars Born from Hydrogen.

The most important of the elements from BB nucleosynthesis was hydrogen which, during the next few hundred thousand years, is believed to have gathered into areas of sufficient density for stellar fusion to commence. Thus stars were born, in which the production of heavier elements commenced, and clusters of stars gathered into galaxies.

Concerns about Quasars and Galaxies Forming Too Soon.

Based on the *accepted interpretation of redshift data*, recent redshift measurements from distant quasars and galaxies indicate that "clumps" of quasars and galactic formations existed within a few hundred million years of the BB. That data is believed to provide support for evolution of the BB universe in general agreement with the above description.

However, as will be discussed in more detail in Chapter 11, there are serious concerns about the possibility of such rapid development.

Concerns about Smoothness.

BB cosmologists believe that the BB was smooth, and that the observed smoothness of the MBR supports that belief. However, some BBers are concerned that the MBR is too smooth to allow for the irregularities of the early universe that were necessary for the formation of galaxies and larger galactic structures. However, Barrow and Silk (in *SCIENTIFIC AMERICAN* in 1980) suggested that, "the radiation [MBR photons] might have been rescattered by the intergalactic medium on its journey to the solar system and hence its variations might have been smoothed," thus solving that problem.

BB cosmologist B. J. Carr, in struggling with that problem, postulated (in 1982) that the BB started out very smooth, as generally accepted, or that it started off chaotic but was smoothed as the result of various "dissipative effects" such as "little-understood quantum gravity" very soon after the BB. In either case, he decided that, whatever the cause, the degree of irregularity was "just right" ("fine-tuned") to result in galaxies and clusters, while retaining large-scale uniformity.

ELS Theory of Galaxy Formation.

The generally accepted ELS theory of galaxy formation, named for its originators (in 1962), Olin Eggen, Donald Lynden-Bell and Allen Sandage, has been described by Canadian astronomers Sidney van den Bergh and James E. Hesser, in *ASTRONOMY* in 1993, as follows:

"The Milky Way formed when a large, rotating gas cloud collapsed rapidly, in about a few hundred million years. As the cloud fell inward on itself, the protogalaxy began to rotate more quickly; the rotation created the spiral arms we see today. At first the cloud consisted entirely of hydrogen and helium atoms, which were forged during the hot, dense initial stages of the BB. Over time the protogalaxy started to form massive, short-lived stars. These stars modified the composition of galactic matter, so that the subsequent generations of stars, including our sun, contain significant amounts of elements heavier than helium."

Formation of Galactic Clusters and Larger Structures.

The calculations of astronomers Edward Shaya, James Peebles & Brent Tully (in *ASTRONOMY* in 1992) show how our local region of the universe started 13 billion years ago as a fairly random scattering of galactic groups. At subsequent times, the gravity of large groups attracted smaller neighboring groups, eventually building the highly structured pattern astronomers call the Local Supercluster.

Astronomers Henry, Briel and Bohringer told us that, "Star clusters merged to form galaxies, which in turn merged to form groups of galaxies, which are now merging to form clusters of galaxies. In the future it will be clusters' turn to merge to form still larger structures."

Because galaxies obviously have formed in some manner, one or more of the ideas presented here have been accepted by BB cosmologists as satisfactory rationale for the formation of stars, galaxies and galactic structures in the universe.

SIX

Proofs of
Big Bang Theory

BB cosmologists believe that there is considerable evidence in support of BBT, much of which is briefly presented in this chapter. The first three items describe below are called the "pillars" of BBT, but other phenomena are believed to provide additional evidence in support of it.

Presence of MBR.

It is claimed that the MBR that is received from all directions of space can only be explained by infrared radiation that came from the hypothetical BB decoupling that is red-shifted by a factor of about 1,000 to the microwave region. It therefore provides powerful evidence of the BB. Its prior prediction by some BB cosmologists is said to add support to that claim.

Theoretical physicist and cosmologist Edward Tryon wrote (in 1973), "Recent observations confirm the 2.7 K background radiation…establishes beyond reasonable doubt that some version of the big bang theory is correct," and virtually every writer on BB cosmology has made statements similar to that.

Because some BB theorists were concerned that the presence of massive bodies such as quasars and black holes might disturb the smoothness of the MBR in space, they have suggested that blackbody radiation didn't come to us directly from the BB decoupling, but that it had been repeatedly absorbed and reradiated to become thermalized, that is, for its temperature to be equalized, producing a black-body spectrum.

However, the generally accepted view is that the MBR came directly from the BB decoupling.

Expansion.

In a 1991 article that was designed to put to rest once and for all any doubt about the credibility of BBT, cosmologists Peebles, Schramm, Turner and Kron have written that, "improvements in the tests of homogeneity and Hubble's law (that is believed to provide proof of expansion)...must be counted as impressive successes for the standard model," meaning Standard BBT.

Overlooked is the fact that, if the universe were expanding, evidence of that might be equally supportive of other cosmologies, such as discarded SST, that also incorporate an expanding universe.

Light Elements.

Some BB cosmologists, including David Schramm and Gary Steigman (in *SCIENTIFIC AMERICAN* in 1988), have written that, "The strongest support for the big-bang model comes from studies of primordial nucleosynthesis; the formation of elements....the strongest evidence for BBT comes from the need for the extremely high temperatures of the BB for "primeval nucleosynthesis'" to "forge" some of the light elements of the universe from neutrons and protons.

At first it was erroneously postulated that all the elements were produced in the period of BB nucleosynthesis. When it was later learned that, with the possible exception of a few light elements, most elements are produced by stellar fusion, BBT was modified to accommodate their observed abundances.

Regardless of such inconsistencies, BB cosmologists believe that the relative abundances of the light elements of the universe provides significant evidence for BBT.

Evolution.

Based on the *accepted interpretation of redshift data* quasars are believed to be "clumped" at great distances. Ignoring the fact that quasar clumping is in conflict with the BB tenet of homogeneity,

BBers consider that clumping provides evidence of an evolving universe, which is considered to be an important attribute of BBT.

Families of Particles.

The reported verification that the number of families of fundamental particles of the universe is limited to just three is also cited as proof of BBT. John Ellis, the head of CERN's Theory Division, has declared, "There are only three—no more, no less."

That limitation has been stated by some cosmologists to provide evidence in support of BBT. However that evidence, like that of Hubble expansion, may be equally supportive of other possible cosmologies.

Gravitational Lensing.

Lensing of radiation from distant bodies by closer matter in space was predicted by Einstein as one of several possible proofs of General Relativity. Because BBT is based on that theory, and because lensing has been observed, it is said to provide proof of BBT.

However, as discussed in Appendix A, because of the great uncertainties regarding the distances of both the lensing matter and the source of the lensed radiation, and because it may merely be due to gravitational "warping" of the path of light rather then to curved space, lensing provides no proof of relativity, BBT, or any other cosmology.

Even if lensing were to occur precisely as believed by BBers, it might provide proof of other possible cosmologies equally well as BBT.

Olbers' Paradox.

BB theorists believe that their solution to Olbers' paradox provides proof of BB: The great departing speeds of distant bodies of the universe redshifts the wavelengths of their radiation to below the visible range, thus dimming the sky; and, if that weren't so, the entire sky would be bright.

However, it seems more reasonable to accept the straightforward solution that Olbers himself had long ago offered, that closer, smaller, cooler matter can obscure radiation from more distant, larger, warmer matter of space. Certainly telescopic images show that "dust" hides more distant matter, and certainly telescopic photographs of many areas of the sky show that dust hides more distant matter. Even BB cosmologist Peebles, in his discussion of C. V. L. Charlier's clustering hierarchical universe, has recognized that the view of distant galaxies is obscured by dust in our galaxy.

John Gribbin has apparently agreed, "what Olbers is telling us is that the universe is not in thermodynamic equilibrium. Most of it is cold, in spite of the efforts of all the stars in the galaxies pouring out energy to warm it up."

Olbers' paradox is no paradox at all. Therefore, it can't support any cosmology.

Other Candidate Proofs.

As discussed in Chapter 3 on BB chronology, a reconciliation of the creation of fundamental particles with quantum theory is believed to lend support to BBT.

Despite the fact that astronomical observations deny it, BBers insist that the universe is smooth; and regarding the smoothness Peebles et al., as an example, tell us that, "In the BB cosmology, particles uniformly fill all of space." That smoothness is said to be supported by the smoothness of the MBR, providing convincing evidence of a smooth BB explosion.

The fact that the age of the oldest stars in the universe are of the same order of magnitude as the age of the BB universe has also been cited as providing support of BBT. The fact that there are stars that are significantly older than the BB universe, as determined by their own methods, which rules out BBT, is overlooked.

Although each of the alleged proofs of BBT are subject to considerable question, when taken as a whole, they are believed by BBers to provide positive proof of BBT.

SEVEN

Singularity Problems

In the early days of BBT, in the excitement of that intriguing new theory, the lack of explanation for a universe out-of-nothing seemed to go unnoticed or unquestioned.

As Joseph Silk told us (in 1980) that, "The pioneers of big bang theory were not greatly concerned about the singularity in space-time that was apparently required by the Friedmann equation." But, as time has passed, there has been increasing awareness that the law of the conservation of mass/energy and related problems should not have been ignored, and that BB proponents had a serious problem on their hands.

Breakdown of Theory.

At the first instant of the microscopic BB universe, in which its density, temperature, and gravity were near infinitely high, there would be what is known to mathematicians as a singularity, which is considered to be a breakdown of theory. That is, it cannot be assumed that the laws of physics as we know them can apply to that event, thus presenting serious questions about it.

More than one BB cosmologist has admitted that a singularity indicates the breakdown of a theory.

W. B. Bonnor (in 1960) wrote that, "a singularity in mathematics is an indication of the breakdown of a theory" that must be done away with, and Cambridge astrophysicist B. J. Carr (in 1982) said that "all known physics breaks down" in a singularity.

Oxford professor of astrophysics Dennis Sciama (in 1967) declared the BB singularity to be "one of the botches" of the universe. Sciama, a former SST advocate, reported that the problem of the "unpleasant singularity" helped motivate Bondi and Gold and Hoyle to develop the SST.

Cosmological philosopher Ernan McMullan warned (in 1981) against such an enormous extrapolation of laboratory physics in his statement, there are "good historical reasons to distrust the applicability of standard theories to extreme conditions."

Out of Nothing.

Possibly the most serious aspect of the BB singularity, of course, is that it is the creation of all the mass and energy of the entire universe out of nothing.

According to Standard BBT, before the BB there was nothing: no space, no time, no matter, no energy. No explanation had been given for that within reasonable bounds of known physical science.

As examples of such utter nonsense was Pagels' explanation of the origin of the universe out of nothing referred to in Chapter 2, and Joseph Silk telling us (in both the 1980 and 1989 editions of *The Big Bang*), to "Imagine a moment so early and a density so high that the gravitational stresses were capable of tearing apart the vacuum."

Although to some, who may have confused their religious ideas with science, the creation of the universe out of nothing is seen as a reasonable interpretation of their religious beliefs. Certainly it was not within the realm of science, and can only have been a gigantic violation of the law of the conservation of mass/energy.

Speeds Greater than Light.

BBers tell us that it is the space between the matter, rather than the matter of the universe that is expanding, the BB didn't involve the travel of mass, and thus its superluminal explosion did not violate the theory of relativity. But how the BB explosion could have displaced all the mass of the universe without physically moving it, defies common understanding.

Regardless of protests to the contrary, a major violation of the prohibition of speeds in excess of that of light seems to be inherent in that process.

Infinities of Energy.

According to Standard BBT, at the instant of creation, the mass of the universe was accelerated to above the speed of light; some say many times the speed of light. Therefore, unless the expansion of empty space is accepted, each particle of matter of the explosion required infinite energy to propel it from the infinite gravity of the infinitely dense universe, or, according to General Relativity, infinite curvature of space.

The total energy required to accelerate those particles to above the speed of light would be many times infinity (in any units you might chose), without considering the energy necessary to overcome the gravitational attraction of the entire mass of the universe.

The Universe as a Black Hole.

We are told that the density of a black hole is so great that—neither matter nor radiation can escape it. But the infinitely dense BB universe would initially be in exactly that state.

In fact, these are theories for the formation and the life of a black hole, in which some theorists, including John Archibald Wheeler (in 1970), have indicated that black holes are "laboratory models" for processes of a collapsing universe. Although it is possible that they gradually dissipate by quantum evaporation (a process called Hawking radiation after its originator in 1974), they are not predicted to explode. European astronomers Thierry J. L. Courvoisier and E. Ian Robson wrote in *SCIENTIFIC AMERICAN* (in 1991) that, "According to the theory of general relativity, a black hole is the ultimate stable configuration for a very massive object."

It seems that the BB explosion could not have occurred.

The Closed Cycling BB Universe.

All singularities are anomalous, and the closed cycling universe case has some additional problems of its own. Among those is the problem of the bounce. Possibly because it appeared to offer a solution to the BB singularity problem, the closed cycling universe once was a favored BB case, and it is still favored by some.

The open, the flat and the non-cycling closed cases of BBT have the immediate problem of a source of energy and matter for their "one-shot" singularity, but the closed cycling case defers the question of the origin of the universe. Those cosmologists who favor a closed cycling BB universe (despite its unlikelihood) believe that, because it didn't come out-of-nothing, but from the remains of a previous universe, the explosion of a collapsed universe eases the singularity problem.

Wheeler suggested a means by which a rebound might occur in accordance with quantum theory, and Peebles suggested that, if there were bounces, each would be cooler and last longer than the previous one. However, there is no theory in physics that can account for the re-explosion, or bounce, of the universe. Edward Tryon (in 1973) wrote that, "No satisfactory mechanism has ever been proposed," and B. J. Carr (in 1981) said that, "physics cannot yet explain what could cause this bounce."

As mentioned above, Wheeler said that a black hole is a laboratory model for a collapsing universe. However, if that were so, why wouldn't it spin as a black hole is believed to do? Because virtually all stellar matter, including satellites, planets, stars, galaxies and clusters spin or orbit or both (not to mention all the particles of modern physics), shouldn't we also expect a collapsing universe to be rotating? Why wouldn't it, upon its collapse, spiral into an enormous black hole, rather than become an exploding singularity?

Wheeler also wrote that, in its collapse and re-explosion, the universe is "squeezed through a knot hole" of Planck length. Furthermore, according to his view of quantum theory, the world that results from the rebound could have a whole new set of physical laws; the outcome subject to the participation of an observer. All of which seems to be a *little* beyond the realm of science.

The Convergence Problem.

There is a possible additional problem for the closed cycling universe that I call the convergence problem.

As evidenced by formations of galaxies spread over hundreds of millions of light-years there are enormous irregularities in the distribution of matter in space in an expanding BB universe. Therefore, upon its collapse, the matter of the universe might not converge. Some of its matter, now crunched to particle size, might arrive at the anticipated site of the next BB somewhat earlier than other matter, and thus proceed to shoot out at relativistic speeds into space in the opposite direction from whence it came.

Later arriving matter, having nothing to impact, would also shoot out in the opposite direction. Therefore, unless there is a spinning collapse, à la black hole, the matter of the universe, might not converge. At the time of the collapse, instead of the envisioned Big Crunch, chaos might result.

(Incidentally, both John Boslough in *Stephen Hawking's Universe* and California Institute of Technology physics professor Kip S. Thorne in *Black Holes & Time Warps* have presented ideas similar to that regarding the collapse of stars to form black holes.)

The Second Law of Thermodynamics.

The closed cycling universe of BBT has the additional problem that, in violation of the Second Law of Thermodynamics, the total entropy of the universe (a measure of the degree of disorder of a system) must in some unknown manner decrease from a very high level to zero, or very nearly zero, in the instant of each new BB.

In his book of 1989, *The Emperors New Mind*, Oxford University mathematician and theoretical physicist Roger Penrose struggles to find a solution to that problem. His concern with that situation, which he apparently agrees is quite serious, is the only acknowledgement of that problem I have found in the literature.

Zero Net Energy Type I.

It has been suggested that the singularity problem can be solved by postulating a universe of zero net energy.

According to Tryon (in 1973) and Davies (in 1984), that is because the negative gravitational energy of the observable universe and the positive energy of the potential, kinetic and the equivalent energy of the mass of the universe are equal, so they cancel each other. However, there are at least two reasons why that idea is unsound:

(1) The energy of the gravity of the universe is very much smaller than the remaining equivalent mass/energy of the entire universe.

It has been estimated that the gravitational energy amounts to as little as one thousandth of the equivalent energy of the observable mass of the observable universe, and that doesn't include the kinetic energy of that matter, or dark matter that might have at least ten times the mass of the observable universe. Quite obviously the energy of its gravity is very much smaller than the rest of the Einsteinian equivalent energy of the universe.

(2) Negative matter, negative energy and negative forces are unknown in nature. There may be opposing energies of forces, so

that one of an opposing pair might be labeled negative for mathematical usage, but none are really negative.

Tryon gave an example of a balloon that is blown up as an analogy of zero net energy, in which the energy of the compressed air within it was equal and opposite to the energy stored in the stretched rubber. But that is a fallacy. The energy in that air and in that rubber are both positive, they merely happen to oppose each other.

In the case of the universe, both the energy of gravity and the energy of all the rest of the universe are also positive energy. In the real world we live in negative energy does not exist.

(A second type of zero net energy is discussed in Chapter 24.)

Inflation to the Rescue.

The incorporation of inflation into BBT theory (that is discussed in Chapters 23 and 24) is claimed to have solved its singularity problem, but that revision of theory doesn't seem sufficient to circumvent the law of conservation of mass/energy. Even Andrei Linde, the originator of new inflation, admitted (in 1985) that a final solution to the singularity problem "will be possible only after the development of a complete quantum theory," meaning a Theory of Everything (TOE).

In Standard BBT, because it was said that before the BB there was nothing—no time, no space, no matter—the BB came out of nothing. Inflation theorists contradict that, saying that the universe came from the energy of space. In a manner similar to the spontaneous appearance of particles (such as electrons and positrons in strong electric fields in the vacuum of laboratory experiments) a sudden "quantum fluctuation" of the vacuum of space is said to have produced all the matter and energy of the universe.

However, with or without inflation, the creation of the entire mass and energy of the universe out of the empty vacuum of space continues to represent an extreme violation of the law of conservation of mass/energy.

EIGHT

The Smoothness and Horizon Problems

Two related problems have plagued BBT for many years: the smoothness and horizon problems.

THE SMOOTHNESS PROBLEM

Despite the fact that it may not be essential to their theory, BB cosmologists have long insisted that the BB explosion was extremely smooth.

Concerns have sometimes arisen regarding the smoothness of such an explosion. As an example, British cosmologist and quantum field theorist Paul Davies and Cambridge University astrophysicist John Gribbin wrote (in 1992), "What agency could have orchestrated the primeval explosion in such a way that all parts of the universe expanded at the same rate everywhere and in every direction?"

Regardless of such questions, other BB cosmologists have generally insisted on a smooth BB explosion. As an example of that, Barrow and Silk wrote (in SCIENTIFIC AMERICAN in 1980), "The large-scale structure of the universe today is regular to within one part in 1,000. There is evidence that it has been that way since 10^{-35} second after the start of the big bang."

In addition to that original smoothness, despite the fact that ever larger galactic formations have been observed in our universe, some BBers have insisted that the present universe is smooth, that is, isotropic and homogeneous, and that the Copernican and Cosmological Principles would apply.

However, because of the discovery of galactic formations of gigantic size, others have recognized those as a more serious problem, and decided that the early BB universe may have been less than perfectly smooth; and their position regarding the present universe has been modified to that "on the very large scale" it will be found to be smooth.

Although those changes may represent an admission of a failure of the early BB thinking, the latter may, in fact, be a proper assessment of the real universe.

Simplifying Assumption.

The belief in smoothness apparently originated as a result of some simplifications that were made in the process of solving the General Theory of Relativity field equations. Friedmann had quite reasonably assumed a uniform universe, without which it would have been much more difficult, and perhaps impossible, to solve Einstein's equations.

That dependence on the uniformity as the result of simplifying assumptions became distorted in the minds of early BB cosmologists. As cosmological philosopher Ernan McMullin wrote (in 1881) that isotropy "is no longer the simplification for the sake of a first calculation that it once was."

Because of his importance as an originator of what became Standard BBT, Gamow's belief that, "the galaxies were spread fairly uniformly in space and the universe as a whole has a smooth general curvature" undoubtedly helped to perpetuate the idea of smoothness, which became a requirement rather than a mathematical expedient.

Even BB cosmologist Heinz Pagels, admitted (in 1985), "Really it is we—the model builders—who artificially put in the uniformity to begin with." However, some cosmologists ignore the fact that smoothness originated as a simplifying assumption and have gone to great lengths to invent theories as to why there is sufficient small-scale nonuniformity to cause the formation of galaxies and clusters of galaxies.

Evidence Against A Smooth Universe.

Although Gamow had reported his belief in the smoothness of the universe, since that time astronomers have discovered evidence of vast galactic formations at great distances that tend to deny that idea. Questions arose as to how galaxies and clusters of galaxies might have started to form as a result of gravitational attraction if there weren't irregularities in the density of the early BB universe.

As time progressed there have been increasing reports regarding very large-scale nonuniformity of the universe; first clusters of galaxies, then superclusters, later voids, relative empty regions estimated at 150 to 300 million light-years across and several billion light-years from us, surrounded by sheets of galaxies, and the 500 million light-year "Great Wall," a structure that spreads 20 degrees across the sky. In 1987 Princeton University astronomer Jeremiah Ostriker is said to have conceded that the conflict of those large galactic formations with the smoothness of the MBR was putting a strain on Standard BBT.

Carnegie Institute astronomer Alan Dressler tells us that the matter of the universe is "clumped together on unimaginably large-scale, reflecting poorly understood events in the early universe" and, "If our results are verified, they will point to structures many times larger than the largest features that have been mapped recently, such as the cells of the 'bubble universe' described in 1986 by astrophysicists John Huchra, Valerie de Lapparent and Margaret Geller of the Harvard-Smithsonian Center for Astrophysics." As reported in Scientific American (in 1992), in the opinion of astrophysicists working the Las Campanas Observatory in Chile, "theorists will still be hard pressed to explain how the once smooth universe gave rise to features as vast as the Great Wall."

Astronomer Vera Rubin of the Carnegie Institution's Department of Terrestrial Magnetism is reported to have said "We know very little about the universe....I personally don't believe it's uniform and the same everywhere. That's like saying the earth is flat," Margaret Geller has been reported to have said, "We don't know how these [giant galactic formations] happened and the answerers are not just around the corner," and science writer Jim Dawson wrote that the findings of Geller, Huchra and De Lapparent of a 500 MLY wall of galaxies challenges the standard model: "The Big Bang itself may never have happened."

Cal Tech Astronomer Alain Picard has reported that his research "indicates that the universe is even more clumpy than indicated by previous work" and that "galaxies are assembled into very large-scale structures whose existence cannot be explained by our current cosmological models," and Jeremiah Ostriker noted that, "Theorists are particularly disturbed by the growing evidence of large scale inhomogeneity in the universe' structure, which conflicts with the uniformity of the comic background radiation."

Professor and American Astronomical Society prize winning astronomer Charles Steidel, also of Cal Tech, who has developed a method for observation of remote galaxies, has discovered hundreds of distant galaxies, some having redshifts as high as 4.2. His latest work, with colleague Mark Dickinson, on a Keck Telescope on the island of Hawaii shows galaxies at those distances, possibly more than 12 billion light-years from us, not to be randomly distributed, but to show considerable clustering.

Bunching of galaxies so soon after a BB, within about a billion years, cannot be explained by any form of BBT.

(As it will later be shown, those of the establishment base their estimates of the velocity and distance of matter in space on the *accepted interpretation of redshift data* which is subject to serious question. Accordingly, the reader is cautioned not to accept the distances given above as gospel.)

If that wasn't enough bad news for BBT, satellite borne X-ray detectors have provided evidence of clusters of quasars that are ten or more billions of years old, that is,—according to the *accepted interpretation of redshift data*—within a few percent of the age of the BB universe. If that is so, such clumping of quasars so soon after the BB also seems to discredit the postulated smoothness of the early BB universe; and, as mentioned, the clumping of quasars at great distances, that BBers believe provides proof of an evolving universe, denies isotropy and the Copernican and Cosmological Principles.

Smoothness Verified by the MBR.

The smoothness of the distribution of the matter of the universe is said to be verified by the smoothness of microwave background radiation that is received from all directions of space, and its presence is often cited as the most important physical evidence, not only for a BB, but for a smooth BB.

Regarding this tie between the smoothness of MBR and the smoothness of the BB, Davies, Gott, Gunn, and Schramm all consider the MBR, that is believed to have come directly from a smooth BB, provides near positive proof of the smoothness of the universe, and Davies (in 1984) wrote, "If the universe were to expand faster in one direction than in others, it would depress the temperature of the background heat radiation coming from that direction and distort the pattern of motion of galaxies as viewed from the Earth. "So not only did the universe commence with a bang of quite precise magnitude, it was a highly orchestrated explosion as well, a simultaneous outburst of exactly uniform vigor in every direction" and that this radiation should "carry the imprint of any departures from uniformity."

Although data from the Cosmic Background Explorer (COBE) satellite and other investigations (to be discussed in Chapter 13) indicate that the level of MBR varies across the sky by only about one part in 100,000, that is said to provide proof of those "departures from uniformity."

However, those variations that were actually gleaned from very poor data that radio engineers would term as "down in the noise," provide little confidence in its worth. But even if that data were good, those variations are far too smooth to account for the formation of galaxies and quasars so soon after the BB, or to account for the presence of giant galactic structure or such things as black holes.

As a possible solution to the problems regarding those early formations, cold dark matter (CDM, hypothetical non-baryonic matter having no postulated characteristics other than gravitational attraction) has been proposed to exist throughout the universe. But the extreme smoothness of MBR, and a failure to discover adequate missing matter in the universe, has discredited cold dark matter theory in the eyes of many cosmologists.

When the MBR was found and accepted by BBers as proof of the photon decoupling, logic forced them to also accept its smoothness as proof of the smoothness of the early BB. As long as they continue to believe that the MBR comes directly from the decoupling, as opposed to the thermalization of radiation in surrounding space, it will be difficult for them to escape that logical trap.

Inflation to the Rescue.

Attempts have been made to utilize quantum mechanics to reconcile small-scale irregularities with large-scale smoothness.

Cambridge astrophysicists Rees and Carr have both suggested that quantum gravitational effects might solve the smoothness problem. Guth's 1981 inflation might stretch out irregularities enough to solve the problem, and Linde's 1985 new inflation, that started out chaotic, was so enormous that it was said to guarantee a smooth BB universe.

Davies (in 1982) agreed that inflation "stretched to death" any initial irregularities, but didn't produce complete uniformity, because a small degree of "clumping" was needed in the early universe to account for the present existence of galaxies, and clusters and Linde agreed (in 1985) fluctuations grew "in just the right way to produce large-scale uniformity without small-scale uniformity."

However, postulating a different kind of expansion doesn't change the present state of the universe, and, as will be discussed further on, it is doubtful whether inflation can provide an explanation for the expansion of the universe at speeds far in excess of that of light. As expressed by Martin Rees, inflation may have caused the smoothness of the universe, but, for an understanding of that, we must await the development of the a "full blown theory of quantum gravity" to explain the events of the first 10^{-23} second of the BB.

Neither quantum theory nor inflation offer a real solution to the BB smoothness problem. The observed irregularities of the universe must not be ignored.

Insistence on Smoothness.

Despite the many problems related to smoothness, some prominent BB cosmologists continue to cling to the tenets of isotropy and homogeneity and go to great lengths to propose rationale for its support.

Astronomer Andrew Chaikin (in 1991), in an article on the Great Wall, reported that P.J. E. Peebles believes that, "if you stand back far enough, the universe will turn out to be smooth," which probably is correct. But Peebles continued to write about the "tranquility of the early universe...as revealed by the observed even distribution of galaxies and quasars in the sky."

Contrary to all human experience, and despite contradictory evidence, many BB cosmologists continue to insist that the BB explosion was very smooth. That is all the more strange because, except that it interferes with a smooth BBT as the cause of smooth MBR, it's not clear that the observed lack of uniformity is harmful to BBT; shouldn't a universe that started by an explosion be expected to be quite nonuniform?

THE HORIZON PROBLEM

BBers fear that there may be another problem that is related to the smoothness of the universe.

The horizon problem is concerned with how matter widely separated in various directions from the BB could mutually interact to cause matter in the universe to appear to be quite similar. Because of the enormous initial rate of expansion of the BB universe, it is thought that faster-than-light signaling would have been necessary for gravitational (or any other) forces to produce or retain that sameness across billions of light-years. Such signaling is believed to be impossible.

The horizon problem is sometimes illustrated in the following manner:

If the radius of the BB universe were, for example, 15 BLYs, two regions at the edge of space are thus 30 billion light-years apart. But because that universe is only 15 BYRs old, it is impossible for those two regions to ever have been in contact with each other.

In another example, groups of quasars may be located more than 10 billion light-years in opposite directions from us in a universe that may be, for example, less than 12 billion light-years old. In order for them to have become as similar as they appear to be, it would have required "information" to have passed between them faster (2/3 faster) than the speed of light during some prolonged period in the past. As plasma theory cosmologist Eric Lerner has written, "Points in the universe separated by more than the distance light can travel since the universe began...can have no effect on one another," or, as Peebles has said, "We can see galaxies that can't see each other. How could they and their environments know to look similar?"

It seems that BB cosmologists have come to believe that it would be necessary for bits of matter to have "communicated" with each other in some mysterious manner in the early BB universe, so as to acquire similar characteristics so that they might "evolve" in a similar manner.

Inflation to the Rescue Again.

Among its other virtues, inflation theory is said to provide a solution to this horizon problem.

Somehow it is theorized that following the BB, but before inflation started, all the matter of the universe was in sufficiently close proximity so that it was then able to communicate, thus solving this problem. The fact that some versions of inflation put the BB after the inflationary expansion is ignored in that explanation.

However, I question whether there is reason for BBers, or any other cosmologists, to be concerned about a perceived horizon problem. If the physical laws of the universe are the same throughout, it would seem reasonable to expect that matter would evolve similarly throughout that universe without the necessity for "communication" of any kind.

NINE

Flatness and Missing Mass Problems

Two additional related problems have also plagued BBT for years: the flatness and the missing mass problems.

THE FLATNESS PROBLEM
A Miraculous Balance.

In the flat BB universe the average density would be at a critical level, that is, at the precise balance between the positively curved space of a closed universe and the negatively curved space of an open universe. That is also at the precise borderline density between that which would cause collapse and that which would cause ever continuing expansion.

According to Davies one of the "remarkable coincidences" of the BBT primeval explosion "is the way in which the strength of the explosion was exactly matched to the gravitational power of the cosmos such that the expansion rate lies today very close to the borderline between collapse and rapid dispersal."

The mystery as to how such flatness might have occurred has been called the flatness problem.

Special Theory Required.

Some BB theorists have said that, for the universe to now be somewhat less than perfectly flat, in order for the universe to be as flat as it now is, in earlier times it would have had to have been very much flatter.

One such theorist claimed that in order for the universe to be as flat as it appears to be—somewhere between one tenth and twice the critical density (Ω between O.1 and 2)—the initial conditions of the universe had to be fine-tuned to within one part in about 10^{18}, and another has said that a present density within a factor of 10 of critical density implies that its deviation from the critical amount must have been even smaller at earlier times, and stated a smoothness within one part in 10^{16} at one second and one part in 10^{60} at 10^{-43} second after the BB. Yet another theorist has calculated that, at one second after the BB the universe would have had to have been flat within one trillionth of one percent; and at 10^{-43} second after the BB it would have to have been flat to within one part in 10^{58}.

If estimates of those kinds truly reflect the universe according to BBT, they should certainly demonstrate the impossibility of a BB universe. As commented by Eric Lerner, even to theoretical cosmologists a crucial number fine-tuned to 58 decimal places should engender suspicion.

Flatness Problem Applies Only to a BB Universe.

The reader should be aware that this flatness problem applies only to a relativity-based universe such as that of Standard BBT.

In the absence of Einstein/Friedmann curved space all the space of the universe would be flat. Regardless of how little, or great, the average density of the universe, it would have flat Euclidean space. Newtonian physics would apply, as it does in our daily lives.

Also, the reader should be aware that, if Einstein's ideas prevailed instead of Friedmann's, the only possibility for a flat universe would be one having an insignificantly low average density: no mass, no space curvature.

MISSING MASS

In a balanced (flat), near balanced (somewhat open) or closed BB universe there is the problem of missing mass.

Astronomical observations show the average density of the universe to be only one to two percent of the critical level required of the flat BB universe (Ω = 0.01 to 0.02). The density inferred from studies of the rotation of spiral galaxies indicates that the presence of missing mass might raise the average density of the universe to about 10 times that amount, or about 10 to 20 percent of the critical level (Ω = 0.1 to 0.2).

That is still far too little mass to support a flat or near flat BB universe. Because of that, it has become necessary for BB cosmologists to postulate that up to 99 percent of the mass in the universe would have to consist of mysterious stuff, perhaps non-baryonic CDM, having no known characteristics other than gravitational attraction.

The Search for Missing Mass.

Regardless of the lack of data, flat universe proponents believe sufficient missing mass exists in space for it to be at critical density, and that it will eventually be found.

Considerable time and effort have been expended to demonstrate theoretically, and to find observationally, sufficient additional matter in space to solve this problem. Although investigators have made valiant efforts in support of missing matter, it hasn't been found.

All sorts of exotic stuff, particles called photinos, axions, winos, zinos, gravatinos, neutralinos, WIMPS (weakly interacting massive particles), CHAMPS (charged massive particles), and MACHOS (massive compact halo objects—a new name for brown dwarfs) have been postulated.

Rees and Silk have suggested that some missing mass might exist in the form of burnt-out galaxies and black holes within them, and others have suggested that some of it might consist of gas, dust grains, low mass stars, large planets, small black holes; all of which might have some merit. Still others have suggested neutrinos, magnetic monopoles, cosmic strings or sheets, or gravitational waves. but there is no significant theoretical or observational support for that stuff.

Cold Dark Matter.

The unseen and unknown dark matter of the BB universe is usually assumed to be CDM.

CDM theory has also provided hope for BBers regarding the formation of galaxies in a universe that is said to be extremely smooth. It was hoped that it might provide the seeds that could in some manner gather in the early universe to start the formation of galaxies. However, the inability to find that missing matter, the observed smoothness of the MBR, and evidence that giant galactic structures had to have started to form too soon after the BB, have resulted in disillusionment regarding CDM.

As reported in *SCIENCE NEWS* (in 1991), "it is difficult to explain how quasars of such great age might have formed from the hypothesized cold dark matter in a period of about one-half to three-quarters of a billion years following the BB decoupling." Also, as reported in *SCIENCE* (IN 1991) "The CDM model slips up because it does not get the galaxy distribution right on scales up to 20 megaparsecs and above: the real sky has more nonrandomness than CDM can provide."

Although Guth indicated that CDM theory must merely be "modified for a better fit," University of Pennsylvania cosmologist Paul Steinhardt, who had worked with both Guth and Linde on inflation theory, has continued to hold out hope for the CDM model, and David Schramm indicated that, even if there were found to be no fluctuations in the MBR, BBT will survive. However, astronomical observations have caused many astronomers and cosmologists to give up on CDM.

Former supporters Carlos Frenk and George Eftathiou haven given up on it, Vera Rubin is skeptical, Margaret Geller announced that, "the cold dark matter model was dead," and although Jeremiah Ostriker believes that "none of that casts any doubt on the Big Bang itself," he is quoted in *SCIENCE* (also in 1991) as saying that the results "sound the death knell" for CDM theory.

Flat Rotation.

According to Newton, the orbital velocity of objects around a central concentration should decrease in proportion to the reciprocal of the square of their distance from the center of rotation. However, the rotation rates of objects in the outer regions of some spiral galaxies have been found to be higher than expected in accordance with that theory, indicating that they contain significant amounts of unseen mass.

University of California at Berkeley astronomy professor Ivan King in his book, *The Universe Unfolding*, (in 1976) has provided data showing that our very own spiral galaxy doesn't have a flat rotation curve, and MIT physicist and science writer Donald Goldsmith tells us, in *Einstein's Greatest Blunder* (in 1995), that the same is true of the relatively nearby elliptical galaxy M105.

On the other hand, there have been a number of reports by other astronomers of spiral galaxies having flat rotation curves, indicating that they are surrounded by unseen matter. That has encouraged cosmologists' expectation of a flat universe. Analysis of the rotation of those galaxies results in a total density in their vicinities on the order of ten times that of their visible matter. As an example, observations have shown that stars at the outer edges of spiral galaxy Andromeda are rotating about as fast as those at its center.

However, if the average density of the universe was as high as that indicated by the matter in those galaxies, it would still be far below that required to support a flat, closed, or somewhat open BB universe.

Candidate Neutrinos.

Regarding one of the favorite missing matter candidates, a team of Columbia University astronomers reported in *ASTRONOMY* (in 1996) that, of 2,000 searches for MACHOS, only 2 showed possible evidence of their presence, essentially ruling them out as the sought after matter. The other preferred candidate has been the neutrinos that were said to have been "decoupled" from the "quantum soup" of the early BB and now "flood" the universe. Those have also been ruled out.

It had been thought that, if those neutrinos had appreciable mass, they could provide the needed missing mass. Because BBT postulates that a hundred or more of them now fill every cubic centimeter of the space of the universe, they have been the primary hope for the solution to the BB flatness problem. But their mass has proven to be to be far too little to meet that expectation.

Regarding another possibility, *SCIENCE* in 1991 reported that Arthur F. Davidson of the Department of Physics and Astronomy at Johns Hopkins University used the Hopkins Ultraviolet Telescope (HUT) to detect radiation from decaying dark matter particles that might dominate the universe. According to Davidson, "The hypothesis of decaying dark matter is a clever attempt to explain a number of disparate facts and ideas from astrophysics, cosmology and particle physics by attributing a mass of about 30 eV to the tau neutrino and assuming that it decays with a life time of about 10^{23} second...(but) no emission was found, limiting the lifetime of any such decaying dark matter particles to at least several times 10^{24} seconds."

As discussed in Chapter 14, according to calculations based on data from BBT, the energy of neutrinos presently in the universe would only be 0.00067 electron volt. Thus, BBT itself denies the possibility that neutrinos might be the missing matter of their universe.

Cosmic Repulsion.

Another suggestion by Peebles is that, either the unknown dark matter of the universe has to be very massive, "or else there has to be something like a cosmological constant, that is necessary to allow the universe we observe to be flat."

However, that is purely speculative.

Furthermore, that would require the cosmological constant to somehow act like positive mass that, in all other sources of which I am familiar, the cosmological constant is presented as an expansive force (anti-gravity) rather than a contractile one; one that might only be presumed to act like negative mass.

Low Density Universe After All.

Astronomer Vera Rubin has been quoted as saying, "We are being driven to the conclusion from dynamics, that we live in a low density, ever-expanding universe," that is, an open BB universe, Marc Postman of the Space Telescope Science Institute, reporting on the results of a recent study of the density of clusters of galaxies in the universe, has stated that, "These numbers imply that...the best theories are wrong, and the universe will keep on blowing up fast and forever," and an article in *ASTRONOMY* (in 1999) declared that, "The latest findings show that the universe is open anyway, so a photon will just travel forever, never circling back."

Those comments, and many more that are found in the literature, deny the possibility of a flat BB universe.

Inflation to the Rescue Yet Again.

The enormous rate of expansion of the early BB universe as postulated by inflation theory is said to provide the solution to a number of BB problems, including the BB flatness problem.

Inflation theorists have postulated that inflations' enormous expansion spreads out the matter of the universe, thus making it flat. But that flatness would necessarily be as Einstein would have expected—flatness due to very low density. The universe would not be flat as Friedmann would have expected—at a much greater density; that of the critical density of BBT.

Flatness resulting from inflation is therefore a contrived solution to the BB flatness problem. Expansion of the universe by an enormous amount could only result in decreased density, not a flat BB universe of critical density.

The searches for missing mass that have been conducted to find support for inflation theory have been totally misguided, but, fortuitously, that effort resulted in the discovery that the mass of some galaxies is greater than previously thought.

TEN

The Hubble Constant, Distance and Velocity

As mentioned in Chapter 1, it had been noticed that the spectrum of the radiation of stars was slightly shifted toward the red, and Carl Wirtz suggested that their distance correlated to their velocity. In the late 1920s and early 1930s American astronomers Edwin Hubble and Milton Humason, working at the Mount Wilson Observatory, provided convincing evidence that the redshift of relatively close galaxies correlated with their distance and velocity.

Hubble was born in Missouri, attended the University of Chicago, went to Oxford University in England as a Rhodes Scholar, and received a PhD degree at the University of Chicago. Humason worked as Hubble's assistant for a number of years.

Redshift.

Redshift has a simple mathematical definition.

It is equal to the fractional shift in wavelength (the wavelength of a received spectral line less the wavelength of that emitted spectral line divided by the wavelength of the emitted spectral line). Although this can be simply stated, and has been made much easier by present day equipment, in Hubble's day measurement of redshift of a distant galaxy was not an easy task. The distance of each galaxy studied had to be estimated by other means. Spectral lines of the received radiation had to be identified and compared to the spectral lines expected of their source.

Even to this day the process of determining redshift is not easy. As Vera Rubin is reported to have said, "It's difficult to make spectroscopic measurements of the velocity of individual stars which are faint even in the galaxies that are fairly close to our own".

It is generally accepted that the rates of departure of other galaxies from ours results in Doppler shifts of radiation received from them; a lengthening of the wavelength of the received radiation (with frequency decreasing in a reciprocal relationship). That affects all bands of electromagnetic radiation (EMR) that are emitted, from gamma rays through radio frequencies. Because the spectrum of visible light from distant bodies would be shifted toward the red, that is, toward longer wavelengths, that shift is called redshift.

The Hubble Constant.

Based on the assumption of Doppler redshift, what is known as the Hubble constant can be determined.

That constant is usually expressed as velocity as a function of distance in units of either kilometers per second per megaparsec (km/sec/Mpc), or in units of kilometers per second per million light years (km/sec/MLYs).

(A megaparsec is a million parsecs. A parsec is defined as the distance to a star that is observed to move an angle of one arc-second in 3 months. One parsec equals 3.26 light-years.)

Even after the passage of several decades since the work of Hubble and Humason, an exact value of the Hubble constant has not been established. Early estimates were as high as several hundred km/sec/Mpc, but have gradually been reduced through the years. Until recently estimates ranged between about 50 to 100 km/sec/Mpc. However, improved methods are now thought to have narrowed that down to the range of 50 to 80 km/sec/Mpc (roughly 15 to 25 km/sec/MLYs).

An interesting note about the Hubble constant is that, according to Standard BBT, it is not really a constant, but has been thought to have been ever greater in the past. Consideration of Figure 2 illustrates that only for a fixed-rate universe would the Hubble constant be constant.

Hubble's Law.

Most astronomers and cosmologists believe that redshift is due to the expansion of the space of the universe and have accepted what is known as Hubble's law.

That law is merely the simple expression that velocity as a fraction of the speed of light is equal to the redshift, usually expressed as $V/c = Z$. For galaxies that are relatively close to ours, which have relative velocities that are only small fractions of the speed of light, their velocities can be determined by that expression. Also, for galaxies that are relatively close to ours, their distance can be determined by use of the Hubble constant. It is equal to redshift times the speed of light divided by the Hubble constant ($D = Zc/H_0$).

However, as will be discussed in Chapter 15, in accordance with the *accepted interpretation of redshift data,* neither the relationship for velocity nor for distance are applicable beyond a few hundred million to one billion light-years. Beyond those distance, the formulas for both velocity and distance, as determined by that method, are corrected for relativistic effects.

Some History of the Hubble Constant.

Hubble's earliest attempts to establish the constant that is named after him are said to have been in the range of 530 to 558 km/sec/Mpc (equal to 162 to 171 km/sec/MLYs).

In 1936, using the best equipment available at that time, he determined relative velocity to Ursa Major II, then thought to be about 260 million light years distant (but now believed to be several times that far), to be about 42,000 kilometers per second (14 percent of the speed of light); for which the Hubble constant would be 161.5 km/sec/MLYs or 526 km/sec/Mpc.

(Lemaitre, who had postulated an expanding universe in 1927, suggested the equivalent of a Hubble constant value of 625 km/km/Mpc. As a result, perhaps the Hubble constant should have been named the Lemaitre constant.)

Following Hubble's death in 1953 astronomer Walter Baade, basing his work on improved Cepheid variable data, found that distances calculated by Hubble had to be increased by a factor of 2.8, which put the value of the Hubble constant at about 190 km/sec/Mpc or about 58 km/sec/MLYs.

Alan Sandage, who, since Hubble's death in 1953, has continued Hubble's work, in 1956 determined a Hubble constant of about 180 km/sec/Mpc, verifying that correction. However, in recent years estimates of that constant by various astronomers have been in the range of about 50 to 80 km/sec/Mpc.

If the universe expanded at the higher of those two values, a fixed rate of expansion would put the BB at about 12 BYRs ago (Hubble time), and if the universe were flat, as accepted by many BB cosmologists, the age of the universe would be about 8 BYRs. Because some stars are admitted to be as old as 16 to 20 BYRs by BB cosmologists (but some are actually much older), that has presented a severe problem for BBT. However, if the universe expanded at the lower of these values, a fixed rate of expansion would put the BB at about 20 BYRs ago, which might solve its age problem. (See Chapter 11 on the BB age problem.)

(Based on Hubble's early estimates, the Hubble time would have been below 2 BYRs. Improved estimates in the early 1950s were on the order of 200 km/sec/Mpc, putting the Hubble time at about 5 BYRs, which was the value Gamow reported in his early work. Obviously, those ages presented a major problem to BBers.)

Because of that problem, which BBers prefer to call the age paradox, they have struggled to find evidence for lower and lower values of the Hubble constant. A major player in that struggle, Alan Sandage, very much an advocate of BBT, has shown a strong bias toward an ever lower Hubble constant as is necessary to increase the age of the BB universe and thus solve the BB age problem. Through the years he gradually reduced his estimate of the Hubble constant to 50 km/sec/Mpc.

(Research of the literature has shown that Sandage's values of the Hubble constant (in km/sec/Mpc) varied over the years approximately as follows: 1956, 180; 1957, 75; 1961, 89; and over the past couple of decades, about 50.)

While other experienced astronomers, including John Huchra and Wendy Freedman of the Carnegie Observatories, and Gerard de Vaucouleurs of the University of Texas have for a number of years found evidence that the Hubble constant is about 80 km/sec/Mpc, Sandage has insisted that his evidence indicates 50 km/sec/Mpc. Even Peebles has based his text and mathematics in *Principles of Physical Cosmology* on a Hubble constant of 80 to 85 km/sec/Mpc throughout.

Very recently, however, a compromise has apparently been

struck. American astronomer Wendy Freedman, who been most prominent among those announcing for the higher value, has reduced her number to about 70, and Sandage has increased his to about 60. However, that compromise seems to be more political than scientific. Apparently it was decided that it would be beneficial to astronomy/cosmology to close a rift among those involved in that dispute.

For convenience I will assume a compromise value of 65 km/sec/Mpc, or its equivalent of about 20 km/sec/ MLYs, throughout this book, which puts the value of the Hubble time at 15 BYRs, and the age of a flat BB universe at 10 BLYs; a somewhat open BB universe at somewhat more; and a closed BB universe at somewhat less to considerably less.

Actually, whether the value of the Hubble constant is 60, 65 or 70 would make little difference to the acceptance or rejection of BBT. At 70 km/sec/Mpc a fixed-rate BB universe would be about 14 BYRs old, and a flat BB universe would be about 9.3 BYRs old. At 60 km/sec/Mpc a fixed-rate BB universe would be about 16 BYRs old, and a flat BB universe would be about 11 BYRs old. Only if a BB universe were of the fixed-rate variety, which is not accepted in Standard BBT, would a Hubble constant at the lowest of those values allow the possibility for BBers, who generally ignore evidence of stars older than about 16 BYRs, to claim a possible solution to the BB age problem.

Distance Measurement.

During this century several sophisticated methods have been developed for measurement of the distance to remote bodies in the universe which, of course, is essential to the determination of an accurate Hubble constant.

The recent deployment of the satellite Hipparcos in a wide 10-hour elliptical Earth orbit has improved astronomers' distance measurement ability. By measurement of their parallax angles, from the earth at 6 month intervals as it circles around the Sun, it has extended the range of parallax measurements by a factor of about 10 over ground-based telescopes, out to several hundred light-years.

Standard Candles.

Several methods, known as standard candle methods, are used by astronomers to extend the measurement of the distance of galaxies to far beyond the limits of the parallax method.

The first and oldest of those, discovered by Henrietta Leavitt in about 1906, and used by Hubble in the 1920s, is the use of Cepheid variables. Those stars have varying luminosity that shows a consistent relationship between their maximum brightness and the cycle of their brightness independently of their distance. By calibrating the distance of Cepheids within the range of parallax measurements, the maximum luminosity of Cepheids can be used to extend the range of accurate distance measurement. (Cepheid variables were named after the constellation Cepheus, where the first star of that type was found.)

An additional measurement means is provided by the Tully-Fisher method, named after Brent Tully and Richard Fisher who discovered it in 1972, which utilizes correlation between the rotational rate and the brightness of large galaxies. This method, the calibration of which is in turn based on Cepheid measurements, has allowed accurate measurments of the distance of galaxies and galactic clusters out to as far as 300 MLYs.

There are two other lesser known standard candle methods.

One of these takes advantage of the fact that luminosity of planetary nebulae does not exceed a maximum limit. In this method the brightest planetary nebula in a galaxy is selected and its observed magnitude used to determine its distance.

(A planetary nebula is the cloud of debris that is blown away from a violent transformation of a red giant—the remains of a burnt-out small to medium sized star—into a white dwarf. That term was formerly used by Hubble to refer to distant galaxies before their identity was known.)

The other of those methods utilizes the fact that the "graininess" of galaxies decreases with distance. Thus the fluctuation of the brightness of a galaxy over its surface provides a measure of its distance. Both of these methods, which are also calibrated by use of Cepheid data, have shown close agreement with the results of the Tully-Fisher method.

The standard candle method that provides the greatest range is the use of Type 1a Supernovas. Because they reach approximately the same peak brilliance, again, independently of their distance, those explosions of dying stars can provide a good indication of distance. Because of their great brilliance, they are believed to extend the range of distance measurement out to as far as 5 BLYs.

(A supernova is the remains of a massive star that has exploded at the end of its life. A nova differs in that it is the result of matter from one star of a binary pair impacting the other; often a white dwarf.)

Because the accuracy of this method is based on a limited number of Cepheid calibrations, and it hasn't been confirmed by an alternate method of measurement out to great distances, its accuracy cannot be considered to be as great as the previously discussed methods.

The accuracy of the Cepheid, Tully-Fisher, planetary nebulae and graininess methods, which have been carefully tied to the parallax methods, is undoubtedly quite high. The calibration and correlation of the data from those methods provide assurance that the accuracy of measurement of the distance of galaxies, galaxy groups and galactic clusters is good out to about 300 million light years. Beyond that (which is about 2 or 3 percent of the postulated radius of the BB universe) measurement grows less accurate as distance increases.

Stellar Magnitude.

Celestial brightness or apparent magnitude of objects in space is the level of brightness that is observed in the visual range of radiation.

It is measured by a system that gives higher numbers to dimmer objects. The "first magnitude" is equivalent to the brightness of a candle at 1,300 feet. Each increase in magnitude of one is equal to a decrease of brightness by a factor of about 2.5 and each increase of 5 is equal to a decrease in brightness of 100. Because brightness varies inversely as the square of distance, a star ten times as far as another of the same actual (absolute) magnitude would appear to be 100 times fainter, and its apparent magnitude would be 5 times higher.

Human eyes can see out to about magnitude 6. The most powerful land-based telescopes with modern sensing devices can "see" to about magnitude 24.

Apparent magnitude does not take into consideration the fact that the brightness of objects in space varies widely from object to object. Therefore, the distance of those objects cannot be determined by apparent magnitude.

If its distance is determined by independent means, the apparent magnitude of an object can then be corrected to determine what is called its "absolute magnitude," to provide an indication of what their brightness would be as compared to other objects at the same distance.

Because apparent magnitude and absolute magnitude have only to do with the energy in the visual range, they do not provide an indication of the total energy of an object in space, which can vary widely depending on its characteristics, such as its temperature.

What is called the "bolometric magnitude" of an object in space is used to describe the total radiant energy received from it. A device called a bolometer is used to make that measurement.

Although all of these magnitude numbers are related to the distance of objects in space, they provide no indication of the relative velocity of an objects.

Velocity Measurement.

Because distances to relatively nearby bodies can be measured, changes of those distances over time can be used to estimate their actual radial velocity, both toward or away from us. (Actually, change in distance and angle data can be used to determine, not only the radial component of their velocity, but their vector velocity and direction.)

The units of the Hubble constant, km/sec/Mpc or km per second per MLYs, indicate its purpose is to provide a method of velocity measurement of distant bodies in space. However, its use is limited to relatively nearby stars and galaxies whose distance and change of distance might be verified by other means.

Because of problems related to the use of the application of Lorentz transformations to the space of the universe (discussed in Chapter 15), the determination of either relative velocity or distance of very distant galaxies or quasars based on a Hubble constant and by the *accepted interpretation of redshift data* is erroneous.

Other Possibilities.

As discussed in more detail in Chapter 15, there are a number of scientists who question whether redshift provides a reliable indication of the velocity of distant galaxies, clusters of galaxies or quasars, and have postulated credible alternate possibilities, such as redshift as a result of Compton effect due to matter in the intergalactic space. Although they deny cosmological redshift, that is, redshift due to the expansion of space, they do not deny Doppler redshift. It undeniably exists, but it may be only a minor factor in producing redshift of very distant bodies, and there is evidence that gravitational redshift—Einstein redshift—makes a significant contribution to the total redshift of distant massive bodies.

ELEVEN

Big Bang
Age Problems

The BB Age Paradox.

One of the most serious of the BB problems is its age problem; the BBer's age paradox: However, it is not a paradox; it's simply a serious problem.

For many years it has been known that the age of some stars and galaxies is as much as 15 to 20 BYRs. The age of the BB universe, based on the Hubble constant, is considerably less than that; and of course, the universe can't be younger than its galaxies. Despite high hopes and continuing efforts, that problem has never been put to bed.

As mentioned in the previous chapter, Hubble's earliest estimates of about 500 km/sec/Mpc, indicated a BB universe age of only about 2 billion years. In continuing attempts by BBers to improve on that low age, over the years they have claimed a gradual decrease of the Hubble constant to about 50 km/sec/Mpc. However, it now seems that, at least temporarily, a value of about 65 km/sec/Mpc has been settled upon.

Hoping to minimize that problem, BBers often quote Sandage's lowest estimate of the Hubble constant of 50 km/sec/Mpc. That value allows them to quote a Hubble age of about 20 BYRs as the age of the universe, while fully aware that the corresponding correct value for a flat or near flat universe should be about 13 BYRs, a value that is too low to solve their age paradox.

In further attempting to minimize their age problems, some BB enthusiasts have predicted that the difference between theory and evidence will soon be eliminated by new interpretation or new data, and some have rationalized that, after all, because the age of their universe is of the same order of magnitude, the ages of stars actually tend to support BBT.

Cheating.

As mentioned above, regardless of which Standard BB case is assumed, and regardless of what the Hubble constant might be, the age of the universe is typically given as that of the Hubble time.

Although BBers are aware that that is mathematically correct only for a fixed rate BB universe, which none of them have ever accepted as valid, they give the age of the universe as the Hubble time. For example, if a BBer believes in the flat universe case and the Hubble constant is believed to be 65 km/sec/Mpc, which is equal to 20 km/sec/MLYs, although they know that its age should be given as 10 BYRs, instead it is typically given as the Hubble time of 15 BYRs.

It should be remembered that these are educated, knowledgeable people who are not simply making errors. The purpose of their deception is to minimize one of the greatest problems of BBT, that of the so-called age paradox; more "purposeful obfuscation."

The Ages of Stars.

There is overwhelming astronomical evidence showing the age of many stars in and around our galaxy to be much older than that admitted by BBers.

Some examples of their age is provide by globular clusters of stars within our own galaxy. As long ago as 1976 American astronomers Gott, Gunn, Schramm and Tinsley (formerly Australian) reported that, "Models of stellar evolution indicate that they are between eight and 16 billion years old." British cosmologist Michael Rowan-Robinson wrote (in 1977) "The oldest known stars in our galaxy are 10 to 20 BYRs old and are composed of about 73 percent hydrogen, 27 percent helium, and almost no other detectable elements." Regarding the age of globular clusters, *NATURE* (in 1994) reported that, "ages have been quoted for some of the oldest clusters up to 20 billion years."

Although Rowan-Robinson stated that the "Big Bang happened 10 to 20 billion years ago," he also suggested that there is a "good possibility" that some stars "are as old as 100 to 200 billion years," and BB cosmologist Silk, apparently accidentally, once referred to "evolving stars over the tens of billions of years of stellar evolution." The Hertzsprung-Russell diagrams published by each of them, and the discussion of white dwarfs below, would seem to confirm those great ages.

Quasars, Galaxies, Clusters and Structures Formed Too Soon

But the BB age problem is much worse than indicated by the admitted age of some stars.

Not only wasn't there enough time since the BB for galaxies and quasars that are observed to be at great distances to have formed, but their clustering, and the formation of gigantic galactic structures, would have required periods far beyond that since the postulated time of the BB.

A quasar having a redshift of about 4.7 has been reported, which is said to be equivalent to a velocity of 94 percent of the speed of light, and to be seen as it was 94 percent of the time and distance back to the BB. Others have been reported at redshifts of 4.9 and 5 putting their ages within about 95 percent of the age of the universe, and indicating that they were seen as they were just a few hundred million years after the BB. It is thought to be impossible for those quasars to have developed so soon after the BB.

Not only the does the presence of individual quasars so soon after the BB present a problem to BBT, but satellite-borne X-ray detectors have provided evidence of clusters of quasars that are ten or more billions of years old, that is, within a few percent of the age of the BB universe. Astronomers have indicated that it might have taken billions of years for quasars to form, and that problem is compounded by the presence of clusters of them which might have taken additional billions of years to form.

SKY & TELESCOPE also reported (in 1997) that, "Astronomers believe that the most distant galaxies in this image were recorded as they looked when the universe was only about a billion years old," SCIENCE NEWS reported (in 1996) a galaxy (HDF 4-473) having a redshift of 5.6, and 3 others having redshifts greater than 5 were reported, putting their ages as seen at about 500 to 700 million years after the BB, *NATURE* (in 1999) reported a galaxy in Ursa Major having a redshift of 6.68, which puts its age as seen at about 400 to 500 million years after the BB, and a team of astronomers from the Universities of Hawaii and Cambridge, England has recently reported finding a galaxy having a redshift of 5.74, which is seen as it was well under one billion years after the Big Bang.

(All of the ages reported here, of course, are the result of application of the *accepted interpretation of redshift data,* which may be quite erroneous.)

SKY & TELESCOPE also reported (in 1997) that, "Astronomers at the University of Chicago have found evidence for superclusters of galaxies at high redshifts....The team's findings...suggest that large-scale clustering exists out to redshifts as high as $z = 3$. This implies that galaxies ... were grouped together within a billion years of the big bang," and astronomers Steidel and Dickinson have reported, "hundreds of extremely distant galaxies at...possibly more than 12 billion light years from us, not to be randomly distributed, but to show considerable clustering. Bunching of galaxies so soon after a BB, within about a billion years, cannot be explained by any form of BBT."

Astronomers using the Hubble Space Telescope (HST) to see farther than ever before have said that, "even at early times there already were galaxies with huge families of stars," and astronomer Marcia Bartusiak has agreed, saying, "This seems to suggest that the major galactic components were in place within a couple of billions years of the Big Bang."

Astronomers deny the possibility for galaxies to have formed in such short periods of time, and it is even more difficult to accept that clusters could have formed that early. But the presence of enormous galactic structures, a half billion light-years or more across, presents an even greater problem.

During the past few decades ever larger stellar formations have been discovered; first clusters of galaxies, clusters of clusters, sheets of galaxies and large voids in space. Results of data collected by satellite infrared detectors indicate the presence of immense galactic formations, including the "Great Wall" and the "Southern Wall" that are said to spread 500 million light years through space, and some galactic structures are thought to span almost a billion light years.

A number of cosmologists have expressed concern about those findings and agreed that it would have taken hundreds of billions of years for the largest of those structures to have evolved. Those have included cosmologist Paul Steinhardt, who is quoted (in 1991) as saying that, "There wasn't enough time in the history of the universe for gravity to pull together these structures," and astrophysicist Edwin Turner said that, "We're starting to find that we just don't have enough time to get the Universe from an early state to the one we're seeing now."

SKY & TELESCOPE (in 1999) stated that, "it has been estimated that their formation (gigantic sheets and voids) would have taken as long as a 100 billion years." Other sources have presented similar, or even longer estimates, and Faye Flam has written (in SCIENCE in 1991) that, "The bigger those structures get, the harder it becomes...to figure out how they could have coalesced in the limited time since the BB."

Elements and Compounds in Space.

Astronomers have discovered significant amounts of heavy elements and compounds of those elements in remote galaxies and quasars and throughout space. Some examples of those findings are presented here.

Using the Infrared Space Observation satellite, astronomers have reported the discovery of gas and dust rings in the Andromeda galaxy and a ring around a star in the constellation that contains complex organic molecules—most likely polycyclic aromatic hydrocarbons; and spectral analysis of radiation from distant galaxies, whose age has been estimated to be as much as 15 billion years, has indicated the presence of carbon monoxide lines.

Hale Observatory astronomers Maarten Schmidt and James Gunn have reported a quasar having a redshift of almost 5. The spectrum of that quasar, which is thought to be as old as about 95 percent of the age of the BB universe, indicates the presence of carbon, nitrogen, oxygen and silicon.

Ancient globular clusters have been found to contain a variety of heavy elements. Ivan R. King has reported that Don A. VandenBerg of the University of Victoria in British Columbia "has concluded that the [globular] clusters are all approximately 16 BYRs old, but even those calculations contain an uncertainty of about 3 BYRs." King also noted that, "Even more of a mystery is how clusters acquired any heavy elements at all given that the Big Bang is thought to have produced only hydrogen and helium," and American physicists Gulkis, Lubin, Meyer and Silverberg reported in 1990 that, "significant amounts of elements heavier than helium have been observed in the oldest known stars."

It has been reported in SKY & TELESCOPE that David M. Mehringer of the University of Illinois and colleagues have found acerbic acid in an interstellar cloud 25,000 light years distant. That article also mentioned that ammonia has been found in interstellar space. Astrophysicist L. H. Aller has reported the presence of organic molecules such as formic acid, methanol and ethanol in the interstellar medium, and astronomer Gary Melnick has reported that a NASA satellite utilizing ,"a band of emissions between infrared and radio wavelengths" has found the presence of water in "regions where stars and planets are born."

A report in ASTRONOMY has confirmed that "polycyclic aromatic hydrocarbons, [is] another compound often found in clouds around stars." That article also reported that, Harold Mutshcke of Jena University in Germany stated that, "the discovery of titanium carbide in space has solved the long-standing mystery of emissions in the 20-micrometer region....[and that] Titanium carbide nanocrystals are also found in certain meteorites."

According to BBT all of the elements and compounds discussed above had to have originated in earlier generations of stars that have blown up within their galaxies. Although BB may insist that the lives of those early stars were relatively short, probably at least several such generations would have been required to produce that matter. That undoubtedly would have taken at least several billion years, adding to an already severe BB age problem.

Galactic Rotation.

Consideration of the dynamics of galactic rotation would seem to present further evidence regarding the great age of our galaxy and, of course other similar spiral galaxies.

Astronomical observations support a period of rotation of our galaxy of 200 to 250 million years. At that rate, if the BB had occurred on the order of 10 billion years ago, there would have been time for only 40 or 50 rotations to reach its present spiral form.

However, because astronomical theory indicates that galactic rotation rate would have been ever slower in the past, the period since the BB universe would have provided time for considerably less than 40 or 50 rotations. That statement is supported by several sources, including astronomer David L. Eisher, "Disks rotate because protogalaxies, very early on, were slowly spinning. The gas that forms disks collapses into these slowly spinning dark halos, and the rate of the spin of the gas increases."

If 40 or 50 revolutions were needed, they would have required much more than 10 billion years. However, as judged by the present spiral form of our galaxy, and others like it, it might be expected that many more revolutions would be required, and perhaps as much as an order of magnitude greater than the age of the BB universe would have been required for their formation. Thus spiral galaxy rotation can be added to the list of BB age problems.

Age of White Dwarfs.

The following paragraphs provides evidence of even greater age of stars.

If one were to examine the Hertzsprung-Russell (H-R) diagram of Figure 2.2 of Michael Rowan-Robinson's book, *Cosmology*, the H-R diagram of Figure 4.3 of Joseph Silk's book, *The Big Bang*, (1980 edition), and American astrophysicist Martin Harwit's book, *Astrophysical Concepts*, on the right edge of each of those diagrams is a time scale. In addition to showing magnitude and luminosity on their vertical scales, they indicate the time it has taken for stars to develop, showing the lives of some main sequence stars to be at least 20 billion years old. But white dwarfs, when shown, are quite far down on those diagrams, indicating lives that are much greater; hundreds of billions of years or more.

Although Rowan-Robinson's H-R diagram shows smaller stars on the main sequence to be as old as 20 billion years, and white dwarfs much older than that, on the very next page he states that the universe is only 15 billion years old. Apparently, he was ashamed to admit to such ages, and an article by physicist/astronomer James Trefil in *ASTRONOMY* of November, 2000, includes an H-R diagram that has a time scale—that, as though ashamed to show it, is barely visible—indicating white dwarfs to be at least hundreds of billions of years old.

That great age is supported by work of University of Michigan physicists Gregory Laughlin and Fred C. Adams and University of California Observatories and Lick Observatory astronomer Peter Bodenheimer, in a paper entitled *The End of the Main Sequence* published in *The Astrophysical Journal*, June 10, 1997. The item of primary importance in that paper was reviewed in a short article entitled *Why the Smallest Stars Stay Small* in *SKY & TELESCOPE* of November, 1997. Evidence is presented in that paper and reviewed in the short article, indicates the lives of at some white dwarfs could be as much as six trillion years old!

Having thus been aired to the astronomical/cosmological community, it seems that an item of such significance should have been responded to more vigorously by cosmologists of the BB persuasion. However, it apparently is ignored, as is most evidence that conflicts with establishment beliefs.

Although not quite so devastating to BBT, similar threats have been presented by astronomers for a number of years. For example, George Abell wrote in *Realm of the Universe* (in 1980) that "stars of about 0.4 solar mass have a main sequence life of some 2×10^{11} years" (200 BYRs), and Herbert Friedman wrote in *The Amazing Universe* in 1975, regarding white dwarfs, "For the smallest stars, evolution off the main sequence may take more than 100 billion years."

Although King admits that it is its, "relatively large store of internal energy [that] keeps a white dwarf shining...the great length of time that it will take it to cool off," and that it might "take an infinite length of time to cool completely," he doesn't suggest an age that is more than that prescribed by the BBT, and Australian astronomer David Campbell wrote in *ASTRONOMY* (in 1999) that it takes an average white dwarf about 10 billion years to cool down from its original temperature to 3,000 K, and thus, "Thus the lack of even cooler white dwarfs is strong testimony for the age of our universe," However, he neglects to mention that cooler white dwarfs, because they are so cool, are not normally seen.

It is suggested here that black holes, if they really exist, and are as stable as Courvoisier and Robson have stated, their age might be equally as great as those of white dwarfs, and the same may be true of neutron stars.

Cosmic Repulsion to the Rescue.

When it became accepted by the establishment that Hubble and Humason showed distant galaxies to be fleeing each other at a rate proportional to their distance, cosmic repulsion was discarded. Gamow reported that Einstein confessed to him that, "the cosmic repulsion idea was the biggest blunder he made in his entire life." But it would seem that BB cosmologists have changed their minds about that blunder. Some BB theorists have recently suggested that cosmic repulsion might provide a solution to the age paradox. As BB supporters Peebles, et al. wrote in 1991, "If objects of the universe prove to be older than 17 billion years, "it would drive us to a cosmological constant."

As touched upon in Chapter 4, if cosmic repulsion were like negative gravity, and of sufficient magnitude, the expansion of the universe in the past may have been sufficiently slow so that the BB may have occurred sufficiently long ago for the universe to be older than some stars are admitted to be. That is, if the universe had a positive cosmological constant for a significant period in the past, its average expansion rate might have been ever slower (an ever lower Hubble constant), providing for an earlier BB, thus rescuing the BB from its age problem.

However, that variety of BBT (illustrated by Curve 4 of Figure 2), would not have been acceptable in the past. According to the Friedmann solution to the Einstein equations, it would require a sufficiently negative cosmic repulsion to cause increasing expansion, meaning a net negative force of gravity (antigravity) and a net negative mass density of the universe. Nevertheless, it has been recently suggested that cosmic repulsion might provide just that as a solution to the BB age paradox.

Actually, that solution is not a new idea, but the revival of one that had been postulated long ago, for example, in the Eddington-Lemaitre cosmological model of about 1930. Quoting History of Science Professor Helge Kragh, "Like his former teacher (Lemaitre) Eddington (in 1933)...strongly believed the necessity of this assumption...in order to avoid the time scale difficulty." Gamow (in 1949) showed that, "with appropriately chosen values of the curvature [of space] and the cosmological constant, any age could be obtained (in order to provide for) agreement with observations," and Lemaitre proposed that the universe had what has been called a "quasistatic phase" that resulted in increased age.

More recently, in 1988, Brandeis University physics professor Larry Abbott suggested that a small positive cosmological constant could cause increased redshifts of remote galaxies to appear more distant than actual, and that it could also cause increasing expansion of the universe, in 1992 University of Chicago physicist Michael Turner agreed that a small cosmological constant could provide added expansive force (acceleration) to the BB universe, and Harvard professor of astronomy John Huchra has agreed, and added that, in view of the recently confirmed large value of the Hubble constant, resulting in the paradox of a universe younger than its galactic formations, the extra push of a small cosmological constant is now required to get BBT out of their age paradox difficulty.

As presented in more detail in Chapter 23, cosmic repulsion had come to the aid of BBT as an essential feature of inflation theory. Upon the advent of that theory, in the early 1980s, which was thought to provide the solution to many of the problems of BBT, Einstein's previously denounced cosmic repulsion, on an enormous scale, was called upon to provide the force necessary for the inflationary expansion of the universe. Instead of the minute force he had proposed as necessary to balance the force of gravity in space, it took on the enormity required to blow up the entire universe.

After decades of rejection, Einstein's cosmic repulsion, has been legitimized by its incorporation into inflation theory, and has now emerged as a possible solution to the BB age problem. Because it has recently been recognized that inflation theory may have failed to provide the desired solutions to many of the problems of BBT, and because of the particular severity of BB age problems, it has become popular to adopt cosmic repulsion as the solution to that problem. Thus a cosmological constant of the required magnitude has again been proposed as the cause of increasing expansion of the universe, extending the age of the BB universe, and solving the BB age problem.

In the accustomed manner of BB cosmologists, in order to meet this new goal, astronomical data previously presented as support for a universe of decelerating expansion is now being reevaluated and presented as support for a universe of accelerating expansion.

As reported in *SCIENTIFIC AMERICAN* reported in 1999,

"Evidence for an accelerating universe continues to pile up," and in 2000, "Contrary to most expectations, they are finding that the expansion of the universe may not be slowing down but rather speeding up."

That, of course, is quite a different BB universe than envisioned in the past: one that had an ever decreasing rate of expansion due to gravitational attraction, or perhaps more properly stated, due to positively curved space. But to BB cosmologists, a solution to the age paradox might warrant the acceptance of a revision to theory. History shows that a number of past revisions have been attempted to cope with their problems. Fear of the age paradox is such that data can be swiftly reinterpreted to provide a solution to it.

As astronomer Geoffrey Burbidge wrote (in *SCIENTIFIC AMERICAN* in 1992) regarding such matters, "Rather than consider alternatives to the big bang, cosmologists contort themselves and propose that the rate of expansion is just small enough to accommodate their oldest well documented stellar ages. Or they vary the big bang model by invoking an arbitrary parameter, the cosmological constant." His comments certainly would apply in the situation described here.

Although Gamow had suggested that a value of the cosmological constant might be chosen for any age that might be desired to solve the age problem, it doesn't seem possible that it could lengthen the age of the BB universe sufficiently to overcome the problem of trillion year old white dwarfs, or even white dwarfs or gigantic galactic structures several hundred billions of years old.

An Old Universe.

The various pieces of evidence presented here tend to support a universe of tens, hundreds or even thousands of billions of years old, far older than envisioned in any BB scenario, and perhaps even infinitely old.

As Rhodes Colleges astronomy professor Gerrit L. Verschuur has said (regarding some astronomers' estimates of globular clusters as old as 17 billion years), "This poses problems for the big bang theory of the origin of the universe. According to that theory, the universe and all it contains is more like 15 billion years, give or take a billion or two. Do astronomers understand the origin of the universe? Not yet, at least not fully."

Even Einstein, the "father of relativistic cosmology" and a firm believer in BBT, is reported to have been willing to give up on his belief in BBT if its age problem could not be solved.

TWELVE

Galaxy Formation Problems

Although some BB cosmologists, including Ostriker, Dressler, and Picard have expressed concerns regarding the formation of galaxies or galactic structures as the result of of gravitational attraction in the BB universe, the inability to present a credible scheme for the formation of those following a smooth BB explosion is generally ignored in establishment literature, or passed off as unimportant or even irrelevant.

Clusters of Galaxies and Quasars Formed Too Soon.

As a result of the *accepted interpretation of redshift data*, not only galaxies and quasars, but clusters of both, are believed to have appeared unreasonably soon after the BB; in as little as a few hundred million years. Furthermore, giant galactic structures may have taken far longer to form than the entire period since the BB is supposed to have occurred.

Science writer Marcia Bartusiak has written, "Particularly imperiled is the notion that virtually all galaxies came into existence at the same moment in the distant past.... Astronomers had once seized on this explanation because it was the simplest," and *SCIENCE NEWS* astronomy writer Ron Cowan wrote (in

1998), "Finding galaxies that existed so soon after the Big Bang puts a bigger burden on theories that seek to explain galaxy formation."

Impossibility of Accretion.

As mentioned in Chapter 7 regarding singularity problems, at the instant of creation all of the particles of the mass of the BB universe were accelerated to above the speed of light, as mentioned in Chapter 5, Gamow calculated that the galaxies are fleeing from each other with a kinetic energy equivalent to about fifty times the gravitational attraction between them, and Paul Davies (in 1984) estimated the "cosmic repulsive force (of inflation) to be 10^{120} times greater than Einstein needed to prop up a static universe".

Although some BBers have estimated the velocity of the initial expansion of the BB universe to be far greater than the speed of light, the analysis of BBT data that is presented in Chapter 21, shows that to be incorrect. For all of the accepted Standard BB cases, the initial velocity of expansion would have been greater than the speed of light, but not at the great many multiples of that speed as often described. However, even at those lower rates, nature provides no known force that could provide for the accretion of matter that would be needed for the formation of galaxies.

That problem undoubtedly became apparent to Gamow who, in disagreement with the smoothness insisted upon by others, postulated that turbulence in the early BB could have been sufficient for the accumulation of matter. However, it is difficult to imagine how, even in the presence of turbulence, how the great departing speed of particles could allow the accretions of matter needed for the formation of galaxies.

As an alternate solution to the BB galaxy formation problem, Peebles suggested that the birth of galaxies might be the result of "primeval magnetic fields." But he added that, "would have to have dissipated before the decoupling", presumably because, otherwise, the MBR—assuming it came from the BB—couldn't be so smooth. Furthermore, that couldn't explain how galaxy formation that came after the decoupling could have occurred.

Regardless of various suggested solutions, it seems impossible that galaxies could have formed in a universe that was expanding at the speed of light or greater.

Inflation to the Rescue.

Over the years BB theorists had developed a variety of scenarios to overcome that difficulty, but none of them had been able to overcome their galaxy formation problem.

However, when inflation theory came along, in addition to its promise to solve several other serious BB problems, it postulated a flat universe of critical density that brought some hope regarding BB galaxy formation: Missing matter, that was postulated to provide for a flat BB universe provided the opportunity to propose all sorts of unknown and undetected matter throughout the universe that could provide for the formation of galaxies and galactic structures.

As Anne Kinney has asked, "How did the universe go from gentle smoothness to chaotic clumpiness?" She suggested the answer to that was, although the universe originally was smooth, density fluctuations produced "the waves of galaxies that formed." But after the advent of inflation, the answer to her question that became widely accepted was that the presence of dark matter provided the gravitational force to overcome the universe's rate of expansion and start the accretion of matter.

With the density of that universe exactly at the critical level, meaning that 98 to 99 percent of the mass of the universe must be unseen dark matter. According to inflation theory that would result in noticeable irregularities: the "seeds" that were necessary to start the process of galaxy formation and cold dark matter became the favored candidate for that mass. Despite the lack of astronomical support of that belief, the majority of BBers accepted it as the solution to their galaxy formation problem: CDM would provide the seeds that were necessary for gravity to form galaxies, clusters and giant galactic structures.

Davies (in 1984) explained that, "The decay of the 'false vacuum' of inflation does not occur at exactly the same instant throughout space...Irregularities will therefore appear in the final state. It is hoped that these irregularities can act as seeds...that lead to galaxies and galactic clusters," and Dennis Overbye, in *Lonely Hearts of the Cosmos* stated that, "In the theory of new inflation authored by Paul Steinhardt, among other things, quantum fluctuations in the first instant of time were revealed to be the source of galaxies."

Details regarding that revelation were not presented. Perhaps it came in a dream.

Doubts about Cold Dark Matter.

As reported in *POPULAR SCIENCE* (in 1993),"Cold dark matter plays a key role in many modern versions of the BB theory in explaining a puzzling paradox. If the universe was smooth and homogeneous at the moment of its creation, why is it now lumpy, filled with aggregates of matter in the form of galaxies?" and perhaps "in the form of clusters, super clusters, voids and sheets of galaxies" should be added to that question.

Henry, Briel and Bohringer have written that, "The inescapable conclusion was that the [galactic] clusters were mostly made of unseen, or 'dark,' matter. But what was the matter?" These two mysteries—the uneven distribution of galaxies in space and the unknown nature of dark matter—continue to confound astronomers." As mentioned in Chapter 5, David Eicher remarked that, "the key question is how the universe went from smooth to lumpy with galaxies."

Various forms of CDM were postulated to cause noticeable irregularities in the smoothness of MBR. But, as reported by Faye Flam in SCIENCE (in 1991), "The cold dark matter model doesn't have what it takes to amass the ever larger cluster of clusters that observers have seen throughout the last 10 years....Cold dark matter, like the blank spaces on a map, is the domain of fanciful entities, so far undetected, with names like 'axions', 'photinos', and 'winos' and 'zinos.'"

John Boslough, in *Masters of Time* told us that Geller and other observational astronomers had said that, "the CDM model was now dead. Neither it nor any other theoretical construct allowed gravity enough time to create the enormous structures such as the Great Wall out of density fluctuations in the early universe that were consistent with a perfectly even background radiation." He quoted Geller as saying that, "We clearly do not know how to make large structures in the context of the big bang."

Quoting Corey S. Powell in *SCIENTIFIC AMERICAN* (in 1992), "Some cosmological models incorporating cold dark matter can account for the existence of large clusters and super-clusters of galaxies. Others can explain the formation of individual galaxies. None can do both. Some researchers therefore suspect that cold dark matter may turn out to be a chimera. 'The physicists have been enormously reluctant to accept what astronomy shows them,' says Arno Penzias, who argues in favor of a less dense universe containing only ordinary matter. 'Cold dark matter is dead,' Peebles agrees.'"

As reported in *SCIENTIFIC AMERICAN* (in 1990), George Eftathiou of the University of Oxford, one of the original advocates of CDM, had concluded that, "The cold dark matter model must be either revised of scrapped."

MBR Too Smooth.

What might have been intended as an optimistic note was sounded by MIT astronomer Edmund Berrschinger (in *SCIENCE* in 1993), who said, "The fact that we have enough data to prove CDM wrong shows we're making progress."

However, efforts to confirm the presence of missing matter, that have been successful only to a limited degree, have failed to confirm a flat universe, and because the MBR has been found too uniform, it has become apparent that CDM theory can't account for galaxy formation.

Although Steinhardt doesn't believe there was enough time for galaxy formation in the BB universe, the article by Faye Flam mentioned above states that, "Steinhardt and many of his colleagues nevertheless hold out hope for the cold dark matter model," and that Schramm was working to find other kinds of seeds, "hoping to find one that can organize matter efficiently enough to explain the structures now being mapped."

Unfortunately for BB inflation advocates, those seeds, the missing matter that is required to support the closed or flat BB universe cases and provide for the formation of galaxies has not materialized, and as a result, as mentioned in Chapter 9, Ostriker has announced the "death knell" of CDM theory.

In a discussion of the "Great Attractor" in a *SCIENTIFIC AMERICAN* article of October, 1998 Cambridge University astronomers Renée C. Kraan-Korteweg and Ofer Lahav wrote, regarding clustering of less distant galaxies, "vast cosmic filaments challenge theories of dark matter and galactic formation" and, repeating from above, Fay Flam has reported that, "The cold dark matter model doesn't have what it takes to amass the ever larger cluster of clusters that observers have seen throughout the last 10 years."

No Explanation for the Formation of galaxies.

American astronomers Margaret and Geoffrey Burbidge have been quoted as saying that, "Undoubtedly one of the greatest shortcoming of cosmological theories is their failure to provide a working model of the formation of galaxies." That of course was true regarding all cosmological theories as of 1963, when that statement was made. As reported in *SCIENCE NEWS* (in 1998) astronomer Arjun Dey of Johns Hopkins University has said that, "The most important science facing astronomers today is how galaxies formed. At the moment there are lots of theories but no observations to constrain any of these theories."

Regarding the BB galaxy formation problem, Carr struggled (in 1982) with "the enigma" of a BB universe that "started off very smooth," but, soon after the BB, "the degree of irregularity was fine-tuned to result in galaxies and clusters in a universe that now has "remarkable large-scale homogeneity."

Peebles, et al. (in 1994) wrote, "Our understanding of the genesis and evolution of the universe is one of the great achievements of 20th-century science." They also wrote, "At present there are no fundamental challenges to the BBT, although there are certain unresolved issues within the theory itself. Astronomers are not sure, for example, how the galaxies were formed, but there is no reason to think that the process did not occur within the framework of the BB. Indeed, the predictions of the theory have survived all tests to date." However, both of those comments are incorrect. There is no such understanding of evolution, many BB predictions have been incorrect, and no actual tests of BB have been performed.

In an article in *ASTRONOMY* (in 1992) Jeff Kanipe quoted astronomer Ethan Vishniac of the Universe of Texas as saying, "I would say the current situation is that we have no believable theory of galaxy formation." Kanipe added, "For some astronomers the downfall of the cold dark matter model has made the Big Bang look guilty by association, a view many astronomers reject. 'Cold dark matter is a theory about the beginning of the formation of structure,' says BB cosmologist James Peebles. 'The Big Bang is something quite different....They [the press] take the discussions about the beginnings of structure and confuse them with the beginning of the universe.'"

In his book, *The Vindication of The Big Bang* (of 1993), professor of physics and astronomy Barry Parker quoted Ostriker as saying, the origin of galaxies and the hot big bang are completely separate issues," and David Schramm was quoted as saying, "It is not the big bang that is having problems, the problems are with galaxy and structure formation. The structure problem has nothing to do with the big bang."

However, physicist and cosmologist Anthony Peratt, who "suggests scrapping the Big Bang altogether," has properly responded to that nonsense with, "The Big Bang theorist attempt to decouple themselves from the problem of galaxy formation. But one must ask what kind of cosmology is it that cannot account for the galaxies and stars that we observe....Big Bang cosmologists have struggled mightily to find a mechanism for galaxy formation in spite of their arguments that it is not their problem." That, I submit, provides yet another example of their lack of intellectual honesty.

Many additional examples from the literature could be presented that illustrate the inability of BB cosmologists to explain the formation of galaxies and gigantic galactic structures, but those that have been presented should be more than sufficient to illustrate that problem.

THIRTEEN

Microwave Background Radiation Problems

BBers insist that the MBR that is received from all directions of space not only provides proof of the BB, but of a very smooth BB. As mentioned in Chapter 6, Edward Tryon had written that the 2.7 K MBR "establishes beyond reasonable doubt" the correctness of some version of BBT. However, serious doubts remain, some of which are presented in this chapter.

MBR from the BB Decoupling.

The reception of microwave radio energy from surrounding space, believed to have originated sometime in the range of 100,000 to one million years after the BB, was predicted by George Gamow in 1954 when he said that a "great event" occurred "when matter took over from radiation, i.e., surpassed it in mass density." As usually stated, the universe was "radiation dominated" before the decoupling and "matter dominated" after it.

Gamow's great event, that became known as the decoupling, is called that because reactions between radiation and matter are said to have virtually ceased after that. At that point the previously opaque universe became clear, and radiation is said to have traveled unscattered through space to become the MBR received today. Because of the postulated expansion of space since that time, its wavelength is said to have red-shifted from the infrared to the microwave band of EMR. Martin Rees stated (in 1976) that, "microwave photons detected on Earth have been propagating uninterruptedly through space for 99.9 percent of the time since the big bang."

Apparently to stress the implication that it comes from the BB decoupling, BBers insist on calling the MBR "cosmological background radiation", or CBR. But that is far from a proven fact, in fact, it cannot be so. Its source its not known, and may originate relatively nearby, so it is called microwave background radiation, or MBR, in this book

Some History of MBR Temperature Estimates.

It is claimed that the prediction of MBR from the BB provides powerful support for BBT, but estimates of the present MBR temperature were scattered and quite inaccurate. Furthermore, the 5 K prediction of Ralph Alpher and Robert Herman that is invariably quoted as providing proof of BBT was based on erroneous assumptions. (It should be understood that, as used by radio engineers, and as it is in this case, signal strength is frequently expressed as an equivalent temperature.)

Kragh has said that Dicke had predicted an MBR temperature of about 20 K in 1946 and had reestimated that to be 40 K in the 1960s. In fairly good agreement with that, physicist Stephen G. Brush, who has taught history of science at University of Maryland, and before that conducted research in theoretical physics at Lawrence Livermore Laboratories, has stated that Dicke had estimated "less than 20 K" in 1946 but, later on, revised that to 45 K. Dicke's estimate was later modified to about 10 K by his colleague Peebles, and following the measurement of about three degrees by Arno Penzias and Robert Wilson of Bell Laboratories in 1965, Peebles adjusted his calculations to agree with that number.

It is well documented that Gamow, using a formula he had devised, predicted a temperature of about 50 K, but in 1948, based on Gamow's work, his students Alpher and Herman reestimated Gamow's prediction to 5 K. However, although it is never mentioned by BBers, a year later they changed their prediction to 28 K. (Gamow's formula was that the temperature of the universe equals 1.5×10^{10} divided by the square root of the age of the universe in seconds, resulting in his estimate of 50 K.

Some sources insist that Gamow stated the MBR temperature to be "a few degrees Kelvin," but that has not been found in the literature.)

Regardless of a wide range of other estimates, only the 5 K estimate of Alpher and Herman is mentioned in BB literature: All other estimates are ignored. Also ignored are the estimates of MBR temperature by scientists that were far more accurate than most of those of BB cosmologists.

Estimates of background temperature by scientists, including Nernst, Eddington, Regener and McKellar, based on actual matter observed in the universe, were closer to the subsequently observed value than most of the estimates by BBers. Others who have agreed with the ideas of those scientists include Narlikar, Peebles, Rowan-Robinson and Hoyle.

Chemist Walther Nernst, Nobel prize winner in 1920 for his work in thermodynamics, estimated 0.75 K in 1938.

In 1926 British astrophysicist and mathematician Sir Arthur Eddington had suggested that the amount of light from stars was equivalent to a thermal background temperature of 3.2 degrees K, in the 1930s cosmologist Ernst Regener concluded that intergalactic space had a background of temperature 2.8 K, and in 1941 Canadian astronomer Andrew McKellar estimated that temperature to be 2.3 K; temperatures that are quite close to what is observed.

Astrophysicist Jayant Narlikar has said that the energy density of MBR "is not too different from the energy densities observed in other astrophysical phenomena in the universe," Peebles has agreed that the energy density of the MBR "is comparable to (that of) starlight near the edge of the Milky Way," and Rowan-Robinson has written, "It is still just about possible, however, to explain the background in terms of the superposition of discrete sources spread throughout the universe."

Hoyle had also estimated that the energy of starlight was of the same order of magnitude as the 3 K radiation, (about 10^{-20} Joules per cubic centimeter), and the *Encyclopedia of Physics* reports that, "the energy density of cosmic rays...is comparable to the energy density of the 2.8 K of cosmic background radiation...whether that is a coincidence or has fundamental significance is an unanswered question."

Temperature Discrepancies.

If the temperature is now about 3K, and about 3,000 at the time of the decoupling, and therefore the redshift since the decoupling is about 1,000, that presents an additional fault in the chronology that is usually presented. As shown in Figure 1, that fault is that the plot of temperature vs. time passes through 1,000 K rather than 3,000 K.

Adrian Webster explained (in 1974) that the 10 to 1 difference between Gamow's predicted present temperature and that derived from current observations (50 K rather than 5 K) is due to changes in the "large-scale dynamics of the universe....the temperature drops off a little faster than before" the great event, and, after abandoning SST just a year before, Dennis Sciama (in 1967) wrote, also without providing further explanation, that an MBR "temperature as high as 30 degrees can be ruled out" because "cosmic ray protons and electrons interacting with such radiation" would produce effects that haven't been observed and "three degrees is about the highest permitted temperature from this point of view."

Those comments, made without further explanation two years after Arno Penzias' and Robert Wilson's discovery of the MBR, apparently were intended to support BBT, providing an excuse for Gamow's poor estimate (and possibly to provide an explanation for the plot of Figure 1 passing through 1,000 K instead of 3,000 K).

The 5 K prediction of Alpher and Herman is forever quoted by BBers as the final proof of BBT. However, not only do they fail to mention that that prediction was later readjusted to 28 K, but they fail to mention that their work was based on the erroneous assumptions mentioned above.

Those assumptions included, not only that the BB and the photon decoupling had occurred at all but, at the time of that prediction, BBers believed that all of the elements of the universe were produced by nucleosynthesis prior to the decoupling. Later on, when it was learned that all the heavier elements of the universe are produced in stars, BBT was revised to allow only the production of helium and small quantities of other light elements by BB fusion. One might guess that so great a misconception regarding BBT would have significant impact on such details as the decoupling of photons.

However, as with the prophecies of Nostradamus and other such seers, if enough predictions are made, some are sure to come to pass, and those that do not are often ignored.

Decoupling Discrepancies.

Various BB sources have postulated that the BB decoupling happened about 100,000 to 1,000,000 years after the BB, at a temperature of about 2,000 to 5,000 degrees; or perhaps it extended over those ranges of time and temperature. Photons from that decoupling, which were "undisturbed from that time on," are said to be the source of the MBR at 2.7 degrees K, that was first detected by Penzias and Wilson who's measurements were made at a wavelength of 7.35 cm (a frequency of 4 GHz).

Adrian Webster said the decoupling occurred about 300,000 years after the BB, producing black-body radiation at a temperature of about 5,000 degrees K; Steven Weinberg *In The First Three Minutes* said that the decoupling occurred 700,000 years after the BB when the temperature of the universe was at 3,000 K; and for some reason, Carr (in 1982) decided that the decoupling took place one million years after the BB when the temperature of the universe was about 4,000 K. At that time, working backward with Gamow's formula, the temperature would be about 2,700 K; and Berkeley physicist Richard A. Muller (in 1978) said that the temperature at the time of the decoupling was 4,500 K and the redshift of its radiation was 1,500.

Some theorists have postulated that the decoupling didn't occur in an instant, but over an extended period encompassing those times and temperatures. For example, Silk (in 1980 and again in 1989) said the decoupling started at 300,000 years and ended at 1,000,000 years after the BB, and Ivan R. King in *The Universe Unfolding* wrote that "The background radiation decoupled when it universe was about a million years old."

Those disagreements among various theorists add to the confusion about the hypothetical decoupling.

Gamow's original postulation of BBT indicated the decoupling occurred at about 250,000 years after the BB, at a temperature of about 170 K. But in most current literature, BBers have settled on the decoupling to have occurred about 300,000 years after the BB, the redshift of radiation from that period to be about 1,000, and the temperature at that time to be about

1,000 times higher than the present MBR temperature, or about 3,000 K.

Goldsmith, in *Einstein's Greatest Blunder?*, tells us that, "high energy gamma-ray photons that emerged in great numbers during the early minutes of the cosmos have become the low-energy photons that the fill the universe today." Joseph Silk in *The Big Bang* agreed that, "As the universe expanded, the background radiation has passed through the entire spectrum from gamma rays to radio."

However, there seems to be some confusion there. According to the generally accepted BB chronology, at the time of the BB decoupling of MBR photons, at a redshift of about 1,000, they would have been in the infrared region; but for them to have been in the gamma ray region would correspond to a redshift of about 10^{11}, and a time of about one minute after the BB—about the postulated time of the postulated BB nucleosynthesis, rather than that of the MBR photon decoupling.

MBR Photon Energy Discrepancy.

Based on the predictions of their temperature by various BB cosmologists, the energy of the MBR photons would vary over a wide range and be far different than that based on the observed temperature. Some estimates of temperature were more than 18 times the measured temperature of 2.7K, and, in accordance with the Stefan-Boltzmann law (which puts energy density proportional to the fourth power of absolute temperature) equals 5 million times as much energy $[(50-2.7)^4 = 5 \times 10^6]$. That wide range of energy would seem to further discredit a scientific basis for MBR from the BB.

MBR Photon Energy Estimate.

Calculations that are presented in Appendix E provide some additional interesting results regarding MBR photon energy. They are based on the Stefan-Boltzmann law and on typical data that is postulated for Standard BBT—not necessarily the real universe. Perhaps because of the embarrassment they might cause, this information is absent from establishment literature.

Three results of those calculation are as follows:
1. The density of MBR photons throughout the space of the present universe results in a MBR photon energy of about 0.0006 eV.

2. The present MBR photon energy would equal about 0.14 percent of the total equivalent energy of the observable universe.
3. The loss of energy of MBR photons in space since the decoupling would equal about 1.4 times the total equivalent energy of the present observable universe.

The first two of the results given above may be only of passing interest, but the third would seem to present a serious problem to BBT.

MBR Photon Missing Energy.

As mentioned above, MBR photons from the decoupling are said to have cooled by a factor of about 1,000 from 3,000 K to about 3 K. The calculations of Appendix E, based on the energy scale of Figure 1, show that the total MBR energy would have been 1,000 times greater at the time of the decoupling than at present. Therefore, they have lost 99.9 percent of their original energy, which is almost twice the equivalent energy of the present observable universe. Therefore, the question arises, "What happened to that enormous amount of energy?"

The only answers to that question I have received from a BB source is, "that it disappears into the 'fine structure of space' [what ever that means] and eventually reappears in the structures of atoms," or as Donald Goldsmith wrote in *Einstein's Greatest Blunder?*, "The only good answer to the question Where has the photon energy gone? is 'Doppler theft,' the robbery of energy by the expanding universe itself." Neither of those answers are supported by Standard BBT nor by any known science.

Radio astronomy pioneer Grote Reber, who had mapped the sky with a home-made antenna at a wavelength of 144 meters (2.08 MHz), discovered (in the early 1940s) that there is considerable energy in the universe at low radio frequencies. Could that be where some of the missing MBR energy has gone? Perhaps; but that energy could have come from a number of natural sources in the universe.

BBers might have seized upon Reber's work to provide at least a partial answer to the question of the missing MBR energy, but because he rejects their theory, they ignore his work, as they do of all of those who don't accept their theory.

Smoothness of the MBR.

According to BBers, photons from the decoupling are raining on the Earth, and on all other bodies of the universe, equally from all directions of space, providing proof of the smoothness of the BB explosion. As Paul Davies assured us (in 1984), "If the universe were to expand faster in one direction than in others, it would depress the temperature of the background heat radiation from that direction....So not only did the universe commence with a bang of precise magnitude, it was a highly orchestrated explosion." However, the directional uniformity of the MBR cannot be reconciled with the observed nonuniformities of matter distribution in the universe.

Scientist such as Tom Van Flandern, who reject BB, agree that the observed irregularities in the distribution of matter in the universe, such as voids and clusters of galaxies, would disrupt the smoothness of MBR from the BB; and, amazingly, a number of BB Cosmologists have also agreed.

Some example are given as follows:

Standard BBT indicates the the MBR has stayed smooth since the decoupling. Its photons were "undisturbed from that time on." However, although they are firm believers in BBT, Rees and Silk wrote (in 1970) that, although prior to the decoupling these photons "attained thermal equilibrium with its surroundings as a result of repeated absorption and reemission," and admitted they "would not all have been redshifted by exactly the same amount; in some directions they might have been scattered off material with a random velocity toward us, whereas in other directions the last-scattering surface may have been receding from us. As a consequence the microwave temperature would be slightly nonuniform over the sky."

Although he is also a firm believer in BBT, Paul Davies (in 1984) wrote that the MBR, "would carry the imprint of any departures from uniformity encountered on the way." Sufficiently large imprints of those departures haven't been found.

In addition to Ostriker's agreement (in Chapter 8) that the growing evidence of large-scale inhomogeneity in the universe's structure conflicts with the uniformity of the MBR, Barrow and Silk have written that, "The strength of the gravitational field of the largest of these inhomogeneities suggests that their ancient precursors would have created an anistropy in the microwave background over a scale of a few angular degrees," which, of course, hasn't been found.

Peebles (in 1993) wrote that, if a black hole "were placed in a nearby void, it would be detectable by the hole it makes in the CBR [cosmic background radiation]." He also wrote that, "if the wave packet falls into a potential well that differs from the one it moves out of, the result is a gravitational redshift or blueshift of the photon energy, and a perturbation to the CBR temperature." Translated into English; "massive bodies in space would have disrupted the smoothness of the MBR and distorted its black body spectrum."

Rather than supporting the postulated BB decoupling as the source of the MBR, its almost perfect black-body spectrum, and its almost perfect smoothness, deny the BB decoupling as its source. The MBR undoubtedly is radiation from sources other than BB that, in some manner, is smoothed in the space that surrounds us to produce the 2.7K black-body spectrum that is observed.

BB Photons from All Direction Not Possible.

Due to the presence of giant galactic formations in the universe, it is inconceivable that MBR photons that came directly from a BB decoupling are now received uniformly from all directions. That would also be true of a BB universe that was less than perfectly spherical.

In addition to those difficulties, the reception of BB photons from all directions can only be attributed to a closed BB universe of the closed space of positive curvature which, due to time constraints and other considerations, has been shown to be impossible. In the other BB universe cases, of uncurved or negatively curved space, those photons would have long ago dispersed at the speed of light out to the edge of the BB universe, never to be seen by us.

(In all my many years of study I have only found one astronomer who agreed with me regarding that statement. In *ASTRONOMY* of August, 1999 Phil Plait acknowledged that, "The latest findings show that the universe is open anyway, so a photon will just travel forever, never circling back.")

Smearing.

There are at least three reasons why it is inconceivable that a black-body spectrum could have been retained if it started from the BB decoupling as black-body radiation:

(1) differences in radiation travel times as a result of giant galactic structures in the universe.

(2) a less than a perfectly spherical universe at any time during or after the BB explosion, and

(3) the nonlinear expansion of the universe during the extended period of the decoupling.

The effect of irregularities in the universe on the MBR would certainly have cause a less than perfect black-body spectrum—a "smeared" spectrum. If MBR photons have been bouncing around the universe for 10 to 15 billion years, with all the possibilities for smearing of their black-body spectrum due to time and temperature differences, the impossibility of an undistorted black-body spectrum should be obvious.

If the expansion BB universe had ever been less than perfectly spherical, that also would certainly have smeared a black-body spectrum.

There are a number of BBers who have postulated that the decoupling occurred over an extended period of time. If that is true, because they believed that the expansion of the universe has ever been decelerating, that deceleration would certainly have resulted in distortion (smearing) of the black-body spectrum of the MBR they believe originated from the decoupling.

Some BB theorist have referred to the decoupling as a "flash." As Halton Arp has written, "upon realization of this problem BBers decided that decoupling happened in a 'very thin shell,'" but other BBers have indicated that it went on for hundreds of thousands of years, during which the radiated spectrum would have been distorted by changing temperature and changing redshift.

As Donald Goldsmith told us in *The Astronomers*, "The time of the decoupling occurred about a million years after the big bang. In truth, this was no single moment, but a phrase like 'the many millenniums of decoupling' lacks firepower." Although he adds that, "Compared to the time that had elapsed since the big bang that was a mere moment," but it is actually a significant length of time.

Undoubtedly it has occurred to some BBers that smearing of a black-body spectrum would result if the decoupling had occurred over an extended period, so the admission of that is carefully avoided by them.

BBers who admit to an extended period of decoupling might assume that those effects would tend to cancel, but unless the universe has the linear characteristics of Figure 1 (or Curve 3 of Figure 2), that is, it is of the fixed-rate variety, rather than closed, flat or somewhat open as they believe (having a decelerating expansion that is quite nonlinear), that cancellation could not be perfect.

Rather than supporting the postulated BB decoupling as the source of the MBR, its almost perfect black-body spectrum and its almost perfect smoothness tend to deny that position.

Thermalization.

As mentioned above, the predictions of the MBR temperature that were made by scientists long before its detection were considerably more accurate than those based on BBT, and the evidence of other sources of energy from space at levels comparable to that of the MBR provide reason to doubt its source was the BB. The nearly correct prediction of MBR temperature (Alpher and Herman's 5 K), only one of many MBR temperature predictions by BBers, provides no proof that it originated in the BB.

However, for the suggested alternate sources of the MBR, as thought possible by those estimators, the observed spectrum and isotropy of the MBR could only be attributed to the thermalization of that energy (the equalization of temperature of the radiation). As Eric Lerner explained, "The energy of the massive stars would be adsorbed by interstellar dust, which would then emit the microwave background."

Paul Marmet, of the Herzberg Institute of Astrophysics and retired physics professor of the University of Ottawa has said, "The existence of the 3 K MBR is no longer valid evidence for the big bang. There is no need to assume, as Big Bang believers do, that this background radiation came from a highly Doppler redshifted black-body at about 3,000 K...The background radiation is simply Planck's black-body radiation emitted naturally by our unlimited universe that is also at a temperature of about 3 K," and as astronomer Tom Van Flandern, who has a PhD degree in celestial mechanics from Yale, summed up the opinion of many who deny MBR from the BB in his statement, "It therefore must be the result from the re-emission of microwaves from the relatively close inter-galactic medium."

Whiskers and Grains.

In support of the idea that MBR can only be explained by radiation that came directly from the hypothetical BB decoupling, some BB cosmologists have attempted to show mathematically that, because the space of the universe surrounding us is "optically thin," it is impossible for it to have been thermalized, and therefore it cannot produce a spectrum that closely resembles that of a black-body. However, it does seems strange that BB cosmologists can postulate that 98 to 99 percent of the mass of the universe exists in the form of unidentified dark matter but, in some mysterious manner, they know that it is optically thin.

Despite the optically thin contention, there is considerable evidence of the presence of what has been called "whiskers" or "grains" in and around our galaxy, that might provide the means of thermalization of EMR. There is theoretical support, and both laboratory and astronomical evidence, for the presence of graphite whiskers or grains that are distributed throughout the space within and around our galaxy. The size of those particles is such that they might absorb and reradiate energy in the band of wavelengths necessary to produce thermalized MBR.

As has been presented in Chapter 11, additional evidence for the presence of whiskers in interstellar space may be provided by metallic flakes that are found, along with bits of silicon, in meteorites that are said to have formed during the birth of the solar system.

Ivan King has written, "We are forced to conclude that the interstellar dust is a mixture of grains of different kinds, one of which is small particles of graphite;" SKY & TELESCOPE reported in 1997 that, "Observations show that AGB (asymptotic giant branch) stars pulsate with periods of 200 to 600 days, and that they lose matter from their surfaces in the form of powerful winds. These winds carry out freshly made carbon and neutron-rich elements as well as dust grains that have been formed in the star's relatively cool outer atmosphere;" ASTRONOMY reported (in 1992) that, "Supporters also argue that the CBR is actually normal radiation from stars, radiation that has been scattered by metallic whiskers sown through the interstellar medium," and Harwit, in *Astrophysical Concepts*, devotes several pages to the discussion of interstellar grains.

Although those sources only mention the presence of whiskers and grains within galaxies, there is little doubt that it is also present the dark matter that that has been found to surround galaxies, and undoubtedly results in the thermalization of radiation from all directions of of space.

Thermalization Accepted By Some BB Cosmologists.

Although some BBers ignore the possibility of the thermalization of radiant energy from matter and processes in space, they have ignored the evidence for grains or whiskers that would support that possibility. But schemes that others have postulated directly support the possibility of thermalization, and the schemes of others, perhaps unintentionally, would require it.

Many BBers insist that the MBR comes directly from the BB decoupling. However, others have indicated that it bounced around the universe ever since the BB, which, of course, implies that it had been thermalized.

As an example of that (as quoted in Chapter 5), Barrow and Silk have suggested that, "the radiation (MBR) might have been rescattered by the intergalactic medium on its journey to the solar system and hence its variations might have been smoothed" which certainly sounds like thermalization, and, although denying the possibility of thermalization, Sciama and Peebles et al. have agreed that the possibility of radiation from space over a wide range of wavelengths might be expected from the creation of matter in space. But of course, that would also have required thermalization.

Regarding the question of how another theory might explain the presence of MBR, BB advocate Dennis Sciama said (in 1967), "It would be reasonable to propose that along with the newly created matter there comes into existence newly created radiation; indeed, some such effect would be expected as a result of the creation process itself." Also regarding that question, Peebles, et al. (in 1991) said, "it would be reasonable to suppose radiation is created along with the continuous creation of baryons, but absurd to suppose the spectrum of the created radiation is just such that the integrated background...adds up to a thermal form," strangely similar to Sciama's comments of 24 years earlier. But it seems that the thermalization of that radiation from space may not be so absurd.

Richard Gott, though a firm believer in BBT, has suggested that MBR might originate as thermal radiation from the event horizons of many black holes that exist throughout the universe. Hawking radiation resembling BB radiation may be scattered evenly throughout the universe. Hawking himself has also suggested that. But if radiation from such sources came directly to us, it could not have a characteristic black-body spectral distribution.

Even if all such radiation from black holes somehow originated at the same temperature, because of the dispersal of black holes in space, the MBR spectrum would be smeared due to differences in redshift. The only manner in which a black-body spectrum could be received as a result of those sources is by thermalization of that radiation.

As demonstrated here, when thermalization is postulated in support of BBT, it is perfectly acceptable. However, when it is presented in opposition to BBT, it has been rejected.*

Ripples in the Cosmos.

On April 24, 1992, newspapers and, within the following couple of weeks, broadcast newsmen and science magazines across the United States announced a great discovery.

It was "ripples...at the edge of the universe" that "have provided the first evidence of how the stars and galaxies were formed." This "strongest support yet for the birth of the universe" was hailed in the news as "one of the major discoveries of the century."

---

* The reader should be aware that reports of smoothness of the MBR have been corrected for the drift of our galaxy toward the Great Attractor at about 600 km per second, for our solar system's motion within our galaxy of about 220 km per second, and for the Earth's orbital speed of about 30 km per second. The directions of these motions, each quite different, are such that our net velocity with respect to the received MBR is about 390 km per second. That motion shows up as a measured signal difference in opposing directions of space equivalent to about 0.0035 degree K.

That temperature differential is of significance to the consideration of the thermalization of radiation from space. Regardless of the source of that radiation, its thermalization must occur due to reactions with matter that is in place in and around our galaxy.

The significance of this "unbelievably important" discovery "cannot be overstated." It's the "Holy Grail of cosmology" that, if true "would have to be considered for a Nobel Prize."

Paul Steinhardt's reaction was quoted as, "These observations tell us about the universe back to the very beginning." Joseph Silk's reaction was, "It's the missing link." And it was later reported that Stephen Hawking said, "it is the discovery of the century, if not of all time."

In that news release, reporting on the results of experiments aboard the Cosmic Background Explorer (COBE) satellite, not only was the importance of those "ripples" overstated, it was overstated by orders of magnitude. The writers of that news release and some important BBers appear to have gotten carried away with the enthusiasm of the experimenters for their work.

University of California astrophysicist and COBE team leader George Smoot was reported as repeatedly declaring this to be "the golden age of cosmology" (a phrase that was used earlier by David Schramm when reporting his reaction to earlier bad news for CDM).

Since its invention years ago a basic tenet of BBT has been that the cosmos began as a perfectly smooth mixture of "primordial matter". In 1965, when the MBR was discovered coming from all directions of space, it has been considered to be the most important evidence, not only in support of the BB, but in support of the smoothness of the BB.

Over the years following that discovery more and more sophisticated detection methods have found that radiation to be increasingly smooth causing BBers to become increasingly pleased with what they considered to be all but positive proof of a smooth BB. But as time progressed some of them had become increasingly concerned about too much smoothness. But, during the past decades greater and greater irregularities have been found in the matter of space, some reaching a half a billion light-years across.

In addition to the comments of Ostriker, Dressler, Picard and others presented in Chapter 8 regarding conflicts between the postulated smoothness of the BB and those irregularities, one science news writer reminded his readers that, as embarrassment grew over the increasingly excessive smoothness of MBR, theorists "obligingly adjusted their models to accommodate the ever smaller initial density fluctuations."

Although cosmologist Robert Oldershaw commented regarding Smoot's tiny ripples that, "Even the strongest piece of evidence (the smoothness of MBR) has turned on it," some BBers haven't given up hope on CDM theory. Smoot, who announced the results of the COBE Differential Microwave Radiometer data on April 23, 1992, is included among those. He is quoted as saying, "the temperature and size of the ripples also provide strong confirmation of the theory that as much as 90 % of the matter of the universe is so-called cold dark matter."

Decades ago each report of increased smoothness was hailed as increased confirmation of BBT. But when smoothness was reported as one part in 1,000, some cosmologist began to express concern about that degree of uniformity. Through the years measurements have gradually increased, causing increasing concern, and with the new measurements, approaching one part in 100,000, the smoothness of MBR became too embarrassingly perfect.

However, it was inevitable that sooner or later, as more precise measurements were made, a limit to the smoothness of MBR would be reached. If a product of nature appears smooth on some scale (like viewing the surface of the earth's oceans from a spacecraft), when examined more and more closely it will eventually be found to have some degree of irregularity (like ocean waves).

Smoot was quoted as saying that, "after considerable computer processing," the results were withheld until his team could "check and recheck for possible errors in 70 million measurements at each of the three radiometers (of COBE)." Although computer processing can retrieve data from poor quality signals (which in this case were below the noise level of the instrumentation), unfortunately, neither computer processing or checking and rechecking poor data can make corrections for unknown system errors.

Certainly Smoot and his team were aware of that, and tried to give them proper consideration. But, even if they did so, isn't it obvious that the reported variations, equivalent to plus or minus 15 millionths of a degree K in radiation from the BB decoupling, are insignificantly small as compared to what might be expected as a result of the presence of the gigantic galactic formations found in space? The reported variations of MBR were so minute that they might have originated from any number of unknown or unsuspected sources.

Although those variations were far too small to have any significance, Smoot was quoted in the October 1992 issue of *DISCOVER* magazine as saying, "If you are religious it's like looking at God...its the Holy Grail of Cosmology, its the birth of the universe, the handwriting of God."

In the original story in April 1992, he was quoted as saying, "I know I'm going out on a limb" but, blinded by enthusiasm for his work, he apparently had no idea how frail that limb might be. His reported ripples change nothing.

FOURTEEN

Neutrino Problems

Several problems regarding the postulated presence of BB neutrinos throughout the space of the universe are presented in this chapter.

Neutrino Decoupling.

According to BBT, in addition to that of MBR photons, a flood of neutrinos was decoupled from the "primordial soup" of the early expanding universe. That is said to have happened at about 300,000 years before the decoupling of black-body photons, at about one second after the BB. At that time the temperature of the tiny (just a few hundred kilometers), violently expanding universe was about 10 billion K. Thus those primordial neutrinos would have had a redshift of about one billion from the time of their decoupling to the present.

It has been also estimated that they presently fill the universe at an energy level of about 70% of that of BB photons, equivalent to a temperature of about 2 K. The estimated number of BB neutrinos present varies from about 100 hundred to two hundred per cubic centimeter throughout the space of the universe (as compared to an estimated 400 or so MBR photons per cc), but based on one authoritative BB source the correct number is 113 per cubic centimeter. They are assumed to be electron neutrinos.

As mentioned in Chapter 9, MACHOS previously had been a favored candidate for missing mass of the BB universe. However, because searches failed to provide sufficient evidence for their presence, BB neutrinos became the favored candidate.

Undetected BB Neutrinos.

The reason given by theorists that those neutrinos haven't been detected is that they were decoupled much earlier than the MBR photons, making their redshift much larger, and their energy too low to be detected.

Neutrinos produced in the nuclear reactions of the Sun can be detected, and are regularly detected (but at only 1/3 to 1/2 the expected numbers). In addition to that, a short burst of neutrinos was detected from Supernova 1987A, the explosion of a blue super-giant star in the Large Magellanic Cloud named Sanduleak) that produced an enormous number of them.*

Because a neutrino background temperature of 2 K is assumed, it must therefore also be assumed that BB neutrinos, like MBR photons, have a black-body spectrum. Although neutrinos are usually thought of as particles, the rationale provided by BB theorists to account for their low energy is that they can also be thought of as waves. Accordingly, they are thought to lose energy due to the expansion of the universe in the same manner as thought of MBR photons.

According to accepted wave/particle duality of quantum theory, photons sometimes appear to behave as particles and sometimes as waves. Thus it is believed that, because the universe expanded by

---

* A burst of neutrinos of (variously reported from 10 to 19 of them) were detected (during a period said to range from 10 to 13 seconds) at various detection facilities throughout the world.

Those facilities are the GALLEX solar neutrino project (at the Gran Sasso underground laboratory in the Mont Blanc Tunnel linking Italy and France), SAGE (for Soviet-American Gallium Experiment, in a tunnel under Mount Elbrus in Russia), the University of Tokyo Kamiokande Detector (in a lead and zinc mine, 200 km west of Tokyo), the Fairfax, Ohio detector in a salt mine under Lake Erie shore, and at a University of Pennsylvania facility in the Homestake gold mine near Lead, South Dakota.

Other than Kamiokande, its not clear from media reports which facilities detected SN1987A neutrinos. One report says also "in the salt mine under Lake Erie" and another says also at Kamiokande, GALLEX, and SAGE.

a factor of 1,000 since their decoupling, the wavelength of BB photons has increased, and their frequency decreased by that amount as they traveled at the velocity of light through time and space from their decoupling.

Neutrino Wavelength.

In accordance with quantum theory, that duality is also said to apply, not only to fundamental particles, including neutrons, protons, and electrons, but to all the matter of the universe. Every object, regardless of size, is said to have its wave function, which includes you and me, planets, moons, stars, and all there is in the universe, including neutrinos.

Accordingly, because the universe is estimated to have expanded by a factor of one billion since their decoupling, BB neutrinos, in their wave guise, are said to have a redshift of about one billion. As a result, their wavelength, that is estimated to have originated at a length of about 0.001 centimeter, is presently about one million centimeters (about 6.2 miles) in the present universe. The frequency (and energy) of those neutrinos would thus be far too low to be detected by any available means.

Those neutrinos, now in the present universe, like MBR photons, would also be expected to have a black body spectrum that is consistent with a temperature of about 2 K.

Neutrino Mass.

Because neutrinos from any source pass virtually unimpeded through all objects, it is impossible to detect more than a small fraction of them by presently available techniques. Vast numbers of them are generated in the nuclear reactions of the Sun, from which they have a negligibly small redshift or energy loss. However, in several neutrino detection sites in the world, only a small number are detected each day.

The reason for such low detection rates is that, although neutrinos react to the weak force, they do not react to the strong force, because they have no charge they do not react to electromagnetism, and, although they may react to gravity, their mass is so low that their reaction to that force is correspondingly small. It has been estimated that a neutrino can pass through the Earth with a chance of only one in 200 million of interacting with matter.

However, the arrival of neutrinos from SN1987A, at a distance estimated to be 166,000 light years, was essentially concurrent with its visual detection, indicating their speed to be at or very near to that of light. Thus their rest mass is either zero, or a very small fraction of an electron volt (eV). According to General Relativity, if the mass of those neutrinos was more than a tiny fraction of an electron volt, they couldn't have been accelerated to such speed.

(Those neutrinos were actually detected a few hours before light from the SN1987A explosion was detected. The explanation that has been given for that is that light—that is, electromagnetic radiation—was delayed in its passage though matter ejected from the supernova explosion, whereas the neutrinos passed through it undelayed.)

Regardless of that, neutrinos from SN 1987A were received here on Earth at essentially the same time as light, providing strong evidence that those neutrinos, in agreement with the long accepted Standard Model of Particle Physics, have little or no mass. Because their primary hope has been that the presence of "massive" BB neutrinos throughout the universe would provide the missing mass that is necessary for a flat universe, that lack of that mass has been a disappointment to many BB cosmologists

BB Neutrino Energy.

Calculations that are presented in Appendix E provide some interesting results regarding BB neutrino energy. As in the discussion regarding MBR photon energy in the previous chapter, the calculations of neutrino energy are based on the Stefan-Boltzmann law and on typical data that is postulated for Standard BBT—not necessarily the real universe.

Three results of those calculations are as follows:

1. The density of BB neutrinos throughout the space of the present universe, estimated to be about 113 per cubic centimeter, or 113,000 per liter, results in a neutrino energy of about 0.00067 eV.

2. The ratio of total BB neutrino energy in the universe to the total equivalent energy of the observable universe would be about 0.043 percent.

3. The loss of energy of BB neutrinos since their decoupling is equal to 430,000 times the total equivalent energy of the present observable universe.

The first and second of those results shows BB neutrinos spread through the universe could contribute to only a small increase in the density of the universe, but the third result would present a much more serious problem to BBT.

BB Neutrino Missing Energy.

Due to expansion since their decoupling, BB neutrinos would have cooled by a factor of about one billion, and their energy would have been one billion times greater than at present.

Therefore, they would have lost all but a tiny fraction of that energy, which Appendix E shows to be about 4.3×10^{73} Joules since their decoupling, as compared to an estimated total energy of the observable universe that has been estimated to be about 10^{68} Joules.

If that estimate is correct, the loss of neutrino energy is would be very nearly 430,000 times the total equivalent energy of the mass of the observable universe. As in the case of the MBR photons, the mystery of what happened to that missing neutrino energy arises, but in this case, the amount of lost energy is utterly ridiculous.

Supernova 1987A Neutrinos.

BBers have suggested that "massive" neutrinos (that is, having a rest mass of more than a few electron volts) might provide the postulated missing mass of the universe that could "close" the universe. If that were true, they might bring the average density of the universe up to the level necessary for the flat or the closed BB universes. Some theorists had suggested that their mass might be as much as 30 eV. But those ideas are known to be incorrect.

The *Encyclopedia of Physics* states that, "A neutrino travels at essentially the speed of light," that its mass is "equal to or less than 10^{-6} eV," but also states that its mass might "lie between 10^{-4} and 10^{-2} eV," in which region my calculated value lies; and the detection of neutrinos from SN 1987A confirms their mass to be extremely low, perhaps on the order of those numbers or less.

An article (in *SCIENTIFIC AMERICAN* of August,1999) on neutrino oscillations, that is, conversions from electron neutrinos to more massive neutrinos (muon or tau neutrinos), by Edward Kearns, Takaaki Kajita and Yoji Totsuka, indicates that neutrino energy is in the range of 0.03 to 0.1 eV. If it was in the middle of that range, say 0.0667 eV for example, or 100 times greater than my calculation (and about 10^4 times greater than that of the *Encyclopedia of Physics*). Based on that estimate the equivalent mass of the of the BB neutrinos would still be only about 4 percent of the equivalent mass of the observable universe, still far from that needed to solve the BB missing mass problem.

It has been suggested by some theorists that neutrino oscillations might result in sufficient mass to close the universe. However, it was reported (in *SCIENCE NEWS* in 1996) that, because it is believed that there should be a correlation between the number of Sun spots and a decrease in the number of solar neutrinos, that would provide evidence of those oscillations. However, observations by University of Tokyo researchers at the Kamiokande Neutrino Detector have failed to observe that correlation.

If the mass of neutrinos is in accordance with standard particle theory, the confirmations of that by neutrinos from SN 1987A, and my calculation of neutrino mass based on BBT, don't provide enough evidence against it, certainly the enormous amount of energy that neutrinos would have lost as they traveled through an expanding BB universe should be sufficient to destroy the credibility of BB neutrinos in space.

Surely scientists and mathematicians of the establishment have been capable of discovering the BB neutrino problems that I have presented here. Could it be that information that discredits BBT is intentionally omitted from their literature; more purposeful obfuscation?

FIFTEEN

Redshift Problems

According to Hubble's law, the wavelength of received radiation increases, and its frequency decreases in an inverse relationship, as functions of the departing velocity of matter in expanding space. Although Hubble never accepted it, the establishment is convinced that the *accepted interpretation of redshift* data provides a proper indication of the distance and velocity of matter throughout the space of the universe, and thus provides proof of an expanding universe.

BBers frequently refer to that redshift as Doppler shift, but that is inconsistent with BBT dogma that claims redshift to be "cosmological," that is, it is the result, not of expanding matter in space, but of the expansion of space itself. However, not only is the expansion of the matter of the universe subject to serious question, but the expansion of space is beyond the realm of reason.

As Halton Arp has said, the relationship between redshift and distance is a "frail assumption in which so much of modern astronomy and cosmology is built."

Doppler Redshift.

Astronomers, astrophysicists, and even BB cosmologists, will tell you that the redshift of stars in our galaxy and the redshift of nearby galaxies, and the blue shift of some, is Doppler shift, that is, it is due to their motion relative to us. However, when it comes to very distant galaxies and quasars, BB cosmologists insist that the redshift of those bodies is primarily due to the expansion of space.

Periodic observations of the distance to stars within our galaxy can determine that the redshift of those receding from us corresponds to their receding velocity, and that the blueshift of those approaching us corresponds to their approaching velocity. Therefore, it cannot be denied that Doppler shifts are real.

Observations of spiral galaxies that are seen edge-on show that the redshifts of radiation from one side of their center differ from that of the radiation from the other side. Not only does that provide a measure of rotational rate of those galaxies, but it demonstrates that Doppler shift provides an indication of the velocity of matter in space.

Present techniques of measurement show that Doppler redshift contributes to the observed redshift of the radiation of bodies out to a million light-years. All concerned are therefore forced to acknowledge that. But for more distant galaxies and quasars, BBers cling to the belief that the redshift of those bodies is primarily cosmological redshift, that is, due to the expansion of space.

Lorentz Transformations Applied to Empty Space.

Figure 4 shows a plot of velocity as a fraction of the speed of light, V/c, as a function of redshift, Z, in accordance with its Equation 4. That equation has been derived from the Lorentz transformations, which are discussed in Appendix A of this book.

In accordance with Hubble's law, for small values of redshift V/c is equal to Z. However, when the relative velocity of a distant body is more than a small percentage of the speed of light, that equation makes a correction for velocity in accordance with Special Relativity, which prevents the speed of the expansion at the edge of space from exceeding the speed of light. However, if it is space that is expanding rather than the matter in that space, that is equivalent to applying the Lorentz transformations to the speed of the space rather than the speed of matter. Although those transformations might apply to speeding matter, there certainly is no justification for their application to empty space. There is no mathematics, experiment or logic in support of that.

In addition to speeds greater than that of light, if the Lorentz transformations were not applied to empty space, the redshift of distant bodies would put them at distances and ages that seriously violate their theory.

As an illustration of that, if a quasar has a redshift of 2, the *accepted interpretation of redshift data* puts V/c at 0.8. Because BBers typically assume the age of the universe to be in the range of 10 to 15 BYRs, that would put that quasar's age in the range of 8 to 12 BYRs, and its distance in the range of 8 to 12 BLYs. But, if space were not curved in accordance with that method, and instead was linear, the Hubble constant (assuming 65 km/sec/Mpc or 20 km/sec/MLY) would put the distance of that quasar at 30 BLYs and its age at 30 BYRs, far more than the BB universe size and age are assumed to be. A redshift of 5 would put the distance of that quasar at 75 BLYs and its age at 75 BYRs.

[Distance in millions of light-years equals the speed of light in km/sec times redshift, divided by the Hubble constant in km/sec/million light years (D = c Z/H). For Z = 2, distance equals 30 MLYs; and for Z = 5, distance equals 75 BLYs.]

Incorrect Ages Assumed.

As discussed in Chapter 11, undoubtedly in order to minimize the impact of the BB age problem, an assumed age of the BB universe is typically chosen to force the age and distance of remote bodies to be as great as possible. The assumed age that is usually chosen is Hubble time. However, that is erroneous for all but a fixed-rate BB universe.

An example of that, as given in that chapter, was, if the Hubble constant was thought to be 65 km/sec/Mpc, regardless of a belief in a flat universe, rather than the proper value of 10 BYRs, its age would be given as 15 BLYS.

To further illustrate the use of that deception, according to Figure 4, a galaxy or quasar having a redshift of 3.5, would have a speed of 90 percent of the speed of light, and a "look back" of 90 percent. In accordance with BBT, its age is said to be 90 percent of the Hubble time, or 13.5 BLYs, and it is be said to be observed as it was at 1.5 BYRs after the BB.

Speed Problem.

In the example given above, that quasar would be reported to have been seen as it existed 13.5 BYRs ago. Because 13.5 BYRs are believed to have elapsed since that quasar was as seen at a distant of 13.5 BLYs, then perhaps it has traveled another 13.5 BLYs from us, putting its present distance at 27 BLYs. If its recessional speed is proportional to its distance, as are all other bodies according to BBT, its relative speed might now be twice as great as it was when observed, or about 1.8 times the speed of light.

(BBers could have no knowledge of what happened to that quasar since it was last seen. Maarten Schmidt suggested that such a quasar would have "burnt out" by now. But, even if it burnt out or blew up, some of its remains might now be 27 BLYs from us.)

Because BBT is based on General Relativity, which denies the possibility of relative speeds greater than that of light, one might think that this anomaly would be troublesome to BBers. But when that problem is presented to them it is characteristically dismissed with an explanation than something like the presenter, "has a poor understanding of the curvature of four-dimensional space-time." (A BBer might also point out that the situation described could only apply to a Euclidean universe; but the flat BB case, that many of them espouse, is claimed to be just that.)

Although the example of a BB speed problem given here has to do with a quasar, this problem applies to distant galaxies as well.

Anomalous Redshift.

Observations over several decades by some highly regarded astronomers have shown many quasars to have considerably greater redshifts than those of neighboring galaxies, which has provided evidence that something is amiss with the present interpretation of the redshifts of massive bodies.

Most notable among those having reported that phenomena is American astronomer Halton Arp, formerly at the Hale Observatory and now at the Max Planck Institute of Astrophysics in Germany, who has provided vast amounts of astronomical data regarding quasars that are associated with nearby galaxies having considerably different redshifts.

Among those quasars that are quite close to galaxies are Markarian 205 (whose redshift indicates a velocity of 13,000 miles per second) and galaxy NGC 4319 (who's velocity is only about 1,000 miles per second) that are connected by a bridge of gas. There are also several quasars in The Third Cambridge Catalog that are extremely close to galaxies listed in the New General Catalog. Some examples are NGC 4651 and 3C275.1, NGC3067 and 3C232, NGC5832 and 3C309.1, NGC7413 and 3C455; and more examples can be found in Arp' books, *Seeing Red* and *Quasars,Redshifts and Controversies.*

Arp has shown that the quantity of quasars found within small angles of galaxies greatly exceeds statistical expectations and, in many instances, they occur in pairs. He has suggested that such anomalous redshift can be explained by younger matter that in some manner produces greater redshifts than older matter.

An additional item (in *SKY & TELESCOPE* in 1995) in support of Arp's findings, was that by astronomer Margaret Burbidge of the University of California at San Diego. Using the 3-meter Shane Telescope at Lick Observatory she found, "two point like X-ray objects that were identified by the ROSAT satellite on opposite sides of the M106. They proved to be quasars with redshifts of 0.398 and 0.653. M106 (NGC 4258), an 8th magnitude spiral in Canes Venatici, that has an active nucleus containing a black hole and emits long braided jets of gas. The symmetry of those QSOs [quasars] with respect to the galaxy nucleus, and the evidence for activity in the galaxy, make it very hard to argue that this is an accidental configuration." (But, of course, that article should have said, "what are thought to be quasars" and, "what are thought to be black holes.")

As is their custom regarding data that might upset their apple-cart, the establishment simply ignores the vast amounts of anomalous redshift data. But sooner or later they will have to acknowledge the validity of, and cope with, the vast amount of such data compiled by Arp and other astronomers regarding anomalous redshifts.

Quantized Redshift.

There have also been reports of quantized redshifts, values of redshift that repeat at certain intervals. That was first reported in 1967 by astronomer William Tifft of the Steward Observatory, who found that galaxy redshift data showed a tendency to peak in steps equivalent to about 72 kilometers per second, that is, at 72, 144 and 216 kilometers per second. Later on, Bruce Guthrie and William Napier of the Royal Observatory at Edinburgh, working with a larger set of more accurate data, found a periodicity of 37.5 kilometers ranging out to over 2,000 kilometers per second.

Because the quantization of redshift supports the idea that redshift is not merely the result of velocity, which would tend to deny BBT, those findings have been ignored. However, impartial study of that data makes it difficult to dismiss. After decades of investigations regarding redshift by a skilled professional astronomer, the establishment should not continue to ignore Arp's anomalous redshift data, nor should they ignore data Tifft and others have presented regarding the quantization of redshift.

Tired Light.

There are a number of highly regarded American scientists who find reason to believe that redshift of radiation from distant bodies in space is due to causes other than Doppler redshift or cosmological redshift.

"Tired light" theories have been advanced by a number of theorists throughout the years that the redshift of radiation from distant bodies is due, at least in part, to the presence in space of an "ether" (or "aether," as of old); matter, forces or fields which, in some manner, cause redshift. Although tired light advocates do not deny that the redshift of stars within our galaxy and of some nearby galaxies is the result of Doppler, they support the idea that, as EMR travels through that ether, it loses energy and its wavelength increases.

University of Chicago astronomer, and proponent of a steady state universe, William MacMillan, who not only questioned the *accepted interpretation of redshift data*, but may have been the first to suggest tired light; that the radiant energy from stars was partly absorbed in the ether of space, and reradiated at lower energy. More currently, Grote Reber of the University of Tasmania and considered to be the father of radio astronomy, Paul Marmet, cosmologist John Kierein, and others, are advocates of ideas, such as Compton scattering, that might be classified as tired light.

(Kierein and Marmet have informed me that it is improper to refer to redshift due to Compton scattering or inelastic collisions as tired light. However, I find it convenient, as others have, to refer to the several theories of redshift resulting from reactions to matter in space under that general heading.)

Some tired light advocates have claimed that all redshift is due to tired light phenomena. However, they would be hard pressed to provide satisfactory explanations for some astronomical observations. For example, blue shifts of radiation from some stars within our galaxy, and from a number of galaxies with our local group indicate that they are moving toward us, some at considerable velocity. For example, M31 (Andromeda), about 2.7 million light years distant that is approaching us at about 266 kilometers per second, and M33, about 3 million light years distant that is approaching us at about 189 kilometers per second.

On the other hand, there are theorists who claim that tired light is illogical because the reactions between photons and any sort of particles in space would result in excessive scattering of radiation. However, they apparently fail to consider that light from a remote source travels through the Earth's atmosphere of oxygen, nitrogen and other matter, without causing a noticeably distorted view of objects, even when seen at great distance by means of telescopes.

It is suggested here that some form of tired light theory might provide a significant portion of the solution to some of the BB problems discussed in this book.

Gravitational Redshift.

As presented in more detail in Chapter 17, gravitational redshift (GRS) and the mathematical formula describing it are well recognized in the astronomical world: The more massive the body and the smaller its radius, the greater is its GRS.

It is accepted that ordinary stars, such as our Sun, produce only very small gravitational redshifts, white dwarfs about an order of magnitude greater, a neutron star thousands of times more, and we are told that black holes produce infinite GRS. But, when it comes to distant galaxies and quasars, BB cosmologists deny that GRS is a significant factor, insisting that their redshift is due to the expansion of the universe.

On the other hand, tired light advocates, who deny an expanding universe, and therefore deny the Doppler (or cosmological) redshift of very distant bodies in space, but generally accept that their redshift is indicative of the distance of very remote matter, may be faced with a another problem.

If tired light advocates were to accept that the Hubble relationship for distance ($D = cZ/H_0$) applies, it results in unreasonable distances of matter in space. As in the example previously given, quasars having the highest observed redshifts would be about 75 BLYs distant. At such great distances, even if they were faintly visible by the most powerful telescopes, it would be impossible to determine their redshifts.

However, if it were accepted that GRS applied to distant bodies, that problem might be solved. They would be much less distant, less massive and less brilliant than they would be perceived to be by the linear application of Hubble's law. Accordingly, the fact that quasars having high redshifts are seen well enough for their redshifts to be determined, would seem to support the applicability of GRS.

If both tired light and GRS were accepted, and the *accepted interpretation of redshift data,* that is, the application of Lorentz transformations to empty space were abandoned, it would provide solutions of some of BB problems, including those related to velocity, distance and age, and the perceived clumping of quasars and galaxies.

Wolf Effect.

A little-known additional cause of redshift is known as the Wolf effect, named after its originator, optical physicist Emil Wolf of the University of Rochester, New York.

According to his theory, light from distant bodies is partially coherent and, that during its propagation through space, radiation from different source atoms can interfere in such a way as to cause its wavelength to be shifted toward the red. Wolf deduced this phenomena mathematically but, as presented at the spring 1988 meeting of the American Physical Society, Wayne Knox of AT&T Bell Laboratories has simulated such a light source and proved that the Wolf effect exists.

Even BB advocate Berry Parker reported in his book that, "Recently, however, Wolf has shown that there is a third way [to produce redshift]. He has shown that if two sources of slightly different frequencies are coupled, the resultant wave tends to assume a lower frequency. In other words, it is redshifted."

Combined Redshift Possibilities.

According to BBT high redshift quasars are observed to be at distances up to 10 to 15 billion light-years. Regardless of the power of any existing telescope, at those distances quasars can only be seen as point sources. Ron Cowan has reported that, "quasars typically look no different than the blob of a Milky Way star in the smudge of a nearby galaxy." However, that can't apply to quasars

10 to 15 billion light-years. They can be seen only as dots of light.

At those distances the brilliance of quasars can only have been roughly estimated, their sizes only estimated by the variations of their brilliance (perhaps one light-week, one light-day, or less in diameter), their mass, sometimes said to be in the range of 100 to 1,000 billion times that of the Sun, can only be be guessed at, and It is impossible to determine the redshifts of objects at those distances.

There must be other causes of their redshifts. It could be due to a combination of those, including tired light, gravitation, or even Wolf effect, or other unknown possibilities that would result in considerable less distance, mass and brilliance than usually presented by BBers.

When the compounded illogical results of the use of the *accepted interpretation of redshift data*, of the application of the characteristics of closed relativistic space to a flat or open BB universe, of an incorrectly assumed age of the universe, and of ignoring other redshift possibilities, the fallacies of determining the characteristics of remote bodies in the accustomed manner should become obvious.

Seeing Stars Too Distant to be Seen.

In review, the application of Lorentz transformations to the empty space of the universe allows BBers to limit the size of their universe to agree with Friedmann's solutions to General Relativity equations. Also, if they hadn't accepted that, Hubble's law would result in the impossible situation that bodies observed to have high redshifts would be too distant for them to be observed by the most powerful telescopes in existence. (Apparently they chose to ignore the fact that the redshift of galaxies and quasars, even at the distances limited by their method, could not be determined.)

Unfortunately, all of the estimates of the distance (and relative velocity) of high redshift bodies in space made by astronomers, and thereafter accepted by the entire establishment, are determined by the method of BBT. In doing so, they have accepted the erroneous concepts of curved space and the justification of that error by the application of Lorentz transformations to empty space.

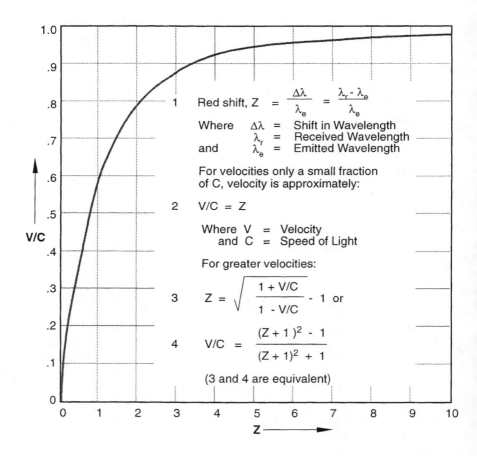

The equations shown in the figure:

1   Red shift, $Z = \dfrac{\Delta\lambda}{\lambda_e} = \dfrac{\lambda_r - \lambda_e}{\lambda_e}$

Where $\Delta\lambda$ = Shift in Wavelength
λ_r = Received Wavelength
and λ_e = Emitted Wavelength

For velocities only a small fraction of C, velocity is approximately:

2   $V/C = Z$

Where V = Velocity
and C = Speed of Light

For greater velocities:

3   $Z = \sqrt{\dfrac{1 + V/C}{1 - V/C}} - 1$ or

4   $V/C = \dfrac{(Z + 1)^2 - 1}{(Z + 1)^2 + 1}$

(3 and 4 are equivalent)

FIGURE 4: VELOCITY AS A FUNCTION OF REDSHIFT
(Velocity as a fraction of the speed of light
as derived from the Lorentz Transformations)

SIXTEEN

Quasar Problems

Inconsistencies regarding the *accepted interpretation of redshift data* in estimating the distances of bodies in space results in many problems to BBT. Some of those have to do with massive bodies that are called quasars.

Quasar Luminosity, Size and Mass.

As presently utilized, redshift data results in the perception of the great distances of some quasars indicating their luminosities to be enormous. It is said that variations in the level of their radiation are as short as one day, indicate their sizes to be about that of the solar system and their masses and luminosities to be enormously great.

A quasar having luminosity variations of one day might have a diameter of about that of the solar system. (The diameter of a quasar having a flare that swept around toward us once a day, might be $1/\pi = 0.318$ light-day, 8.25×10^9 kilometers which is about 70 percent of the size of the solar system based on the diameter of the orbit of Pluto.)

Based on that size, and on distances determined by the *accepted interpretation of redshift data*, the brilliance of some quasars has been estimated to be as great as that of 10^{14} suns, equal to that of 1,000 average galaxies. For example, Astronomers Courvoisier and

Robson have estimated regarding quasar 3C 273 that, "On an average day, it is more luminous than 1,000 galaxies, each containing 100 billion stars."

The extreme estimates of luminosity, size and mass that are made regarding quasars suggest that the *accepted interpretation of redshift data* doesn't tell the whole story about the speed and distance of remote massive bodies in space.

Quasar Clumping and Evolution.

As presented in Chapter 11, based on that method distant quasars are believed to be seen as they were within as little as a few hundred million years after the BB. However, it seems impossible for them to have formed so soon after the BB, and, worse than that, that data is said to show them to be "clumped" at great distances, requiring large numbers of them to have been formed and amassed too soon after the big bang.

That clumping also conflicts with a basic tenant of BBT of smoothness, that is, homogeneity and isotropy. The universe might appear to be the same in all directions (isotropic), but it could not be the same throughout the universe (homogeneous).

The clumping of quasars as evidence of an evolving BB universe assumed importance to BBers in the past as evidence against a competing SST that denied evolution. As a result, they insist that the matter of the universe is smoothly distributed, while ignoring the obvious conclusion that clumping and smoothness are contradictory ideas.

The Copernican Problem.

The clumping of distant quasars and Seyfert galaxies (called active galactic nuclei or AGNs) in all directions also puts BBers at the center of their universe. That situation, known as the Copernican Problem, is in direct conflict with the basic tenets of BBT that we occupy no special place in the universe (Copernican Principle), and that the BB universe has no center.

Some BBers have denied clumping. For example, Cal Tech astronomer Patrick S. Osmer (in 1982) said that, "statistical analysis is consistent with quasars being distributed uniformly at random....These findings are evidence in favor of an assumption ...that on a large scale the universe is homogeneous."

On the other hand, some of them have admitted to the lack of homogeneity due to clumping. For example, South African astronomer and cosmologist G. F. R. Ellis (in 1975) suggested that, "It would certainly be consistent with the present observations that we were at the center of the universe," and as Joseph Silk wrote in 1980 and 1989, "If the universe possesses a center we must be very close to it...otherwise we would detect more radiation from one direction than from the other direction."

Of course, Silk, a firm believer in homogeneity, didn't seriously consider that possibility. But If BBers were truthful, they would admit that quasar clumping puts them at the center of their universe.

In an article entitled *Everyone's Guide to Cosmology* in *SKY & TELESCOPE* of March 1991, Paul Davies wrote, "In the real universe there is not the slightest hint of a center or edge." But if quasars were clumped at great distances as other BBers believe, that statement could not be true. BBers can't have it both ways; either the quasars are clumped, or the universe is smooth and centerless.

Clumping Due to Lorentz Transformations.

The BBers relationship of velocity and distance as functions of redshift is based on the Lorentz transformations, as given in the equations of Figure 4 and illustrated by the graph of that figure. The perception of the clumping of distant quasars, that is believed to provide evidence for the evolution of the BB universe, is a result of that unrealistic application of those transformations.

Due to the determination of their distance based on that *accepted interpretation of redshift data*, plots of the distance of quasars as a function of redshift are forced to take a nonlinear shape similar to that of the curve of Figure 4 which results in the appearance of greater density, that is, clumping, at great distances.

A typical example of the result of that is shown in an article in *SCIENTIFIC AMERICAN* of June, 1998, by Professor of Astronomy at the University of Wales Michael Disney, who presented a plot of quasar distribution versus distance. (His plot must be rotated 90 degrees to illustrate that effect.) Furthermore, the perception of the sudden end of such clumping beyond a certain large redshift is not because quasars are "rare in the very early history of the universe," as he states, but merely because they are too distant to be seen.

Quasar Distribution in a Smooth BB Universe.

Despite the fact that they insist that quasars are clumped at great distances, and despite astronomical evidence to the contrary, BBers insist that the universe is isotropic and homogeneous.

As an example, Peebles, et al. (in 1994) stated in no uncertain terms, "in the big bang cosmology, particles uniformly fill all space". But if the stars, galaxies and the rest of the matter and energy of the universe, including BB photons and neutrinos, are also said to have departed the BB and spread in all directions with the expansion of space, and are said to be smoothly scattered through the BB universe, that must also apply to quasars.

Under BBT, or any other known cosmology, there is no more reason for greater percentages of them to be departing from us at great distances than there is for nearby galaxies, or any other matter in space, regardless of its age. That is an important consideration that should not be ignored,

Similarity of Quasar Characteristics.

There have been reports regarding the similarity of some of the characteristics of quasars that do not correlate with their perceived distance and age.

Not only is there a lack of correlation between quasar luminocity and distance, but the spectra of radiation from some quasars, thought to be at various distances and ages, have been reported to have similarities. That is, the relationships of their spectral lines (when adjusted for their apparent velocity) are similar, indicating their composition to be similar, which is not explained by BBT.

In a related example, Van Flandern (in 1993) has reported that, "the highest redshift galaxy to date, z = 1.02, and the highest redshift quasar to date, Z = 4.9, both have ordinary spectra implying roughly the same materials and evolution as later galaxies."

Those reports add to doubts about the determination of quasar distance by means of the *accepted interpretation of redshift data.*

Superluminal Quasar Flares.

An additional redshift problem has to do with quasar flares that appear, as observed by radio astronomy, to exceed the velocity of light. That appearance is the result of the perceived great distances of the quasars from which those flares originate. However, it can

ERRATA   Corrections shown in Blue

Page 141, 4th full paragraph:

The erroneous perception of superluminal flares is illustrated by an example of a quasar flare traveling at 95 percent of the speed of light, but at an angle of 36.87 degrees from directly toward us (using a 3-4-5 right triangle for this example, which has been chosen merely for convenience.) Analysis shows that, when observed at intervals, that flare would appear to travel an arc that is proportional to 0.57c (= 3/5 X 0.95c), in an interval that is proportional to its speed in the direction of the Earth of 0.24c (= c - 4/5 X 0.95c). Thus it would appear to travel across the sky at a speed of 0.57/0.24 = 1.375 times the speed of light.

Page 141, 5th full paragraph:

In another example, a quasar flare at that same angle, traveling at 90 percent of the speed of light, determined in the same manner as above, would result in an apparent speed across the sky equal to 1.929c [(3/5 X 0.9c)/(c - 4/5 X 0.9c) = 0.54c/0.28c]. If the flare speed was 0.9 c, but at an angle 30 degrees, the apparent velocity would be 2.04c [(0.5 X 0.9c)/(c - 0.866 X 0.9c) = 0.45c/0.2206c]. At that same speed, but at an angle of 45 degrees, the apparent velocity would be 1.75 c [(0.707 X 0.9c)/(c - 0.707 X 0.9c) = 0.6363c/0.3637c].

Page 142, 2nd and 3rd lines:
Change "if course" to "of course"

Page 191, 2nd full paragraph, 4th line:
Change "H_T" to "T_H"

Page 199: 4th full paragraph, 2nd last line:
Change "years" to "billion light years"

be shown, by some simple, but somehow quite confusing trigonometry, that flares having relativistic velocities that are ejected at angles of less than 90 degrees toward (or away from) the observer can create the appearance of superluminal velocities.

Because of the great energies required to propel flares to near superluminal speed it is difficult to account for the large number of quasar flares that are reported to exhibit that phenomenon. One might expect such flares to be observed only infrequently; and because the acceleration of particles of matter to superluminal speed requires infinite energy, it is impossible to account for those that might actually exceed the speed of light.

It may be more reasonable to conclude that the perception of flares at such speeds is due to the *accepted interpretation of redshift data*. The mathematics that is used to provide the appearance of those great speeds is directly dependent on the perceived distance of the quasar under consideration, which, in turn, is dependent on that method.

The trigonometry mentioned above can show that flares having near relativistic velocities, that are ejected at angles of less than 90 degrees toward (or away from) the observer, can create the appearance of superluminal velocities. Furthermore, mathematical investigation of the velocity relationships of those quasars and their associated superluminal flares, provides unintelligible results.

The erroneous perception of superluminal flares is illustrated by an example of a quasar flare traveling at 95 percent of the speed of light, but at an angle of 36.87 degrees from directly toward us (using a 3-4-5 right triangle for this example, which has been chosen merely for convenience.) Analysis shows that, when observed at intervals, that flare would appear to travel an arc of 0.57 light-years (3/5 x 0.95 c) in an interval of 0.24 year (the speed of light less the transverse component of travel = 1- (4/5 x 0.95 c), thus appearing to travel at a speed of about 2.375 times the speed of light across the sky.

In another example, a flare at that same angle, traveling at 90 percent of the speed of light, would appear to travel an arc of 0.54 light-years (3/5 x 0.9c) in an interval of 0.28 year (the speed of light less the transverse component of travel = 1- (4/5 x 0.9 c), thus appearing to travel at a speed of about 1.929 times the speed of light. If the flare speed was 0.9 c, but at an angle 30 degrees, the apparent velocity works out to 2.04 c. At that same speed, but at an angle of 45 degrees, the apparent velocity would be 1.75 c.

Examples of other angles and other flare speeds would, if course, produce different apparent velocities. But it appears that, depending on the actual speed and relative angle of travel, quasar flare apparent speeds of about twice the speed of light might be common.

Because the speed of a quasar flare can only be observed by the astronomer as an angular speed, its apparent transverse speed can only be determined by knowledge of its distance. That information is provided by the distance of the associated quasar that, in turn, is determined by *the accepted interpretation of redshift data* for that quasar. If that quasar has a redshift of 2, for example, it might have been thought to be at 8 BYRs distant (perhaps 80 percent of 10 billion light years) that might result in a flare having an apparent transverse velocity of 2.375 c. But, if it was 800 MLYs distant, the velocity of the flare would be 10 times less, or only 23.75 percent of the speed of light.

Because flares might be expected to depart in opposite directions from a quasar with approximately equal speeds, the examination of that possibility illustrates a serious difficulty regarding the observation of apparent velocities of quasar flares. In the first example given above, the same apparent tangential speed would also be observed, in the opposite direction, for a flare of the same quasar that travels away from us, and appearing to travel at the same speed in the opposite direction.

The radial speed of the flare moving toward us would be 0.76 c (4/5 x 0.95). If the associated quasar also had a flare in the opposite direction at the same speed relative to the quasar, its radial speed would be at 0.76 c away from us. If the quasar had a redshift of of 2, and thus, in accordance with Figure 4, a speed away from us of 0.8 c, the flare traveling radially away from us at 0.76 c would have a radial speed of 0.04 c (toward us!) relative to its quasar; and the flare traveling radially toward us at 0.76 c would have a radial speed of 1.56 c toward us relative to its quasar.

The only reasonable explanation that can be suggested for those results is that the present method of determining the relative speed and distance of remote massive bodies is incorrect.

As an example of a related topic, John Gribbin in *Space Warps* wrote that "although radio galaxy 4C 345 is 5 BLYs away [according to the *accepted interpretation of redshift data*]," its enormous lobe of radio emission "is twice as large in the night sky as the moon." If it were at that distance, the length of that lobe would be "an astonishing 78 million light-years." If that galaxy were the size of the Milky Way the tangent of its observed angle would be about 4 arc-seconds. The angle of the moon is about 32 arc-minutes. If the galaxy were at the the stated distance, the flare would be about 960 times the size of its galaxy, or about 96 million light-years. That great length should also prompt question about the accepted method of velocity and distance determination.

The only possible explanation for the perceived irrational relationships between quasars and their flares is that those quasars are not moving away from us with the great speed that has been determined by the accepted method. On the large scale, the universe cannot not be expanding at the perceived great rates.

Quasars with Opposing Flares.

When I first examined the problem of superluminal quasar flares, I knew of no instance of a quasar having what were thought to be superluminal flares in opposite directions, and had therefore suggested that, if such a configuration were to be found, it might be used to provide some answers regarding the discrepancies described above. I suggested that might be done by determining and analyzing the redshifts and angular velocities of opposing flares of quasars from their source quasar.

Several years later observation of superluminal "gas jets" in opposite directions from a source known as GRS 1915+105, estimated to be 40,000 light years distant, and thought to be either a small black hole or a "microquasar", were reported. (In this case GRS doesn't mean gravitational redshift.) Those observations were made in England in 1997 using an array of radio telescope that is called MERLIN (for multi-element radio-linked interferometer network). The combined signals from those telescopes is reported to result in a resolution of 40 milliarcseconds.

Calculations based on the inbound flare estimated at 0.9 c, appearing to be at at a speed of 2c, and on similar geometry to that described above, show the GRS 1915+105 inbound flare coming toward us at an angle of about 30 degrees from radial, and outbound flare going away from us in the opposite direction.

Unfortunately GRS 1915+105 is not at a "cosmic" distance, but within our own galaxy. Because of its very low redshift, observations of it and its flares can't contribute to the solution of possible redshift problems regarding opposing flares of quasars that are billions of light years distant and thought to be departing at relativistic speeds.

A similar appearing nearby, "mini-quasar" or miniature black hole, having jets in opposite directions had been reported in 1995. The jets of GRO 1655-40, estimated to be 10,000 to 15,000 light-years distant are reported to appear to have speeds of 1.5 c.

I recently discovered a report (of 1997) that distant quasar NGC 6251 has "two monstrous jets of gas in opposite directions." If the redshift of that quasar, and the angular velocity of its two jets relative to the quasar, were to be determined, that information might shed some light on the true nature of the problem of the measurement of distance (and velocity) of remote bodies in intergalactic space (IGS).

Now that such a quasar has been found, it provides hope that efforts might be made to determine and analyze the relative velocities of a quasar and its flares in order to explain the inconsistencies described above. Unfortunately, rather than just weeks required for the measurement GRS 1915+105 flare speeds, it might take much longer to obtain adequate data regarding the flares of quasars at great distances. But the results of that investigation might provide valuable information regarding the interpretation of redshift data of distant quasars.

An investigation of the kind that I proposed years ago, and again propose here, might provide convincing evidence that the presently *accepted interpretation of redshift data* is invalid, and that the universe on the whole is not expanding. That would be worth knowing!

Quasars as Points of Light.

The current belief of the establishment is that quasars are radiated energy from the accretion of matter by black holes in the centers of galaxies. But there is little evidence in support of that belief, and considerable evidence that denies it.

Over the years a number of scientists have indicated that distant quasars are seen only as points of light. Ivan King told us (in 1976) that quasars, "look very faint and are superficially indistinguishable from faint stars," and, as mentioned above, University of Alabama astronomers have reported that, "at the highest redshifts, even the

Hubble telescope fails to show galaxies surrounding quasars," and Astronomer George Abell et al in *Realm of the Universe* wrote that quasars are unresolved optically, that is, they appear to be stellar, and Halton Arp in (in 1987) commented that quasars are so small that, "Optically they looked like point sources of light—like stars—hence the name 'quasi-stellar' radio source."

Dennis Overbye (in 1992) wrote that, " Quasars were points of light, like stars, everyone agreed, but nobody knew what they really were or even if they were made out of ordinary matter," Donald Goldsmith (in 1995) told us that, "Although quasars have sizes much smaller than galaxies their name, an acronym for 'quasi-stellar radio sources,' testifies to their point like appearance," and *SKY & TELESCOPE* reported (in 1997), "Even nearby quasars have shown no evidence of a having a host galaxy."

SCIENCE NEWS reported (in 1992) that, "Hubble [the HST] was able to resolve the bright red giant stars in the outskirts of M 15, enabling the researchers to subtract them out of the image. What remained was a core region containing thousands of faint stars spread out over a surprisingly large radius of about 0.4 light-years, 10 times that predicted by the black hole models. The Hubble results strongly suggest that M 15 does not harbor a black hole at its center....That finding comes as a relief to those of us made uncomfortable by the popular tendency to invoke an invisible black hole to explain every powerful object in the universe."

Regardless of those opinions, many BBers have insisted that "fuzz" is seen around what they believe to be quasars, and that fuzz provides proof that those quasars are the result of accretion of matter around black holes that exist in the center of galaxies. As stated in *DISCOVER* (in 1992), "No one knows for sure what a quasar is. It looks like a point of light,...yet most astronomers agree that it is probably a galaxy with a black hole in its center."

Some reports regarding fuzz are presented here.

Belinda Wilkes reported in *ASTRONOMY* (in 1991) that "many quasars had a fuzzy appearance around the bright central object. The spectrum of the fuzz appeared similar to that of a galaxy at the same redshift as the quasar. Thus the quasars seemed to lie in the central region of galaxies but, because they were so much brighter than their host galaxies, fuzz could be seen only in those closest to earth."

Notice that she said that they "seemed to lie in central regions," which is not very definitive: and also that kind of observation could only have been made at a limited range. As will be shown below, the appearance of distant quasars cannot be resolved by the most powerful telescopes available.

An article in *SKY & TELESCOPE* reported (in 1996) that HST, "had failed to find some of the galaxies in which every quasar is thought to reside." Investigators "failed to find the hosts for 11 of the brightest, closest quasars." But now they have managed to subtract the glare of the center of the images "for a few of the nominally naked quasars," and have been able to see light from the host galaxies. But it was stated that, "subtracting one Hubble image from that of another can leave extended residuals that might be mistaken for diffuse emissions."

John N. Bahcall of the Institute for Advanced Study in Princeton, N.J. appears to have been a tireless worker in the effort to find proof of the establishment position regarding quasars. Some media reports on his efforts are presented here.

SCIENCE NEWS reported in March, 1996, "regarding last year's report that images of 11 of 15 nearby quasars showed no evidence of host galaxies," Bahcall had commented that, "This is a giant step backward towards the understanding of quasars." But when "many of the same quasars" were examined in the near infrared by other astronomers, "The images reveal fuzzy blobs that fit the description of host galaxies." However, notice the term "fit the description," which again is not very definitive.

On that subject (in *ASTRONOMY* in 1997) Bahcall said, "If we thought we had a complete theory of quasars before, now we know we don't. No coherent single pattern of quasar behavior emerges."

As Halton Arp has commented, "When the Space Telescope started taking high-resolution pictures of quasars, John Bahcall called a press conference to report that a number of them did not have any host galaxies at all! Gasp! *Naked quasars!!* The community was horrified. What was going to sustain the enormous luminosity of distant quasars if they did not have a host galaxy to fuel them?" Arp further reported that Bahcall went on to produce some quasars with "host galaxies", [and] everyone decided to paper over the issue." In his latest book, *Seeing Red,* (1998) Arp has stated that, "Observed with seeing better than 1 arc sec. [a more powerful telescope], many [quasars] showed no fuzz at all."

ASTRONOMY of July 1997 reported that, "Observation with the two largest telescopes in the world (Keck I and Keck II) confirm that many quasars lie at the center of normal galaxies" and astronomers also took spectra of the "nebulous blobs surrounding bright and reasonable nearby quasars" showing them to be "aggregates of stars" at the same distance as the quasars. In this article Joseph Miller of the Lick Observatory went off in a different direction to suggest that his quasars are the result of galactic collisions, that could be throwing fuel onto the supermassive black hole that presumably powers the quasars." Note the word "presumably."

However, further on in the same issue of that magazine, a report by University of Alabama astronomers said that, "But at the highest redshifts, even the Hubble telescope fails to show galaxies surrounding quasars." In fact, it is impossible for the Keck telescopes or the HST to show distant quasars as more than points of light.

Award winning astrophysicist Robert Zimmerman reported in *ASTRONOMY* in May, 2001 that the Chandra X-ray Observatory has shown that neither spiral galaxy M33 nor star-burst galaxy M82 have central massive black holes. He also reported that astronomer Richard Mushotzky, using Chandra, had observed, "four of the nearest, brightest and biggest elliptical galaxies...which should all have big supermassive black holes. Yet Chandra saw no evidence of them. Instead sampling of x-ray point sources appear scattered across the face of each galaxy."

Telescopic Resolution.

Although quasars at great distances can be seen only as points of light, it is often claimed that they appear to be surrounded by fuzz, providing evidence that they are in the centers of galaxies. However, there are reports that deny that possibility.

Ivan King has stated that, "Quasars are so far away that the limited resolving power of our optical telescopes makes even a kiloparsec look like a stellar point," and a kiloparsec equals 307 light-years, far larger than any quasar is imagined to be, and in the report mentioned above, Michael Disney agrees with that: "The typical quasar is so far away from Earth that its image in the largest ground based telescope would be 100 million times too small to be resolved."

It can readily be shown that quasars in the center of distant galaxies cannot be seen.

Consider the example of a quasar having a redshift of 2, that is thought to have a velocity of about 0.8c and be at a distance of 10 BLYs. As shown in the calculations of Appendix E, if its size was one light-week in diameter, it would be seen to have an angle in space of only about 4×10^{-7} arc-second, which is far beyond the resolving ability of any existing telescope. Almost certainly that quasar could not be seen at all. At best, it might be seen as a faint point of light.

(The resolving ability of the HST is often reported to be about 0.1 arc-second.)

If that quasar was in the center of a galaxy the size of the Milky Way, about 100,000 light-years across, that galaxy would be seen to have an angle in space of about 2 arc-seconds, which is within the resolving ability of existing telescopes; about 20 times larger than the resolving ability of the HST. Thus some features of an average sized galaxy might be seen at a distance of 10 BLYs. But a quasar in that galaxy, having a diameter of one light-week couldn't possible be seen.

In agreement with that, astronomer William Keel has been quoted in *ASTRONOMY* (of July 1997) as having said, "Clearly quasars are intimately related to galaxies. They probably represent the energetic centers of infant galaxies. But at the highest redshifts, even the Hubble telescope fails to show galaxies surrounding quasars." Not only is he correct about HST not being able to see distant host galaxies, but he seems to have hit upon the truth that, what are thought to be quasars in the center of galaxies, are really the enormous levels of radiation from the violent star-forming centers of galaxies.

A *SKY & TELESCOPE* article of 1998 shows a photograph of an image 17 arc-seconds wide, that is said to be of a "quasar host" a billion light-years distant. However, calculations of Appendix E show that quasar host to be 82,166 light-years across. If there were a quasar in its center that was one light-week in diameter, its diameter would be seen to have an angle in space of only about 4×10^{-6} arc-second, which again is far beyond the resolving ability of any existing telescope. Because it would be impossible to have determined that galaxy to have a quasar within it, there must be a serious discrepancy in the caption of that picture; either an inadvertent error, or another case of purposeful obfuscation

Distant Quasars Are Observed.

If the space of the universe were not curved (which it certainly is not), if the Lorentz transformations didn't apply to empty space (which they certainly do not), and if the universe were not expanding, the situation would be far different than visualized by the establishment.

In the example given above, a quasar having a redshift of 2, thought to be at a distance of about 10 BLYs, and to have a diameter of one light-week, would appear to be about 250,000 $(0.1 \div 4 \times 10^{-7})$ times smaller than could be resolved by the HST. Not only would it be impossible to observe such distant quasars, but it would be impossible to determine their redshift. Recall Vera Rubin's comment of Chapter 10: "It's difficult to make spectroscopic measurements of the velocity of individual stars which are faint even in the galaxies that are fairly close to our own".

Nevertheless, what are thought to be quasars having redshifts of 2, or even as much as 5, are observed, and astronomers manage to determine their redshift, presenting quite a mystery.

For those who believe in the tired light theories in a non-expanding universe, in which the Hubble law is thought to apply, that would still present a mystery. However the solution to this mystery is quite straightforward. Those quasars are much closer than indicated by the *accepted interpretation of redshift data* or by the linear application of Hubble's law. Although redshifts of distant bodies in space may be primarily due to tired light phenomena, a large portion of the redshift of massive quasars is due to GRS, which causes them to appear much further than their actual distances.

Thus the acceptance of redshift due to its travels through the matter (the ether?) of space, and the acceptance of GRS, in accordance with well established theory, would allow the world to escape the ridiculousness of both curved space, and of that of the application of Lorentz transformations to it.

Quasars as Black Holes.

Although BB cosmologists insist that quasars are the result of the accretion of matter around black holes in the center of galaxies, some excerpts from the media that tend to deny that premise are presented here.

Halton Arp tells us in *Quasars, Redshifts and Controversies* that, "The conventional view of quasars is that they are normal galaxies which have, for some reason, superluminmous nuclei which enable them to be seen at great distances. But if quasars really were these kinds of galaxies, we should expect to see them clumping into the clusters or superclusters that characterize the distribution of galaxies on the largest scale....The conclusion forced on the conventional believers is that quasars are so rare that we seldom see a cluster of galaxies with one, that is, far less than one quasar exists per average supercluster." In other words, why are quasars not seen in a large percentage of the galaxies that are observed in gigantic structures?

SCIENTIFIC AMERICAN editor Russell Ruthen (in 1992) asked an important question regarding active galactic nuclei: "How does a black hole in an AGN [active galactic nucleus] attract enough gas to satisfy its voracious appetite, and how does it manage to generate long jets of particles?....astronomers have difficulty devising a mechanism that produces enough friction so that at least one star, or the equivalent, falls into the hole every year for a billion years....'There are no good answers, admits theorist Julian H. Krolik of Johns Hopkins University.'"

But, of course, there are good answers. What is thought to be quasars in the center of galaxies is radiation that is produced in their violent centers.

It was reported in *DISCOVER* (in 1994) that it is not just extremely energetic young galaxies that emitted X-ray, but that "normal, run-of-the-mill" galaxies are the source of the X-ray background from all directions of the universe. Steve Holt of NASA's Goddard Space Flight Center has said, "Every galaxy may be a source of these X-rays." But in answer to the question, "Does that mean that a black hole lies at the heart of every galaxy," Holt stressed that those results are no more than a suggestive clue. If each galaxy is a source of X-rays, black holes are one explanation. But this is certainly not meant to be proof that there are black holes in all galaxies."

As reported in *SCIENCE NEWS* (in 1998), "Quasars are rare, however. Many researchers view them as cosmic oddballs fueled by galactic black holes that drown out the light from the stars in a galaxy. But Esther Hu of the University of Hawaii was quoted as stating that, "It's a lot easier to look at something blazingly bright, even if it is extremely rare—perhaps one (galaxy) in ten million houses a quasar."

It is also important to consider that, whether it is in the center of a galaxy or elsewhere, there is reason to doubt that matter in orbit around a black hole would spiral into it. As stated by physicist and astronomer Neil F. Comins (in *ASTRONOMY* of April, 2001), "Even billion solar-mass galactic black holes only act gravitationally on the rest of the universe; astronomers see gas and stars orbiting around such bodies, without being sucked in. So black holes have no magical ability to suck in external matter."

Astronomical evidence indicates that planets might sometimes get into orbits that are too low and therefore fall into their stars. For the same reason matter orbiting black holes might fall into them. But once nearby matter has cleared out by that process, why should more distant matter continue to "feed" a black hole?

Although quasars (such as GRS 1915+105 discussed above) may be present in space, and some within galaxies, the belief that quasars are the result of black holes in the center of galaxies is far from convincing. Rather than that idea, it is more likely that what is believed to be those quasars are not quasars at all but simply the brilliance of violent star forming centers of young galaxies.

Some astronomers have indicated agreement with that. *SCIENCE NEWS* (in 1995) reported that Stanislav G. Djorgovski of Cal Tech has said, "Some bright objects identified as distant quasars may in fact represent infant galaxies fiery starbirth," and Donald Goldsmith has written, "Quasars may be the central regions of young galaxies....(they) are probably galaxies in the process of forming."

However, there probably are at least two types of massive objects that have been identified as quasars; those that are erroneously identified as radiation from the accretion of matter around giant black holes in the centers of galaxies, that have fuzz; and those that have been called grey holes, that have no fuzz.

SEVENTEEN

Gravitational Redshift

Although it has long ago been ruled out by BB cosmologists as an important factor, the solution to many of the problems related to quasars and other massive bodies in space may lie in proper consideration of GRS.

Gravitational Redshift as Accepted Science.

According to General Relativity, gravitation causes a tiny redshift in the radiation we receive from the Sun. It equals G times M divided by R times c squared, where M and R are the mass and radius of the Sun, G is the gravitational constant, and c is the speed of light. (GRS = GM/Rc^2)

Gravity is also believed to increase the wavelength (decrease the frequency) of radiation from the matter of black holes enough to prevent its escape, that is, their GRS is infinite. Obviously, it must also contribute to the total redshift of radiation from other massive bodies.

Using the formula given above, the redshift of the Sun, as calculated in Appendix E, equals about 2×10^{-6}. Even the gravity of the Earth causes a small amount of redshift of radiation that leaves it. The calculations of Appendix E show that to be about 7×10^{-10}, and show the GRS of radiation from white dwarf Sirius B, whose mass is said to be 1.05 times that of the Sun, and whose circumference is said to be 31,000 kilometers, to be 10^{-4}; about 50 times that of the Sun. Those are relatively insignificant redshifts, but a typical neutron star, having a mass about the same as that of the Sun, but only about 10 miles in diameter, would have a GRS of about 0.18, or about 90,000 times that of the Sun.

Belinda J. Wilkes of the Harvard-Smithsonian Center for Astrophysics in Cambridge, Mass., wrote (in *ASTRONOMY* in 1991) that, "quasars are only about 1 light-day in diameter or roughly the size of our solar system" and, "the typical amount of light generated by a quasar—some 100 billion to 10 trillion times that of the Sun—requires a central black hole of 100 million times the mass of the Sun." As calculated in Appendix E, the GRS of the quasar Wilkes describes would be 0.00572.

But, if the mass of a quasar was just a few times greater, and its diameter just a few times smaller than Wilkes' conjecture, or some combination of those, its GRS might be in the range of that of a neutron star or greater; a major fraction of the highest redshift ever determined for a quasar.

In support of that possibility *ASTRONOMY* (in 1998) reported that Australian graduate student Lucyna Kedziora-Chudczer and her advisor David F. Jauncey "discovered one that varies 50 percent in less than an hour." That could provide a bit of evidence of quasars of considerably smaller size than usually reported (perhaps smaller by a factor of about 100).

Denials of Quasar Gravitational Redshift.

Regardless of evidence in support of GRS, and regardless of the fact that BBers accept it when they believe it is either benign or supports their theory, denials of its application to quasars are common. Some examples are given here.

The *Encyclopedia of Physics* tells us, without providing any rationalization, that, "It has long been known that gravitational redshifts are insufficient, but there is currently no generally accepted theory of non-cosmological redshift for quasars."

Silk agreed that the bodies mentioned above produce redshift but adds, "No compelling evidence has ever been presented to cast doubt on the cosmological nature of quasar redshift," meaning that the gravity of distant massive quasars is for some unknown reason exempt from producing any appreciable gravitational redshift.

Barrow and Silk in *The Left Hand of Creation* (1993 edition) tell us, "The actual redshift of the most remote galaxies… is so much greater than any possible gravitational red-shifts that no model of a galaxy could yield a red-shift value that was due to gravity alone." Although they have written "due to gravity alone," they, like many other BBers, clearly deny that GRS makes any significant addition to their cosmological redshift of distant bodies in space. However, it should be quite obvious that it could be significant.

(William Kaufmann strayed from BB dogma by mentioning that, "If we assume that the redshift is due to general relativity in the form of gravitational redshift, then quasars should rapidly form black holes and disappear from the universe." But, as discussed below regarding "grey holes," that wouldn't be true if insufficient nearby matter was available to produce a black hole.)

Halton Arp wrote in *Quasars, Redshifts and Controversies* (in 1987) that GRS was "quickly discarded" as the source of their red-shift, but further on wrote, "Perhaps they [quasars] are redshifted by a strong magnetic field…[and] evidence points to the fact that galaxies can also have nonvelocity redshifts," and further on yet, "No internal gravitational fields can be responsible for these red-shifts." Thus, even Arp, who probably has produced more astronomical evidence against the *accepted interpretation of redshift data* than anyone else in the world, has been influenced against the possibility of the GRS of radiation from distant quasars.

Because the redshift of radiation from that fuzz is the same as that of its quasar, it has also been claimed that it provides evidence against gravitation as the cause of quasar redshift. However, the "reflection" of quasar radiation from surrounding dust denies that claim.

In support of that, it was reported in *SCIENCE NEWS* (in 1994) that British astronomers Richard G. McMahan, Michael Irwin and their colleagues found 40 distant quasars, observed in the radio frequency range that have, "evidence that huge amounts of dust surrounding two of the quasars….[They] propose that a warm dust cloud more massive than a hundred million Suns surrounds the quasar and produces the extra emissions…. *The quasar itself may provide the heat.*" (Italics added for emphasis), and an article in *SKY & TELESCOPE* in June, 2001, reported that, "In much the same way clouds hiding the Sun can show bright linings, the quasar [a "Type II" quasar] identified by the VLT [European

Southern Observatory's Very Large Telescope] is hidden but lights up the dust clouds around it."

In Support of Gravitational Redshift.

Many sources in the literature, by well-regarded scientists and science writers, have supported gravitation as a possible cause of the redshift of radiation from massive objects in space.

BB astronomer William Kaufman wrote in *Relativity and Cosmology* (in 1973), who at that time was the director of the Griffith Observatory, "Perhaps quasars are extremely massive objects, and the redshift comes from the intense gravitational field of the object." Although he later denied that possibility, he might have been correct the first time.

Science writer and astrophysicist John Gribbin in *Space Warps* (in 1983) wrote that, "And there is a second, completely different way (in addition to Doppler or cosmological redshift) to produce a large redshift, through the gravitational effect of a supermassive object." But he, also a member of the establishment, also couldn't seriously consider that explanation.

Physicist James Paul Wesley in his book *Advanced Fundamental Physics* (in 1991) has written that, "The large redshift of quasars is immediately explained by the [his] present model as primarily a gravitational redshift due to [their] compact super massive bodies....The present theory which says that quasars are distributed like ordinary galaxies, indicates radiation rates much less than ordinary galaxies, as would be expected for small objects with large gravitational redshifts."

Even BB cosmologist Peebles accepts GRS when it might suit his purpose. As mentioned in Chapter 13, he wrote about "a packet" of MBR photons being gravitationally red- or blue-shifted due to their "falling into a potential well" of matter in space, and SST cosmologist Fred Hoyle, published a paper in 1983 entitled *A Gravitational Model for QSOs*, presenting his ideas in support of the gravitational redshift of quasars.

Van Flandern, has written in *Dark Matter, Missing Planets and New Comets* (in 1991) regarding the collapse of supermassive star-like objects, such as radio galaxies and quasars, "one would expect the result of the collapse to be an object with a very intense gravitational field. Light leaving it would be highly redshifted. Its predicted properties would not in any obvious way differ from the

observed properties of quasars, which may be just highly redshifted objects."

Kip Thorne wrote in *Black Holes and Time Warps* (in 1994), "It
is still possible to explain all the observed properties of radio galaxies and quasars using an alternative non-black-hole engine: a
rapidly spinning, magnetized, supermassive star, one weighing millions or billions of times as much as the Sun—a type of star that
has never been seen by astronomers, but that theory suggests might
form at the center of galaxies. Such a supermassive star would
behave much like a hole's accretion disk. By contracting to a small
size…, it could release a huge amount of gravitational energy, by
way of friction, could heat the star so it shines brightly like an
accretion disk; and magnetic field lines anchored in the star could
spin and fling out plasma in jets."

NATURE reported (in 1995) that Yasuo Tanaka of the Japanese
Institute of Space and Aeronautical Science, found that the redshift
of gas in the neighborhood of a Seyfert galaxy 110 million light-
years distant, provides data that shows the GRS of photons
climbing out of a strong gravitational field; an admission of such
phenomena that rarely appears in establishment media.

Ron Cowan reported on an item in the October 20, 1997
Astrophysical Journal Letters regarding X-ray radiation from quasars
"that are thought to be powered by massive, central black holes" as
follows: "The indicator [of how rapidly black holes devour their
surroundings] consists of x-rays emitted by iron atoms after they
fall onto a swirling disk of matter surrounding a black hole. This
emission, first detected in the early 1990s in a group of nearby
galaxies that are relatively dim but have bright centers, is shifted in
wavelength by a strong gravitational field—a tip-off that these
galaxies house black holes."

Although he (or whoever was the source of that material) has
assumed quasars to be the result of black hole accretion, he has
accepted GRS of radiation from matter that surrounds them.

SKY & TELESCOPE (in 1998) reported that, "An ordinary
looking spiral galaxy in Centaurus, MCG-6-30-15, has become a
test bed of General Relativity. In 1995 the Advanced Satellite for
Cosmology and Astrophysics (ASCA) observed the galaxy and
found enormous redshifts in X-rays emitted by iron ions in the
galaxy's nucleus. This testified to the ultra-strong gravitational field
of a black hole in the galaxy's center. In fact, some of the x-rays

appeared to have lost more than half of their energy climbing out of the black holes's "gravity well." [That seems to be a recognition of GRS but, on the other hand, demonstrates some confusion: Accepted theory is that nothing can escape ("climb out" of) the gravitational clutch of a black hole.]

Quite obviously, there are many scientists who believe that GRS plays a significant role in the redshift of various massive bodies in space.

Types of Stars.

Astronomers generally recognize several stable states of large stellar bodies of the universe.

One of those is main sequence stars in which nuclear reactions are taking place. Another of those is white dwarfs that are formed when relatively small stars cease their normal processes and collapse to that state. Another is neutron stars that result from the collapse of stars somewhat larger than the Sun, and yet another is black holes. Stars that have a mass more than several times greater than the Sun are believed to collapse to that state. Although their existence is not entirely proven, theory and observational evidence tend to support the reality of that state of massive matter in space.

GRS effect on the first and second of those types of stars might not be of much significance, but in the case of neutron stars it becomes quite significant; and, in the case of black holes, it becomes great enough to prevent all radiation, that is, their GRS in infinite.

That progression suggests the possibility of (at least) a fifth type, that has been called a grey hole, better known as a quasar; a compact massive object whose gravity falls short of preventing the escape of radiation, but whose redshift is very large.

Grey Holes.

Boston University astronomer Kenneth Brecher (in 1994) suggested massive bodies that fall short of becoming black holes, can produce redshifts in excess of Doppler shifts due to gravitational effects. He has called the result of that process a grey hole.

Amazingly, that is exactly the process I had long ago described for the birth of quasars!

Regarding grey holes: "These, Brecher proposes, are massive stars that did not collapse enough to form black holes yet have smaller radii and greater densities than typical neutron stars." The article says, "To become a black hole a star would have to collapse below its Schwarzschild radius." Their Schwarzschild radii of his grey holes would therefore be within their surface, just as I had written long ago.

Although Brecher suggests that his grey holes would be quite dim, because their surface could be well outside of their Schwarzchild radii, they (quasars) could be very brilliant and produce violent flares.

Speculating about "the rate at which gas accretes" into a black hole accretion disk, astronomer Virginia Trimble of the University of California and the University of Maryland has written (in *SKY & TELESCOPE* in 2000) regarding the formation of quasars, "How much gas is available to make the disk and how much stuff the jets encounter on the way out depends on the host galaxy's type and probably on the previous history of the accretion, which could have cleared out all the central gas and left a starving black hole." That sounds just like what I had postulated for a possible black hole that didn't make it and became a grey hole, that is, a quasar.

Astronomer Rowland van der Marel, specialist in the study of black holes, had decided (in 1999) that quasars are really the result of radiation from the processes of black holes in the centers of galaxies acquiring matter from their surrounding. Therefore, his explanation for some galaxies, such as M87, which he assumes were brighter in the past, have now lost their central brightness because "the quasar turned off," and "Maybe it doesn't have enough fuel to be a quasar anymore," and he suggests that, "Apparently not all black holes are still eating."

If van der Marel is correct, and the process of the accretion of matter by a black hole ceases due to "starvation," certainly that might also happen to collapsing stars on the way to becoming black holes, resulting in what Brecher calls grey holes, and that I suggest results in quasars.

I had written (in 1994) the following in support of my belief that quasars are massive bodies (like Brecher's grey holes) that couldn't quite make it as black holes, about a quasar going forward to become a black hole rather than turning off, as van der Marel has presented:

"Of course, it is possible that more evidence will be discovered [regarding quasars]. If, for example, it should be determined that objects previously identified as quasars cannot again be found, or the character of their radiation has changed rather suddenly, it may be that they have grown into black holes. (Perhaps such observations have already occurred but gone unreported or insufficiently publicized.)"

Although van der Marel's findings that some galaxies might not have "enough fuel to be a quasar anymore," might have hinted at phenomena related to that, I have continued to search for that evidence in the literature—so far without success—that quasars might disappear because they have become black holes. I still have hope that some astronomer might someday report that he has discovered that. It's possible that van der Marel's quasars turned off because they became black holes.

American astronomers Moore, Katz, Lake, Dressler and Oemler reported (in 1996) that "Recent HST images suggest that many quasar hosts are not as luminous as [the Milky way]," that is, they exist in environments lacking sufficient matter to fuel black holes that might generate quasars. According to Moore et al, "That is surprising because simple energy considerations imply that quasars need [100 million to a billion] solar masses to feed the black hole engine." They have concluded that, for quasars to form in the center of galaxies, that requires host galaxies like the Milky Way, to provide a gas of several billion solar masses. But some spiral galaxies provide only 100 million solar masses of gas, "and a quasar needs nearly all of it for fuel."

Moore et al. of course believe, like most of the establishment, that quasars are the result of the accretion of galactic matter into the clutches of a central black hole. What puzzles them is how quasars can exist in those small galaxies. Therefore, they have postulated a elaborate scheme of "galaxy harassment" deigned to solve that problem. (By harassment they mean galactic collision, but how is it possible for galaxies to have collided in a relativistically expanding BB universe?)

It is suggested here that, if quasars have formed from the accretion of surrounding matter, it would provide support for Brecher's grey holes, that is, the formation of quasars as the result of insufficient "fuel" to form black holes.

The active galactic nuclei (AGN) in the center of some galaxies, considered to be quasars by many of the establishment, are thought to be powered by the in-fall of surrounding matter toward black holes that produces enormous amounts of radiation. However, as mentioned in the previous chapter, Russell Ruthen had asked how a black hole might be fed enough to satisfy its voracious appetite: How does a massive body acquire enough matter to grow into a black hole? It would seem that, if sufficient matter is not available, its growth might be limited to that of Brecher's grey holes; one of the forms of matter that have been called quasars.

Quasar Flares.

It is suggested that nonuniformity of surface luminosity, perhaps giant flares, and faster rotational rates of bodies that are closer and smaller than those that have been perceived in the past, are responsible for the observed large variations of quasar radiation intensity.

As presented in the previous chapter, if a quasar had a flare that was seen once a day by us as it rotated, its diameter would be only about 3/10 of a light-day. That is about 70 percent of that of the solar system—just a few percent of the often estimated one light-week size of a quasar—and there have been reports of luminosity variations of considerably shorter periods than once a day. That is consistent with Herbert Friedman's statement that astronomer Halton Arp has said that, "Quasars are not as distant as their redshifts indicate, therefore they do not have to release such unprecedented amounts of energy."

The turbulence of the surface of the Sun is relatively mild, and its flares tend to loop back to its surface. Flares of neutron stars have greater strength and escape from the fields that tend to confine them, some producing pulsar flashes as these stars rotate at high rates. Therefore, flares of even greater velocities might also be expected to emanate from quasars as they are described here.

It may be possible for some of those flares to reach an appreciable fraction of the speed of light, and, as described in the previous chapter, it is possible for relativistic flares from very distant bodies to appear to be superluminal. But, because infinite energy would be required, superluminal flares are ruled out.

Schwarzschild Radius/Event Horizon.

One might think of large stars that ultimately collapse to become black holes as initially having a Schwarzschild radius, or event horizon, that is far inside its surface, where its effect would be of little significance.

As the star collapses, and its density increases, its event horizon becomes progressively closer to its surface, and, when collapse is complete, its event horizon has moved out beyond the surface of the black hole. At that time, regardless of how hot and how radiant the mass might be, the event horizon, a phenomenon of gravitational force, prevents the escape of radiation. It follows that a main sequence star may be thought of as having its event horizon only a small percentage of the radial distance from its center, a white dwarf perhaps as having its event horizon at a greater percentage of its radius from its center, and that of a neutron star having its event horizon at an even greater percentage of its radius from its center.

It is suggested that quasars (or grey holes) may be objects that have their event horizon at a large percentage of its radial distance from their center, but not beyond their surface. If "fed" enough, they might collapse to become black holes, but because they haven't acquired sufficient matter to become full-fledged black holes, their development ceases and their event horizon remains below their surface, far enough below to allow a large amount of radiation to escape.

It is therefore postulated that there is a family of objects that may be thought of as having the equivalent of event horizons at various depths below their surfaces, that result in quasars having a wide range of high redshifts, and therefore appearing to have a wide range of velocities.

As has been called to my attention by cosmologist Steve Newman, "Plots of redshift versus magnitude produce a scatter rather than a straight line as nearby galaxies do." That scatter can't be explained by BBT. However, it can be explained by quasars that have a rather wide range of gravitational redshifts.

Perhaps some of those objects gradually accumulate enough nearby matter to become black holes and are thereafter no longer visible; or perhaps a scarcity of matter in the vicinity of some of them retards their growth, keeping their event horizon below their surface for an extended period; or perhaps matter in the vicinity of some is so sparse that they can never become black holes.

That concept is in agreement with stellar theory, as can be confirmed by many sources, including the following quotation from the McGraw Hill *Encyclopedia of Science and Technology* under the subject of GRS, "neutron stars (and white dwarfs as well) which had been formed earlier could accrete enough matter to become more massive than the maximum mass of a neutron star. In these cases the only known alternative is for such stars to collapse to a black hole."

But if the matter that is available for accretion falls short of enough to form a black hole, what might be the result? The answer to that question might simply be "a quasar."

Meanwhile, it should be recognized that there are other "things" that are thought to be quasars; one of which is what goes on in the violent star-forming centers of galaxies.

Redshift Difference Across the Sun.

Careful measurements of the redshift of the Sun's radiation has shown some surprising results.

As stated above, it is about 0.000002. However, redshift radiation from across the face of the Sun has been found to differ slightly. A plot of redshift from the center of its surface to its limb shows at first a gradual increase and then greater and greater increase in redshift as the limb is reached, where it is at its greatest.

The relatively large (0.000002) redshift of the center of the Sun increases by a relatively small amount toward its limb. Although that amount is quite small, when plotted on an expanded scale its accelerating increase is quite pronounced and resembles a secant curve. The shape of a plot of redshift versus distance from the Sun's center is exactly what would be expected due to gravitation.

Some of those who espouse tired light theories attempt to explain this by postulating increasingly dense matter (their ether) near the Sun (due to gravity) that might result in the observed solar redshift curve. However, the presence of hydrogen throughout space, perhaps the most likely candidate for ether, has not been shown to accumulate in the gravitational fields of stars, and the violence of solar flares would certainly disrupt that, or any other ether, that might be present. However, that would not noticeably affect the Sun's gravitational field.

It's much more reasonable to believe the observed increase in redshift of that radiation as it leaves the Sun from points increasingly far from its center is because it travels an increasing distance and time through the Sun's gravitational field.

In Einstein's *The Meaning of Relativity* he says that the spectral lines are displaced toward the red "on the Sun's surface." But that should have read, "by the gravitational field on its surface and within its gravitational influence." If just "on the Sun's surface" was correct, how could he have predicted the "bending" of light rays from a star as they pass near the Sun?

Clifford Will tells us in *Was Einstein Right?* that, "Once he [Einstein] understood...that gravity could have an effect on light (the GRS), he attempted to construct a theory of gravity in which the speed of light would vary in the vicinity of a gravitational body." Notice that he said, "in the vicinity of," not "leaving the surface of." As in the bending of light rays as they pass a massive object in space, it is the gravitation field "in the vicinity of" the Sun that does the bending, and it is not just the gravity at the surface of the the Sun that affects the redshift of light that leaves it. It is the effect of the Sun's gravitation during its entire path through that field.

In support of that, there is considerable astronomical evidence that the path of light and its spectrum is shifted as it travels through a gravitational field. That has been demonstrated by the observation of starlight passing by the Sun and by the "lensing" of the light from more distant sources as it passes through the gravitational fields of closer massive bodies. As Kip Thorne explained in *Black Holes & Time Warps*, "As a particle moves upward through the atmosphere, gravity pulls on it, reducing its energy of motion, correspondingly, as a wave moves upward, it becomes gravitationally redshifted to longer and longer wavelengths."

(As discussed in Appendix A, those effects are claimed to be due to the curved space of relativity, but hard evidence for that is lacking. In all probability they are the result of Newtonian gravitational effects.)

It is clear that the redshift of light from the Sun, is not only the result of its gravitational field at the point from which it departs, but that it is further shifted due to the gravitational field through which it passes as it leaves the Sun. The light from the center of the Sun travels a shorter distance through the field surrounding it, and further from the center of the Sun it travels increasing distances through the Sun's gravitational field.

The redshift of radiation from the center of the Sun is in accordance with gravitational theory. If the variation of the Sun's redshift across its face were due to an ether of some kind, that would require two causes of redshift; one real and one ad hoc.

Different Centers of Rotation of Binary Pairs.

The redshift data of stars of some binary pairs results in the perception that the centers of their orbits are not at the same distance from us, which, according to the laws of physics, they must be. But that happens to be what would be expected due to GRS if those stars were of different masses and sizes.

Although other causes have been postulated, the differences in the GRS of a binary pair provides the only straightforward explanation for that perception. However, in order to prove or disprove GRS as the cause of the perceived differences in centers of rotation of binary pairs perhaps the mass of each would somehow have to be accurately determined.

Possible Evidence of Galaxy Mass Loss.

From a paper entitled *Cosmic Perspective* by astronomer/cosmologist Harold Allen: "To the astonishment of the astronomical community, it has been reported that the redshift of certain members of our Local Supercluster are actually declining with the passage of time! (See W. G. Tifft, *The Astronomical Journal* Dec. 1, 1991, Pgs. 396-415) Through analysis of observational data, compiled during the course of the past decade or two, it is claimed that [in that period] a reduction of typically up to 2 km/s is probably the rule rather that the exception. Should future studies uphold this amazing claim, it will clearly present astronomers with a puzzle to end all puzzles."

If that report is correct, it certainly would present a puzzle.

For example, if the Hubble constant is 20 kilometers per second per million years, and if it were assumed that those galaxies were one million light-years distant, their redshift would be decreasing by a factor of about 0.1 kilometer per second per year. If that decreasing redshift was due to Doppler, that is, they were to continue departing from us at about 20 kilometers per second, their relative velocity would go to zero in 200 years (and perhaps they would start to approach us). On the other hand, if they were not departing from us at all, and their redshift was GRS and entirely due to mass loss, their mass would go to zero in 200 years. Of course, a decrease in GRS could also be due to increasing size or a combination of decreasing mass and increasing size.

Because those possibilities make no sense. it would seem that Tifft's data must be erroneous. However, that subject suggests the possibility that if "future studies" confirm deceasing redshift of radiation from bodies in the IGS, they might provide evidence in support of GRS due to their mass loss. The 200 year period resulting from Tifft's data are unrealistically short. However, as will be discussed in Chapter 28, the rate of mass loss of some objects in space is quite high, which could result in measurable decreases of their mass.

The Acceptance of Alternate Causes of Redshift.

Although GRS was long ago been ruled by BB cosmologists to have no significant impact on cosmological theory, astronomical evidence, science and logic show that to be erroneous.

As determined by the *accepted interpretation of redshift data*, quasars appear to have greater than their actual relative velocity, distance, luminosity and mass, and those faults result in other problems, such as the perception of excessive numbers of superluminal flares. However, if GRS and other possible causes of redshift were given proper consideration, a number of such problems might be solved. Some additional misconceptions, like those related to the Sun's GRS and that of binary stars, might also be cleared up.

Hopefully, gravitational redshift, long denied by BBers to be of significance in cosmological matters, may soon come into its own.

EIGHTEEN

Big Bang Chronology Problems

The chronology of the universe that is typically presented by BBers provides an inadequate and false representation of BBT.

Erroneous Age.

The BB chronology, which is described in Chapter 3 and illustrated in Figure 1, shows a universe having a fixed rate of expansion and an age of 15 billion years, which requires a Hubble time of 15 BYRs and a Hubble constant of about 65 km/sec/Mpc (20 km/sec/MLYs).

But that is not the age of the accepted BB cosmological cases—closed, flat or somewhat open. For those, a Hubble constant of 65 km/sec/Mpc would require the BB to have occurred at about 2/3 of that Hubble time or about 10 billion years ago, considerably less than an age that is acceptable to BBers.

Erroneous Linear Expansion.

Although astronomical evidence indicates that the density of the universe falls far short of the critical amount required for a flat BB universe, many BBers believe that enough missing mass exists in space to cause its average density to approach the critical amount, and that the flat universe is the most likely of the possible BB cases. The closed universe case, requiring somewhat more than critical density, and the open universe case, requiring some-what less than critical density, each have had some supporters. All of those require a universe of nonlinear decreasing expansion. But the fixed-rate universe that is typically portrayed by BBer chronol-ogy diagrams is not included in Standard BB.

Inflation Theory Ignored.

Since the general acceptance of inflation theory, that requires it, most BBers have accepted the flat universe case. Therefore, they believe in a considerable degree of deceleration of the expansion of the universe since the BB. For that reason, a proper plot of energy and temperature versus time would require a decreasing slope as time progressed since the BB, rather than the linear expansion of Figure 1. Furthermore, the nonlinearity required for a decelerating expansion, would require considerable modification to occur-rences such as the creation of various particles, the BB thermonucleosynthesis, neutrino and photon decouplings, and other events of that chronology.

But even more incongruous than that, although they must be aware of its impact, BBers continue to describe events essentially in accordance with that chronology, which is not only inconsistent with pre-inflation BBT, but fails to incorporate the vast non-linear expansion introduced by inflation.

For typical examples of that inconsistency, see *Masters of Time* by John Boslough for a sketch of that chronology as envisioned by BBers; or see Barrow and Silk in *The Left Hand of Creation* who presented inflation as virtual fact, but included chronology dia-grams that ignore the changes required to accommodate inflation.

Certainly astronomers and cosmologists must be aware of the inconsistencies presented in chronologies similar to that of Figure 1, but they are overlooked, and continue to appear in the literature.

Event of Any Energy Accommodated.

If the discrepancies mentioned above are ignored, the elaborate BB chronology described in Chapter 3, that was generated by a host of skilled theoreticians, might at first appear to be on firm ground. However, upon careful consideration that ground appears to be quite shaky.

The postulated higher temperature, and thus higher energy

level that increases toward infinity as we go farther back in time to the BB, can accommodate the creation of particles requiring any conceivable degree of energy. Thus, the various quantum particle creation events, at any level of energy that is postulated or experimentally produced in an accelerator, can be, and have been, assigned a point in time on the BB time scale. Regardless of what their energy level might be, those events are indicated to have occurred at the time when their energy corresponded to the energy of the BB, somewhere between the infinite energy (infinite temperature and density) of the singularity and the present low energy level of space (a temperature of 2.7 K).

Although it has been said that "reconciliation of the creation of fundamental particles with quantum theory" is believed to lend support to BBT, the placing of various particle creation events, both experimental and theoretical, on that chronology appears to be an arbitrarily contrived attempt at that reconciliation. An event of virtually any amount of energy can be placed between the time of a BB of infinite energy and the present low level, making that attempted reconciliation a meaningless exercise.

Regarding that matter, as Ernan McMullin wrote in the *American Philosophies* (in 1981) that, "in the past decade, much effort has been expended on applying quantum and elementary particle theories to the problem of how the universe developed in the first moments after the Big Bang. An immensely detailed scenario has been developed....There are, of course, good historical reasons to distrust the applicability of standard theories to extreme conditions. Furthermore, no adequate theory of quantum gravity has yet been devised. So there is every reason to suppose that present constructions of the early universe ought not to be taken too seriously as history."

A Tested Chronology.

In a book written by Edward W. Kolb, and reviewed by Peebles, Kolb wrote something like the following paragraph. Peebles agreed with it, and presented it as follows:

"If we trace the expansion of the universe back in time to a redshift of $z = 10^{10}$, when the temperature...would have been $T = 10^{10}$ K $= 10^6$ eV, we find neutrons and protons reacting to form new elements up to lithium in amounts that agree with the observed abundances in the oldest stars. This is evidence that we understand the outlines of the behavior of the universe when it was just 1 second old, a remarkable accomplishment indeed."

Similarly, in a 1991 article that was designed to put to rest once and for all any doubt about the credibility of BBT, Peebles et al. stated that equations describing the temperature and the density of the universe "have been tested back to z [redshift] equal to 10^{10}." A redshift of that amount is equivalent to a tiny fraction of a second after the BB.

Those statements, of course, are not true. The "evidence" of that "tracing" is nonexistent, and, not only have such tests not been performed, but it is impossible to perform them. (To some modern theorists "tested" has apparently come to mean "believed to conform to favored theory.") Furthermore, the various particle creation events of the BB chronology have often been referred to as "predictions," but they are not predictions at all. That chronology was created in recent decades,10 billion years after those events are claimed to have occurred.

It took years of effort by teams of geniuses to synthesize the amazing BB chronology, but there is no reason to believe a word of it!

When a representation of the chronology of the BB universe is presented, whether or not it includes a represention of inflation, it should be carefully examined to determine whether it is a genuine representation of what is claimed. Experience has shown that BB chronology diagrams of the past have been poor representations of their stated intent. Although lack of understanding of their own theory may be a factor in that misrepresentation, I suspect that often it is another case of the purposeful obfuscation that is prevalent in BB literature.

NINETEEN

Big Bang Element Problems

As mentioned in Chapter 6, BB cosmologists believe the abundance of elements observed in the universe provides evidence in support of BBT.

Early in the history of BBT it was believed that all the elements were produced by BB nucleosynthesis. When it was later learned that, with the possible exception of a few of the lightest elements, most are produced by stellar fusion, BBT was modified to accommodate that discovery. Although there is considerable evidence that even these few light elements also originate from other sources, BBers haven't been swayed from that belief.

THE SOURCE OF LIGHT ELEMENTS

The Abundance of Light Elements.

Regardless of conflicting evidence, BB theorists insist that the relative abundance of the light elements in the universe provides strong evidence in support of BBT.

We are told that studies have predicted the abundance of light elements, including helium 3, helium 4, deuterium (the heavy isotope of hydrogen), and lithium. According to Schramm and Steigman, "The behavior of atom nuclei under the conditions of big-bang nucleosynthesis is not a matter of guesswork; it is precisely known." In accordance with the BB chronology of Figure 1, all the forces and particles of quantum theory, and the generation of those elements, occurred as a known function of time, temperature and density since the BB.

However, the previous chapter shows that there is considerable reason to doubt that.

Helium to Hydrogen Ratio.

The reported ratios of the light elements, calculated from a postulated ratio of neutrons to photons (seven to one) at about one second after the BB, agrees with the presently observed amount: helium about 20 percent, deuterium about one part in 10,000 and lithium about one part in ten trillion. However, the ratios of those elements were worked out after the observations were made, and are based on a hypothetical baryon to photon ratio (the baryon number).

BB enthusiasts have repeatedly attempted to use a postulated ratio of helium to hydrogen in the universe as further evidence of the validity of BBT. According to calculations by Rees in 1976, Davies in 1981, and Carr in 1982, after the first second or so after the BB "one expects" roughly 25 percent of the mass of the universe to be helium and all the rest, but "a tiny residue of deuterium," to be of hydrogen.

Except for his ratio of about 50 percent each of hydrogen and helium, Gamow had made similar statements in the 1950s. An estimate in the 1960s by Hoyle and others came in at 36 percent helium, later adjusted to 25 percent. Regardless of the variety of estimates, Schramm and Steigman have agreed that the predicted ratios agree with the currently understood composition of the universe.

Overbye tells us that Peebles "jiggled the numbers" until the "helium abundance came out right," and Arp, et al. have written that documentation shows the baryon number in the early universe was selected to predict an abundance of helium that agreed with what was observed at that time. It's quite obvious that the "predicted" ratios, and corresponding baryon numbers, have been periodically adjusted to agree with the latest observations of the real universe.

Regardless of those inconsistencies, BB cosmologists continue to believe that the abundances of the light elements of the universe provide significant evidence in support of BBT.

Light Elements from other Sources.

Although BBers insist that those light elements could only have come from the BB, there is considerable opinion among astronomers that they could have come from other sources.

• Helium.

Adding doubts about BB nucleosynthesis, University of Texas at Austin astronomer Jeff Kanipe has reported that the abundance of helium in galaxies is less than that allowed by the Standard BBT model, and other researches have found similar results. Other investigators have agreed that the generation of helium, deuterium and lithium by BB nucleosynthesis would require more baryonic matter in the observable universe than is seen by astronomers.

It is known that helium is produced in the nuclear reactions in stars. British astrophysicist Martin Rees agreed that massive stars could, in a few hundred million years, produce the abundance of helium now observed, and distribute it into space when they explode as supernovas. Peebles also agreed that the present helium abundance could have been produced "in an earlier generation of supermassive stars." In fact, some astronomers have suggested that all elements are synthesized in stellar reactions and spread by supernovas.

• Lithium.

Evidence has been reported suggesting that lithium may also be created in substantial quantities in the "modern" universe.

A number of astronomers, including Michael Rowan-Robinson, Martin Harwit, and Douglas Duncan of the Space Telescope Science Institute, have indicated that cosmic rays can split atoms of matter to produce elements such as boron, beryllium and lithium.

An additional item of interest regarding lithium, is that University of California, Berkeley professor of astronomy Stuart Bowyer has reported (in *SCIENTIFIC AMERICAN* in 1994) regarding the work of Andrea K. Dupree of the Harvard-Smithsonian Center for Astrophysics and her colleagues on the extreme ultraviolet spectrum of Capella, 45 light-years away, which has "two coronally active yellow giant stars." They have "observed a large amount of plasma at a temperature close to six million degrees C in the Capella system...Plasma confined by magnetic fields may undergo fusion near one or both of the stars, releasing energy." All sorts of elements, including lithium, might be produced in that process.

The presence of lithium is important to BBers. They maintain that, because of its high volatility, it can't survive the high temperatures inside of stars and thus, it could only have been generated by BB nucleosynthesis, providing support for BBT. However, the temperature at the center of the Sun is said to be 15 million K, and is less and less further away from the its center. On the other hand, the postulated temperature during BB nucleosynthesis is from about 10 billion K down to about one billion K. If lithium can't survive the Sun's temperature, how could it have survived those temperatures?

• Deuterium.

BBers have also insisted that deuterium could only have been produced in BB nucleosynthesis.

Peebles, et al. have written that, "significant amounts" of deuterium "cannot be produced in known non-cosmological processes" (meaning non-BB fusion processes) But, like lithium, it may be possible for deuterium to be produced by other processes throughout the universe; Silk has stated in the *Big Bang* that, "It is possible to conceive of other non-stellar sources of deuterium at early stages of evolution of galaxies....The net result of attempts to synthesize deuterium in the Big Bang remains distressingly inconclusive...just because deuterium is not produced in ordinary stars does not rule out a possible pregalactic phase involving massive stars that might have produced deuterium;" and Steven Weinberg wrote in *The First Three Minutes,* "We can imagine that...deuterium was produced in "recent" astrophysical phenomena—supernovas, cosmic rays, perhaps even quasi-stellar objects."

Adding further doubts about the source of deuterium in the universe, University of Washington astronomy professor Craig J. Hogan has reported (in *SCIENTIFIC AMERICAN* in 1996) that the investigations by a team of University of California and Columbia astronomers have found the abundance of deuterium to be a factor of 10 lower than previous estimates.

THE SOURCE OF HEAVY ELEMENTS

Beryllium, Boron and Iron.

In addition to the light element problems mentioned above, observations have shown that the abundances of beryllium and boron are inconsistent with BBT. (Beryllium, having an atomic number of 4, is also sometimes referred to as a light element.)

Observations of a very old "fossil" star located outside of the plane of our galaxy have resulted in the discovery of both boron and beryllium in it. That star has only about 0.2 percent of the iron and less than one percent of the oxygen found in the Sun, indicating that it is about 15 billion years old.

HST observations have confirmed those findings in three of the oldest stars within our galaxy that are said to be about 13 to 15 billion years old. In those stars the ratio of beryllium to iron was found to be 1,000 times greater than it would have been if it had originated in stars. That ratio indicates that the beryllium could have been produced either by BB nucleosynthesis, or by the action of cosmic rays to produce boron and beryllium (by fission rather than by fusion).

However, Gerard Gilmore of the Institute of Astronomy in Cambridge, England, and his colleagues, have reported that a star called HD 140283, 200 million light-years distant, contains little iron, indicating that it formed 10 to 15 BYRs ago. Its spectrum has shown it to contain "far more beryllium than the standard model of the big bang predicts," and Astronomer Sean Ryan of the University of Texas is quoted as saying, "There appears to be a lot more beryllium in the early universe than we expected based on predictions of the standard model of the Big Bang....The standard picture of the Big Bang implies that the very first stars to form should be entirely free of beryllium and boron.... Observations of old stars in the Milky Way halo have shown 1,000 times more beryllium than should be expected from cosmic rays alone."

In addition to problems regarding their abundance, it should noted that some heavy elements are observed in stars that are thought to be older than the calculated age of the BB universe.

New Adjustments Required for BBT.

Going in a different direction, Richard Boyd of Ohio State University was quoted as saying, "Nuclear processes during the first second after the Big Bang might have made everything in the periodic table." He suggested that, "Instead of the uniform sea of particles usually pictured, the newborn universe may have been riddled with zones of higher and lower density, where nuclear processes could have formed heavier elements...[Thus] the universe contains more matter than the standard Big Bang allows," and David Schramm is quoted as saying, "the early universe was much lumpier than generally believed...that could have sparked a cascade of nuclear reactions that generated the extra beryllium.

Those ideas called for some new adjustments to BBT.

Accordingly, near instantaneous suggestions have been forthcoming. It has been suggested that at about the first minute after the BB, in a universe more "lumpy" than previously thought, beryllium was produced in the higher density regions of the universe. But, of course, that lumpiness, would have cleared up long before the decoupling so that the MBR would still be smooth, thus avoiding another dilemma for BBers.

As Schramm stated, "those lumps would have vanished after the first 100 seconds of the universe, so they wouldn't affect today's clustering of stars and galaxies. Nor would they have left a trace in the universe's pervasive background of radiation, which appears perfectly smooth in current observations."

Elements heavier than beryllium might also have been produced in those lumps. Some astronomers are now suggesting that many elements of the periodic table might have been so produced. Opinions regarding BB nucleosynthesis might now have completed a full circle regarding the generation of the elements. As in the past, as soon as a problem is encountered, an assortment of adjustments to theory are postulated in order to circumvent it.

ELEMENTS FROM WITHIN OUR GALAXY

As mentioned above, after it had been determined that most of the elements of the universe are produced by the nuclear processes within stars, BB cosmologists had conceded that only a few light elements, such as helium, deuterium and lithium might have been produced by BB nucleosynthesis.

Thereupon they, and the rest of the establishment, decided that all of the heavy elements of the galaxies, including all of those in the Sun, the planets, and even our bodies, came from other sources within the galaxy. Those sources include supernovas, novas, red giants, cosmic rays, and perhaps plasma such as that of the Capella system; but supernovas appear to be their favorite source of that matter.

Elements from Supernovas.

Those of the establishment seem to agree that most of the heavy elements found in the universe were created in previous generations of stars that had exploded as supernovas.

As mentioned in Chapter 11, there have been a number of reports of heavy elements in remote galaxies and quasars. According to BBT, the only possible source of those is previous generations of stars that have blown up within their associated galaxies.

Some examples of those opinions are:

Herman Bondi and American nuclear astrophysicist Edwin Salpeter concluded (in 1951), that stellar reactions and supernova explosions might account for all the elements in the universe.

Based on data compiled by American chemist Harold Urey and German-American Physicist Hans Suess, astronomers Geoffrey and Margaret Burbidge, Hoyle and Fowler concluded (in 1957) that, "We have found it possible to explain, in a general way, the abundances of practically all the isotopes of the elements from hydrogen through uranium by synthesis in stars and supernovas."

Astronomer Robert Noah (in 1997) told us, "Ironically, the death of a star seeds the galaxy with the raw ingredients for the next generation of stars, planets, and life."

Physicists Gulkis, Lubin, Meyer and Silverberg speculated about it having taken at least several such cycles before our solar system formed in order to account for the variety and quantity of heavy elements; Gerrit Verschuur told us that the estimated age of some globular cluster is about 17 billion years, and yet they contain "metals that came from previous generations of stars;" and as mentioned in Chapter 11, astronomers Schmidt and Gunn have reported a quasar having a red shift of almost 5 that contains carbon, nitrogen, oxygen and silicon. They all believe that such elements could only come from previous generations of stars.

(Astronomers refer to elements heavier than lithium as "metals.")

James Kaler's of the University of Illinois wrote (in 1999), "We estimate that supernovas occur about once every 30 years or so in the Milky Way Galaxy. If the galaxy is now about 15 billion years old, it has seen about 500 million supernovas. The mass of the galaxy is about 200 billion suns. The heavy elements constitute about a hundredth of that, so the galaxy contains about 2 billion solar masses of the stuff. Each supernova has therefore contributed a few solar masses of heavy elements, give or take a very large fraction (to produce the elements that exist today), which is consistent with theoretical estimates."

On the surface, all of that seems to be reasonable, but the calculations shown in Appendix E deny its validity.

The Impossibility of Stellar Systems from Supernovas.

Perhaps for the first time, some questions regarding that possibility are presented here.

The above statement about each supernova contributing a few solar masses of heavy elements to each of the 200 billion Suns of the Milky Way is totally unreasonable. The typical supernova, that might have only a "few solar masses" of heavy elements to begin with, loses most of its mass in radiation and neutrinos, and much of its other matter flies off into space at greater than escape velocity.

Let's assume that a supernova the size of SN1987A, that is estimated to have a mass about 20 times that of the Sun were to explode and all of that mass remains evenly distributed throughout an area the size of the solar system. Ignoring the fact that some of its mass might remain as a neutron star or a black hole, let's also assume that all of its mass were to remain evenly distributed throughout an area the size of the solar system.

According to the calculations of Appendix E, taking the radius of the solar system to be that of the distance of Pluto from the Sun (about 5.9×10^9 kilometers), the average density of the matter from that supernova in space of that size would only be on the order of one 100 billionth of that of the Sun. Certainly that density is low enough to deny the possibility of the accretion of matter from such a supernova to form a stellar system.

In addition to that, because much of the matter of a supernova leaves it at very high velocity—far greater than its escape velocity—that would tend to deny that more than a small percentage of it would remain within the space of our solar system.

Furthermore, a major portion of the mass of a supernova leaves it in the form of electromagnetic radiation and neutrinos. The velocity of those is at, or very near, the speed of light. Therefore, virtually none of it would remain in the space of our solar system, but would speed on out of the Milky Way.

Icko Iben, Jr., University of Illinois professor of astronomy and physics, and Alexander V. Tutukov head of the Department of Stellar Evolution at the Institute for Astronomy in Moscow (in 1997) have stated that, "Observations suggest that a Type II supernova should occur roughly every 50 years in our Milky Way," *SKY & TELESCOPE* reported (in 1999) that, "astronomers calculate that a supernova goes off in the Milky Way roughly once every 40 years," and *ASTRONOMY* reported (also in 1999) that, "Supernovae in our galaxy are rare, occurring perhaps once every 30 to 50 years."

Probably only one of those in millions of years is likely to be close enough to shower our solar system with a few particles of matter.

If only one supernova in 30 to 50 years might explode anywhere within our entire galaxy, that would seem to rule out the possibility of matter from more than one supernova explosion gathering to a significant density within the space of a future solar system. (According to the calculations of Appendix E, if a supernova the size of SN1987A exploded within the Milky Way, and its matter was evenly distributed in that space, its average density would be only about 10^{-33} times that of the Sun.)

An additional major factor is that a star like the Sun is estimated to contain over 99 percent of the mass of the solar system, and it is initially composed almost entirely of hydrogen. Because a star uses up much of its hydrogen before it explodes as a supernova, it can provide, at most, only a fraction of the amount of hydrogen that is required to form a new star.

It is known that hydrogen is present in interstellar space. However, there is no reason to expect that a supernova explosion could cause it to accrete to form a new star; and, even if there were sufficient hydrogen, it is not clear how that could cause it to accumulate to form a star while most other elements and compounds are separated to form planets and satellites.

The idea of star-birth from supernovas within a galaxy, having once been suggested by an establishment "authority," and without providing a shred of scientific evidence, has apparently been accepted without ever being critically examined by others of the establishment.

It appears that, not only the ideas regarding light and heavy elements from the BB, but also ideas regarding elements from exploding stars within galaxies, are in deep trouble.

TWENTY

Curved
Space
Problems

When Albert Einstein's work on General Relativity was published in 1916 there was no mention of negative curvature of
space: Space curvature was simply a function of the density of matter. If no matter was present, there would be zero gravitational
force, and space would be uncurved. If the average mass of the universe were greater than zero, gravity and the curvature of space
would be proportionately greater.

No Negative Curvature Before Friedmann Solution.

Not until Friedmann came along did we have the nonsense of
negatively curved space. No references to negatively curved space
can be found in Einstein's *Relativity, The Special and General
Theories*, or in other early books on Einstein's work such as
Biography of Physics by George Gamow or *Understanding Relativity*
by Stanley Goldberg, and there is no mention of it in other early
books on Einstein's work. In all of those there is only discussion of
positively curved space resulting from gravitational attraction (or
equivalent acceleration).

Einstein's book, *The Meaning of Relativity*, of 1922, and its subsequent editions of 1945 and 1950, were published without
mention of negative curvature. As Barry Parker wrote, Einstein's
initial reaction to Friedmann's solution to his equations had been

that it was, "nothing more than an exercise in mathematics." That is confirmed by Einstein's own words in the 1957 edition of *The Meaning of Relativity*, in the *Appendix to the Second Edition*, in which he presented Friedmann's work, but stated it to be, "essentially nothing but an exposition of Friedmann's work."

No Physical Basis for Friedmann Solutions.

In that appendix Einstein presented a discussion of Friedmann's 1922 solution to the equations of General Relativity wherein he presented the concept of negative curvature. However, he made no attempt to provide a physical basis for negatively curved space, nor have I been able to find that in any subsequent literature on the subject. To my knowledge, neither Friedmann, Einstein, nor anyone else, has provided any physical rationale for negatively curved space.

Without that rationale, Einstein's assessment of Friedmann's negative curvature as merely an exercise in mathematics retains its validity. Einstein himself said, "The skeptic will say, 'It may well be true that [a] system of equations is reasonable from a logical standpoint. But this does not prove that it corresponds to nature. 'You are right, dear skeptic. Experience alone can decide on truth.'"

As Kragh has written, "The mathematical character of Friedmann's work is further illustrated by the fact that he [Friedmann] indicated a solution with negative density as one of the possible solutions to his equations. That such a solution is physically inadmissible (or at least problematical) does not seem to have interested him."

But regardless of the lack of a physical basis for Friedmann's solutions to Einstein's equations, they have been readily accepted by the establishment.

Acceptance of the Friedmann Solutions.

It had taken years of study and debate for Einstein's positively curved space to be generally accepted, but Friedmann's negatively curved space seems to have been accepted with little critical examination. Thus BB cosmologists have not only accepted the Einstein's positively curved, closed space, that provided only for a closed universe, but also Friedmann's negatively curved space that provides for an open or flat universe. Accordingly, the closed

BB universe was ascribed positively curved space; the open BB universe, negatively curved "saddle shaped" space; and the flat BB universe, uncurved space: a fine balance between positive and negative curvature.

According to Einstein's original work, the idea of a flat universe as a balance between a closed and an open universe would be illogical. A flat universe could only be the result of zero density, and a near flat universe could only be the result of low density; quite a different situation than the accepted cosmological possibilities that result from Friedmann's work. (As in the Friedmann solution, zero density would result in a fixed rate of expansion but, unless Einstein's cosmic repulsion were at work, there could be no possibility of a BB universe of increasing expansion, as has recently become a popular theme.)

Even B. J. Carr, a leading advocate of BBT who accepts the negative curvature of an open universe, in a lengthy paper on that theory has written the conflicting statement that, "matter curves space". If that is so, the presence of matter in the universe denies the possibility of negatively curved space, and Carr omits discussion of the cause of negative curvature. Neither he nor his fellow BB theorists seem to recognize the inconsistencies inherent in negatively curved space.

However, if space is uncurved or negatively curved, a la Friedmann, there must be something in the BB universe to overcome the positive curvature resulting from the presence of the matter. If the BB universe is flat ("flat" meaning a balanced state between an "open" and a "closed" universe, as intended by BBers), that "something" must be just sufficient to compensate for the gravitational influence of the matter of the universe and, if the BB universe is open, it must be sufficient to overpower that influence. That something must be some kind of antigravity; perhaps a small positive cosmological constant, Einstein's cosmic repulsion.

If negatively curved space is to be accepted, it should be demonstrated that Friedmann's solution to Einstein's equations represents something that is known to exist in nature. There must be more than a set of equations to provide the rationale for either a flat or open BB universe, where space is uncurved or negatively curved. Unless mathematics represents actual physical phenomena it is meaningless.

Cosmic Repulsion and Inflation Theory.

As reported in a number of sources, because Einstein did his work on relativity before the universe was believed to be expanding, he inserted a term (as a constant of integration of unknown magnitude) in his equations in order to provide for a universe that was thought to be static. That term, thought to represent a force that opposes gravity, was needed to reconcile his mathematics with that universe. In the absence of a belief in an expanding universe, it might have seemed plausible for a cosmic repulsive force to be present throughout the universe.

Some writers have indicated that Einstein gratuitously added the repulsion term to his equations. But others deny that. Silk, for example, has said that Einstein's equations "in their most general form contain this term," and Davies has said that Einstein "didn't conjure up cosmic repulsion in an ad hoc way. He found that his gravitational field equations contained an optional term which gave rise to a force with exactly the desired properties." However, Einstein himself admitted (in 1917) that it was not justified by actual knowledge of gravitation, but was "necessary for the purpose of making a quasi-static distribution of matter."

As mentioned in Chapter 11, when it became accepted by the establishment that Hubble and Humason had shown galaxies to be fleeing each other at a rate proportional to their distance, cosmic repulsion was abandoned by all concerned.

But the acceptance of the three BB cases resulting from Friedmann's work required something akin to it, and, although Paul Davies wrote (in 1973) that cosmic repulsion provided the expansive force that overcame gravity to cause the expansion of the universe, that idea was rarely stated by mainstream cosmologists. So it would seem that BB theorists' acceptance of uncurved space of a flat universe, or the negatively curved space of an open universe, unknowingly by most of them, implicitly acknowledged that concept. For many years following that it was rarely, if ever, found in their literature.

Actually, cosmic repulsion began to be taken seriously in the early 1980s when it was resurrected to provide the force that fueled the inflation of the universe. As Davies wrote (in 1984) regarding inflation theory, "The quantum vacuum behaves exactly like the previously hypothetical medium which produces cosmic repulsion" and, "The antigravity Einstein threw out the door has come back in through the window." Although Donald Goldsmith in *Einstein's Greatest Blunder?* wrote that, "Negative mass, or at least 'negative gravity,' plays a role in more than one novel, but physicists do not regard the concept as a serious possibility for the real world," apparently that didn't apply to inflation theorists.

Cosmic Repulsion and Increasing Expansion.

Cosmic repulsion thus reemerged on a grand scale, and, apparently in order to avoid the embarrassment of its previous rejection, and to make it sound more respectably scientific, it was given its new name, the cosmological constant.

However, although it had difficulties all along, inflation theory's problems have increased, resulting in increasing loss of credibility. As a result, it has become popular among BBers to consider the possibility that the expansion of the universe is increasing rather than decreasing; and the cosmological constant, has been claimed to be responsible for that.

As discussed in Chapter 11, if the BB universe had expanded slower in the past, it might be much older than previously thought based on the Hubble constant. Its age might be pushed out beyond that of its stars. If there had been a positive cosmological constant for a significant period in the past (possibly continuing to the present and future), that would mean that its average expansion rate might have been slower in the past, and thus the time since the BB might have been longer than indicated by the previously accepted rate of expansion.

Although a universe of increasing expansion is outside of the norm for Standard BBT, this isn't the first time in recent years that BBT has been readjusted to aid in overcoming its problems. Cosmic repulsion itself, has been proposed as the salvation of BBT for a second time; first to establish inflation theory, and now to provide a new solution to the BB age problem.

Negative Matter, Energy and Force.

However, getting back to Standard BBT, although BBers had long declared their rejection of the "troublesome cosmic repulsion," logic would have required its presence. If space has negative curvature, it would have to contain negative matter (negative density) that has negative energy. That negative energy would be anti-gravity much like that of Einstein's cosmic repulsion.

As mentioned above, in an expanding BB universe that is flat, that negative energy would have to be just sufficient to compensate for the positive gravitational influence of the positive matter of the universe; and, in an open universe, it must be sufficient to overpower that influence.

Helge Kragh relates that, in the 1930s, "Irish mathematician and cosmologist William Hunter McCrea, professor of mathematics at the Royal Holloway College of the University London, explained the expansion [of the universe] as a result of negative pressure which corresponds to a negative gravitational mass between the observer and a galaxy," and, as mentioned in Chapter 7, BB cosmologists Tryon and Davies both wrote that the negative energy of gravity opposes all the other positive forces of the universe to result in zero net energy, and others, including Friedmann, himself once suggested that negative density might provide a solution to his equations.

If there is negative curvature of space it would seem that there must be something like negative matter or negative energy that provides the negative force (anti-gravity) needed to produce negative curvature of space. But, unfortunately for BBT, those things just don't exist in the real world. As stated in Chapter 7, negative matter, negative energy and negative forces are unknown in nature. There may be opposing energies or forces, so that one of an opposing pair might be labeled negative for mathematical usage, but none are really negative.

Infinite Curvature.

Regarding the singularity of a black hole, or of the BB itself, space would have infinite or near infinite positive curvature, which presents some difficulties. In the case of a black hole, in-falling matter would reach infinite mass and zero speed as it reaches its event horizon, so nothing could ever fall into it; and, in the case of a BB, nothing could have ever escaped such gravity—or such great Einsteinian curvature.

Ivan King in *The Universe Unfolding* agrees that, "If someone were to fall into a black hole,...watching him from the outside, the events of his demise would appear to run more and more slowly, so that for us, he would take an infinite length of time to reach the point of no return." Those who claim to understand such matters confirm that in-falling matter would appear to slow to a stop. To the outside observer—us—that process would take forever. The fact that it is believed that time for the one falling in would not slow is not a consideration. We are the ones who are considering the events of the cosmos.

But cosmology need not be greatly concerned with hypothetical ideas regarding matter entering the infinite gravity of a black hole, but conversely, it should be greatly concerned with the impossibility of matter to have escaped the infinite gravity of a BB. According to relativity, on which BBT is based, there could have been no BB explosion!

Curved Space Not Acceptable.

In addition to problems concerning the existence of negative curvature in the space of the universe, some aspects of relativity are far from being proven facts. Because the evolution of the BB universe is based on relativity, operating in that environment is subject to considerable question. Certainly it has not been tested under the extreme conditions of a BB.

Many question remain about relativity, both special and general. Those include questions, not only about negatively curved space, but also about positively curved space.

As in our daily lives, and in most practical scientific endeavors, there is no need for cosmologists to consider any effects of any space curvature. In fact, it may ultimately be found that it is unnecessary for any scientists even to consider it as a possibility. Although GRS was predicted by Einstein, there is little reason to believe that the "warping" of the path of light is the result of the curvature of space, but simply the reaction of the equivalent mass of photons, traveling at the speed of light, to gravity.

As Kragh has told us about British mathematician and cosmologist Edward Arthur Milne, based on his work in the early thirties, "Milne found the general theory of relativity to be mathematically as well as philosophically monstrous....Space was for him not an object of observation, but a system of reference, and thus could not have structure, curved or not. His own model of the universe supposed a flat, infinite Euclidean space and simple kinematic considerations."

Milne's opinion undoubtedly is correct. The concept of curved space of any kind is unacceptable.

TWENTY ONE

Expansion Problems

In this chapter some ideas are presented that question the BB concept of an expanding universe, especially the expansion of the space of their universe.

Redshift Interpretation.

For those who believe that redshift is Doppler redshift, or in the case of BBers who believe that it is cosmological, redshift provides an indication of relative velocity and distance of bodies in space.

For those who believe in one of the tired light theories, and reject the expansion of the universe, redshift is thought to be indicative of distance throughout the universe, but not velocity. They may accept the Hubble constant as indicative of distance ($D = cZ/H_0$), but they don't accept the Hubble relationship ($V = Zc$) for relative velocity.

For BBers, small values of redshift, velocities and distances are proportional to redshift in accordance with Hubble's law, but, when the relative velocity of a distant body is more than a small percentage of the speed of light, a correction is made for that in accordance with Special Relativity as illustrated in Figure 4; that is, by the application of Lorentz transformations to empty space. However, as presented in Chapters 15 and 16, the redshift problems related to quasars show that, for very distant bodies in space, to be improper. The BBer's *interpretation of redshift data*, which is accepted by most of the establishment, is voodoo science.

Tired light adherents are correct in denying expansion—redshift is not indicative of the velocity of distant bodies—but because some other phenomena must account for the redshift of distant massive bodies, their distance cannot be determined by redshift alone.

Doppler Not All Wrong.

As mentioned in Chapter 15, Doppler effect as the cause of the redshift of radiation resulting from the relative velocity of nearby bodies in the universe is known to be valid.

That is demonstrated by the fact that some stars within our galaxy, and some galaxies within the local group of galaxies, whose velocities have been measured by other means, have redshifts that correspond to those velocities. It has been similarly demonstrated that some stars within our galaxy and some galaxies, such as Andromeda, within the local group of galaxies, that have approaching velocities exhibit blue shifts also corresponding to their observed velocities.

Confirmation of Doppler effect is also provided by the differences in redshifts of stars on opposite sides of rotating galaxies that are viewed on edge, and the differences in redshift of stars of binary pairs that orbit each other provides further evidence of that. However, there remain serious doubts about the cause of redshift of distant massive bodies. It appears that there might be more than one cause, perhaps including velocity, one or more tired light concepts, gravitation, and possibly other unknown phenomena.

Cosmological Redshift and Expanding Space.

Most BBers insist that the redshift of distant bodies in space is not Doppler, but that it is primarily cosmological. Their choice of cosmological redshift rather than Doppler is due to BBT's basis in General Relativity which requires the space of the universe to have closed curvature, resulting in a universe in which its matter is not expanding, but space itself is expanding. As mentioned in Chapter 2, Einstein ultimately agreed that General Relativity "demands the expansion of space."

The belief of BB proponents that the space of the universe has closed curvature in accordance with General Relativity and is uniform (isotropic and homogeneous) is said to be consistent with the idea that we are no more in the center of the universe than any other "observer" in another part of the universe might be. That is also said to be consistent with the idea of expanding closed curved space.

(Perhaps one of the worst violations of logic and science in all of BBT is the belief that the space of the universe is expanding. However, in fairness to some BBers, such as Steven Weinberg who said, "Cosmologists sometimes talk about expanding space but they should know better," there are BBers who know better.)

Size of the BB Universe.

According to BBT, if there had been a fixed-rate BB universe, with a Hubble constant equal to 20 Km/sec/MYRs, Hubble time, T_H, would be 15 BYRs, that is, the BB would have occurred that long ago. ($H_T = c/H_0 = 3 \times 10^5$ Km/sec ÷ 20 Km/sec/10^6 years = 15 BYRs.)

[The present rate of expansion at the edge of the universe would, of course, be 20 Km/sec/10^6 years times 15×10^9 years which equals c (3×10^5 Km/sec).]

In the case of that universe, having ever expanded at the Hubble rate, its size would now be equal to that rate of expansion times the age of the universe (in km) divided by the number of kilometers in a light-light year, which equals 15 BLYs.

[{(3×10^5 Km/sec) x (15×10^9 years) x (3.1558×10^7 sec/year)} ÷ {(3×10^5 Km/sec) x (3.1558×10^7 sec/year)} = 15×10^9 light-years.]

The rate of expansion of that fixed-rate BB universe would have been at that same speed, c, ever since the BB. But, as is evident in Figure 2, the initial expansion rate of the flat BB universe, might be about twice that rate, or about 2c. The rate of expansion of the open BB universe case might be somewhere between c and 2c, and for a closed BB universe case, it might be somewhere between 2c and several times c.

Although those rates are enormous, they are far less than the initial rates of expansion that been postulated for a BB universe, which have been as high as 1,000 c.

Superluminal Expansion.

BBers believe that it is the space between distant galaxies that is expanding, and insist that those galaxies have no velocity, and that, because it is space rather than the matter of the early BB universe, that expanded faster than the speed of light, there has been no violation of relativity's prohibition of speeds greater than light.

(But strangely, while continuing to report on their velocity based on redshift data, they insist that those galaxies have no velocity.)

BB cosmologists who have indicated that the expansion of the BB universe would be as much as 1,000 times faster than c have attempted to justify that by claiming that (as stated by Peebles et al.) faster than light speed expansion of the young universe does not violate Special Relativity. It only says that *information* cannot be transmitted faster than light. Space Sciences Laboratory research physicist Richard A. Muller wrote, "The concept that the distance between two objects can change without the objects themselves moving seems strange because it is completely foreign to our everyday experience. It is hardly stranger, however, than the curvature of space itself."

Those, of course, are distortions of "not even information can be transmitted faster than the speed of light." Relativity clearly indicates that, because its mass would increase to infinity, matter cannot be accelerated to the speed of light or beyond.

As in Standard BBT, how inflation theory can in some manner claim to displace all the mass of the universe without physically moving it, defies common understanding.

Superluminal Quasar Flares.

As discussed in Chapter 16, inconsistencies regarding the perceived velocity of quasars and their flares, that appear to be superluminal, can only be explained by a universe that, on the large scale, is not expanding.

Infinities of Energy Required.

As discussed in Chapter 7, if at the instant of creation all of the BB universe was accelerated to or above the speed of light, each particle of its mass would have required infinities of energy.

Of course, BBers insist that it wasn't the particles of the universe that were accelerated; it was the space between them, and thus little or no energy was required. However, that reasoning is erroneous. Even to this day the rate of expansion of matter at the BBers' edge of space relative to us is at the speed of light which, if we are to believe Einstein regarding this matter, must have required infinities of energy.

BBers, side-step that requirement by citing expanding space, so that General Relativity's prohibition doesn't apply to the BB explosion; or they dismiss it with comments like, "a proper understanding of closed curved space-time avoids that problem," ignoring the fact that their comment might only apply to the closed BB universe case, which very few of them accept.

The Accretion Problem.

As discussed in Chapter 12, no known force, gravitational, electromagnetic or other, could be great to enough to cause the accretion of particles of matter that are departing from each other at the expansion rates that have been postulated for the BB. (The formation of galaxies is said to have started at only a small fraction of the time since the BB—only about 500,000 years as compared to the present age of 10 or more billion years—when the rate of expansion was still very close to its initial rate.)

Even if one were to accept a turbulent BB as suggested by Gamow, it would have been impossible for accretion to have started. At such rates of expansion unbelievably violent turbulence would be required—in a BB explosion that is claimed to be unbelievably smooth.

Even if some particles of matter could have somehow started to accumulate they would soon be flying apart; and even now the planets that orbit the stars would be flying into space. Peebles' suggestion that the birth of galaxies might be the result of "primeval magnetic fields" would have suffered the same difficulty.

As usual, BBers side-step this problem by citing expanding space. The force of expansion, which BBers themselves estimate to have been enormously great, is ignored. Until inflation theory came along, no solution had been postulated for this galaxy formation problem. Unless one were to accept that theory, which is purely ad hoc, no solution to the problem of matter accretion in the early BB universe has been provided.

Whether it is the expansion of the space of the universe, or merely the expansion of the matter of the universe, it should be quite apparent that the increasing distance between galaxies can provide no explanation for the formation of giant galactic structures, nor can it explain the collisions of galaxies that are sometimes reported in astronomical/cosmological literature.

Olbers' Paradox.

BBers insist that if it weren't for the expansion of the universe causing great redshift of remote starlight the sky would ever be brilliant. However, there is overwhelming astronomical evidence that the simple fact is that smaller, cooler, closer matter blocks the radiation from larger, hotter, more distant bodies.

Some of the many examples of that evidence, both old and new, are presented here.

Robert J. Trumpler of the Lick observatory (in 1930), reported interstellar absorption to be a general phenomena, even Peebles recognized (in 1983) that dust obscures our view of both distant parts of our galaxy and distant galaxies, and Ivan King wrote in *SCIENTIFIC AMERICAN* (in 1985), "Interstellar dust absorbs starlight, making the stars appear more distant than they really are."

SCIENCE NEWS reported (in 1997) that, "Located 25,000 light-years from Earth, the star [Pistol] is intrinsically bright… but intervening dust prevents it from being seen in visible light." *SCIENCE NEWS* also reported (in 1998), that Mark E. Dickinson of Johns Hopkins University has said, "If many more galaxies show up in the near infrared than in visible light, it would indicate that dust plays a major role in hiding distant galaxies," and (in 1998) regarding the HST infrared camera finding of several galaxies not seen before, "About 1000 of the galaxies found in the near-infrared had not been seen in visible light. Most are not believed to be very far away but were hidden by dust, which absorbs visible light and reradiates it in the infrared."

Astronomers Kraan-Korteweg and Lehav wrote (in 1998) that, "Over a fifth of the universe is hidden from view, blocked by dust and stars in the disk of our galaxy," and *SKY & TELESCOPE* reported (in 1999), "Bok globules are dark, roughly spherical clouds of interstellar gas and dust that are collapsing to form new stars. They are named after the late Dutch-American astronomer

Bart Bok," and astrophysicist Robert Zimmerman wrote (in 2000) regarding Eta Carinae, "It has never been viewed directly, hidden as it is within the gigantic cloud that surrounds it,"

Although many more could be presented, that sampling of items should be more than sufficient to destroy the BB premise regarding the so-called Olbers' paradox (which isn't a paradox at all) that the sky is dark due to the expansion of their universe.

Gravity Holds Galaxies, Groups and Cluster Together.

The force of gravity is sufficiently strong to keep our solar system and our galaxy, and clusters of galaxies together. Galaxies within our local group, and undoubtedly within other groups, are not only attracted to each other by gravity, but some are actually moving toward each other. As mentioned in Chapter 15, Andromeda, has been estimated to be approaching us at about 266 kilometers per second Also, the weak, the strong, and electromagnetic forces aid gravity in holding together local pieces of matter, such as humans and their measuring devices. Otherwise it might be impossible to determine the relative velocity of other matter of the universe.

Gravity is not only strong enough to hold together stellar systems and galaxies, but also galactic clusters and gigantic galactic formations. Some of those formations span hundreds of millions of light-years of space, indicating that the gravitational forces that hold them together must be infinitesimal. The existence of those accumulations provides denial of the expansion forces of the BB universe.

The gravitational attraction between the matter of those formations at such distances could not be strong enough to overcome the rates of expansion postulated for a BB universe, or even that of a universe having a far lower rate. Even if some galactic structures had somehow formed in the early BB universe, those expansion forces would overcome the weak gravitational attraction of matter at the edges of such accumulations, and gradually destroy them.

Any other cosmology, such as SST, that postulates an expanding universe also faces those problems.

A New Fly in the BB Ointment.

If the space of the universe is expanding, it must be expanding at essentially the same rate in all "local" areas, such as those of stellar systems, galaxies and cluster of galaxies. But BB theorists tell us that gravity is sufficiently strong to overcome the force of expansion in those areas, which implies that in all of those areas, regardless of their mass or their size, gravity must be sufficient, to exactly overcome expansion.

In order to maintain their fixed orbital relationship the gravitational attraction between the Earth and the Sun, for example, must be of just the proper strength to overcome the expansion of their surrounding space. They must have an equal and opposite force of attraction to overcome the force of expansion. The same would also have to be said, for example, of the relationship of the Earth and the Moon. But the magnitude of the gravitational attraction between the Earth and the Moon is quite different than that between the Sun and the Earth.

Likewise, the various gravitational attractions between the many bodies in orbital relationships of galaxies and galactic clusters throughout the universe must all be of exactly the magnitude necessary to overcome the rate of expansion of their space—but they are all different. As a result of that impossible situation, one can only conclude that, on the large scale, there is no general expansion of either space or the matter of space.

Lorentz Transformations Applied to Empty Space.

The BBers' belief in the application of the Lorentz transformations to empty space is inappropriate. They may apply to matter, but not to the empty space of the BB universe. Einstein never intended that.

Because the BBers' *interpretation of redshift data*, based on that fallacy, is accepted by all of the establishment, all that is presented in the media regarding the velocity, distance, mass, luminosity and other characteristics of distant bodies in space is distorted to agree with those incorrect ideas.

In addition to the perception of quasar clumping as a result of applying Lorentz transformations to empty space, as explained in Chapter 11, it also results in other erroneous perceptions such as the formation of galaxies impossibly soon after the BB. Just one recently reported example of such nonsense (in *SCIENCE NEWS* of May 1998) is a galaxy having a redshift of 5.46, that is assumed to be seen as it was about a half billion years after the BB.

Because of the erroneous ways of BBT, the whole world is presented with erroneous astronomical data.

The Energy of Empty Space.

Although Standard BBT postulates that there there was nothing before the BB—no matter, energy, space, or time—in inflation theory, the energy of that space is said to be the source of all the matter and energy of the the universe. Inflation theorists tell us that quantum theory indicates that empty space isn't really empty at all: It contains lots of energy.

Perhaps it could be claimed that it is the equivalent matter of quantum theory's energy of vacuum to which the Lorentz transformations applies. But it would seem unlikely that the equivalent mass of its energy could be sufficiently great to justify that idea. It seems more appropriate to conclude that "the energy of empty space" is an oxymoron, or just plain ridiculous.

The Momentum of Empty Space.

A new BB problem regarding the expansion of space has occurred to me, that I call the momentum problem.

BBers who might have thought about this subject, including Davies and Gribbin, will tell you that it is momentum that keeps the space of the universe expanding. BB inflation theorists, who deny the nothingness of the universe before the BB, might claim that it is the equivalent matter of the energy in empty space that has the momentum. However, as above, even if empty space isn't empty, it seems unlikely that the equivalent mass of its energy could be sufficient to have the necessary momentum. However, I have found no realistic theory of physics that can explain how massless space can have momentum.

The Deceleration of Empty Space.

In addition to a BB momentum problem, a related problem has occurred to me, that I call the deceleration problem.

It is clear that BBers believe (at least in the past, have believed) that the expansion of the space of the universe is slowing due to gravitation. If that is so, it must be the expansion of space that is decelerating. As in the case of momentum, I have found no physical law that explains how the nothingness of space can react to gravity. Again, inflation theorists might claim that it is the equivalent matter of the energy of empty space that is decelerated by gravity. And again, even if empty space wasn't empty, it seems unlikely that the equivalent mass of its energy could be sufficient to have the necessary gravitational attraction.

The c-Barrier Problem.

In any ever-expanding universe, matter that is increasingly distant from any particular point in space has correspondingly increasing relative speed. At very great distances those relative speeds reach the speed of light, c; and beyond that, they would exceed the speed of light, which I call 'the c-barrier'.*

If Einstein was correct, that is prohibited; thus denying the possibility of cosmologies that postulate an ever expanding universe, such as BBT and SST.

Some BBers will insist that prohibition doesn't apply to their universe of closed, positively curved space in which no matter exceeds the speed of light relative to any other observer. However, they ignore the fact that the Standard BB flat and open cases, don't have closed curved space but have Euclidean or saddle-shaped space. They erroneously assume that matter in the expanding curved space applies to all cases of BBT, and that all of the BB cases avoid Einstein's prohibition. Furthermore, those cosmologists who

---

* I have recently discovered that American cosmologist Gerald James Whitrow had noted this problem that has been called "Whitrow's Paradox" and referred to my c-barrier as the "world horizon," Thus, matter that approaches the speed of light relative to some "observers" can be well beyond the speed of light relative to them; well beyond that horizon.

Quoting from the source of that discovery, Helge Kragh wrote that in 1953, "Whitrow had challenged the steady state protagonists with what he believed is a paradoxical situation specifically connected with their world model. If the paradox was real it would imply an inconsistency in the logic of SST....Whitrow pointed out that the steady state model had what he called a world horizon, a distance from each fundamental observer (galaxy) at which matter receded with the velocity of light, so that signals outside or originating inside the sphere can never reach the observer." Kragh also stated that, "Hoyle had noticed the existence of a horizon in steady state theory, but without making its meaning clear or considering it a problematic feature."

have accepted inflation theory, and thus accept that the universe extends far beyond my c-barrier, must also admit to speeds far in excess of light speed.

As stated by Ernan McMullin, "On the Big Bang view, there is a 'world horizon' about ten billion light-years from us at which the galaxies are receding from us at velocities close to that of light. Since according to this same model many more galaxies lie beyond this horizon, it follows that the greater part of the universe cannot be observed here now."

It seems clear and incontestable that all cosmologies that postulate an expanding universe, including BBT, should be ruled out for that reason alone.

The following example provides a quantitative illustration of one ramification of the c-barrier problem.

If the BB universe were either open or flat, unlike the closed type, wherein the space of the universe is not closed, but is flat or saddle-shaped; it has no edge. In that universe, if astronomers were to observe a quasar having a redshift of 5 (z = 5), BB cosmologists would report that it is receding from us at a speed of about 95 percent of the speed of light. If they believe that the BB happened 15 billion years ago, as many of them presently do, they would say that the quasar was seen as it existed 0.95 x 15 = 14.25 billion years ago (only 0.75 billion years after the BB) when it was 14.25 light-years distant. (Its light traveled toward us at c for 14.25 billion years, so it must have been 14.25 years distant when that light was emitted.)

Because 14.25 years are believed have elapsed since that quasar was as seen at a distance of 14.25 light-years, then perhaps that quasar (or its debris) has traveled another 14.25 light-years, putting its present distance at about 28.5 light-years. Its average speed relative to us would therefore have been 28.5 light-years in 14.25 years, or twice the speed of light. (Actually, according to BBT, because its relative speed might be greater at greater distance, the situation might be far worse than that.)

Although a BB advocate, astronomer Charles Steidel has agreed that, "a galaxy that is said to be 15 BLYs away is actually at a distance of about 30 BLYs right now."

Because BBT is based on General Relativity, which insists velocities greater than c are impossible, one might think that this anomaly should be particularly troublesome to BB theorists. But when it is presented it is typically dismissed with the comment that it merely demonstrates an inadequate understanding of the curvature of Einstein's four-dimensional space-time.

Look-back.

In a BB universe that was, for example, about 14 BYRs old, if a galaxy were found to have a redshift of 0.1, Figure 4 shows its velocity relative to us would be about 0.1c, or 30,000 kilometers per second, and it would have been about 1.4 BLYs from us, at the time the light received from it had left it. "Look-back" is 1.4 BYRs or 10 percent. Because its light would have taken 1.4 BYRs to reach us, and assuming, as BBers would, that it was "born" shortly after the decoupling, we see it as it was 1.4 BYRs ago; that is, when it was about 12 BYRs old. If that galaxy continued to travel at approximately 0.1 c during the 1.4 BYRs it took for its light to reach us, it would have traveled an additional 0.14 billion light-years (BLYs) and now be 1.54 BYRs from us, all of which appears to present no problem.

However, in an example of a quasar having a redshift of 3.5, according to Figure 4, its velocity away from us is about 0.9c, or 270,000 kilometers per second. If the BB happened 14 BYRs ago, that quasar is assumed to have been about 12.6 BLYs distant when the received light left it. Its light would have taken about 12.6 BYRs to reach us, and would be seen as it was when it was 1.4 BYRs old (1.4 BYRs after the BB). Look-back is 90 percent.

Using the age for a BB universe of a fixed rate of expansion, as normally utilized by BBers in their calculations (however erroneous) during that 12.6 BYRs, if that quasar still existed, it might have traveled another 11.34 BLYs, and it would now be 23.96 BLYs from us. Although redshift indicated the relative velocity of the quasar to be 0.9 c, it, or its remains, might have traveled a total of about 24 BLYs in its lifetime of 14 BYRs, and its speed relative to us would be about 1.7 c, a velocity that is not allowed by relativity. (Actually, because during the elapsed 12.6 years the velocity of the quasar relative to us, according to BBT, may have been increasing, what I call the look-back problem might be far worse than that.)

As in the case of the c-barrier problem, this look-back problem would also apply to any cosmology that postulates an expanding universe, and would also tend to deny the possibility of that cosmology.

Going Backward in Time.

In their discussions of the evolution of their universe, BBers apparently like to consider the reversal of time back to the BB. In a question that has been asked by American cosmologist Steve Newman, that method has been turned against them to reveal a new problem regarding the expansion of the universe.

Newman has asked, "If clusters of galaxies don't expand when time goes forward, they won't shrink when time goes backward; so how does the infinite density of the BB origin become the end point from the present condition?" The answer of course is, if galaxies, clusters of galaxies, and giant galactic formations that are held together by gravity don't expand as time goes forward, perhaps they wouldn't shrink as time is reversed, and therefore the universe wouldn't shrink back to a BB.

That line of reasoning would seem to provide another illustration of the implausibility of the expansion of the BB universe as time has gone forward.

Accelerating Expansion.

As discussed in some detail in Chapter 11, and reviewed in Chapter 20, a current major quest of BBers is to glean evidence in support of accelerating expansion of the universe in an attempt to solve their age problem. All Type 1a Supernovas are believed to reach about the same peak luminosity, allowing them to be used as standard candles. The goal of BBers is to show that those supernovas are increasingly dim at greater distances to provide evidence of the presence of a cosmological constant that causes increasing expansion of the universe.

For decades astronomical data has been interpreted to support Standard BBT wherein the universe may have been open, flat or closed. Following the advent of inflation that data has been reinterpreted to support only the flat universe of inflation. But now that data is again being reinterpreted in support of increasing expansion. Success has been claimed in finding evidence of increasing dimness, and thus increasing age, of those supernova. However, there is considerable doubt regarding the reliability of that data.

As Anthony N. Aguirre of Harvard-Smithsonian Center for Astrophysics, in SKY & TELESCOPE of August 1999, is quoted as saying that due to, "diffuse halos of dust that extend hundreds of thousands of light-years from many of the universe's galaxies," and, although "the universe's expansion appears to be accelerating....galaxies could plausibly cough up enough dust to take a 20 to 30 percent bite out of light from the supernovas which lie several billion light-years away....We shouldn't jump on the (accelerating universe) band wagon too fast." He believes that there could be enough dust, extending hundreds of thousands of light-years around galaxies, for that decrease in brightness of distant supernovas, to make them appear more distant and younger than they are.

SCIENTIFIC AMERICAN science writer George Musser has reported, "New doubts about whether cosmic expansion is accelerating....All this hinges on differences in brightness of about 25 percent. As it happens, supernova of the type used by cosmologists naturally vary by about the [that] same amount, probably because of the differences in mass and composition of the stars that give rise to such explosions," and *NEW YORK TIMES* science writer George Johnson wrote (in 1998), "It is still possible that the astronomers have been victims of an optical illusion, as Hubble was with the Cepheids.

Also, it should not be forgotten that distance and age of distant supernovas, as perceived by the establishment, is based on the erroneous *accepted interpretation of redshift data*, adding considerable question about the age and distance of supernovas.

Meanwhile theorists are preparing for more tinkering in support of their quest. Some cosmologists are proposing a hypothetical stuff called "quintessence" that "fills the nooks and crannies of space." Quintessence was the name for Aristotle's fifth element, beyond earth, air, fire and water, the etheric substance of the heavenly spheres.

TWENTY TWO

Quantum Theory Problems

Q uantum theory has presented a number of concepts that provide evidence of an incomplete and imperfect understanding of particle physics. Of those, the one that would seem to have the most significance to cosmology is the inequality of matter and antimatter in the universe, is discussed in the following section. Other quantum theory topics that may impact cosmology are presented following that.

The Missing Antimatter.

Of the several problems of quantum theory, because it appeared to have a direct bearing on BBT, the problem of the missing antimatter has received the greatest amount of attention.

Quantum theorists generally believe that the amount of antimatter in the universe should be equal to the amount of matter. Therefore, the observed lack of antimatter in our surroundings has been perceived to present a significant cosmological problem. Because the early processes in the BB chronology are thought to be dependent on a solution to that problem, cosmologists have been motivated to find an explanation for the lack of antimatter in the universe. However, no acceptable solution to it has been found.

Some examples of attempted solutions are presented here.

Barrow and Silk wrote (in 1980), "the asymmetry of one part in

10^8 of matter over antimatter must have been built into the initial structure of the big bang," and guessed that, in the first 10^{-35} of a second after the BB, "when the processes that mediate the the decay of protons are abundant," they might have decayed leaving an excess of matter over antimatter of one part in 10^8, but no real explanation was given how that could have occurred.

Princeton Institute for Advanced Study particle physicist Frank Wilczek later (also in 1980) suggested that the asymmetry between matter and antimatter came about because the law of conservation of baryon number was occasionally violated. According to him that involved hypothetical massive unstable X particles, vector bosons 10^{15} times more massive than protons, that existed before 10^{-35} second, just before the formation of quarks in accordance with GUTs.

Prior to 1980, a theory of symmetry called CP, for charge conjugation and parity, that applied to the behavior of antiparticles versus particles, had been hypothesized. CP symmetry means mirror image symmetry: If an experiment is conducted and watched in a mirror and then another experiment conducted that is the mirror image of the first experiment, replacing all particles by their antiparticles, the results would be the same as in the mirror image of the first experiment.

It was later decided that the rules of CP symmetry are occasionally violated. Therefore, Wilczek suggested that in some cases, upon their decay, X particles were among those that violated CP symmetry. When that happened the law of baryon conservation was violated, resulting in an inequality of particles and antiparticles. By the time the universe cooled to the GUT temperature, all of the X particles had decayed, leaving an excess of about one proton for every billion antiprotons. That happened in just the right ratio to leave the number of protons that remain in the universe today. (The theory of CP symmetry is also responsible for postulating the existence of axions as a candidate for the dark matter of the universe.)

B. J. Carr said (in 1982) that GUTs predict "that the generation of a tiny asymmetry between the amount of matter and antimatter is inevitable, and it could well be sufficient to explain the excess of protons over antiprotons." But it turns out that GUTs require the decay of protons (in about 10^{30} seconds), and experiments performed to confirm their decay, and thus confirm GUTs, have failed to do so, tending to discredit the ability of GUTs to explain the excess of matter.

American physicists Dicus, Letaw, Teplitz and Teplitz (in 1983) suggested that, in the first 10^{-35} second after the BB, the observed excess of matter was generated; and that is because, at temperatures above 10^{27} degrees, quarks can disintegrate into electrons and protons. They added that, "If the universe is cyclic each cycle can give rise to the excess of nuclear particles over antiparticles that is observed today."

According to some cycling BB universe advocates the collapse of the universe is like the formation of a black hole in which baryon number is not conserved. (We are told that all that is preserved in the collapse of black holes is mass, charge and angular momentum.) But it would seem that, based on the evidence presented herein, the possibility of a cycling BB universe has now vanished.

If Hawking's idea of billions of small black holes resulting from the BB is valid, as the matter of the early universe collapsed to form these black holes, he has suggested that, unequal amounts of matter and antimatter were caught in the gravitational clutches of each of them. Unequal amounts of matter and antimatter would then have disappeared into each hole. The subsequent collapse of these short-lived holes might have resulted in the excess of matter that is presently in the world. But it's not clear why matter and antimatter would be treated unequally on average in that scheme.

Based on the assumption that some "domains" of matter and others of antimatter exist in the universe, thereby explaining the absence of antimatter in our surroundings, Astronomers Andrew G. Cohen of Boston University, Alvaro De Rujula of CERN, and Sheldon Glashow of Harvard University have suggested (in 1995) that wherever matter and antimatter "abutted" one another they would have produced "copious amounts of photons and particles" which would have made "a measurable imprint in the gamma ray spectrum of today's skies" and "therefore a matter-antimatter symmetric universe is empirically excluded, [but] There are a couple of 'outs'...Completely empty zones could have separated matter and antimatter parcels, preventing annihilation. But maps of the microwave sky made by COBE satellite rule out this contrived hypothesis."

In attempting to explain the processes of the BB, Adrian Webster suggested that in its early stages, "the equilibrium between the photons and the pairs of particles was disrupted; positrons and electrons that recombined to produce photons were no longer replaced by the reverse action. The positrons were steadily annihilated leaving a small excess of electrons," but he later admitted that he knew of nothing in physics that would lead us to believe there should be an excess of either matter or antimatter, and said, "the most likely possibility is that the excess was always there and that it has been a characteristic feature of the universe at all times." It seems that Webster might have finally got it right, but in an infinitely old and infinitely large universe how would we ever know?

None of the attempts to explain an excess of matter over antimatter presented above, or any others that have appeared in the literature, are convincing. All of them have come to naught, and what is perceived as the problem of missing antimatter remains unsolved.

Other Quantum Mysteries.

Although they may prove to be of importance to cosmology, other aspects of quantum theory have not been given nearly as much attention by cosmologists in the past.

Among those items are such mystifying topics as particle/wave duality, the uncertainty principle, observer participation, Schrodinger's wave function, fields as probability waves, particle pair creation from the energy of empty space, hypothetical particles, renormalization, symmetry breaking, GUTs and TOE.

Attempts to reconcile some aspects of quantum theory with BBT, such as the creation of particles by the hypothetical process of symmetry breaking, are rather far fetched, and attempts to reconcile quantum theory with General Relativity, upon which BBT is based, have failed completely.

Additional information regarding the mysteries of quantum theory are presented in Appendix C.

General Concerns About Quantum Theory.

The various problems of quantum theory provide considerable reason for uneasiness regarding its adequacy.

It seems that Einstein's reluctance to accept quantum theory was well founded. Roger Penrose has related that, in response to a letter from Max Born in1926, Einstein wrote, "Quantum mechanics is very impressive. But an inner voice tells me that it is not yet the real thing. The theory produces a good deal but hardly brings us closer to the secret of the Old One. I am at all events convinced that He does not play dice."

Some later work by American physicist David J. Bohm may have provided support for Einstein's uneasiness with quantum theory. In 1952 he published his ideas based on Louis de Broglie's pilot-wave model, that provided an objective and deterministic account of quantum phenomena that was not dependent on observer participation nor subject to Heisenberg uncertainty. However, that alternative, that eliminated some of the paradoxes of the Copenhagen interpretation, has been ignored by most quantum theorists to this day.

Perhaps the philosophy of Niels Bohr, a key figure in the development of quantum theory, was sound. His opinion was that there isn't really a quantum world, virtually all knowledge is provisional, and quantum theory only provides an interim means of describing the behavior of the fundamental particles of nature. Richard Feynman seemed to agree, saying that, "Scientific knowledge is a body of statements of varying degrees of certainty—some most unsure, some nearly sure, but none absolutely sure." Another wise man, French diarist Andre Gide, once said, "Believe those who are seeking truth, but doubt those who find it."

(In keeping with those thoughts, I have often suggested that for each bit of scientific knowledge, each individual, depending on his or her own judgment, might assign a "probability of certainty factor." For example, the statement, "The Sun will rise tomorrow" might have a PCF of over 99.99999%, but for "Black holes exist" the PCF might be only about 99%. That practice could serve to remind us of the tentativeness of our knowledge.)

As Austrian born science philosopher Karl Popper had suggested in the 1930s, and as the history of science has shown, theories come and go. They are postulated and provisionally accepted. They might be modified over time, discarded if disproven, and replaced by better theory.

Quantum theory—as well as BBT—will undoubtedly follow that pattern.

BBT Dependence on Modern Theories.

With the advent of quantum theory it was hoped that it might rescue BBT from some of its problems.

All of the theories of natural physical behavior that have been accepted over the previous few centuries have met the tests of human understanding and straightforward demonstration. It seems that in this century scientists have for the first time accepted theories that are contrary to everyday human experience and what is known as common sense.

Some aspects of quantum theory have proven to be acceptable for their predictive capabilities for Earthly phenomena but, until other aspects of those theories are subjected to controlled testing and can be reconciled with the mental processes that have served man so well in the past, full acceptance of them, even for Earthly processes, is suspect. Extending the application of General Relativity and quantum theory to a cosmological phenomena as alien as the explosive birth of a universe out-of-nothing certainly isn't justified.

McMullin added to his remarks (of Chapter 8) regarding the applicability of standard theory to conditions of a BB singularity that, "no adequate theory of quantum gravity has yet been devised. So there is every reason to suppose that present reconstructions of the early universe ought not to be taken too seriously." Although Hawking told us many years ago that a quantum theory of gravity, "could easily come within twenty years" and "maybe the end is in sight for theoretical physicists if not for theoretical physics," none of that has yet occurred.

With the advent of quantum theory it was hoped that it might rescue BBT from some of its problems. Since that time great effort has been expended in tailoring BB scenarios to fit quantum particle physics and quantum mechanics, and various features of quantum theory have provided the basis for inflation scenarios. But how can that theory, which, like curved space, defies human intuitive understanding, and has only been partially tested on a small scale in environments very different than that of the hypothetical BB, be depended upon to function on a grand scale in that alien situation?

The inadequacy of the Grand Unification Theories and the lack of a Theory of Everything provide more examples of our lack of understanding. The unification of the electroweak and strong nuclear forces is far from an accomplished fact, and the difficulties of incorporating relativity and the force of gravity into a unified field theory seems overwhelming. As one of the outstanding scientists of our time, Richard Feynman, is quoted as saying,"I think it is safe to say that no one understands quantum mechanics."

TWENTY THREE

Inflation
Theory

This chapter presents an abbreviated introduction to inflation theory. Although Appendices C and D on Quantum Theory and Flights of Fantasy might provide some help, this book can't hope to provide a thorough understanding of inflation theory. But it is hoped it that it will provide an adequate introduction to the subject.

Sometime after 1970 BBT cosmologists began to recognize the possibilities presented by quantum mechanics with its concepts of probability amplitude and vacuum fluctuations to solve some of the problems of the BBT. Now what are considered the two major achievements of the century in physics, general relativity and quantum theory, might be combined to describe the origin and evolution of the universe. One result of this marriage of quantum theory and BB cosmology was a new development called inflation, perhaps the ultimate flight of fantasy.

As might be expected under quantum theory, BB cosmologist decided that almost any conceivable event might have some degree of probability. Accordingly, each cycle of the rebounding universe can be a whole new ball game, and multiple worlds, domains or universes can result from each BB, and each of these can have different sets of physical laws, physical constants, sizes and life cycles. Those worlds or domains don't have to be sequential. They can occur at any time or place, be far apart in time or space, or occupy the same time and space, with no interference, communication or knowledge of each other. Each of them can be created out-of-nothing, now allowed by quantum vacuum energy, and a BB could happen anywhere at any time.

Those are just some of the extreme ideas that have resulted from the quest to utilize quantum theory for the elimination of problems of the previous BB model. Although much of Standard BBT was based on his ideas, Einstein's reluctance to accept quantum theory was ignored in this frenzy.

John Wheeler had suggested that the probability amplitude concept of quantum theory might be applied to the collapse of the universe, and the world that results from the rebound could have a whole new set of physical laws. Somewhat later Tryon proposed that the universe resulted from a giant quantum vacuum fluctuation. He tells us that quantum fluctuations are "utterly commonplace in quantum field theory," and, although probably quite rare on the scale of our universe, "Our Universe is simply one of those things that happen from time to time." According to the probabilities of quantum field theory "those things" arise on various scales and, although they come from nowhere, they do not violate the law of conservation of mass/energy.

Similar to the zero net energy postulated for Standard BBT, Davies and Gribbin tell us (in 1992) that, "The universe has only been borrowed from the vacuum...but eventually the debt will have to be paid." (This is a second type of zero net energy, Type II, which is discussed further in Chapter 24. In Chapter 7 it was indicated that Davies had supported Type I. Now we find that he had supported both types. How is that possible? They are two separate, conflicting ideas.)

In 1976 astronomer Martin Rees made some suggestions that may have been precursors to inflation theory. Those included, that in a tiny fraction of a second after the BB, "quantum gravitational effects" may have caused the "global isotropy and homogeneity" of the universe, and during that period, "When the space curvature becomes sufficiently great....small amplitude fluctuations...developed into galaxies." He suggested that quantum gravitational effects might also solve the BB singularity problem. But "Einstein's theory cannot [provide] an adequate description;" for that we must await the development of "a full theory of quantum gravity" (a Theory of Everything) to explain the events of the first 10^{-23} second of the BB. (See Appendix D on TOE.)

Carr in 1982 mentioned quantum mechanics and the many-worlds concept as they related to his involvement with the Anthropic Principle (which is discussed Chapter 25). But, perhaps in his preoccupation with that topic, he failed to appreciate quantum mechanics' potential to provide an explanation for the energy to fuel the BB. If fact, he expressed his uneasiness regarding the probability amplitude aspect of quantum theory when he wrote, "This concept is very strange, especially when applied to situations where the quantum uncertainty on a microscopic level can manifest itself on a macroscopic level."

Guth's Inflation.

However, MIT physics professor Alan Guth didn't miss the implications of quantum theory. His concept of the universe, published in 1981, marked a radical change in the direction of BBT.

The BB was no longer thought of simply as an explosion. It started as an expansion of energy out of false vacuum (vacuum can become excited and adopt various levels of energy), which behaved like the repulsion force once proposed by Albert Einstein, but was of enormous magnitude. It had negative energy that fed on itself to expand exponentially or, as Dennis Overbye explained, the repulsion of negative pressure blew the universe apart, doubling its size every 10^{-34} second. All of the energy and equivalent energy of the mass of the resulting universe came from the quantum energy of the vacuum of space.

Unlike Standard BBT, which postulated absolute nothingness before the BB, inflation theory required a previous vacuum that contained untold quantities of energy. That process is claimed to solve the BB singularity problem.

After the vast inflationary expansion, because false vacuum is unstable, like the sudden freezing of supercooled water, it decayed into true vacuum in an enormous flash of radiation that turned into matter and antimatter. Inflation ceased, but the expansion of the universe continued. As in Standard BBT, expansion then gradually slowed due to gravitation. Although the cosmological constant is said to have been enormous in the early universe, it would now have to be very small or zero in order to be consistent with the present flat universe as postulated by inflation theorists.

For many years it had been thought that a term in Einstein's equations known as cosmic repulsion was his greatest mistake; even he had reached that conclusion. Guth's idea for inflation may have come from Dutch astronomer Willem de Sitter who in 1916 had suggested a cosmology in which there had been a runaway expansion of the universe, presumable due to Einstein's cosmic repulsion.

Cosmic Repulsion.

The "ugly" cosmic repulsion, as it has been called by Peebles, came to the aid of BBT as an essential feature of inflation theory. Upon the advent of that theory in the early 1980s, which was thought to provide the solution to many of the problems of BBT. As mentioned in Chapter 11, Einstein's cosmic repulsion was called upon to provide the force for the inflationary expansion of the universe.

As Paul Davies had indicated, the quantum vacuum of inflation theory acts just like Einstein's cosmic repulsion and, "The anti-gravity Einstein threw out the door has come back in through the window" and he added, "The way now lies open for an explanation of the big bang....The universe would be subject to a cosmic repulsion force of such magnitude that it would cause headlong expansion at a high rate." Instead of the minute force that Einstein had proposed as necessary to balance the force of gravity in space, it now took on the enormity required to blow up the entire universe.

Cosmic repulsion, now exclusively referred to by the more esoteric sounding term, "cosmological constant," became an essential feature of inflation theory.

Returning to Guth's Inflation.

Guth's inflationary theory, which was developed in 1980 and published in 1981, described an expansion by a factor of 10^{50} that occurred between 10^{-35} and 10^{-32} second after the BB. The speed of that inflation was orders of magnitude greater than the speed of light. (Although other figures have been given, Guth's expansion of the universe might have been from 10^{-25} cm to 10^{25} cm, which is about 10^7 light-years, or about 100 times the size of our galaxy.)

Guth's inspiration for inflation theory came as he studied the problem of the absence of enormously massive magnetic monopoles that were predicted by SU(5) GUT to fill the universe, but they have never been observed, creating a problem for GUT. (See Appendix D on GUTs and monopoles.) It is said that he originally intended only to solve that problem. He thought that his inflation might "dilute" magnetic monopoles so that there would be only about one per observable universe. He later fortuitously found that it also might solve the BB flatness, smoothness and horizon problems.

(British mathematician and theoretical physicist Paul Dirac had found that mathematics indicated the possibility of magnetic monopole existence. If so, they would have a magnetic charge analogous to the electrical charge of an electron. As mentioned in Appendix D, physicists t'Hooft and Polyakof showed that when symmetries of some of the gauge field theories are broken, monopoles would be produced, and that their properties could be calculated.)

The strange series of events of the inflationary process also provided the remarkable situation that the force of expansion exactly matches the opposing force of gravity (zero net energy), and thus also solves the flatness problem. (This is Zero Net Energy Type I. Both Type I & Type II have been ascribed to inflation. I have invented this nomenclature to identify them.)

We are also told that, because of the enormous expansion of the inflation, the small portion of the universe we observe must appear to be flat. In addition, during the inflationary process, any initial irregularities in the early universe are stretched out sufficiently to provide for large-scale uniformity, but not enough to prevent the formation of galaxies and clusters, thus solving the smoothness problem.

Until inflation theory came along there was no generally accepted explanation for the formation of galaxies in the BB universe. But now quantum irregularities of inflation theory were said to provide the seeds for the accretion of matter that was needed for the start of galaxy formation, thus solving another serious BB problem.

As mentioned in Chapter 8, inflation is also said to solve the horizon problem. The explanation given for that is, because all matter was causally connected in the tiny space of the small universe at the beginning of inflation, it remained so in the enormous area of space at the end of the inflation period. Thus all of the events in the formation of the universe, such as the formation of galaxies and clusters of galaxies, are causally connected.

Alternately, some theorists have suggested that inflation didn't start until after the BB singularity. According to their explanation of the horizon problem, all the matter of the universe was in causal contact before being blasted apart by inflation. ("Causally connected" was intended to mean close enough to "communicate" at speeds less than that of light.)

Linde's New Inflation.

However, it was later theorized that, because the phase change from false vacuum to true vacuum would not occur all at once, Guth's inflation would result in a number of "bubbles" in the universe. Because the boundaries of those are not observed in our universe, a new problem was created.

In the mid-1980s physicist Linde, while working on that problem, invented a modified inflation theory, chaotic hyper-expansion inflation, that would solve the bubble problem.

His new inflation took advantage of the unproven concept of scalar fields, like that of the hypothetical Higgs boson of gauge theory, that fill the universe. Those fields, that are without direction, polarity or spin, and have only scalar magnitude, are responsible in modern field theory for "breaking the symmetry" to release nature's basic forces, the weak, the strong, the electromagnetic, and possibly the gravitational force as well, depending on the development of a totally unified theory. Before these forces were separated in this manner they were indistinguishable. In the instant following the creation of the universe the scaler fields were weak, and thus the fundamental forces were unified and the universe was symmetrical. But, as the universe expanded and cooled, symmetry breaking proceeded.

The result of the scalar fields in the early universe was a chaotic, $10^{1,000,000}$ inflation that occurred before the hot BB started. That expansion is so great that upon its completion only an instant after the BB the universe would be on the order of $10^{1,000,000}$ times the size of the present observable universe.

During the new inflation period, lasting less than 10^{-30} second, oscillations of scalar fields caused the generation of not only our domain but many others (mini-universes) having a wide variety of characteristics about which, being confined in our own domain, we can learn nothing.

According to that theory, our domain just happened to develop three-dimensionality (or 4-dimensional space-time) and the physical laws that we observe, while other domains may have different quantities of dimensions and different sets of physical laws. Reactions (symmetry breaking) in our domain "just happened" to have been broken into the strong, weak and electromagnetic and gravitational forces of our domain. We are told that, because of their different characteristics, it is impossible for inhabitants of different domains to communicate or obtain information about each other.

Linde tells us, although it's not obvious how, that his new chaotic inflationary scenario provides simple solutions to most of the problems of the Standard BB model. Among those are the BB singularity problem, which merely awaits the development of a complete quantum theory of gravity.

The tremendous expansion during the inflationary period smoothed out the universe to solve the flatness problem and, although its start was chaotic, it also solved the smoothness and horizon problems. During inflation the quantum fluctuations grew "in just the right way" to produce the relatively small inhomogeneities that we call galaxies and clusters, but not larger nonuniformities.

Guth's original reason for inventing inflation was to address the problem of the generation of large numbers of magnetic monopoles. In our present domain they are not a problem; magnetic poles invariably occur in pairs. But troublesome hypothetical single magnetic poles were predicted by GUTs to occur in profusion in the early BB universe.

It is said that Guth's inflation failed to satisfactorily solve that problem, and also that of bubble walls (which under new inflation became massive domain walls). Linde claimed that new inflation theory solved those problems by dispersing the magnetic monopoles so thinly that they became insignificant, and domain walls are sent far beyond any observable distance. Davies tells us that in addition to magnetic monopoles, which are three dimensional, GUTs would also produce massive cosmic strings and walls that are one- and two-dimensional analogs of magnetic monopoles. Those problematic flights of fantasy (neglected in Appendix D) would also be dispersed to insignificance by new inflation.

Those vibrating strings and walls are of enormous density, and, like magnetic monopoles, they are hypothetical quantum constructions. They should not be confused with actual galactic formations that are found in intergalactic space.

Simple Solution to BB Problems.

Because of its advertised ability to provide, not only solutions, but simple solutions to the major problems of Standard BBT, inflation theories gained considerable popularity in the years following 1980. In addition to BBT's singularity, smoothness, horizon, flatness, and galaxy formation problems, said to be solved by Guth's inflation, Linde's new inflation is said to correct magnetic monopole, domain walls, and similar problems, and to put inflation theory on firm ground.

TWENTY FOUR

Inflation
Problems

For nearly two decades inflation has been regarded as the savior of the BBT. It was claimed to have solved several of the serious problems of BBT. However there is considerable doubt about that ability, and inflation theory has introduced some problems of its own.

A Vacuum Fluctuation Provided the Matter.

Although Standard BBT postulated nothing before the BB, no space, no matter, no energy, no time, inflation theory calls upon the fluctuations of the energy of empty vacuum of space to provide the energy and matter for the birth of the universe.

The vacuum energy of space, previously postulated by quantum theory only to deal with the spontaneous generation of the tiny fundamental particles of modern physics, was claimed by inflation theorists to instantaneously produce the entire universe. Linde has said that quantum fluctuations "grow in just the right way to produce the relatively small inhomogeneities that we call galaxies," and, although, he did wonder, "how a vacuum fluctuation could occur on such a grand scale," he and other BBers ignore the fact that the presence of the energy of empty space is far from a demonstrated fact. In fact, the presence of anything in "empty space" is a contradiction of terms.

The symmetry breaking process that is said to produce all of the fundamental particles in the early BB universe is an enormous exaggeration of quantum theory's postulated creation of particle pairs out of the energy of the vacuum of space.

Cosmic Repulsion Provided the Force.

Although inflation theory postulates quantum fluctuations as the source of the energy that is converted to all the mass of the universe, a source was still needed to provide its expansive power of the universe, and the cosmic repulsion was resurrected to fill that need.

Einstein had thought the cosmic repulsion was just strong enough to prevent gravity from causing the collapse of a static universe. By contrast, the cosmological constant now had to be powerful enough to blast all the matter of the universe apart at a velocity many orders of magnitude greater than the speed of light. It then had to suddenly drop, at about 10^{-32} seconds after the BB, to some very small value that might be consistent with the present flat universe postulated by inflation theory.

It should be obvious that the reemergence of cosmic repulsion on a grand scale to provide for the inflationary expansion of the universe is a purely an ad hoc idea that has no basis in legitimate science.

Far Faster Than the Speed of Light.

The inflation of the early universe is said to have been as great as 10 to the 50th (Guth's original inflation) or even as great as 10 to the millionth (Linde's new inflation) times greater than the speed of light, all within a tiny fraction of a second.

As in Standard BBT, inflation theorists claim that didn't involve the travel of matter, and therefore it didn't violate relativity's prohibition of speeds greater than that of light. As usual, that is said to be permissible because it is space that is expanding, not the matter in that space. However, Einstein tells us that not even information can be transmitted faster than the speed of light. As in standard BBT, how inflation can in some manner displace all the mass or energy of the universe without physically moving it, defies common understanding.

Zero Net Energy Type II.

As mentioned in Chapter 7, Zero Net Energy Type I postulates that the negative energy of gravity is equal and opposite to all the remaining energy of the BB universe, but quite obviously it is far less. Not only does that scheme retain the appearance of a violation of the conservation of mass/energy, but, also as previously discussed, the idea of negative energy is false. And as mentioned in the previous chapter, not only have some theorists postulated that Type I zero net energy also applies to the BB inflationary universe, but others have postulated a second type of zero net energy (Type II) is applicable to the inflationary universe.

In this second scheme, all the energy, including the equivalent energy of the mass of the entire universe, is merely borrowed from the energy of empty space, to be repaid upon the collapse of the universe. Davies and Gribbin told us (in 1992) that, "The universe has only been borrowed from the vacuum...but eventually the debt will have to be paid."

That seems to make a little sense.

In this case, if you were to blow up a balloon, as in Zero Net Energy Type I, energy is saved in the the compressed breath. When the breath is released the input energy (except for some heat losses) can be retrieved. The energy you put into the balloon might be thought of as being temporarily borrowed. However, borrowing an amount of energy equal to all the equivalent mass and energy of the entire universe from the vacuum of space, to be repaid upon its collapse, scores of billions of years later, doesn't avoid the appearance of a violation of the conservation of mass/energy.

Furthermore, not only might that be an excessively long term loan if collapse should occur, but few BBers believe in that collapse. The loan might never be repaid.

A little analysis shows both of the zero net energy schemes to be far beyond the realm of science.

Infinite Energy for Each Particle of Matter.

As discussed in Chapter 7, each particle of matter that was blasted from the infinite gravity of the BB might require an infinite force to propel it. That is reinforced by the premise that the redshift of radiation from matter at the edge of the BB universe (the c-barrier or world horizon) would be infinite.

Inflation theorists might, as in Standard BBT, claim that no energy was required for their inflationary expansion, and for the continuing expansion that followed it. But that theory postulates an enormously vast universe that extends far beyond the limit of the BB infinite redshift. That requires speeds far in excess of that of light; requiring every particle of matter beyond the c-barrier to have acquired far greater than infinite energy.

Inflation didn't solve the problem of infinite energies required for the expansion of the universe; it made it far worse.

The BB Age Problem.

As discussed in some detail in Chapters 11, 20 and 21, there recently has been much ado about the possibility of a cosmological constant that might cause increasing expansion, thus solving the BB age paradox. After many years of insistence on a flat inflationary universe with its density at the critical level, and that astronomical data would provide proof of that density, BBers have suddenly changed their tune and have reinterpreted that data to provide proof of a universe of increasing expansion, as represented by Curve 4 of Figure 2.

Because it would require negative density, a universe of that type was not considered possible under Standard BB. However, theorists have now devised a scheme postulating that the space of the universe contains some mysterious matter having the required amount of mass for a flat universe while also producing antigravity something like Einstein's cosmic repulsion. The mass of that matter and the strength of its antigravity are just right to accelerate the expansion of the universe to extend its age and solve the BB age problem, while also providing the critical density required by inflation theory.

As explained in *ASTRONOMY* of August, 2000 by science writer Diana Steele, "There's just enough mass to keep the universe flat." University of California astronomer Alexei Filippenko is quoted as saying, "It doesn't take a genius to recognize that there's 65 percent of something else....That something else cannot be any kind of gravitating matter. Thus, something like dark energy is a good possibility, and what ever the stuff is, it will have a repulsive effect." Steele goes on to say, "If most of the universe's energy takes this form, which also goes by the names cosmological constant and quintessence, the universe will expand forever."

Amazingly, while BBers claim that cosmic repulsion results in the negative force necessary to cause increasing expansion, they also claim the universe has the critical density postulated by inflation theory. The fallacy in doing that is the failure to recognize that, by any logic that may apply to such madness, only negative mass could be responsible for the negative force (antigravity) that might result in accelerating expansion. But of course, such negative things don't exist in the real world.

Singularity Problem.

Inflation theory postulates the creation of the entire universe out of a single enormous vacuum fluctuation and an enormous cosmic repulsive force from the energy of empty space that resulted in the sudden exponential expansion of the universe, thus solving one of BBT major problems, that of the singularity. However, the idea that the concept of a quantum theory vacuum fluctuation could be extended to the scale required for the instantaneous creation of all the matter and energy of the universe is a totally unreasonable interpretation of quantum theory.

Guth referred to his inflation as a "free lunch," and Davies referred to it as "cosmic bootstrap;" but those expressions are merely euphemisms for a "serious violation of the conservation of mass/energy."

Andre Linde told us (in 1985) that, because of zero net energy, the singularity problem is solved, but then he contradicted that by adding, "A final solution to this problem will be possible only after the development of a complete quantum theory of gravity (meaning a TOE)". But of course, that hasn't happened. There is little likelihood that it will happen in the foreseeable future; and neither of the previously described zero net energy schemes can hope to circumvent that violation.

Smoothness Problem.

The observation of gigantic galactic formations and voids in the universe deny that an enormous rapid expansion of the universe solved the BB smoothness problem. The belief that inflation smoothed the universe by stretching out irregularities of the first instant of the BB, but left just enough of them to provide the seeds for the later formation of galaxies, is a matter of faith, not science.

It is unreasonable to believe that a universe that started with an explosion could be less than extremely irregular. If those who believe the MBR came from the BB decoupling, would look at the sky, they would see that it is too irregular to provide support for either a standard or an inflationary BB universe explosion; or that the MBR might have come from either of those.

Horizon Problem.

The explanation given for inflation's ability to solve the horizon problem is that all the particles of matter were close to each other in the tiny space of the universe at (or before) the beginning of inflation, were casually connected, and thus they were able to acquire similar characteristics that they retained ever after.

In addition to the absurdity of particles' ability to communicate in any way, the belief that inflationary expansion, at orders of magnitude faster than the speed of light, solved the BB horizon problem that had been attributed to the high rate of expansion of standard BBT is also ridiculous.

Professor Peebles suggested that the horizon problem can be put aside because, "the recent tendency is to assume this embarrassment can be resolved by inflation or some other adjustment of the physics of the very early universe," but that doesn't seem to avoid any embarrassment.

Flatness Problem.

It isn't clear how an enormously fast and vast expansion might result in the critical density of a flat universe as required by inflation theory. One might expect that, the greater the expansion, the thinner the density might be.

The belief that an exponential expansion of inflation theory would cause anything greater than a minutely low average density, far less than the critical density required for a flat BB universe, is absurd. Furthermore, the observed density of the universe is too low and the Hubble constant too high (its age is too short) to support the possibility of a flat BB universe.

Ripples.

Smoot's report of variations equivalent to plus or minus about 15 millionths of a degree K in the MBR, that was gleaned from data that was below of the level of noise (a negative signal-to-noise ratio), is not only insignificant, but untrustworthy.

As mentioned in Chapter 8, Ostriker had suggested that the presence of large galactic formations conflicted with the smoothness of the MBR and was putting a strain on BBT.

In what seems to be an amazing contradiction, Pagels in *Perfect Symmetry*, long before COBE's measurements of MBR temperature variations, wrote, "Unfortunately detailed calculations showed that these fluctuations were too small by factors of billions to have gone on to produce galaxies in the BB model." However, there was no need for concern about that. He went on to say, "Subsequently, clever physicists found field theory models that even gave the right size for fluctuations" for the formation of galaxies. (But perhaps *really* clever physicists could produce models in support of most anything.)

According to Goldsmith in *Einstein's Greatest Blunder?*, in an inflationary universe, "we should find irregularities of all sizes in about the same numbers; the super rapid expansion of the universe would have "inflated" all the irregularities in the same (Gaussian) way. The prediction of equal numbers of irregularities of different sizes was a by-product of the basic inflationary model, made at a time when no one expected irregularities to be measured soon."

SCIENTIFIC AMERICAN of September, 1999 agreed, matter should have a Gaussian distribution according to inflation, that of a bell curve, and that, finding "non-random features could sink inflation." However, it reported that in the past year, non-Gaussianity has emerged in studies of the COBE data by teams of scientists of CERN, the Strasbourg Observatory, the University of Kansas, and the Canadian Institute for Theoretical Astrophysics.

Smoot and all concerned had insisted that COBE data provided excellent support for inflation theory. But now it appears that it failed to provide the distribution of irregularities required to support that theory.

Galaxy Formation and Missing Mass.

According to inflation theory, tiny quantum fluctuations provided the seeds that are needed for the formation of galaxies. As Dennis Overbye has stated, "In the theory of new inflation authored by Paul Steinhardt, among others, quantum fluctuations in the first instant of time were revealed to be the source of galaxies." (But I can't help wondering what the source of that revelation might have been; perhaps a dream, or the Almighty?)

That theory also requires the presence of sufficient CDM to bring the density of the universe up to the critical level as required by inflation theory. However, as mentioned in Chapter 13, evidence and support for CDM seeds appears to be lacking.

The flat inflationary universe (at that critical density) would require up to 99 percent of the mass of the universe to be of mysterious non-baryonic matter of no known characteristics other than gravitational attraction. But, after recent years of frantic searching, astronomical observations have found the density of the universe to be only five to ten percent of the "critical" amount postulated by inflation theory.

That shortfall of missing matter had provided the incentive for a frantic search for it. All sorts of exotic stuff had been proposed as that matter. Unfortunately for inflation and BBT, that search has been unsuccessful. The BB galaxy formation problem remains unsolved.

Neutrinos.

As discussed in Chapter 14, although there is no evidence in support of the neutrinos that are said to have come from the early BB, and now "flood" the universe, they have been a favorite candidate for the missing BB matter. However, efforts to show that they have enough mass to "close" the universe have failed. Their transit time from Supernova 1987A was found to be essentially the same as that of light, indicating their mass to be, at most, a tiny fraction of one electron volt. That, and my calculations based on data presented by BB cosmologists, showing their mass to be only 0.00067 eV, would seem to rule them out as a candidate for any significant amount of the missing matter of the BB universe.

Chronology Problem.

As discussed in Chapter 18, BB cosmologists who have accepted inflation, typically continue to describe events essentially in accordance with a chronology of a BB universe having a linear decrease in temperature (energy) and a linear increase in size as functions of time, (like that shown in Figure 1) without consideration of the appropriate changes necessary to accommodate inflation.

Perhaps that is simply because it is too difficult to attempt a diagram that could properly illustrate a theory that has no basis in science or logic.

Momentum and Deceleration Problems.

As presented in Chapter 22, according to BBT, it has been claimed by BB cosmologists that the expansion of the universe has continued due to momentum. The same must undoubtedly apply to an inflationary universe following its initial exponential expansion. However, there is no physics that can explain how massless space can have momentum.

Also as presented in that chapter, according to BBT, the expansion of the universe is decelerating due to gravitation. As in the case of momentum, the same must also apply to an inflationary universe. But again, there is no law of physics that relates massless space to gravity.

Inflation theory has contributed nothing to the solution of those problems.

We See Only a Small Part of the Universe.

Yet another problem that I have discovered has to do with the size of the universe.

Inflation theorists tell us that the universe has expanded to unimaginable size, "trillions upon trillions of light-years in diameter," but that we can observe only a tiny portion of it. However, they continue to tell us that galaxies and quasars having very high redshifts are observed as they were shortly after the BB, that is, within a few percent of the edge of the universe.

A typical report by BBers has been that astronomers are able to observe quasars, as they were within a few percent of the time since the BB, that is, within several hundred million years after a BB that happened 10 to 15 billion years ago and within a several hundred million light-years from the edge of the BB universe, which is 10 to 15 billion light-years distant. However, within the same document, it might also be stated that only an infinitesimally small portion of the enormous inflationary universe is within range of astronomer's telescopes.

As an example of that discrepancy, Barrow and Silk wrote (in 1993), long after they had accepted that inflation "emerged to rescue cosmology," that, "Our vision of outer space is limited by a natural horizon, prescribed by the distance light has traveled since the big bang," clearly denying the vast size of the inflationary universe.

Additional Unsolved Problems.

In addition to the problems of inflation discussed in this chapter, there are a number of other BB problems that have not been solved by inflation theory. Those include problems having to do with redshift, quasars, curved space, light and heavy elements, expansion, quantum theory, and possibly others that I have omitted.

Poor Understanding of Their Own Theory.

Much of the establishment literature demonstrates that their understanding of inflation theory is grossly inadequate.

As an illustration of abysmally poor understanding of inflation theory, COBE team leader, George Smoot, has stated that the early universe inflated, at greater than the speed of light, from an initial tiny size to about 100 meters, a tiny fraction of the sizes suggested by Guth or Linde.

In a statement that would be humorous is it weren't so pathetically ridiculous, Smoot also declared that "inflation is a transcendental concept linking the very small with the very large." He apparently thought that he might clear up any doubts about inflation in one brilliant phrase.

Another discrepancy that frequently shows up is that some of the establishment literature indicates inflation occurred immediately following a giant quantum vacuum fluctuation, as did Linde, while others indicate that it happened some time latter, typically at about 10^{-35} seconds after the BB universe had been in existence. That may seem like an insignificant amount of time, but the concept is vastly different.

Amazingly, BBers who have accepted inflation, and that the matter of the universe came from the energy of empty space, will, when it suits their purpose of the moment, still revert to stating that there was nothing before the BB. One wonders whether that is merely due to habit, due to lack of understanding of their own theory, or is just more purposeful obfuscation.

New Problems Introduced by Inflation Theory.

In addition to its apparent failure to solve pre-inflation BB problems, inflation has introduced some new problems and complexities. As an example of new complexities, multiple domains (multiple worlds or universes) have been introduced, and with them, massive domain walls. The fix for this problem is that domain walls, along with magnetic monopoles, a theoretical problem of early inflation theory, are dispersed to great distances where they no longer trouble us.

Those are just a couple of the many fanciful ideas that have resulted from speculation about such things as GUTs and a TOE in the quest for support of BBT.

Universe in a Basement.

Perhaps the most outrageous examples of illogical fantasy ever stated has been that of the inventors of inflation. Both Linde and Guth have written that they could produce a new universe by compressing a small amount of matter.

In *SCIENTIFIC AMERICAN* in 1994 Linde wrote that, "One would have to compress some matter in such a way to allow quantum fluctuations to trigger inflation. Simple estimates in the context of chaotic inflation suggest that less than one milligram of matter may initiate an eternal, self reproducing universe."

Guth is reported to have said, "In fact, our own universe might have been started in somebody's basement." Overbye has reported that, Guth and another MIT professor, Ed Fahri, found that. "If you could compress 25 pounds of matter into 10^{-24} centimeters, making a mass 10^{75} times the density of water...a bubble of false vacuum, or what Guth called a 'child universe' would be formed. From the outside it would look like a black hole. From the inside it would look like an inflating universe."

Can you believe that garbage?

Inflation Fails to Rescue BBT.

Based on media reports, from scientific journals down to the popular media, it seems that throughout much of the past two decades, inflation theory had become accepted by the establishment as the salvation of BBT. But, at last, its many problems have taken their toll on its credibility.

Many members of the establishment, who have for years put their hope and faith in it have been abandoning it. Although it had been claimed that inflation provided simple solutions to a number of Standard BBT problems, that has turned out to false. In fact, it turned out to be ridiculously complex, and to introduce several new problems of its own.

Giant vacuum fluctuation as the source of all the matter and energy of the universe, and enormous cosmic repulsive force as the source of an exponential expansion of the universe are not simplifications. They are complications; and furthermore, they are not science, but purely speculative ideas with no means of verification.

Although Linde doesn't believe that, "God could miss such a good possibility to improve the creation of the universe," *Encyclopedia of Physics* says, regarding inflation theory, "It is to be emphasized that there is no very strong reason to believe that any of this really happened; this is a scenario rather than a theory." As Geoffrey Burbidge wrote in *SCIENTIFIC AMERICAN* (in 1992), "The inflationary model, a pet of the past decade, holds that a period of extremely rapid expansion of the early universe accounts for both the smoothness of the cosmic background radiation and the amount of matter present in the universe. But, again, inflation is an untestable addition to the lore of the big bang," and as Fermi National Accelerator Laboratory astrophysicist Edward W. Kolb was quoted as saying, in *ASTRONOMY* of June, 2001 "All the theories of inflation amount to proof that we don't have one good theory yet."

Inflation was invented and tailored to solve BB problems; but, like many other theorist's flights of fantasy, it cannot be proved or disproved. All of the old problems of BBT remain. Inflation has provided no viable solution for them.

TWENTY FIVE

Problems
of Logic

This chapter presents a kind of laundry list of miscellaneous items that show logical errors, oversights, and distortions of fact in comments made by BB cosmologists. Some of these are new items and some have been previously discussed.

The Singularity.

According to Standard BBT, all the matter and energy of the universe came out of nothing, for which there is no logical explanation.

Each particle of matter that was blasted from the infinite gravity of the BB might require as much as an infinite force to propel it, an item that is ignored by BBers.

Under inflation, all of the matter and energy of the BB universe, rather than from out of nothing, is said to have come from the energy of empty space, thus solving the BB singularity problem. But, empty space, being nothing, can't have energy, so we're back to a universe out of nothing.

Age Problems.

BBers frequently state the age of the universe to be at the Hubble time, knowing full well that, according to BBT, the age of the flat, or near flat, universe that they believe in should equal only two thirds of Hubble time

It is also often suggested that, because their calculated age of the universe is of the same order of magnitude as the oldest stars, their age paradox is not a significant problem; that the difference between theory and evidence will soon be eliminated by new interpretation or new data.

BB theorists have in the past indicated that all galactic formation had started within the first billion years following the BB while astronomical evidence for the continuing formation of galaxies is ignored. It seems impossible for galaxies to have formed within that short time since the BB, and it certainly must be impossible for the giant galactic structures that are observed to have formed in the 10 to 15 billion years that are said to have elapsed since the BB.

In addition, evidence of a much older universe, at least several tens of BYRs, and probably hundreds of BYRs is ignored

A Smooth BB Universe.

It is said that the BB explosion was perfectly smooth, and that the present universe retains that smoothness. In addition to the fact that such a smooth explosion is completely alien to human experience, smoothness of the present universe is belied by observations of gigantic galactic formations and voids throughout its space.

As an illustration of the lack of logic of BBers regarding a smooth universe, in discussing the plasma universe explosion postulated by Hannes Alfvén, Peebles wrote, "it would be hard to imagine that the explosion produced a spherically symmetric system of galaxies," but he clearly thinks that's all right for a BB universe.

Zero Net energy.

In order to solve the BB singularity problems, zero net energy has been postulated.

According to Zero Net Energy, Type I, gravitational force is negative and equal and opposite to all the other energy of the universe, so they cancel each other. However, it would seem that the positive energy of the universe must be far greater than the negative energy of its gravity. Furthermore, the idea of negative energy is fallacious. There may be opposing forces but, in the real world, negative energy does not exist.

Inflation theorists have postulated a second type of zero net energy, Type II, in which the amount of energy equivalent to all the mass and energy of the universe is merely on loan from the energy of the vacuum, to be repaid upon the collapse of the universe. However, inflation theory denies that the universe will collapse, but continue to expand forever. In that case that energy debt would never be paid, and the violation of the law of conservation of mass/energy persists.

The Distribution of Matter in Space.

BBers claim that all of the matter of the universe is evenly dispersed throughout the universe. But, by their reckoning, redshift data indicates that does not apply to distant quasars, which shows them to be clumped in distant space. Therefore, either the *accepted interpretation of redshift data* is faulty, or the perceived clumping of distant quasar denies the smoothness of the universe, and puts us at the center of their universe.

BBers can't have quasar clumping, that is believed to provide proof of an evolving universe and, at the same time, have a BB that happened everywhere in a smooth universe without a center.

The Horizon Problem.

Inflation theorists believe that their theory solves the BB horizon problem, but they haven't made it clear how a much greater speed of expansion can solve a problem that is said to be due to rapid expansion following the BB explosion.

It has been said that inflation solves the horizon problem because it gives particles the opportunity to communicate before they are blown apart by the BB. But they fail to describe what new science provides particles with the ability to interact in order to acquire similar characteristics.

It has been suggested that an "adjustment of the physics of the very early universe" might come along to solve this problem, but that hasn't yet occurred.

Expanding Space.

BBers accept that redshifts (and blueshifts) of stars in our galaxy, and galaxies in the local group, are Doppler shifts. Beyond those areas, BBT dogma is that the observed redshifts are "cosmological," that is, they are due to the expansion of the space of the universe.

BB cosmologists also accept gravitational redshift in regard to bodies such as the Earth, the Sun, white dwarfs, neutron stars and black holes, but they refuse to acknowledge that it must also apply to very massive distant bodies such as quasars. Instead, they insist that it is due to the cosmological redshift of expanding space.

But the belief that space is expanding is folly. Empty space is nothing, and nothing can't expand.

Lorentz Transformations Applied to Empty Space.

In order to be consistent with their acceptance of relativity, BBers have applied the Lorentz transformations to the expanding, closed, curved, empty space of their universe. However, Einstein never intended that, and there is no basis for it in any science.

Unfortunately for astronomy and cosmology, all of the establishment has accepted that nonsense.

Negatively Things.

Friedmann's solution to Einstein's equations introduced negative curvature of space to cosmology. Although Einstein had postulated the curvature of space, he intended only positive curvature due to the presence of matter.

Although any curvature of empty space is illogical, the negative curvature of space is ridiculous. That would require the presence of negative matter to produce negative gravity, and negative gravity to produce negative curvature, all of which are pipe dreams.

Opposing forces may be labeled positive and negative for mathematical purposes, but all are actually positive.

Closed Universe Characteristics
Attributed to Other BB Universe Cases.

Most BBers have accepted either a flat or a somewhat open BB universe. However, the flat BB universe is said to have uncurved space, and the open universe to have negatively curved saddle-shaped space. Therefore, the space of neither of those can close upon itself. Neither of them would have an edge, and both would have a center where the BB happened.

Unless a BBer believes that the universe will collapse, when he states that the universe has closed curved space with no edge and no center, and that the BB happened all over, it is a distortion of his own theory.

MBR Isotropy and Spectrum.

The combination of a less than perfectly symmetrical expansion of the universe ever since the BB, the presence of gigantic galactic structures in space, and the nonlinearity of expansion during the decoupling would have resulted in disturbed isotropy and smearing of the MBR black-body spectrum.

MBR from all Directions.

It is thought that photons from the BB arrive at the Earth from all directions. However, that can only apply to a BB universe of the closed space of positive curvature, not a flat or open universe. However, due to time constraints and other considerations, the closed universe case has been shown to be impossible, leaving BBers with another set of conflicting ideas.

Discovery of MBR.

Steven Weinberg has written that, "The most important thing accomplished by the ultimate discovery of the 3 K radiation background in 1965 was to force us all to take seriously the idea that there was an early universe." Apparently, before learning of the MBR, some folks hadn't previously considered the possibility that an earlier universe had existed.

Galaxy Formation.

It is impossible for galaxies to have formed from particles of matter that were initially departing from a smooth BB at or above the speed of light. No known force, gravity, electromagnetic or other, would have been strong enough to cause particles to accrete.

That problem has been recognized by some BB theorists in the past who have suggested that turbulence could have started the accretion of matter needed for galaxy formation. However, it is difficult to imagine how turbulence could overcome the great departing speed of particles to allow their accretion.

The BB galaxy formation problem is dismissed by Peebles, who wrote that, "It is generally believed that the massive structures observed on scales greater than a few megaparsecs grew by gravitational instability out of smaller density fluctuations present at the decoupling...because no one has been able to think of any other reasonably effective force on such large scales."

Other BBers have dismissed that problem on the grounds that galaxy formation, "has nothing to do with the big Bang."

The Origin of the Universe.

BB advocates criticized the once competing SST because it provided no explanation for the origin of the universe. However, those who made that criticism are also subject to it. Those cosmologists who accept the possibility of a previously closed cycling BB universe, who clearly have no theory for its origin are subject to the same criticism.

Actually, that is true of all BBT models. There is no credible explanation for the origin of the BB universe.

Predictions and Tests.

BBers frequently write about the predictions regarding BBT that have been proven to be correct, and about the tests of BBT that have been performed in support of it.

As a couple of examples of distortions of facts regarding such matters, Schramm and Steigman wrote that, "predictions based on the evolution of the universe...are consistent with observations made 10 billion years later," and, as mentioned in Chapter 18, Peebles et al. have written that equations describing the universe "have been tested back to z [redshift] equal to 10^{10}," that is, back to a tiny instant after the BB.

But of course, those weren't predictions; they were "retrodictions" made "10 billion years later," and, not only have such tests not been performed, but it is impossible to perform them.

The Abundance of Light Elements.

Regarding the abundance of light elements in the universe (helium, deuterium and lithium) we are told that, "The behavior of atomic nuclei under the conditions of big-bang nucleosynthesis is not a matter of guesswork; it is precisely known."

But, of course, that is not precisely known. It is merely conjecture based on unproven theory.

The Creation of Matter in Space.

Alpher and Herman have written that, "the three of us (BBT pioneers Gamow, Alpher and Herman) did discuss the steady state approach in depth and often....but were concerned that it, (SST) required continuous creation at a rate which would probably never be observable."

Apparently it didn't concern them, or others who have made similar comments, that the BB rate of creation hadn't been observed.

Balloon and Cake Analogies.

BBers frequently present an expanding balloon or rising raisin cake to represent the four-dimensional space-time of their universe but those are ridiculously inadequate.

It is impossible for anyone to visualize Einstein's four-dimensional space-time on which BBT is based. Even if those representations were of some value, they would fail to show the formation of galaxies or the clumping of quasars. Furthermore, in disagreement with BBT, they depict a universe having a center and an edge, and a BB explosion that occurred, not everywhere, but at its center.

North Pole Analogy.

As stated by Barrow and Silk, "On a terrestrial globe there is a coordinate singularity at the North and South poles, where the grid squares of longitude and latitude vanish as the meridians of the globe intersect. Yet the fabric of the world does not physically break down at the poles."

However, there is no singularity at the poles. The meridians are merely artificial lines drawn on a globe by humans as navigational aids. There is no similarity between the intersection of those lines and an infinitely small point in space having infinite temperature, energy, density, and gravity.

Black Holes, White Holes and Worm Holes.

Cosmologists have resorted to serious consideration of some fanciful ideas in support of BBT. Some of these have resulted from speculation about such things as GUTs and TOE.

For example, black holes in the universe provide mass/energy that travels through worm holes in space to other universes or domains, where it is released through white holes to produce new galaxies, or even new a universe, that are likely to start as quasars. And, of course, the opposite occurs, matter from other universes or domains arrives in our universe by the same process, perhaps some of the things called quasars are white holes through which they arrive.

That nonsense is referred to as advanced theoretical physics, but, as George Orwell was quoted as saying, "There are some ideas so wrong that only a very intelligent person could believe them."

The Universe in a Basement.

As presented in the previous chapter, the inventors of inflation, Guth and Linde, have both stated their belief that, if a small amount of matter could be compressed sufficiently, a new universe could be born of the inflation process. Guth even suggested that might have been how our universe came about. Can "science" get more absurd than that?

Proofs of BBT.

BB cosmologists believe that there is considerable evidence in support of BBT. Each of the following ideas, that have been presented in Chapter 6 as providing that proof, fail in one respect or another. Some cosmologists consider the MBR to be the most important evidence in support of BBT. However, the detailed discussion of BB MBR problems presented in Chapter 13, provides ample reason to deny its ability to provide proof of BBT. The source of the MBR is simply radiation from space that is thermalized within the matter that surrounds galaxies.

Expansion of the universe is also thought to provide important evidence in support of BBT. However, the discussions of redshift problems, quasar problems, the Hubble constant and expansion as presented in Chapter 21 (and reviewed in the previous chapter) should be more than sufficient to discourage a belief in an expanding universe.

Because the abundances of the light elements in the universe have been predicted by BB theorists they are also thought to provide proof of BBT. However, early predictions were based on false understanding of stellar nuclear processes, later predictions have been repeatedly adjusted to coincide with changing observations, and astronomical observations have shown many of those predictions to be erroneous.

BBers consider that the clumping of quasars at great distances provides evidence of an evolving universe. However, that perceived clumping is the result of the fallacious application of Lorentz transformations to empty space.

The similarity of spectrograms (when adjusted for their apparent velocity) and the similarity of luminosity of quasars having a wide range of redshift values also tends to deny the postulated evolution of the BB universe.

The reported verification that the numbers of families of fundamental particles of the universe is limited to three is also cited as proof of BBT. However, that provides no more proof of BBT than it might of other cosmological theories.

Lensing of radiation from distant bodies by closer matter in space that was predicted by Einstein is presented as proof of BBT as well as proof of General Relativity. However, because of the uncertainties of the distances of the matter involved in these observations, and because it may merely be due to gravitational deflection of the path of light rather than to curved space, it provides proof of neither relativity nor of BBT.

It is thought that their solution to Olbers' paradox, that the large redshifts of distant bodies accounts for the dark night sky, provides proof of BBT. But astronomical evidence shows that closer, smaller, cooler matter obscures visible radiation from more distant, larger, warmer matter of space.

It is apparent that the so-called proofs of BBT, when carefully examined, don't hold up. They are the result of such erroneous beliefs as curved space, an expanding universe, photons and elements from the BB, the erroneous *accepted interpretation of redshift data*, and a large amount of faulty logic.

The reconciliation of the creation of the fundamental particles of matter with BBT in accordance with quantum theory is also said to support BBT. However, that appears to have been a feeble attempt to place those events in a flawed chronology.

Evidence That Discredits BBT is Ignored.

There has been a consistent pattern of neglect of evidence that might tend to discredit the prevailing BB cosmology. Although many of the flaws of BBT that are discussed in this book are well known to BB cosmologists, they are ignored, and every attempt is made to discredit the integrity of those who air them.

A few examples of prominent BB cosmologists persistently ignoring evidence against BBT are presented as follows:

In his text, *Principles of Physical Cosmology*, Peebles, who is a theoretician, not an astronomer, dismisses the life's work of career astronomer Halton Arp in essentially one sentence.

An article in *SCIENCE NEWS* (in May, 1991) reported that the CDM theory can't account for how "primordial matter" could have developed fast enough to produce "very early quasars," but James Gunn was quoted as saying that those reports, "cannot over-turn—or even force major alterations in—accepted cosmological theories," and regarding a report of far greater abundances of beryl-lium in old stars than BBT predicts, David Schramm is quoted as saying (in *SCIENCE* of January 1992), "The data so far do not force one away from the standard picture."

As discussed in Chapter 11, the great age of stars, such as that of white dwarfs, that has been reported by some astronomers is simply ignored by BB cosmologists.

Mathematics as the Master.

During this century, ever since Einstein came along, it has become fashionable for theorists to write equations and then, because it was possible to write them, decide they must represent reality. They have apparently forgotten that mathematics is merely a tool that can be used as an aid in describing reality.

Some theoretical physicists have come to believe that, if they can write an equation for their wild ideas, their validity is assured. As American experimental physicist Thomas Phipps has written in *Heretical Verities*, "The mathematical servant has become the mas-ter. Physics has become the private property of mathematical 'experts.'"

Commenting on this topic in *Physics and Our View of The World* (in 1994), professor of the history of mathematics and science at the University of Utrecht, Jan Hilgevoord wrote, "I think that the figure of Einstein and the success he achieved have...seduced theo-retical physicists into believing that Nature has a fixed 'deep' structure,...and the way to discover it is to do as Einstein did: sit down at your desk and just think deeply."

Inconsistencies in The Media.

In *Perfect Symmetry*, Heinz Pagels states that, "The appearance of such a singularity is a good reason for rejecting the standard model of the very origin of the universe altogether," but he then proceeded to ignore that rejection throughout most of the book, and to base his ideas on just that.

A close contender for the illogical comment prize must be Fermi National Accelerator Laboratory cosmologist David Schramm, who is reported to have said, "We have trouble predicting tornadoes, but that doesn't mean that we in any way doubt that the earth is round. Similarly we have trouble making galaxies, but we don't doubt that there was a big bang."

However, for shear volume of illogical output, the top prize must go to Peebles' 718 page university text, *Principles of Physical Cosmology.*

On some pages of that book he denies the BB, and on some pages he fully accepts it. (For examples of acceptance see Pages 3, 101, and 394; and for examples of denials see Pages xvii, 6, 101, and 138. On one page (Page 77) his words both accept and deny the BB.

However, regardless of his denials of a singularity, much of the mathematics he presents is directly based on that improbable event, and is filled with mathematics that is specifically designed to prove BBT. The frequent presence of words such as "if" and "assuming" preceding its mathematics, testify to bias in favor of, and apriori conviction of its truth

Peebles admits that his quest is not impartial science, but proof of BBT. He wrote (on Page 227), "we may hope that eventually it will yield meaningful and detailed tests of the relativity theory underlying the standard cosmology model," and (on Page 311) he indicated that the purpose of his "program" is to "test the consistency of the standard relativistic expanding cosmological model."

What is disturbing about that sort of thing is that it is a corruption of the scientific method; one that is common in cosmological literature, taught throughout academia, and spread throughout the world.

TWENTY SIX

On the
Scientific Method

Since the invention of BBT cosmologists have spent untold effort and dollars to overcome their problems. In that struggle a number of innovations have been attempted and, in many cases, biased efforts made to find supporting evidence and theory while contrary evidence and logic have been ignored. Because the validity of BBT is considered by all but a few of the establishment to be a virtual proven fact, those violations of scientific method are ignored.

In addition to violations that have been discussed in previous chapters, some examples of biased opinion in favor of BBT that have shown up in the literature are presented here.

Bias for BBT.

Adrian Webster has written, "The canonical big-bang-theory is the framework within which many astrophysicists are currently attempting to understand all the events in the evolution of the universe....These questions and many others are all being attacked by trying to find explanatory processes in the universe described by the canonical hot-big-bang model," and in *The Big Bang*, Silk told us, "Today the central questions of cosmology and cosmogony are being explored within the framework of Big Bang theory." In the forward of that book, written by Sciama, we are told, "no doubt future research will enable us to rationalize even the Big Bang itself."

Schramm is reported to have said, "We have the basic framework. We just need to fill in the gaps," Barrow and Silk have stated that, "our goal is to unveil the shrouded secrets of the earlier instants of the [BB] universe," and Peebles is quoted as having said, "By being a little more clever in the invention of theories a person can find a way around the problems and continue to look for a way to build within the Big Bang framework."

Clearly the intent is to employ even more cleverness in finding support for BBT in the future.

Bias for the BB Singularity.

The fact that the singularity of the BB lacks any basis in science seems of little consequence to many of those of the establishment. It's perfectly okay with them for the whole universe to have come out of nothing (or out of the energy of empty space that has no energy) to provide all the mass and energy of the entire universe.

In defending the BB singularity "out of nothing," Peebles tells us that, "energy conservation is a good local concept" but there isn't "a general global energy conservation law in general relativity theory," and, as mentioned in Chapter 24, Edward Tryon stated that "such an event (as the BB) need not have violated any of the conventional laws of physics," and passes it off as a mere vacuum fluctuation in empty space.

Perhaps that kind of fantasy is acceptable to theorists who spend their lives sitting and speculating about all sorts of wild possibilities, but for engineers who earn their living by adherence to the laws of physics such ideas are hard to swallow. That is especially so after BBers had insisted for decades that there was no space, time, matter or energy before the BB in which vacuum fluctuations might occur.

Regarding the BB singularity, Barrow and Silk have written that the "singularity theorem" of Penrose and Hawking, "employs no assumptions that cannot be tested by observation," but, of course they didn't identify any such tests—because there are none. They merely mentioned some theoretical notions, and declared that, "these are not unreasonable assumptions."

Bias for Smoothness.

Regardless of the conflicting astronomical evidence and logical difficulties regarding large-scale nonuniformity found in the universe, as quoted in Chapter 6, Peebles, et al. told us that, "improvements in the tests of homogeneity and Hubble's law… must be counted as impressive successes for the standard model," and in defiance of astronomical data, BB cosmologist Carlos Frenk has called the Great Wall rubbish, and Peebles has warned that, "One should beware of Great Walls."

Davies explained (in 1984) that quantum fluctuations grew in just the right way to produce large-scale uniformity without small-scale uniformity," and Linde rationalized (in 1985) that, "the computed irregularities are too pronounced. But the models used are crude, and a more refined approach could prove successful" to explain large-scale uniformity while allowing small-scale nonuniformity.

Concerning the smoothness of the MBR, without providing any supporting data or logic, Rees and Silk wrote (in 1970), "Some wavelengths will be attenuated more smoothly than others, so that the inhomogeneities of favored size will be preserved, whereas those less favored will tend to be destroyed," and added that, as evidence of their bias, "The aim of recent work has been to determine what scales of perturbation are most likely to survive the various damping until the scattering of photons comes to an end."

Rees and Silk also wrote that, "The search for the smoothing processes that would require fewer special conditions is part of the continuing work in chaotic cosmology" (apparently then referring to inflation), and that, "It would be conceptually attractive if there were processes that would transform an initially chaotic universe into one that displayed the large-scale uniformity of a Friedmann model."

Bias for the Formation of Galaxies.

Repeating several items from previous chapters, Faye Flam wrote that, "The bigger those structures get, the harder it becomes for cosmologists to figure out how they could have coalesced in the limited time since the big bang," Steinhardt was quoted as saying that, "There wasn't enough time in the history of the BB universe for gravity to pull together these structures," and Edwin Turner has said that, "We're starting to find that we just don't have enough time to get the Universe from an early state to the one we're seeing now."

But, regardless of those comments, Schramm is working to find seeds that can organize matter "efficiently enough to explain the structures now being mapped,"

Despite the impossibility of galactic formation under BBT, efforts to support it have continued. An example of that is Peebles' ridiculous comment, that gravity caused the growth of large galactic structures out of smaller irregularities "because no one has been able to think of any other reasonably effective force on such large scales."

Bias for Inflation.

Heinz Pagels wrote that, even before inflation was invented, physicists knew "that galaxies could have grown from fluctuations in the density of matter in the very early universe." Quantum fluctuations were always present, thus there was "no need to explain where they came from."

However, he found that inflation provided a "new way of examining the problem," and he wrote that calculations showed "fluctuations were too big by a factor of 1,000...[but] even the wrong result seemed like progress," and, "Subsequently clever physicists found field theory models that even gave the right size for fluctuations. For the first time, a rather simple theoretical model based on field theory could explain the origin and evolution of the fluctuations from which galaxies could eventually form."

Although Pagels presented that as a triumph for BBT, it is really nothing more than another struggle to manipulate theory in support of BBT.

Guth reported an inflationary expansion by a factor of 10^{50}. That was minor league speculation as compared to Linde's ridiculous new inflation expansion of $10^{1,000,000}$, both of those numbers having been provided without any rationale.

Among Linde's other scientific work, was his previously mentioned comment that he couldn't believe that, "God would miss such a good possibility to improve the creation of the universe."

Inflation theory was invented and tailored to solve BB problems but, like many other theorist's flights of fantasy, it cannot be proved or disproved.

Bias for Missing Matter and CDM.

Cosmologists and astromomers have spent vast amounts of time and energy in the search for the missing matter that would bring the average density of the universe up to a level that is acceptable to BBT. As a result of that biased objective, a vast assortment of candidates for missing matter have been proposed.

Those candidates include cold dark matter, massive "cold" neutrinos, or hot dark matter, maybe fast moving "hot" neutrinos, or perhaps previously mentioned suggestions such as, burnt-out galaxies, low mass stars, large planets, black holes, magnetic monopoles, cosmic strings and sheets, gravitational waves, WIMPS, MACHOS, CHAMPS, axions, gravitinos, neutralinos, photinos, winos and zinos.

The presence of CDM, that is thought necessary to explain giant galactic formations, has been of particular importance to inflation theorists who postulate a flat universe.

But because of a recent realization that the amount of CDM that would be present in the universe is insufficient to account for the development of the giant formations within the BB time frame, belief in CDM has been abandoned by some. However, as mentioned in Chapter 9, Alan Guth has suggested that CDM theory might merely be "modified for a better fit," and David Schramm is reported to have said that, even if there were found to be no fluctuations in the microwave background (indicating little or no CDM) BBT will survive; and that eventuality could favor "more exotic and bizarre" BBT models.

Regardless of the fact that the accretion of matter necessary for galaxy formation would be impossible in the superluminal speed of expansion of the the BB universe, Barrow and Silk tell us that CDM is "testable by simulating the cosmological process of gravitational instability and the ensuing structure formation in large computer simulations." However, any such simulation can only be successful if it neglects the extreme speed at which matter is said to depart from the BB.

Although Paul Steinhardt declared that there was not enough time for gravity to pull together those structures, he added that, "many of his colleagues nevertheless hold out hope for the CDM model."

Science writer Tim Appenzeller wrote (in *SCIENCE* in 1991), regarding a quasar having a redshift of 4.733 that CDM, "is hard pressed to explain how something so massive could have formed so quickly" after the BB (less than a billion years). However, he quoted Jeremiah Ostriker as saying, "You have to stretch to make cold dark matter work...although, of course, none of this casts doubts on the Big Bang itself."

Bias for Neutrinos.

The neutrinos that are said to flood the BB universe have been the favored candidate for the missing matter of the BB universe. However, as has been presented in Chapter 14, mathematical and astronomical evidence shows the mass of neutrinos to be far too low to provide for the desired level of density of the BB universe.

Physicist and BBer Dennis Overbye has related in *Lonely Hearts of The Cosmos* (in 1994) that, "Schramm, a neutrino advocate, was one who claimed to know the big picture. He liked neutrinos because they could close the universe and make omega a perfect 1.0. That was the answer required by inflation. If you know anything about grand unified theories and inflation, you could think no other way....The cosmologists job is to reconcile the observations to that number" (thereby demonstrating impartial scientific method at its very best).

As one example of the extraordinary theoretical and experimental efforts that have been made to find the missing mass, Sciama has gone so far as to make precise predictions regarding tau neutrinos. His calculations showed them to have a mass sufficient to close the universe (30 eV), and a lifetime of 10^{23} seconds.

However, satellite (Hopkins Ultraviolet Telescope) experimental searches for the radiation that would result from the decay of those neutrinos has produced only negative results. Furthermore the arrival of neutrinos from Supernova 1987A at or near the speed of light puts their speed far too high for galaxy formation, and their mass far too low to close the BB universe.

Despite these facts, the belief in missing mass, including BB neutrinos, persists.

Bias for BB Chronology.

The BB chronology discussed in Chapter 3, and some of its problems discussed in Chapter 18, provide some examples of the amazing lack of scientific method of the establishment.

The energy levels, either experimental or theoretical, required for the creation of quantum particles, real or hypothetical, have been used to place them at the time on a hypothetical plot of BB history, where their energy matches the energy of the plot; a totally contrived, arbitrary process. Because any level of energy required for the creation of quantum particles can be fitted between the infinite energy of the BB and the present low level, their placement in that BB chronology has no scientific validity.

As an example of that kind of warped science, as mentioned in Chapter 18, Peebles has written that, if we trace back to an instant after the BB, "we find" that the formation of light elements provides evidence that "we understand" what went on when the universe was just 12 seconds old, "a remarkable accomplishment indeed." Considering the fact that his "trace" consists of the arbitrary placement of events on an inaccurate representation of the evolution of a purely hypothetical BB universe, that understanding certainly is remarkable.

Although Peebles, et al. have declared our understanding of the development of the BB universe to be one of the great achievements of 20th-century science, Ernan McMullin described the process leading to Peebles' "understanding" more correctly when (in 1981) he wrote, "In the last decade much effort has been expended on applying quantum and elementary particle theories to the problem of how the universe developed in the first moments after the big bang. An immensely detailed scenario has been developed...." McMullin has politely used the word "developed" rather than "contrived," which describes that process more accurately.

The Anthropic Principle.

Some scientists' thoughts have apparently strayed far from science, allowing them to seriously consider the possibility that the universe was created for their existence.

A number of perceived coincidences among various physical constants and other factors causes them to ponder the possibility that divine intervention had a hand in shaping things for the benefit of the human race. Carr has written, "Indeed the evidence for the Anthropic Principle (AP) rests almost entirely on the large number of numerical coincidences in physics which seem to be prerequisites of the emergence of life."

When some of the physical constants of nature, such as the

speed-of-light and the mass of the electron or the proton, are adjusted to a dimensionless form, that is, by factoring them by other appropriate fundamental constants, the approximate values of some of them are roughly related by various multiples of 10^{40}. For example, the ratio of the mass of the universe to that of a proton is about 10^{40} squared, and the dimensionless Hubble age of the universe is equal to about 10^{40}. (How can age be dimensionless?)

Paul Dirac suggested (in 1938) that those relationships might have physical significance. Theoretical physicist R. H. Dicke became involved in this "large number hypothesis", and (in 1961) suggested that, if these numbers weren't as they were, human minds wouldn't have had a time and a place to evolve the ability to consider such things. For example, stars that produced the heavy elements that are essential to animal chemistry wouldn't have had time for that process if the Hubble constant were much larger, and life could not have evolved.

Thus was born the concept of the Anthropic Principle.

University of Cambridge cosmologist Brandon Carter (in 1974) further developed the idea. He defined two categories of AP, the weak and the strong. The Weak Principle is defined by the statement that the universe happened to be such that it allowed us to be observers, and the Strong Principle is defined by the statement that the universe was somehow compelled to allow us to be here.

He presented more examples of constants of physics that he considered to be remarkable relationships, and Carr (in 1982) added that, if the relationships of the dimensionless constants pertaining to the BB weren't precisely as they were, the universe would be drastically different, and couldn't possibly support human life. Thus the universe was fine-tuned to provide for our existence. The relationships of those numbers might be the result of physics as yet unknown to us.

If the physical constants of our universe weren't just as they are, we wouldn't be here. An example that is given is that, if the gravitational constant were a little larger the stars would have burnt out too fast for life to evolve, and if it were a little smaller the Sun would be too cool for life to start.

As mentioned in Chapter 9, Carr had said that because "the fact the density [of the universe] is within a factor of 10 of the critical value now implies that its deviation from the critical value must have been even smaller at earlier times" and stated a smoothness within one part in 10^{16} at one second and one part in 10^{60} at 10^{-43} second after the BB. He presented that as evidence of fine tuning, and thus of the AP.

To summarize, some BB cosmologists have reached the conclusion that, rather than conditions just happening to be such as to allow the appearance of life on earth, from which man eventually evolved, the BB and everything following it had been precisely tailored for the development of intelligent life. Philosopher Richard Swinburne, in 1989, finally took the bull by the horns and suggested that divine intervention (by the "Fine Tuner") may have played a part in establishing the universe for our occupancy.

Believers in the Anthropic Principle apparently feel that they have uncovered some of God's methodology for producing life and humanity on the Earth. However, mankind has been fooled over and over again by such magic numbers in support of erroneous ideas. From chance numerical anomalies he has a tendency to select those that agree with satisfying results, and to distort data to support his views.

There might be about 10^{22} planets in the observable universe-; perhaps an average of about one planet for each of an estimated 100 billion stars in each of an estimated average of 100 billion galaxies within telescopic range of our planet. If there were a possibility of life, say, on one in a billion of those planets, there could be life of some form on as many as a 10,000 billion of them.

As another guess, there might be about 10,000 (one in a billion) of them that are old enough and have environments sufficiently hospitable to have evolved some form of intelligent life. There might therefore be a chance that intelligent life on about 100 planets within our own galaxy could be smart enough, and close enough, to ponder cosmology while scanning our galaxy with their telescopes. (However, if they were there, chances are, they would be at least tens of light years distant, meaning it would take twice that long for message exchange.)

So perhaps we are not as special as some cosmologists like to think.

As cosmologists Robert Shapiro and Gerald Feinberg in their book of 1980, *Life Beyond Earth*, have suggested, those who embrace the Anthropic Principle are akin to microscopic rotifers living in a muddy little puddle who view the world as having been designed to meet their needs. Cosmologists, more so than bugs, should be aware that there is much evidence of life adapting to harsh environments, but little evidence of environments changing to meet the needs of organisms.

The inappropriate consideration of fine tuning and AP as science was accurately stated by Heinz Pagels who said, it's "needless clutter" is "deeply flawed and has no place in physics or cosmology," and the most eloquent comment I have come across regarding AP is that of physicist Paul K. Feyerabend was quoted as having said, "this one day fly, a human being, this little bit of nothing discovering the secret of existence is crazy."

Gibberish.

The use of terms commonly used by BB cosmologists, such as, "fabric of space/time," gravity "tearing apart the vacuum" and "the fine structure of space," that have no meaning whatsoever, are a disgrace to science.

As examples of such utterly unscientific nonsense, Heinz Pagels (as mentioned in Chapter 5) explained how, "the very origin of the universe—how the fabric of space/time and matter can be created out of nothing", and Silk tells the reader (as mentioned in Chapter 7) to "Imagine a moment so early and a density so high that that the gravitational stresses were capable of tearing apart the vacuum."

Barrows and Silk wrote that, "Space-time might have an intricate crenelated structure with handles and loops joining back upon itself;" using such scientific expressions as "crenelated," and "handles and loops;" to convey their conception of the "fabric of space-time."

James Trefil's description is somewhat different: "Think of the fabric of space as being something like the membrane of a very special kind of balloon. The presence of any matter, causes the fabric to bulge, and this drains energy from the gravitational field...."

The use of such phrases, commonly found in BB literature, is more purposeful obfuscation. The message intended is that those of us outside of the establishment are not sufficiently knowledgeable or intelligent to understand such esoteric matters. But the truth is that it merely hides an inability to describe some aspects of BBT in a logical, scientific manner.

Beauty and Elegance.

Quantum physicist Paul Dirac is quoted to have said, "It is more important to have beauty in one's equations than to have them fit experiment." Roger Penrose wrote in *The Emperor's New Mind* that Dirac, "is unabashed in his claim that it was his keen sense of beauty that enabled him to devise his equation [the Dirac equation] while others have searched in vain," and Peebles tells us that, "the standard presumption is that deeper physics yet to be discovered will someday give us an elegantly reasonable, and testable picture for what happened before the big bang."

The common theme in all of this is that beauty and elegance of theory and mathematics have become more important than experimental data, logic and proven scientific principles.

However, an article in *NEW SCIENTIST* once stated that, "theory is far out pacing experimental observations...a hypothesis can become to be regarded as being so convincing and elegant that it simply has to be right...A classic example is surely our relentless devotion to the traditional paradigm of the big bang in cosmology," and John Boslough has stated that, "Another troubling trend is that physicists have resorted to concocting complicated mathematical hypotheses to explain the universe. They justify these excruciatingly difficult equations on the basis of their 'elegance' or 'inner truth and harmony.'"

Religion.

A few decades ago it was thought that BBT provided a possible model for the origin and evolution of the universe, but the matter provided to the media by the establishment for its dissemination has resulted in its almost universal acceptance as scientific fact.

Perhaps aided by the Pope Pius IX's endorsement, BBT has been absorbed by the Judeo-Christian world, and by those of other religions as an acceptable version of God's creation of the universe. After hearing of BBT in 1951, that pope is said to have written, "True science to an ever increasing degree discovers God as though God were waiting behind each door opened by science."

BB opponents Hoyle and Narlikar have written that. "Many people are happy to accept this position. they accept [the big-bang picture] without looking for any physical explanation for the abrupt beginning...[which is] deliberately regarded as *metaphysical*—that is, *outside* physics," and BB cosmologist W. B. Bonner explained that, "The underlying motive is, of course, to bring in God as creator....It seems like the opportunity Christianity has been awaiting for ever since science began to depose religion from the minds of rational men in the seventeenth century."

Regardless of how it happened, BBT has been accepted as religious faith by many of those in the establishment. As Geoffrey Burbidge has commented, BB has become a faith, not a science.

The proof of that has been demonstrated to me many times. When I have been so tactless to suggest to BBers that there may be some flaws in BBT, invariably the response has been hostile and insulting; the kind of response you might expect if you were to make a derogatory comment about a person's religion. The acceptance of BBT has lead to the conclusion that only God could have caused the BB. To question that has become heresy, and those who do so are treated with ridicule, insults and contempt.

The Need for Common Sense.

Those who reject the many errors of present day cosmology, that is based on theoretical innovation that lacks the support of experimental data, have some very good company.

William MacMillan, believed the universe to be Newtonian and rejected Einstein's relativity as outside of common sense, said (in 1927), "The exclusive use of mathematics is a dangerous thing," and Arthur Eddington wrote (in 1928), "As a scientist I simply do not believe that the Universe began with a bang."

Astronomer and physicist, and president of the Royal Astronomical Society from 1951 to 1953, Herbert Dingle (in 1961) declared that mathematical physicists, "have simply lost the power of understanding of what they are doing...(and) have substituted mathematics for reasoning"

BB cosmologist Michael Rowan-Robertson admitted in his university text (in 1977), *Cosmology*, "most of the models of the universe described in this [his] book are based on general relativity, which cannot be said to rest on a very solid experimental basis."

British astronomer Fred Hoyle wrote (in 1982) concerning cosmology, "Over the past seventeen years astronomers and physicists the world over have made numerous investigations, with the outcome essentially nil. It has been a fruitless churning of mathematical symbols, exactly the hallmark of an incorrect theory."

Those comments apply to this day.

Scientific Method Goes Out the Window.

Joseph Silk has written that, "Practically all known astronomical phenomena can be understood in the context of the Big Bang cosmology," and Peebles has written that here is "no generally accepted list of the most serious challenges to each of the more popular models" of BBT.

Those are just a couple of examples that are typical of the lack of scientific fact that is perpetuated by leading figures in the BB cosmology.

Long ago I read something like, "The history of cosmology is largely a history of careful selection and the manufacture of data in support of BBT, and of the continuous ignoring of all evidence against it," and Halton Arp has written, "Cosmology is unique in science in that it is a very large intellectual edifice based on very few facts."

My studies certainly have verified those comments.

Often those violations of scientific method are admitted; the perpetrators apparently proud of their special efforts in support of the favored theory, as they make a good living teaching, lecturing, and writing articles and books.

It is assumed that the occurrence of the BB is not to be questioned; only how the universe can be explained within BBT, and when difficulties are encountered BB theorists merely reinterpret old data and patch up BBT with new ad hoc modifications. Experimental data, proven science, and common sense are not required. Scientific method goes out the window.

As physical chemist and science writer Jim Baggott has written in *The Meaning of Quantum Theory*, "An otherwise objective scientist may defend an entrenched view (as a favorite theory, for example) long after overwhelming experimental evidence suggests that such views are logically indefensible."

Tom Van Flandern, formerly of the U. S. Naval observatory and Jet Propulsion laboratory, in *Dark Matter, Missing Planets and New Comets* has "noted a regular practice of not reexamining the fundamental assumptions underlying a theory once it has gained 'accepted' status, almost no matter how incompatible some new observations or experiments might be." (He has also noticed that "professional peer pressure" is "designed to isolate and repress those who choose to criticize an accepted theory.")

Frank Wilczek wrote (in 1991) that, "new theoretical ideas seem increasingly abstract and untestable, some are incomprehensible even to most physicists," and that theoretical physicists, "wander far from convincingly understood territory in their efforts to break new ground. Their theories take us into increasingly abstract realms such as curled-up ten dimensional space-time," and that, "the true test of a scientific theory is that it should illuminate concrete features of publicly shared reality."

In 1987 Thomas Kuhn expressed the opinion that science is a political rather than a rational process, and, in an article in *SCIENCE NEWS* in 1992, Ivars Peterson wrote that some historians, philosophers and sociologists "argue that science has an undeserved reputation for objectivity...that social interests determine not only how science it done but also its content....Science itself is a matter of opinion—decided on the basis of personal or political beliefs...a social construction, perhaps even a group self delusion."

Those thoughts certainly apply to the field of cosmology where scientific method is often considered to be an unnecessary annoyance.

TWENTY SEVEN

Previous Alternatives to the Big Bang

If, as I suggest, BBT is invalid, the question arises as to what might replace it. In response to that, some theories have competed or continue to compete with BBT. Some of those that might have some validity, are briefly presented.

Steady State Cosmology.

The oldest of the alternatives to BBT is the SST which was devised over 40 years ago, primarily by Bondi, Gold and Hoyle, who couldn't accept the flaws of BBT.

According to SST new matter is continuously generated in space, thus providing new material for the evolution of new stars and galaxies as old ones die, and keeping the density of the universe constant throughout the ages. That cosmology incorporated what was called the "Perfect Cosmological Principle" that included a constant rate of expansion throughout the universe, and the large-scale smoothness. However, SST failed to provide a credible rationale for the creation of matter in space or for the expansion of the universe, and, when BBers presented evidence that quasars were clumped at great distances, and claimed that it provided evidence for an evolving universe, that couldn't be easily countered by SST.

When the MBR was discovered in the mid 1960s, and SST also

provided no explanation for that, it was abandoned by all but a few diehards.

New Steady State Theory.

When writing a previous book, *The Cult of the Big Bang*, a number of years ago, having recognized no reason to disbelieve the majority of the famous men of astronomy, I had accepted their belief that the universe was expanding. However, as presented in that book, I had found sufficient reason to doubt the so-called proofs of BBT. As a result of that, and a long list of unresolved BBT and inflation theory problems, I postulated a "new steady state theory" (NSST) that included a universe that is expanding, but that was only as smooth as it was observed to be.

NSST differed from old SST in that, based on quantum theory, its matter was created from the energy of space, and its expansion was caused by cosmic repulsion. Because of inflation theory's acceptance of the energy of empty space and of cosmic repulsion, both on gigantic levels, as the source of a BB universe, I felt that it would be reasonable to suppose that, on a minute scale, it might provide for a revised SST.

However, having since learned of many reasons to deny the expansion of the universe, and many additional errors of BBT, and having hit upon a cosmological concept that is far superior to BBT, SST or NSST, I have abandoned all of those.

Plasma Cosmology.

One of the more well known alternatives to BBT that deserves more attention is that presented by Anthony Peratt and Eric Lerner; a plasma cosmology based on the earlier work of Hannes Alfvén, Nobel Prize winner for his work in magnetohydrodynamics. In that theory electromagnetic forces dominated the evolution of the universe rather than gravitational force.

As in the case of SST, the problems of BBT were undoubtedly a factor leading to Danish plasma physicist Hannes Alfvén's invention of plasma cosmology.

According to that theory, at some time in the distant past the universe was a dilute plasma—a gas of electrically charged particles—negatively charged electrons and positively charged ions. That plasma slowly contracted into clouds of matter and antimatter, and, as it contracted, matter and antimatter annihilated. The pressure of radiation from those annihilations eventually, in some manner, became high enough to cause accumulations of matter that eventually formed into galaxies. All of that occurred in a non-expanding universe that had no beginning and has no end, and which now contains both matter and antimatter galaxies.

Those plasma processes also resulted in the radiation that became the MBR that now fills the universe; and it is claimed to have produced the relative abundances of elements that are observed in the universe.

Not only does plasma theory provide an explanation of galaxy formation, that is seriously lacking in BBT, but many of the old problems, such as, singularity, smoothness, horizon, flatness, missing mass, and age problems, are absent from that theory.

It cannot be denied that plasma exists in the IGS, and, although, plasma theory may not provide the complete answer, it undoubtedly plays a major roll in the formation of galaxies.

Of course, BB cosmologists don't accept plasma theory. In fact, they hardly acknowledge its existence. However, Peebles made an exception to that and had written regarding a plasma universe explosion, "It would be hard to imagine that the explosion produced a spherically symmetric expanding system of galaxies," leaving the reader to wonder why he didn't express similar doubts about a smooth BB.

Quasi Steady State Cosmology.

Another cosmological theory that has been considered in recent years is that Quasi Steady State Cosmology (QSSC), sometimes called Small Bang Theory, that was proposed by Hoyle, Burbidge and Narlikar in 1993.

Rather than one gigantic blast that instantaneously produced all the matter and energy of the cosmos, why not a continuing series of smaller explosions? Small Bang proponents suggest that there may be associated areas of high gravitational force causing gravitational redshifts that result in the appearance of quasars at increased distance.

The discovery of voids and sheets of galaxies could be seen as support for the idea of multiple small bangs in space. Each of those bangs is said to involve masses 10^{16} times that of the Sun, at least a million times smaller than that of BBT.

The QSS universe is said to be expanding, but not uniformly.

Its Hubble constant would be about 65 kilometers per second per million parsecs, very close to the present most favored value. Like plasma cosmologists, QSSC cosmologists claim that their theory explains the MBR and the relative abundances of light elements in the universe, that it can explain MBR as due to thermalization by iron whiskers created by supernovas, and that it lacks many of the problems of BBT and Plasma Cosmology. However, it may have some singularity problems.

If one can accept one enormous bang of BBT, certainly a series of Small Bangs should be easier to accept than a single blast that was large enough to produce the entire universe in one instant. However, it seems unlikely that energy from explosions distributed in time and space could have produced MBR of the smoothness and the near perfect black-body spectrum that is observed. Furthermore, it would seem that blue shifts of radiation from the matter of those explosions would be seen as well as great redshifts, but that has not been observed.

Anomalous Redshifts and Quantized Redshifts.

As discussed in Chapter 15, observations over several decades have shown many quasars to have considerably higher redshift than those of galaxies that are within small angles of them. The statistics of those sightings provide evidence that they occur many times more often than would be expected of the angular distribution of quasars in space. That, and the observation of bridges of matter between some of those quasars, and the observation of configurations of pairs of such quasars, has led to the conclusion that those quasars are spawned from their associated galaxies. That situation also leads to the conclusion that the higher redshift of radiation from newly formed quasars is red-shifted by other than Doppler (or cosmological) effects.

Halton Arp, who is responsible for a vast amount of data concerning anomalous redshifts over several decades, has suggested a process by which the younger matter of newly formed quasars produces greater redshifts than older matter.

Also as discussed in Chapter 15, Arp, Tifft and others have discovered considerable evidence of quantized redshifts; redshifts that repeat at certain intervals of wavelength.

As in the case of anomalous redshift, there is no accepted explanation for the quantization of redshifts. Arp has said that, "there is no obvious reason why gravitational redshift or photon debilitation by scattering should be quantized." There would seem to be no possibility that "photon debilitation" (tired light schemes) could cause quantization. (But, it is suggested here that GRS may provide the answer. It may simply be that nature favors certain mass-to-radius ratios that result in the observed quantization.)

Astronomical data regarding both anomalous redshift and quantized redshift data are simply ignored by BB cosmologists, as seems to be their custom regarding data that might present additional problems to BBT.

Although neither anomalous redshift or quantized redshifts are cosmological theories, they represent unexploited opportunities of investigation that, if pursued might lead to some new ideas regarding cosmological processes.

Tired Light Theories.

"Tired light" is used here as a general term that includes a variety of ideas regarding loss of energy of photons in their travels through space resulting in the redshift of the spectral lines of radiated energy.

There are a number of highly regarded American scientists who find reason to believe that redshift is due to other than the unimpeded travel of EMR through space since a BB. Those include, William MacMillan, as mentioned in Chapter 15, perhaps the first to suggest tired light, and more recently Grote Reber, Paul Marmet and John Kierein, all of whom support various tired light concepts.

Swiss-American astronomer Fritz Zwicky made a similar suggestion in 1929 that he called gravitational drag in which photons transfer energy to intergalactic matter resulting in the redshift of radiation.

Some of the current tired light ideas include Compton scattering of photons by particles of matter (electrons, protons and "other free particles") distributed in space, and inelastic collisions of photons with those particles. Both of those are believed to result in energy losses and wavelengths that are redshifted in proportion to distance traveled. Some theorists have suggested that the resulting energy loss shows up as long wavelength radiation from space that is detected by radio reception.

Marmet has long proposed that the matter in space that is involved in those inelastic collisions of photons is molecular hydrogen. As time has progressed, astronomical evidence for the presence of hydrogen in the IGS has increased, adding to the credibility of that concept.

The list of those supporting tired light concepts includes Physics professor A. K. T. Assis of the State University of Brazil's Institute of Physics. In his recent book, *Relational Mechanics*, he wrote, "Our own point of view, however, is the cosmological redshift...is due to some kind of effect known in the literature as 'tired light' and not to a Doppler effect....We're not sure what kind of mechanism is at work here (Photon-photon interaction, inelastic collisions between photons and particles and free electrons, or between photons and molecules, etc."

Tired light theorists generally deny the large-scale expansion of the universe.

Although the work of Reber, Marmet, Kierein, Assis, and others involved in tired light concepts is ignored by the establishment, it may prove to be of great importance to the future of cosmology.

Other Theories.

A number of scientists have developed other less prominent cosmological theories, such as C-field cosmology and the Charlier hierarchal cosmology that may be of some value, but they are omitted here. For those who might be interested, discussion of those ideas can be found in a number of books on cosmology.

The cosmological ideas discussed above, and others, may have faults of one kind or another. However, some good and useful concepts are embodied in some of those. One or more of them, combinations or portions of those or others, unknown or omitted here, may yet prove to be viable.

In view of the many problems of BBT, the alternative cosmological possibilities discussed above certainly deserve consideration. That is especially true of tired light theories; and it cannot be denied that plasma exists in the IGS and plays a role in the formation of galaxies. Similarly, anomalous redshifts and quantized redshifts should not be ignored. Efforts to acquire understanding of those observations should be continued.

TWENTY EIGHT

A New Alternative: Reality

Portions this chapter have been taken from a paper, The Recycling Universe, first given at a Natural Philosophy Alliance session at the April, 1999 meeting of the American Association of the Advancement of Science in Santa Fe, New Mexico. At that meeting the concept of a Recycling Universe Cosmology—since then revised and strengthened— was first presented by the author of this book.

As a result of my studies of cosmology over many years I have uncovered overwhelming evidence against BBT. But, more importantly, during that time I have also gathered enough general information about astronomy on a cosmological scale that I have been able to postulate a cosmology that may provide solutions to many of the problems that plague the field of cosmology; not just a cycling universe, like a Big Bang closed exploding universe, but an ever changing, recycling universe.

This chapter presents the results of those efforts.

Everything in the preceding chapters of this book, and its appendixes, is presented in preparation for the presentation of this new Recycling Universe Cosmology (RUC).

IN THIS CHAPTER

Several factors, that have been overlooked by many others, and have resulted in this theory, are listed as follows:

(1) Old galaxies die,

(2) but they have very long lives.

(3) The universe is very much older; perhaps infinitely old.

(4) Enormous amounts of matter and radiant energy are spewed into intergalactic space (IGS) from all the galaxies of the universe, every second of their lives.

(5) Vast amounts of hydrogen are present throughout IGS
(6) New galaxies continue to form in IGS.
(7) The universe is not expanding,
(8) and it is not doomed to heat death.

Old galaxies die, but the universe doesn't. New galaxies have ever continued to form.

The source of that new life is the matter and energy from older *dead and dying galaxies*, plus other matter and energy that fills all of space. Most importantly, much of that is in the form of hydrogen that has been found to be abundant throughout space.

- This chapter presents a discussion of the lives and ages of stars, galaxies and the universe.
- Following that, evidence is presented regarding the loss of matter and energy from galaxies, and the accumulation of those in IGS, that is necessary for the formation of new galaxies.
- That is followed by discussions of the formation of those galaxies and their stellar systems, and the evidence that supports those processes.
- Discussions of other related matters are then presented. Those include such topics as the expansion of the universe, denial of its heat death, the presence of dark matter, the source of background radiation from space, and some other related items.

Much of the text of this chapter is lengthy and difficult, but perhaps the struggle through it will be worthwhile if the reader discovers a new cosmology that is based on evidence and logic rather than theory and fantasy.

THE AGING AND DEATH OF GALAXIES

Radiation and Matter Into Intergalactic Space.

The establishment (shorthand for mainstream cosmologists, astronomers, astrophysicists and theoretical physicists) has accepted the idea that new stars are formed from matter and energy that result from the explosions of older stars, such as supernovas. However, it has gone unrecognized that, at the tremendous speeds of matter, and at the speed-of-light of radiant energy exiting those explosions, all but a small portion of that matter and energy are blown way from their source galaxies.

Of course, not all the matter and energy of stars is blasted off as novas or supernovas. Some stars evolve into other forms, including neutron stars, quasars, and possibly black holes. Nothing seems certain about the fate of those, but it is likely that they are also eventually destroyed by explosion (or possibly by quantum evaporation—Hawking radiation). Perhaps their remains are also eventually blown into IGS.

When stars like our Sun use up their nuclear fuel they explode as red giants, the remains of which collapse into white dwarfs. A large percentage of the matter and radiation from red giant explosions is also blown into IGS, and all of the EMR (from gamma through long radio wavelengths) from all the stars that exist in all the galaxies in the universe, adds to the matter that spews into space, but at the speed of light.

Stellar flares can have velocities of thousands of kilometers per second, far greater than the escape velocity of their stars. Some solar flares have velocities of over 1,000 kilometers per second, considerably greater than its escape velocity of about 620 kilometers per second. Undoubtedly a portion of the matter of the flares of ordinary stars also escapes into IGS. However, stars similar to our Sun have been discovered that generate "superflares"—huge explosions that produce massive quantities of particles and radiation. The superflares release millions of times more energy than the largest flares ever observed from the Sun.

As reported by astronomers Iben and Tutukov, a large percentage of stars having masses in the range of about 1 to 10 times that of the Sun, 90 percent of all stars, "evolve off the main sequence within a 15 billion year time frame to become AGB [asymptotic giant branch] stars" that lose matter in "powerful winds" containing particles, carbon and other elements that spew into IGS. Those stars also eventually die.

Some of the largest stars in the universe, luminous blue variables (LBVs) lose mass at an enormous rate. One of those, Eta Carinae (NC 3372), for example, has been estimated to lose 6 trillion trillion tons of mass per day (equal to about 70 million trillion tons per second, or 17.5 trillion times rate of mass loss of the Sun).

University of California at Berkeley astronomers Brenda Frye and Tom Broadhurst (in 1999) reported finding ten distant "baby galaxies" that "were seething with star forming, exploding stars, and powerful winds...Spectra reveal that the gas in these mini-galaxies is highly blue shifted...meaning that gas is moving toward Earth at speeds up to 1.7 million miles per hour (750 kilometers per second)...Dark lines in the spectra betray the presence of heavy elements such as carbon, oxygen, and silicon....The winds from these distant galaxies are moving fast enough and contain enough heavy elements to pollute the vast regions between galaxies in just 300 million years. This would explain why galactic space contains a surprisingly high abundance of heavy elements."

The enormous amount of matter and energy escaping from the centers of galaxies (thought to be quasars that are the result of giant black holes) adds to that blasted into IGS. Some of that matter departs at speeds in excess of the escape velocity of their sources. Some of it is believed to be emitted at "relativistic" speeds. In the past it has apparently been assumed that such matter remains within its galaxy but, if it can escape its source, a portion of that must escape its galaxy without being captured by the gravitation of other bodies.

When stars blow up as novas or supernovas much of their mass is lost in the form of EMR and neutrinos. The velocity of those is at, or very near, the speed of light. Therefore, virtually none of it would remain in the space of their galaxies. That might apply to some extent to other active stars such as neutron stars. Essentially all of the radiation from all the stars that exist in all the galaxies in the universe, adds to that which spews into IGS at the speed of light.

The Death of Stars and Galaxies.

The radiant energy escaping from a typical star like our Sun is estimated to be equivalent to 4 million tons per second, equal to 1.26×10^{14} tons per year or 1.145×10^{17} kilograms per year. Escaping its star at the speed of light, most of that undoubtedly continues on out of its galaxy.

The mass loss of stars in the form of stellar wind has been estimated to be much greater than the loss due to radiation. According to Heinz Pagels, "the solar wind dumps hundreds of million of tons of solar material into outer space each second." If the mass loss due to solar wind were just 100 times that of the loss due to radiation, the Sun would loose about 10^{19} kilograms of mass per year.

The mass of a typical star like the Sun has been estimated to be about to 2×10^{30} kilograms. At that rate of mass loss, the Sun might last 200 billion years. But, of course, it is scheduled to blow up as a red giant long before that, when its nuclear fuel runs out. (It is believed that a star like the Sun will use up its hydrogen fuel and explode at an age of 10 to 20 billion years.)

Regarding the length of life that might be expected of galaxies, if an average galaxy were to continue to have an average of about 100 billion average stars of 2×10^{30} kilograms of mass during its lifetime, and each of those stars lost 10^{19} kilograms of mass per year, it might last about 200 billion years. (A galaxy might start with many more stars, and end with many less, but the average might be like that of the middle-aged Milky Way.)

(Concerning the recycling universe that is postulated in this book, if there are, as estimated, 100 billion such galaxies in the observable universe, their total mass would be 2×10^{52} kilograms, and their total mass loss would be about 10^{41} kilograms per year. Thus, on average, the total mass of the observable universe would be "recycled" during a period equal to the 200 billion year age of a typical galaxy.)

When the various ways in which the stars within galaxies lose their matter and energy are given consideration, it becomes apparent that the great bulk of galactic matter and energy is eventually blown into IGS. Over many billions of years, with less and less matter and energy remaining, old galaxies must fade away and die. Although debris undoubtedly remains, the death of galaxies is inevitable, and most of their matter and energy is dispersed throughout the universe.

Actually, galaxies are doomed from the moment they are born. Their stars start to die when they reach the mass that allows the start of their nuclear furnaces. As soon as their fusion process start they begin to lose mass to IGS. Thus galaxies also start dying at that point in their formation.

As reported in *ASTRONOMY* of January 1997, Augustus Oemler, director of the Observatories of the Carnegie Institute, and an international team of astronomers have reported that spiral galaxies fade and die over time, leaving just dim remains. In his words, "Astronomers have recently been finding hordes of dim galaxies that contain very few stars," and suggested that, "Maybe these are the ghostly remains of those distant blue spirals that once burned brightly many eons ago."

THE AGE OF STARS, GALAXIES AND THE UNIVERSE

The Age of Stars.

Although the lives of stars and galaxies are limited by the loss of matter and energy, many of them live far longer than generally believed.

As mentioned in Chapter 11, the work of Laughlin, Bodenheimer and Adams indicates some white dwarfs might live as long as six trillion years, and Silk has referred to "evolving stars over the tens of billions of years of stellar evolution."

Also mentioned in that chapter, Hertzsprung-Russell diagrams in Rowan-Robinson's and Silk's books indicate the life of some main sequence stars to be as much as 100 billion years and the lives of white dwarfs to be much longer. Similar great ages are also indicated in a the H-R diagram in *The Universe Unfolding* by Ivan R. King, who also states that some stars could reach the age of 10^{14} years (100 trillion years).

Herbert Friedman wrote that, "For the smallest stars, evolution off the main sequence may take more than 100 billion years," and, in an *ASTRONOMY* article Trefil has presented an H-R diagram showing the age of white dwarfs to be hundreds of billions of years.

The Age of Galaxies.

If all the stars of a galaxy were of the same age (which they are not), and all of them lived about 15 billion years (which they do not), the life of a galaxy might be only about 15 billion years. But, because it is evident that new stars are continually forming in galaxies, the age of galaxies must be much greater than 15 billion years. Although galaxies eventually must die due to loss of matter to IGS, because the original mass and energy from which they formed is sufficient for the continuing birth of many generations of new stars, galaxies might survive for a couple of hundred billion years.

A neglected item that also seems to indicate the great age of galaxies, is that astronomical observations support a period of rotation of our galaxy of about 250 million years. As presented in Chapter 11, if it took just a few dozen rotations for it to reach its present spiral form, its age might be 10 to 15 billion years as postulated by BBT. But, because astronomical theory indicates that galactic rotation rates would have been ever slower in the past, its age might be considerably greater than that; and it would seem that more than a few dozen rotations would have been required to shape our galaxy and other spiral galaxies, indicating their age to be even greater.

The Age and Size of Galactic Formations.

As discussed in previous chapters (8, 11 and 12), giant galactic formations have been discovered that include sheets of galaxies, large voids in space, and "walls" that might spread as much as a billion light-years through space. As mentioned in Chapter 11, it has been estimated that the gigantic sheets and voids found in space would have taken as long as 100 billion years to form. Other astronomers have estimated that it would have taken hundreds of billion of years for those structures to evolve. (Based on reports of galaxies at relative speeds of 750 kilometers per second and structures as large as 500 million light-year, it might have taken 200 billion years for those structures to form.)

The Age of the Universe.

If there were just a few generations of galaxies in the history of the universe, it might have existed for a trillion years; but there may have been more than a few. If galactic formations required a couple of hundred billion years to develop, and more hundreds of billions of years to live and die, perhaps that process might have gone on for at least several trillions of years.

A number of scientists in the past have suggested such great ages for the universe. As mentioned in Chapter 1, those include Alexander Friedmann, who suggested "tens of billions of our ordinary years," and British mathematician, astronomer and physicist Sir James Jeans, who suggested a much greater age.

Jeans, who may have been the first to propose the continuous creation of matter throughout the universe, thought that the galactic cycle might be considerably longer. He is quoted as having said (in 1922), "The time for the condensation of...nebula to form stars...is of the order of 10^{13} years" (10 trillion years), and (in 1928), "A dynamical investigation has shown that the time necessary to break up the formation of less massive stars would again be of the order of 10^{13} years" and the beginning of the universe was "two hundred million million years" (200 trillion years).

As American cosmologist Richard Tolman (in 1929), in attempting to account for the distribution of nebulae, wrote his "hypothesis of continuous creation" in which new galaxies are formed at a rate that keeps the average density of the universe constant. He also wrote (in 1934), "I see at present no evidence against the assumption that the material universe has always existed."

Of course, those scientists had little in the way of evidence to support those great ages, but BBers have no evidence to deny them.

MATTER AND ENERGY IN SPACE

Astronomers have long accepted that the heavy elements of our world were produced in now dead stars or in supernova explosions. As mentioned in Chapter 19, the Burbidges with Hoyle and Fowler wrote, "the abundances of practically all the isotopes of the elements from hydrogen through uranium by synthesis in stars and supernovas."

That may be correct, but it has been overlooked that most of the matter and radiation from all the stars in all the past and present galaxies of the universe has, for hundreds of billions of years or more, been blown into IGS where it accumulates to start the formation of new galaxies.

Heavy Elements in Powerful Winds.

Over the years there have been many reports of astronomical observations supporting the spewing of galactic matter and energy into IGS. Those have been increasing in recent years. Several of them are reviewed in the following paragraphs.

Astronomer E. N. Parker reported (in *SCIENTIFIC AMERICAN* in 1984) that, "clouds of ions [are] ejected from the Sun, traveling at 1,000 to 2,000 kilometers per second...those solar flares are "known to emit very energetic protons, or hydrogen nuclei." Such speeds are far above the escape velocity of the Sun. Thus that matter would escape the Sun's gravity, and much of that escapes into IGS.

Yale University astronomer Bradley Schaefer reported at the January, 1999 meeting of the American Astronomical Society in Austin, Texas that, "Nine stars similar to our Sun have generated 'superflares'—huge explosions that produce massive quantities of subatomic particles and radiation. The superflares release between 100 and 10 million times more energy that the largest flares ever observed on the Sun," and senior lecturer at the Tel Aviv University School of Physics and Astronomy Sara C. Beck tells (in *SCIENTIFIC AMERICAN* in 2000) of massive young stars between 2 and 10 million years old that, "expel most of their initial mass at speeds of a few thousand kilometers per second."

An article on solar flares (in *ASTRONOMY* in 2000) reported that, "When the Sun's surface erupts in a flare or its larger cousin, a coronal ejection, particles speed away from the star like a gust of wind. But these winds, which consist mostly of electrons and protons, blow at hundreds of miles per second," and astrophysicist James L. Burch reported (in *SCIENTIFIC AMERICAN* in 2001) a coronal mass ejection (CME), "directly toward the earth, has an estimated speed of 1,700 kilometers per second," far above the escape velocity of the Sun.

Heinz Pagels in *Perfect Symmetry* (in 1985) wrote: "Astronomers indirectly observe two fast moving streams flowing in opposite directions from newborn stars; these streams are millions of times more intense than the solar wind blowing away from the Sun."

Astronomer Robert Zimmerman reported (in *ASTRONOMY* in 2000) that giant star Eta Carinae (NC 3373) has a jet that is shooting away from it at a velocity estimated at 3.4 million miles per hour. That speed, which equals 1,520 km/sec, is about ten times its escape velocity when the star erupts to its greatest size, and about twice its escape velocity when it's at its smallest size. "During its 20-year Great Eruption [cycle], it spits out two or three Sun's worth of material." (3.4 x 10^6 mi/hr x 1.609 km/mi ÷ 3,600 sec/hr = 1,519.6 km/sec.)

Astronomers Sylvain Veilleux, Gerald Cecil and Jonathan Bland-Hawthorne reported (in 1996) that "narrow radio jets...extend millions of light-years from the core of some active galaxies," and "Colossal forces at work in the center of an active galaxy can make themselves felt half a million light-years or more away as jets of gas moving at relativistic speeds plow into the intergalactic medium."

ASTRONOMY reported (in 1997) that starburst galaxy M82's, "massive young stars and supernovae give off furious winds of hot gas, which combine to form an even more powerful galactic wind…(which) escapes above and below the galactic plain," *SKY & TELESCOPE* reported (in 1999) the HST observation of M87's 5,000 light-year-long jet of relativistic plasma first discovered in 1916. It "travels at near light speed along a line that points nearly at Earth," and regarding spiral galaxy NGC 3079 in Ursa Minor, about 50 million light-years from Earth, *ASTRONOMY* reported (in 2000) that it produces "a superwind with an energy equivalent to that of 2,000 supernovas."

Reporting on a paper in *The Astrophysical Journal,* ASTRON-OMY stated (in 2000) that high velocity winds of active starburst galaxies such as M82, NGC 253, NGC 1569 and Arp 220 spew stellar products such as oxygen, silicon, and iron, into IGS via superwinds that escape the gravity of those galaxies, and that, "star-forming rates in galaxies…strongly hint that superwinds flowing out of young galaxies may have played an integral role in the early history of the universe." That article neglects to realize that process is going on now—not just in the "early history of the universe."

As long ago as 1977 Rowan-Robertson stated that, "In some cases there is evidence for the violent ejection of material [from Seyfert galaxies] at several thousand kilometres per second," and an article in *SCIENTIFIC AMERICAN* (in 1997) stated that astronomers at the University of Maryland and the Max Planck Institute for Radio Astronomy have found "evidence of jets of plasma emerging from quasars at almost the speed of light."

Astronomical evidence in support of matter spewing into IGS has been increasing in recent years to the point were it should no longer be ignored.

The Creation of Matter in Space.

In the literature there is a long history of various ideas regarding the creation of matter in space. Some of those ideas may be somewhat fanciful, but there is considerable relatively recent evidence in support of that general concept.

As an example (mentioned in Chapter 19), it has been suggested that new elements may be produced by fusion due to magnetic fields in the ionized plasma of the Capella system. If that is true, certainly in the centers of existing galaxies and in the centers of developing galaxies that are observed in IGS, there must be environments considerably more violent than those observed in Capella, where new elements can be born and add to those from *dead and dying galaxies.*

A number of scientists have indicated that comic rays might be responsible for the generation of some heavier elements within galaxies. Also as reported in Chapter 19, those include Harwit and Rowan-Robinson who have said that cosmic rays can split atoms to produce such elements as boron, beryllium and lithium. If those ideas are valid, one would expect cosmic ray fusion and other processes to be responsible for the generation of new elements and new compounds, in violent galaxy-forming clouds, and within the violent centers of existing galaxies.

In addition to the formation of elements in those violent environments, new compounds are also formed.

The compounds that are found in IGS are not manufactured in stars. A portion of them might come from planets and satellites previously blown into space by stellar explosions, but their quantities could not have been adequate for newly forming planets and satellites. Those compounds, some of which are quite complex, must also be produced in great quantities in the violent centers of galaxy-forming areas of IGS, and continue to be produced in the centers of galaxies as they age.

Although the exact processes by which new elements and compounds are formed are unknown, it seems that fusion and compound formation might readily occur in the violence of those areas.

The uncertainties about quantum theory that were discussed in Chapter 22 provide doubts about the exact processes of matter creation in space. That must occur, but the source of energy for that process, is not that of the vacuum of space of quantum theory, but is the radiant energy from *dead and dying galaxies.* As evidence of that creation, many elements and compounds of carbon, nitrogen, oxygen and silicon, and many others, that are common in the planets and satellites of the Sun, and undoubtedly in the other planets of our galaxy and of other galaxies, are found in clouds of matter in IGS.

The quantities of those elements and compounds undoubtedly are sufficiently abundant to provide for the formation of new planets and satellites, but the necessary abundance of hydrogen for the formation of stars is a different matter. Because the exploded stars of *dead and dying galaxies* use up much of their hydrogen before they explode, they could not provide the amounts of hydrogen required for the formation of new stars. Thus an explanation is needed for the presence of vast amounts of that element.

The Source of Hydrogen in Space.

Unlike planets and satellites, new stars are composed almost entirely of hydrogen. They might contain only small percentages of heavier elements. For example, the Sun, even at an age of several billion years, is observed to be composed of on the order of 98 percent hydrogen, and at an earlier age that percentage may have been even greater.

Because the stars of *dead and dying galaxies* cannot provide the necessary hydrogen, it must be present in the star-forming areas of both newly forming and older galaxies. That has been found to be so. If there ever had been a presence in a primeval universe, it must have been hydrogen, its component particles or their source of energy. Hydrogen is found to be abundant in that universe to this day, providing an inexhaustible supply for the formation of new stars.

Paul Marmet tells us, and other sources confirm, that, "Although hydrogen in the atomic form (H) is easily detected through radio astronomy, the molecular form is difficult to detect," atomic hydrogen emits radiation at 21 centimeters, or an absorption line at that wavelength in background radiation, but two-atom molecular hydrogen (H_2) is invisible at that wavelength, and that, "It is generally accepted that atomic hydrogen is by far the most abundant particle in the universe. It is also well established that there is about 10 times as much molecular hydrogen as there is atomic hydrogen."

Evidence of the all pervasiveness of hydrogen is supported by the work of American chemist Paul E. Rowe who has written a series of papers documenting his experiments, and those of several other researchers, that demonstrate the unexplained appearance of hydrogen in laboratory experiments involving explosions, electrical discharges and heating of metals.

Astronomers have frequently reported on the presence of atomic hydrogen in space, which is readily observable, but they neglect to consider the presence of molecular hydrogen that is difficult to observe. Atomic hydrogen reacts to produce molecular hydrogen, and that reaction should be expected to result in a ratio of molecular form to atomic form of about ten to one. The total amount of hydrogen in IGS would therefore be considerably greater than has been reported in the past, and it is undoubtedly by far the most abundant matter in the universe.

Its presence not only provides for the formation of new stars in the "gas" clouds of space, but its pervasiveness throughout all of space seems to make it the most likely candidate for the "ether" that causes the redshift of EMR.

Evidence for the Presence of Hydrogen in Space.

There have many reports in the literature over the years concerning the presence of hydrogen clouds in IGS, a few of which are mentioned here.

As stated by Bart J. Bok in *The Encyclopedia of Physics,* "It is now recognized that star formation is actively taking place deep inside large complexes of cosmic dust and associated gas. Most of the gas inside such complexes is molecular hydrogen," and *DISCOVER* (in 1994) reported that, "In the 1960s astronomers discovered isolated, galaxy-size clouds of hydrogen out there. Now an observation made by the repaired Hubble Space Telescope has revealed that intergalactic space is also permeated by a thin fog of ionized hydrogen." A team headed by Danish astronomer Peter Jakobsen of the European Space Agency made that discovery while analyzing ultraviolet light from a remote quasar, thought to be more than 10 BLYs away.

It was reported in *SCIENCE NEWS* (in 1994) that astronomer Arthur M. Wolfe of the University of California made the amazing discovery that high density hydrogen clouds, "collectively contain enough neutral hydrogen gas to equal all the gas and stars found today in spiral galaxies, and possibly elliptical galaxies as well," and *SKY & TELESCOPE* (in 1989) reported that, "The Large Magellan Cloud is one of the Milky Way's nearest companion galaxies, merely 170,000 light-years distant. It is home to 30 Doradus, a vast expanse of glowing ionized hydrogen larger than anything of its kind in our own galaxy."

As reported in *SCIENTIFIC AMERICAN* (in 1995) astronomer Nadine Dinshaw of the Stewart Observatory in Tucson, Arizona and her co-workers, using the HST, have found "in the vast stretches between galaxies...that the gas permeating those voids is not a formless smear but rather is organized into huge clouds" of hydrogen that have a minimum diameter of about a million light-years, and *SCIENCE NEWS* (in 1995) reported that astronomer John T. Stocke of the University of Colorado and coworkers have, "established that galaxies in relatively nearby parts of the universe arrange themselves in thin sheets separated by giant bubbles or voids....(they) found that two of the nine hydrogen clouds they detected lie in what appear to be empty regions of space. Extrapolating from their observations, the team estimates that low-density hydrogen clouds could collectively contain as much mass as the known population of galaxies," and "*Any theory of galaxy formation must still come to terms with this distribution of material, the researchers note.*" (Italics added for emphasis.)

It was reported in (in 1995) that European Southern Observatory (ESO) astronomers used the color and brightness of what is thought to be a faint galaxy near to galaxy BR122202-07250, "to argue that it is primeval and may account for a huge cloud of hydrogen gas that resides at a distance corresponding to a redshift of 4.38," and Carnegie Institute astronomers Ray Weymann and Lisa Storrie-Lombardi of the Carnegie Institute reported (in 1998) that the distant galaxy known as HDF 4-4743, as viewed by the HST, "did not show up in a picture taken in yellow light, appeared only as a dim blob in an image at slightly longer wavelength, and was considerably brighter viewed in near-infrared. That's because a galaxy whose short-wavelength emissions are...absorbed by hydrogen gas, which is plentiful between Earth and distant galaxies."

Dutch astronomers Edwin A. Valentijn and Paul P. van der Werf (in 1999), using the European Space Agency's Infrared Space Observatory, have detected huge amounts of hydrogen in a galaxy in Andromeda; and that their "study of galaxy NGC 891 reveals that molecular hydrogen is all over the place," and it was reported (in 2000) that Australian radio astronomers, "have imaged the entire southern sky at the so-called HII radio wavelength emitted by atomic hydrogen gas...by detecting gas clouds that emit little visible light yet that each weigh as much as several hundred million Suns. The team may have found building blocks left over from the formation of the Milky Way and its neighbors."

There seems to be little doubt about the presence of vast

amounts of hydrogen throughout the universe.

A Long History of Ideas on the Creation of Matter in Space.

One might think that the idea of new matter in space would rarely be advanced by scientists, but, as shown in the following examples, there is a long history of their ideas concerning the creation of matter in space as necessary for the continuing life of the universe. All of them have to do with the creation of new particles one at a time on the microscopic level required for the replenishment of matter in space; none on the creation of all the mass of the universe in one increment as postulated by BBT. (The first few of these items have been taken from science historian Helge Kragh's book, *Cosmology and Controversy*.)

According to British chemist William Crookes (in 1886), "the universe was in continual creation, with the genesis of matter taking place perpetually in space as a result of radiant energy transmitted into protyle." (The protyle was his idea of hypothetical primordial matter, which presumably could be hydrogen or its component particles as suggested above.)

French metaphysicist Henri Bergson is quoted as saying (in 1907), "the universe is not made, but is being made continuously. It is growing, perhaps indefinitely, by the addition of new worlds," and University of Glasgow chemist Frederick Soddy suggested (in 1908) that, "matter is breaking down and its energy being evolved and degraded in one part of a cycle of evolution, and in another part still unknown to us, the matter is being built up with the utilization of the waste energy. The consequence would be that, in spite of the incessant changes, an equilibrium condition would result, and continue indefinitely."

William Duncan MacMillan (in 1918) suggested that, as photons lose energy in their travels through space, that perhaps the energy emitted into space eventually reappears as new atoms, the later portion of which certainly agrees with what is proposed in this book, and James Jeans (in 1928) considered it "not impossible" that matter could be created continually. He said, "We are free to think of stars and other astronomical bodies as passing in an endless steady stream from creation to extinction, just as human beings pass from birth to the grave, with a new generation always ready to step into the place vacated by the old," and (in 1930) he suggested a cycling universe "being built, not out of the ashes of the old, but out of the radiation set free by the combustion of the old."

William Hunter McCrea, who favored his own version of a steady state universe, "that is forever renewing itself from its own resources," agreed (in 1952) that, "a continuous creation process can exist" (albeit "in a suitably chosen General Relativity model of the universe"). Except for the "relativity model," those ideas would be in good agreement with RUC. According to Kragh, George C. McVittie, professor of mathematics at Queen Mary College, the University of London, a leading cosmologist, who tended to favor mainstream relativistic cosmology, wrote (in 1952), "It will be shown that a 'continuous' creation process can exist in a suitably chosen relativity model of the universe."

As reported in *NATURE* (in 1967) Edwin Salpeter stated that, "It is reasonable to expect that all elements were produced, in the observed proportions, within the galaxies or within the intergalactic space of an ancient universe." Even BB cosmologists Rees and Silk (in 1970) agreed, "that some form of continuous creation of matter may not be ruled out," and Paul Davies agreed (in 1980) that, "particles of all types are produced by this mechanism ."

Davies wrote that, "the spontaneous appearance of matter out of empty space is often referred to as creation out of nothing...for the physicist, however, empty space is a far cry from nothing" and he assured us that, "The spontaneous production of new sub-atomic particles out of empty space...can happen because the energy of motion of space can be converted into matter according to the ideas of quantum theory and relativity...Calculations show that particles of all types are produced by this mechanism—electrons, neutrinos, protons, neutrons, photons, mesons and even gravitons." (Rather than the inane "energy of the motion of space," the "energy of the radiation from *dead and dying galaxies*" would be a lot more rational.)

As mentioned in Chapter 13, Sciama suggested (in 1967) that, "with newly created matter there comes into existence newly created radiation in space," Peebles et al. suggested (in 1991) that, "It would be reasonable to suppose radiation is created along with the continuous creation of baryons in space," and Martin Harwit apparently agreed with the ideas presented here regarding matter creation, wrote (in 1991) that "gravity alone can't account for galaxy formation, the only escape would be to postulate new matter created locally."

Perhaps the ideas of some well known scientists that lend support to the idea of a recycling universe should not be disregarded.

Evidence of Matter and Energy in Space.

In addition to the astronomical evidence of matter that is blown into IGS by powerful winds, and the evidence of hydrogen in IGS, there have been observations that provide direct evidence for concentrations of other matter and energy in the clouds of "gas" and "dust" in IGS.

As mentioned in Chapter 11, there have been reports of elements and compounds found in space. Some additional reports of those are presented here.

It was reported that the ROSAT X-ray observatory satellite detected (in 1993) a huge, hot gas cloud in NGC 2300 that emits X-rays—but not visible light—that was found to have a diameter of 1.3 MLYs and an average temperature of 10 million degrees. They calculated the mass of NGC 2300 to be 10 to 30 times that of the visible mass of its trio of galaxies, and it was reported in *DISCOVER* (in 1994) that astronomer Jason Cardelli of the University of Wisconsin at Madison, using the HST, has discovered traces of lead and thallium, the heaviest elements ever found beyond the solar system.

SCIENCE NEWS reported (in July,1995) that University of California astronomers Wolfe and Prochaska have, "inferred the presence of faraway clouds by analyzing the absorption of light emitted by quasars behind them. [They] found characteristic asymmetries in the shape of absorption lines created by silicon, nickel, and iron in the clouds," and, regarding four groupings of galaxies observed by the Japanese X-ray satellite ASCA, *SCIENCE NEWS* reported (also in July,1995) that, "Analysis of these data now reveals that the four clusters...contain enormous amounts of silicon and oxygen. Only massive stars can forge these elements. When such stars explode as Type II supernovas, they hurl silicon and oxygen into space, enriching the intergalactic medium."

It was reported in *ASTRONOMY* (in 1996) that, "NASA and the European Space Agency announced that the SOHO solar probe has discovered seven new elements in the solar wind: phosphorus, chlorine, potassium, titanium, chromium, manganese and nickel." Certainly, some of those solar elements must be blown into IGS.

In addition to those elements, a number of organic compounds, including carbon monoxide, carbon dioxide, methane, methanol, ethane, ethanol, ammonia, and formic acid have been found in space that could not have come from exploding stellar systems, but were somehow formed in space. (It is interesting that all of the elements and compounds that are necessary for the start of life on Earth are present in IGS. Could that be mere coincidence?)

Astronomer Marcia Bartusiak (in 1997) has reported, "Both French and Japanese astronomers have detected carbon molecules in the distant universe, which could possibly be the residue of star bursts in an even earlier era."

Henry, Briel and Bohringer reported (in 1998) to have found clusters in space that consist, not only of galaxies, but also of huge amounts of hot gas. That gas cannot be seen in visible light, but it is so hot—more than 25 million degrees Celsius—that it pours out X-rays, and science writer David Graham reported in *ASTRONOMY* (in 1999) that Jack Burns, an astronomer at the University of Missouri, has found that, "Intergalactic ionized gas is tens of millions of degrees and a bright source of X-rays. The mass of this gas is huge—three to five times the mass of the stars shining in galaxies."

Although a portion of the matter found in space may have come from *dead and dying galaxies* to accumulate in the areas of new galaxy formation, in order to provide the abundance of elements and compounds found in planets and satellites, most of them would have to be produced in the violent centers of newly forming and young galaxies.

The Density of Matter in Space.

The calculations of Appendix E show the average density of the observable universe might be about 5.6×10^{-30} grams per cubic centimeter. But the universe contains, not only the visible matter that makes up that average density, but much of the vast amounts of matter that has spewed out of generations of *dead and dying galaxies*. Therefore, its average density might be a couple of orders of magnitude greater than that of its visible mass.

An article in *ASTRONOMY* (in 1999) by David J. Eicher

reported that astronomer Chris Impey estimated that, "The stars in all of them [all galaxies] amount to only 0.3 percent of the mass of the universe." His estimate, that is equal to 333 times the visible mass, would seem to support my estimate of a "couple of orders of magnitude."

Even at that greater average density, if that matter remained evenly distributed in space, it would probably not be visible until it becomes concentrated in galaxy-forming areas in IGS (and of course those concentrations could not occur in a universe that was expanding at more than a relative low rate.)

Elements and Compounds Found in Meteorites.

There have been numerous reports of a variety of elements and compounds found in meteorites, adding to the evidence of the great age of the universe. Those have included salty water, nitrogen, oxygen, silicon, aluminum, carbon, complex carbon molecules including polycyclic hydrocarbons, diamond particles, titanium carbide, and thorium, uranium and plutonium isotopes. Some reports regarding meteorites that have struck the Earth are presented in the following paragraphs.

Edward Ander and Ernst Zinner of the University of Chicago in 1987 found tiny grains of diamond, silicon carbide and graphite in meteorites which they have suggested to have traveled through IGS for eons, and Don Eisenhour and Peter Buseck of the University of Arizona in 1993 found millimeter-size bits of silicate, called chrondrules, and tiny metal flakes in meteorites

SCIENCE NEWS (in August, 1996) stated that, "Scientists have known since the 1970s that significant amounts of aluminum-26 resided in some meteorites that have fallen to earth," and later that year reported "radioactive aluminum associated with clouds of gas near the center of the [our] galaxy," and it was reported in SCIENTIFIC AMERICAN (in 1998) that, in addition to tiny diamond particles ("microdiamonds") found in the Earth's crust, they have also been found in meteorites.

It was reported in SCIENCE NEWS in 1999 that minute quantities of thorium, uranium and plutonium isotopes have also been found in meteorites. Their relative abundances have provided evidence that the age of our galaxy might be as much as 20 BYRs, and NASA Astrochemists Max P. Bernstein, Scott A. Sandford and Louis J. Allamandola in SCIENTIFIC AMERICAN (in 1999) reported on meteorites that have been found to contain carbon molecules and carbon compounds such as methane, ethane, nucleobases, ketones, quinones, carboxylic acids, amines, amides, amino acids, and polycyclic aromatic hydrocarbons.

NASA scientists have recently reported breaking open a meteorite and finding salt crystals and a minute amount of salty water inside. Regarding the presence of salty water inside a meteorite, cosmologist Robert Clayton of the University of Chicago has commented, "This is the first real sample of the solar nebula gas, the gas from which all the planets formed." However, those are the first real samples only if previous samples that include all the matter of the Earth, Moon and other meteorites is ignored. All of their matter came from the "the solar nebula gas" of the Milky Way when it formed in IGS at least tens of billions of years ago. Those samples have been around for a long time.

Because the Earth consists largely of oxygen, silicon, carbon, aluminum and iron, their presence is no surprise. The mystery regarding the presence of those elements, other heavy elements and compounds found in meteorites, stars, globular clusters, and galaxies is solved. (Ivan R. King had written that, "Even more of a mystery is how clusters acquired any heavy elements at all, given that the Big Bang is thought to have produced only hydrogen and helium." But now that has been solved.)

The establishment is convinced that the elements and compounds in meteorites, stars, planets and satellites within our galaxy, and those of other galaxies, originated in earlier generations of stars within those galaxies. But, because of BB age problems and other considerations, it is more reasonable to believe that most of them came from *dead and dying galaxies* or were produced in the violent galaxy-forming regions of space.

NEW GALAXIES AND GALACTIC STRUCTURES

The Formation of New Galaxies.

As galaxies start to form one would expect that they would initially be of an approximately spherical or elliptical shape. But they would be in an unstable state. Like the water draining from a bath tub, the slightest disturbance in a transverse direction will start rotation, and everything starts to spin.

As mentioned in Chapter 5, Collins and Hawking have showed that, "a highly but not perfectly regular universe is unstable. The slightest deviation from regularity would tend to grow in time as the universe expanded." Although their ideas have (at least) two flaws (irregularities could not grow in a universe that was expanding at relativistic velocity, and, furthermore the universe has not expanded at such speeds), the later of those two sentences make sense.

The article cited above by Nadine Dinshaw and co-workers regarding million light-year clouds of hydrogen in the voids of IGS also stated that, "these nonluminous clouds may be part of a ghostly network of sheets and filaments that fill the universe and trace the process by which galaxies formed," and recall (from Chapter 21) the Kraan-Korteweg and Lehav mention of Bok globules that are dark clouds of interstellar gas and dust collapsing to form new stars.

As described by Vera Rubin in *SCIENTIFIC AMERICAN* (in 1983), "Galaxies designated Sa have a large central bulge surrounded by tightly wound smooth arms in which "knots" or bright regions are barely resolved. Sb galaxies have a less pronounced central bulge and more open arms with more pronounced knots. Sc galaxies have a small central bulge and well-separated arms speckled with distinct luminous segments. The progression from Sa to Sc is one of decreasing prominence of the central bulge and increasing prominence of the disk rotating about it." Her words provide an excellent description of the process of spiral galaxy formation that would be expected in a non-expanding recycling universe.

As matter gathers, the rate of rotation increases, causing the spherical cloud to flatten and expand, leaving a bulge at its center, that of an Sa galaxy. As that process continues, the rotation rate grows and the galaxy grows in diameter as its central bulge continues to shrink, to become an Sb galaxy. Eventually the galaxy becomes quite flat with a small central bulge resulting in an Sc galaxy like our Milky Way.

The words of astronomer David Eicher (in 1999) would seem to support that evolutionary process. He wrote that, "Many astronomers also believe that the central bulges in spiral galaxies are older than the galaxies' disks. Disks rotate because protogalaxies, very early on, were slowly spinning. The gas that forms disks collapses into these slowly spinning dark halos and the rate of the spin of the gas increases."

As a feeble explanation of the rotation of galaxies, Peebles has written, "The conventional picture is that the rotational angular moments of the galaxies come from tidal interactions with neighboring protogalaxies." But the regions of galaxy formation are far from each other; and in a Peebles' universe they would be rapidly growing further apart. Thus "gravitation tides" of adjacent newly-forming galaxies could have little effect on each other. Even if they were close to each other, it is not clear how that might cause young galaxies to spin up into spiral shapes.

But the process isn't as ideal as described above. There may be distortions due to nearby concentrations of matter and collisions that result in highly irregular shapes. The Eicher article also quoted University of Hawaii astronomer John Kormendy as saying that not all ellipticals are ancient. "They are also forming now when big galaxies collide violently and merge." However, it should be noted that, although it assumed that collisions could distort the shapes of galaxies, the postulated high rates of expansion of an early BB universe would rule out the possibility of galactic collisions.

ELS Theory of Galaxy Formation.

The spiral galaxy formation process presented here is essentially in agreement with the ELS theory as described by van den Bergh and Hesser in Chapter 5, except that they were convinced of BBT, and thus were forced to shorten the time for galaxy formation to a period of "about a few hundred million years" in order to maintain consistency with that theory.

In a manner similar to that theory, RUC postulates that spiral galaxies form as rotating clouds collapse, perhaps over tens to hundreds of millions of years. Their rates of rotation gradually increase, eventually creating the spiral arms that appear similar to that of a pinwheel. The clouds from which they form consist of hydrogen that exists throughout space, matter that is newly formed in the violent galaxy-forming process, and the matter and radiant energy from *dead and dying galaxies.*

Although very weak at intergalactic distances, in the absence of a force of expansion, over billions of years gravitation is sufficient to cause the increasing concentration matter and energy from old galaxies to accumulate in space. Astrophysicist L. H. Aller (in the

Encyclopedia of Physics, in 1991) has correctly concluded that, "Concentrations of the normally tenuous dust and gas are accentuated by gravitational action to form protostars which eventually shine by thermonuclear reactions." (Although he must have been aware of the acceptance of the relativistic expansion of the BB universe, perhaps he realized the impossibility of the accretion of matter in that environment, and therefore avoided mentioning that theory.)

The galaxy formation process may take billions of years, but in a universe that is at least hundreds of BYRs old, that is not a problem. And, of course, galaxies may form over a wide range of sizes depending on the quantity of matter and energy there might be in their region of space.

Although gravity provides the initial accumulation of matter in the galaxy formation process, other phenomena undoubtedly have roles in the generation of new matter, and in the dynamics of galactic formation and subsequent process. Plasma theory must certainly be involved in those processes. The ideas from the originator of plasma cosmology, Hannes Alfvén, and from a current leader in the field of plasma physics, Anthony Peratt, whose theoretical work and computer simulations have provided evidence that plasma theory might play an important role in the formation of galaxies. As a further consideration, August E. Evrard of the University of Michigan, reporting on his efforts regarding computer modeling the history of the BB universe, offers the possibility that, in order to "incorporate galaxy formation, the models would have to include effects other than gravity, notably gas pressure, heat and radiation."

Galactic Cycles.

Matter and energy from *dead and dying galaxies* accumulates in space in turbulent violence. Their matter and energy combine with hydrogen to produce violent swirling patterns; and new galaxies are born. As those galaxies mature, matter and energy spreads like that of pinwheels as violent star formation continues in their centers. New stars continue to be born in central regions, and continue to spiral outward. Although stars continue to form for some time in clumps in the galactic arms, all of them gradually die.

After a hundred or more billion years much of the galactic energy is dissipated. The rate of star formation decreases and ultimately stops, the remaining stars gradually expire, ultimately leaving little but swirling dead remnants and long lived stars such as white dwarfs, neutron stars, and other debris.

All during the life of one galaxy, and while others are in various stages of the galactic aging process, new galaxies are being formed. As with much in our experience of natural processes, galaxies have a life cycle and rebirth. But their rebirth can only spring from the matter and energy of past galaxies and that of IGS; not out-of-nothing, as in BBT, and not out of inflation's giant quantum fluctuation.

Just as it has been believed that new generations of stars continually formed within galaxies from the debris of old stars that have ended their lives in nova and supernova explosions, new generations of galaxies continually form from the debris. As Andre Assis has written, "in any large region of space...we should find approximately the same number of galaxies dying out and being formed.

Evidence for the Continuing Formation of Galaxies.

In the past, BBers have insisted all galaxies were formed within a billion years or so after the BB and therefore are about the same age. However, recent astronomical observations have indicated much later and continuing formation of galaxies in IGS. Although much of the establishment has chosen to ignore that data, some have paid attention.

Oxford University astronomer George Eftathiou was quoted in *SCIENCE* (in 1982) as saying, "People used to think that there was a certain time in the early universe when it [galaxy formation] all happened, [but] galaxies have been forming throughout the history of the universe," and as mentioned in Chapter 12, Marcia Bartusiak wrote that the idea that almost all galaxies came into existence at the same time in the distant past is "particularly imperiled," and that, "Astronomers had once seized on this explanation because it was the simplest;" but astronomical evidence shows that idea to be false.

Some of the many articles reporting evidence for the continuing formation of galaxies that have been appearing at an accelerating rate are reviewed in the following paragraphs.

As early as 1970, in a paper on the origin of galaxies, although it was contrary to accepted theory, Rees and Silk wrote that,

"Other arguments indicate the apparent youthfulness of some galaxies stem from observations of clusters of galaxies....One seems forced to the conclusion that there are newly formed galaxies born within the past 100 million years." They also stated that astronomers Halton C. Arp and Erik B. Holberg had discovered phenomena suggesting that "violent events, involving perhaps the birth of galaxies, are continually taking place."

Cornell astronomers Riccardo Giovanelli and Martha Haynes reported (in 1989) finding a "ghost of a galaxy," an immense slowly rotating cloud of hydrogen gas about 65 million light-years from us, providing evidence that galaxies could have formed "throughout the history of the universe—not just in some early, special period," as presumed by BBers.

An item in SCIENTIFIC AMERICAN (in 1993) reported, "disks of matter surrounding young stars...in the Orion Nebula...that include some of the youngest stars ever seen—about 500,000 years old," and Faye Flam reported in SCIENCE (in 1993) that, "recent observations are turning up clusters that shine with the blue light of newborn stars. NGC 7252 consists of 40 spherical globular clusters, each holding up to a million tightly packed stars." In that article astronomer Brad Whitmore of the Space Telescope Science Institute (in 1993) is quoted as saying, "The clusters in NGC 7252 are only about 50 million to 500 million years old....To an astronomer, that's just yesterday."

It was reported (also in 1993) that the ROSAT X-ray satellite observed "a small group of galaxies 150 million light-years from Earth (that) is immersed in a cloud of gas about 1.3 million light-years in diameter." It was estimated that the cloud has a mass equal to 500 billion times that of the Sun and has a temperature of about 18 million degrees Fahrenheit." Richard Mushotzky of NASA's Goddard commented on that, "such a concentration defies conventional explanation." But, of course, it is perfectly explainable as the observation of a galaxy forming area in IGS.

DISCOVER reported (in 1992) that, despite the fact that globular clusters "are supposed to be old," Jon Holtzman of the Lovell Observatory was quoted as saying that, regarding galaxy NGC 1275, about 200 million light-years distant, that, "What we have found was a group of bright objects around the galaxy's core that appear to be young globular clusters. It was totally unexpected….[and] hints at unimaginable violence in the past of our own placid galaxy, the Milky Way."

As reported in *SCIENCE NEWS* (in 1998), Joseph Silk has said, "Recent studies with the Infrared Space Observatory bolster the belief that the infrared background indeed comes from dust associated with distant objects making stars at a feverish rate," and Sara Beck has reported (in 2000) that, "Spiral Galaxies have giant clouds of molecular hydrogen, helium and dust that can readily form stars." Dwarf galaxy NCG 5253, for example, "is in the midst of extreme starbirth—it is forming stars at a fantastic pace….In recent years astronomers have discovered that dwarf galaxies such as NGC 5253 are much more common than previously supposed," and that star formation in our own galaxy, "is a slow, steady process involving the contraction of vast clouds of interstellar gas and dust."

Quoting Corey Powell, "a class of objects known as low surface brightness (LSB) galaxies has been languishing from neglect," and a group of researchers led by physics professor Gregory Bothun realized that a "previously unidentified dwarf galaxy [an LSB]…is roughly a trillion times the mass of the Sun and more than twice the size of own galaxy." Powell also reported that astronomer Stephen E. Schneider of the University of Massachusetts, "notes that the disks of these [LSB] galaxies appear very blue, implying that their stars are young and deficient in heavy elements."

DISCOVER also reported (in 1994) that, "there appear to be more far-off galaxies only because astronomers have been missing most of the near-by ones that contain so few stars that they are intrinsically dim…low surface brightness (LSB) galaxies….It's only recently that they have been revealed as a whole new class of galaxies whose members actually outnumber the more familiar galaxies we see in books and posters."

Astronomers Chris Impey of the University of Arizona and Greg Bothun of the University of Oregon, point out that, "the few stars that are found in LSB galaxies are mostly hot and blue indicating that they are young and suggesting that…[they] were probably even dimmer in the past and are just now getting around to forming stars," and Bothun (in 1997) reported that astronomers have found more than 1,000 LSB galaxies—faint blue diffuse galaxies that are deficient in heavy elements—over the past decade. "We found that in clusters of galaxies—and perhaps in the universe at large—low-surface-brightness galaxies seem to be much more numerous than conventional ones," and *SKY & TELE-SCOPE* reported (in 1994) that, "Dim, blue, diffuse (LSB) galaxies do indeed populate our part of space. They simply haven't been noticed because their surface brightnesses are very low—typically 10 to 20 times dimmer than the Earth's darkest night sky;" all of which provides support of the continuing birth of new galaxies.

SCIENCE NEWS reported (in 1995) that, "Some bright objects identified as distant quasars may in fact represent infant galaxies fiery with star birth, and *ASTRONOMY* (in 1997) reported that, "In our neighborhood astronomers still see examples of galaxies merging" and "Galaxy formation by this process is still going on." But the brilliance of the center of galaxies is merely due to the violence of that star-forming region, not the presence of black holes or quasars. As mentioned in Chapter 16, Stanislav G. Djorgovski of Cal Tech has agreed that, "Some bright objects identified as distant quasars may in fact represent infant galaxies' fiery birth."

In view of such overwhelming astronomical evidence in support the continuing formation of new stars and galaxies, some cosmologists have felt it necessary to deny Standard BBT regarding this matter. As Halton Arp has asked, "Astronomers are gradually coming to accept them (objects that seem to be very young) as recently formed…[but] what material exists to form them? Where is the leftover, remnant material out of which they were formed?"

Matter and energy from *dead and dying galaxies* plus the hydrogen that permeates all of space provides the answer to those questions.

The Nuclei of Galaxies.

It's suggested here that, in order for the matter and energy for the formation of new galaxies to accumulate in space, a gravitational nucleus is required. It is further suggested that long-lived white dwarfs, neutron stars, quasars and black holes (if they really exist), and other matter left over from dead galaxies might survive for hundreds of billions of years or more, long after their original galaxies have disappeared. Much of that matter remains in the location of their former galaxies to provide the gravitational core about which new galaxies form. (Even if that matter were to stray due to external forces, it would undoubtedly stray together.)

Astronomer Roberto Méndez has stated that, "Some of the stars might be older than the galaxies themselves. There is good reason to believe such an ancient population exists somewhere…all the stars we see in our galaxy are partly made of stuff that must have been created inside an earlier generation of stars." It is suggested here that some of those old stars are from older galaxies.

As reported in *SCIENCE NEWS* (in 1999) two teams of astronomers, Rodrigo Ibata of the European Southern Observatory and Harvey Richer of the University of British Columbia and their colleagues, in searching for MACHOS, thought to be the missing dark matter of the universe, believe they have instead found that white dwarfs might account for about half of the Milky Way's missing matter. Ben R. Oppenheimer of the University of California at Berkeley and his colleagues reported (in *SCIENTIFIC AMERICAN* in 2001) "38 white dwarfs within 480 light years of the Sun," and Ibata stated that they, "may trace the oldest building blocks of the galaxy," The great numbers of white dwarfs that have recently been found would tend to support the idea that there were large contributors to the gravitational center around which our galaxy formed.

Neutron stars might lose their mass, in the form of beams of matter and radiation, faster than black holes might lose theirs by the hypothesized Hawking radiation process, but that process might be slow enough for both of those to survive for hundreds of billions of years.

Stars of such great age might be Augustus Oemler's "ghostly remains" of spiral galaxies mentioned above that provide the gravitation needed for the formation of new galaxies. Not only might that explain the initial accretion of matter for some new galaxies, but might explain the vast numbers of white dwarfs that are found in our galaxy. It might also explain the presence of some, possibly very old, neutron stars, quasars, and even black holes.

SKY & TELESCOPE of August, 1998 stated that, "Theoreticians tell us that any star less massive than 8 times the mass of the Sun will end its life as a white dwarf," Matt Burleigh of the University of Leichester, England has said, "That means that over 90 percent of stars will eventually become white dwarfs," and *ASTRONOMY* of April, 2000, stated that our galaxy "may harbor an enormous population" of white dwarfs," and asked, "Where did (they) come from?" That article suggested that they could be the MACHOs [previously postulated to be brown dwarfs] that could "solve the dark matter problem in the galaxy," but it is much more likely that they are remains of old stars in a galaxy that is hundreds of billions of years old.

Donald Goldsmith (in 1991) wrote that, "Since nearly every star has become or will become a white dwarf, they exist by the billions throughout the Milky Way. To be honest, astronomers have found white dwarfs only by the thousands, but since white dwarfs are intrinsically faint, we know that we have found only those closest to us and thus can extrapolate with confidence to derive an enormous total for the number of white dwarfs." Based on their great abundance and great age it seems logical to presume that white dwarfs remaining in the area of an old galaxy would contribute significantly to the mass needed for the nucleus of a new galaxy.

Goldsmith went on to say that, "The density of matter in a neutron star makes the density of a white dwarf look like a vacuum: At 100 trillion grams per cubic centimeter, the neutron-star density is a hundred million times greater than the density of a white dwarf." Thus, due to such great mass their lives might be extremely long and, if their numbers are great enough, they might also contribute to the gravitational nuclei of newly forming galaxies.

If black holes should evaporate by Hawking radiation, or by some other unknown process, that would seem to occur at an extremely slow rate, resulting in enormously long lives. Therefore, the gravity of their masses might also contribute to the nuclei of new galaxies.

SCIENCE NEWS reported (In 2000) that Richard Mushotzky has said that, "The big thing we have learned in the last 2 years from the Hubble [HST] and the Keck telescopes...and now Chandra [Chandra X-ray observatory satellite] is that massive black holes and the galaxies [they reside in] are intimately related to each other." But exactly how is a mystery. "Does the galaxy come first, or does the massive black hole become the seed around which the galaxy will originate?" RUC might now provide the answer to Mushotzky's question.

Regarding the galactic nuclei in a different vein, although quasars may be present within galaxies, the belief that quasars are radiated energy from the accretion of matter by black holes in the center of galaxies is highly questionable. As discussed in Chapter 16, many distant bodies that are thought to be quasars are observed only as points of light, so that their form cannot be resolved. There apparently are at least two types of brilliant, massive kinds of objects that have been called quasars; those that appear to be "naked " and those that appear to have "fuzz."

Those that appear to be naked would be those that have been called grey holes: possibly massive stars that weren't able to acquire enough matter to develop into black holes. The others, that are thought to be the radiation emanating from matter falling into the clutches of black holes in the centers of galaxies are entirely different. However, it is much more reasonable to believe that they are not quasars, but the violent star-forming centers of galaxies.

(The calculations of Appendix E show a quasar that is thought to be one light-day in diameter, and having the mass of 100 million average stars, would have an average density that is about 3.6×10^{17} times greater than the average density of a galaxy like the Milky Way. If the centers of galaxies really are violent star-forming areas—rather than quasars as believed by BBers—those areas might be expected to have such great densities.)

As discussed in Chapter 17, Kip Thorne wrote that, "It is still possible to explain all the observed properties of radio galaxies and quasars using an alternative non-black-hole engine...[that] might form at the center of galaxies...[and] behave much like a hole's accretion disk...and magnetic field lines anchored in the star could spin and fling out plasma in jets. " (He had assumed a single giant star, rather than the central star-forming area of a galaxy.)

As mentioned in Chapter 16, Neil Comins has written that massive black holes can only act gravitationally on the rest of the universe. They have no "magical ability to suck in" gas and stars orbiting around them.

Those comments by Thorne and Comins would tend to support violent star-forming centers rather than black holes in the center of galaxies.

Galactic Structures.

In a very large and very old universe, it is suggested that over tens of billion of years, galaxies gather into clusters, in additional tens of billions years, clusters form into superclusters and, in many more tens of billions of years, superclusters form into the structures that have been called walls, or sheets, and voids.

The energy and matter of the universe spewed into IGS from billions of galaxies for hundreds of billion of years. That, combined with the hydrogen (or the particles that make up hydrogen, and possibly other elementary particles) that permeate all of space provide what is often referred to as the "gas" and "dust" that accumulate due to gravitation to start to form new galaxies.

Although the gravitational attraction between the masses in those regions would be extremely small, over the billions of years of their development, it could be sufficient to cause galactic "clustering." In some cases they might eventually become close enough so that the shapes of some galaxies would become distorted due to gravity, and collisions might occasionally occur.

Over even more billions of years the feeble gravitational attraction between such clusters would result in larger formations, and so on, until structures such as the Great Wall and giant voids are formed (which, of course, couldn't happen in a BB universe that was expanding at relativistic speed).

Astronomer John Kormendy has stated that, the Sloan Digital Sky Survey "should soon nail down our understanding of large scale structure" and that, "It's suspicious that the largest scale things we see, voids and superclusters, are almost always as large as the survey volume. That suggests that maybe we haven't found the largest things that exist out there yet."

If that were found to be true, it would be bad news for RUC. However, a team of Yale, Harvard and MIT astronomers reported (in *SCIENTIFIC AMERICAN* in 1992) on the results of the Las Campanas Redshift Survey. One member of the team, Robert Kirshner, said, "Although the survey has revealed voids and clusters comparable to the Great Wall, it has found nothing larger. Our preliminary look at the data doesn't suggest there are any hyperstructures." And *SCIENCE NEWS* reported (in 2000) that the 2dF [for 2 degree field] Galaxy Redshift Survey, reveals that the largest clusters in the universe (superclusters) are no larger than 250 million light-years in length. That article also reported that that analysis of data from the Las Campanas Redshift Survey, completed in 1990 had indicated that, "there were no structures larger than the Great Wall and Great Void."

In support of that, as stated in Chapter 16, astronomer Patrick Osmer reported that, statistical analysis show quasars randomly distributed; findings that favor the assumption that, on a large scale, the universe is homogeneous. Even Paul Davies had written that "In the real universe there is not the slightest hint of a center or edge." The absence of the discovery of larger structures as the range of telescopes is increased—a homogeneous universe—and one without a discernible center or edge, are what would be expected of the extremely large, extremely old, recycling universe that is postulated in this book.

A Galactic Structure Problem.

It is believed that giant galactic structures have formed due to mutual gravitational attraction, which would apply to RUC as well as all other cosmologies. However, that belief presents an unsolved problem. If it is correct, why hasn't that accumulation continued, and resulted in the collapse of those structures?

Although BBT provides no answer, there must be a counter-force of some kind that prevents that collapse. In the case of stellar systems and galaxies, orbital relationships provide an explanation for non-collapse, but that doesn't provide an explanation for giant galactic structures.

No positive explanation is offered here. However, it is suggested that the necessary repulsion may be the result of matter and radiation departing from the galaxies in a manner similar to that of stellar winds that exert pressure on their surroundings. That pressure may be sufficient to overcome their minute mutual gravitational attraction and prevent their collapse. (It is also possible that, if there is any net expansion of large areas of the universe, it might be due to that force.)

If that answer isn't adequate, regardless of what the true cosmology might be, there must be some other unknown force that prevents the collapse of galactic formations.

NEW STARS AND PLANETS

In addition to evidence that stars form in intergalactic accumulations of matter and energy, there is also reason to believe that they continue to form in maturing galaxies. However, that process is quite different than envisioned by the establishment.

New Stars and Planets Not from Supernovas.

As discussed in Chapter 19, the widely accepted belief that new stars are formed from the remains of supernovas within their galaxy is not only faulty, but totally impossible.

A review of the outcome of that discussion is presented as follows:

- If a supernova the size of SN1987A were to explode within the space of our solar system, and all its matter were to stay in that space, its average density would only be on the order of 100 billionth of that of the Sun, far too low for the formation of a solar system.
- Even if such a supernova were to occur within the space of our galaxy, its exploding matter would not remain in that space.
- Much of the matter of a supernova leaves it, in the form of radiation at the speed of light, neutrinos at or near to that speed, and matter that is ejected at greater than its escape velocity.
- If a supernova the size of SN1987A exploded within the Milky Way, and its matter were evenly distributed in that space, its average density would be only about one part in 10^{33} times that of the Sun.
- Because only about one supernova per 40 years occurs within the space of our entire galaxy, only one supernova in millions of years might be close enough to shower our solar system with a few particles of matter.
- Because the stars that explode as supernovas, or other exploding stars, have expended much of their hydrogen, they cannot supply the element that is essential for the formation of new stars.
- It is known that hydrogen is present in interstellar space, but there is no reason to expect that a supernova explosion could cause it to accrete to form a new star.

The Abundance of Elements.

It is clear that the various elements of the universe could not have been produced in BB fusion, and that the matter for new stars could not have come from exploding stars within their own galaxies.

There is little doubt that the source matter for new stars and planets comes from energy and matter from the remains of *dead and dying galaxies*, the hydrogen that permeates all of space, and matter newly generated in the the violent star-forming areas, in both newly forming galaxies and throughout their lives.

The RUC cosmology presented here doesn't provide quantitative abundances of elements, but it does provide a qualitative explanation for the presence of the matter found in our surroundings, in other galaxies, and in space. It is reasonable to expect that all of the elements except hydrogen were produced in the observed proportions within old galaxies or in all of those areas.

The fact that many of the common elements of the Earth, and compounds consisting of common elements, have been detected in clouds of matter in IGS, and in newly forming galaxies within those clouds, provides support for that opinion.

Those compounds are not manufactured in stellar processes, and their quantities, and those of heavy elements found in space, are greater than could have come from planets and satellites blown up by exploding stars. Both those compounds and those elements must be produced in the violent centers of newly forming galaxies, and they continue to be produced in the centers of galaxies in decreasing amounts as they age.

Elliptical Galaxies.

Some reports have suggested that elliptical galaxies are relatively old, but there appears to be considerable evidence which denies that.

As mentioned above, as galaxies start to form in IGS one would expect them to be of an approximately spherical or elliptical shape, and as John Kormendy stated, not all ellipticals are ancient, "They are also forming now," and, as astronomers Robin Ciardillo and George Jacoby of Pennsylvania State University have reported (in 1993) that, "Elliptical Galaxy M105 in Leo—long considered to be a prototype of its class—has been found to contain little if any dark matter....The fastest moving objects tend to occur near the center, while slower ones generally lie farther out."

In the recycling universe postulated here, the young stars of young galaxies would be expected to eject less matter into surrounding space. Therefore, the observation of little or no dark matter in the vicinity of elliptical galaxies would confirm their young age.

John Kormendy indicated that ellipticals are the result of collisions, and it was reported in *SCIENTIFIC AMERICAN* (in 1991) that, "Computer models and observations indicate that these cosmic collisions may form elliptical galaxies and activate quasars." But it would be expected that such collisions would result in irregular shapes rather than symmetrical ellipses. It is more reasonable to believe that galaxies that had not been disturbed might be elliptical, that is, until they had spun up enough to become significantly flattened. (Although galactic collisions might occur in a non-expanding universe, that seems impossible in an expanding BB universe.}

New Stellar System Formation.

Over many billions of years, weak gravity causes the sparse matter in IGS to start to accrete. As it accretes, density increases; as density increases, gravity increases, and so on, until the density of the matter in surrounding areas becomes too sparse. During that process a swirling cloud forms and continues to grow in mass and energy. Matter and energy continue to gather until it becomes sufficiently dense for the birth of stars to commence throughout the cloud. As explained in *SCIENCE NEWS* (In 1995), "A star forms when an interstellar cloud collapses under its own weight, forming a ball dense enough to ignite nuclear fuel at its core."

Because the quantity of hydrogen far exceeds that of other matter in those galaxy-forming areas, its density and pressure become sufficiently great for fusion to start in localized areas, and stars are born. Those dense concentrations of hydrogen reject or exclude other forms of matter that is left to orbit them and eventually accumulate into planets and their satellites.

Just how that might occur is somewhat of a mystery. Astronomers admit that they don't know how planets form around stars, but a description of that process might be similar to that of astrophysicists Bernstein, Sandford and Allamandola who wrote, "the stage for life was set more than four billion years ago when a cold, dark interstellar cloud collapsed into the swirling disk of fiery gas and dust that spawned our solar system....According to this theory, ice from the mother cloud boiled off, and molecules broke apart and were rearranged in the violence of planet formation."

Astronomer Virginia Trimble declared that, "Galaxies, in all their beauty and variety, come from large lumps of gas....Somehow the mass of a cold cloud, the distribution in it of magnetic fields, turbulence, dust, and probably other things suffice to determine when stars will form, how many, what their masses will be, and how many will be parts of binary systems of different types." She wrote that the star formation process, "is a collective one, yielding groups and clusters of dozens to millions of stars." Her description is also similar to the processes described for RUC.

Regarding planet formation, Trimble also wrote, "Either something had acted on the Sun from outside to tear loose the planets, or a single structure had evolved into both the Sun and planets at the same time." But no explanation was given how such "tearing" might have occurred, or how the matter of an early Sun, composed almost entirely of hydrogen, could have provided the elements that are found in planets.

Ron Cowan (in *SCIENCE NEWS* in May 2001) quoted Adam S. Burrows of the University of Arizona as saying that, "Ultimately...astronomers may be able to use such properties as rotation, the abundance of heavy elements, and orbital motion to distinguish a planet from an object that formed in a starlike manner. For now we don't know in detail how stars (and planets) form."

Not only do they not know in detail, but they don't have more than a vague idea. However, the acceptance of the recycling universe presented in this book may enable astronomers to achieve clearer understanding of that process.

Continuing Star Formation within Galaxies.

The violent interior of our galaxy, and similar galaxies, contains much of what remains of the hydrogen, other matter and energy that accumulated during their formation in IGS, and continues to produce new stellar systems. The centers of such galaxies, rather than being giant quasars, are violent star-forming areas that continue to exist, but with decreasing intensity as they age.

In addition to Kip Thorne's comment mentioned above about galaxy centers behaving like black hole accretion disks, *SCIENCE NEWS* reported (in 1995) that, "Some bright objects identified as distant quasars may in fact represent infant galaxies fiery starbirth," and Ivan King tells us that there are galaxies called Seyferts that have bright "energetic" centers and they are members of a class of galaxies whose centers are so bright that "they completely dominate the appearance of the galaxy," and their spectral lines "seem to indicate rapid motion toward and away from us, as if the gas were expanding out of the nucleus at thousands of kilometers per second."

King doesn't know the reason for that behavior, "except that some energetic event is going on at the center of the galaxy." But what is going on in the centers of those galaxies should now be apparent.

Veilleux, Cecil and Bland-Hawthorne reported (in 1996) that, "M82, about 10 million light-years from the earth, is distinguished by an outpouring of incandescent gas from the area around its core. Astronomers have deduced that the upheaval is caused by the rapid formation of stars near the galactic nucleus. The resulting heat and radiation cause dust and gas from the galactic disk to rush into intergalactic space." What could provide a better description of the formation of stars in the centers of galaxies—emitting jets of matter—in accordance with RUC?

Veilleux et al. went on to mention that, "prodigious luminosity—and the spectacular 'radio jets' [highly focused streams of energetic material] that stretch over millions of light-years from the centers of hyperactive young galaxies known as quasars," providing further support for RUC.

In reference to the jets that are thought to result from the matter that has accreted by black hole gravitational force, E. N. Parker has written regarding Peratt's work on plasma cosmology, that "In conventional astronomy it is assumed that these jets were caused by huge black holes in the center of galaxies, Peratt claims that exotic explanations such as this are not necessary, magnetic energy trapped and squeezed as a result of the 'pinch effect' can produce jets."

SKY & TELESCOPE reported (in 1997) that there are "dark roughly spherical clouds of interstellar dust that are collapsing to form new stars," and as reported in SCIENCE NEWS (in 1997), David Spergel of Princeton University has said that, "Our galaxy continues to form huge numbers of stars, but no one has identified the reservoir of gas required to sustain such activity....Now, researchers say that a collection of high-speed, wispy hydrogen clouds, discovered in 1963, is the remnant of the gaseous reservoir that built the Milky way, Andromeda, and the rest of the nearby galaxies known collectively as the Local Group. In addition, these clouds could fuel starbirth in the Milky Way for another 3 billion years or so. Spergel's "reservoir of gas" has now been identified!

Although Marcia Bartusiak (in *ASTRONOMY* in 1998) declared that, "when the universe was several billion years younger, galaxies were producing 50 to 100 solar masses worth of stars each year....[but] The Milky Way now manufacturers only about two new stars a year." However, it would seem that she might have based her estimate of the star-forming rate on areas that surround us, perhaps neglecting to consider what is going on in central portions of our galaxy.

SCIENCE NEWS reported (in May, 1998) a galaxy 10 million light-years distant that has a disk of gas 130 light-years in diameter that is thought to surround a black hole. Although hidden by "dust" in the visual range, it is observed in infrared. "The images indicate that most of the radiation comes from the birth of stars rather than from material spiraling into the galaxy's black hole," and (in October 1998), "infrared images reveal that many of these [bluish knots of light] are in fact star-forming regions within much larger, older galaxies." As mentioned in Chapter 21, *SKY & TELESCOPE* has reported that Bok globules, "clouds of interstellar gas and dust...are collapsing to form new stars."

The End of Star Formation.

Although stars continue to form in the centers of galaxies, where most their matter and energy is the concentrated, as they age, the matter and energy needed for that process eventually becomes too sparse for that process to continue.

Galaxies like ours, for example, that are in their mid-life continue to produce stars in their violent centers, but in many more billions of years that will cease. All of those stars will continue to lose matter and energy to space. Most of them will eventually use up their hydrogen, blow up and spread much of their remains into IGS.

Observations indicate that star-forming areas continue to exist in molecular clouds within the spiral arms of the Milky

Way, and undoubtedly the same is true of other spiral galaxies. But star formation is less prevalent in less violent regions further and further from the centers of galaxies, which is consistent with stars of greater average age that are found in the outer portions of galaxies.

As reported by Mark Dickinson of the University of California and Peter R. Eisenhardt of the Jet Propulsion laboratories in the *ASTROPHYSICAL JOURNAL* (in 1992), a study of distant radio galaxy B2 0902+34, "revealed an unsettling finding." The team detected what appears to be a bright red halo around that galaxy. If that halo is confirmed, it suggests that stars at the outskirts of the galaxy are redder, and possibly older than those at the core—a phenomena never before observed."

However, it has long been observed that there are greater quantities of young blue stars within the disks of spiral galaxies and greater numbers of older red stars in the outer regions of those galaxies. That had been noted many years ago by Walter Baade who had classified bright blue stars as Population I stars, and faint red stars as Population II stars. That is consistent with a report by B. Chen of the University of Barcelona in the *ASTROPHYSICAL JOURNAL LETTERS* (in 1998) on a study showing that stars within the Milky Way's disk are, on average, considerably younger than those in its halo.

Case Western University physicists/cosmologists Lawrence M. Krauss and Glenn D. Starkman wrote (in 1999), "But stars will eventually die, and their birth rate has declined dramatically since an initial burst about 10 billion years ago." (They also wrote that, "About 100 trillion years from now, the last conventionally formed star will wink out," which is their guess about the future life of the universe based on an assumption of a BB universe, as opposed to that of a universe that might recycle forever.)

Eventually the matter and energy in the central star-forming areas of galaxies becomes insufficient for star birth to continue. Most of the stars in the galaxy gradually expire, leaving only remnants of stars, old white dwarfs, neutron stars and other debris, possibly including the remains of planets and satellites that weren't destroyed by the explosions of their stars. The remains of such burnt-out galaxies might last for eons in the space of the universe, to eventually provide the nuclei of new galaxies.

EXPANSION OF THE UNIVERSE

A Non-Expanding Universe.

It shouldn't be surprising that Doppler redshift shows the distance between many stars in a spiral galaxy is increasing (or decreasing), or that the distance between some galaxies in the local group is increasing (or decreasing), perhaps due to rotation or unknown disturbances. But there could not be more than a very low rate of expansion throughout the universe as a whole.

Some of the reasoning that denies more than that low rate, and in particular denies that of the extreme rates postulated for the expansion of a BB universe, that have been presented in Chapter 21 are reviewed here.

- If the universe is expanding at any more than a fraction of the rates postulated by BBT, the accretion of matter that is necessary for the formation of galaxies would be impossible.
- Increasing distance between galaxies can provide no explanation for the formation of giant galactic structures, nor can it explain the collisions of galaxies that are often reported in the literature.
- If accumulations of matter had somehow occurred, the extremely weak gravitational attraction of matter at their edges couldn't overcome the force of expansion, and they would gradually be destroyed.
- The local gravitational attraction of various bodies, such as galaxy-star, star-planet and planet-satellite systems, is said to overcome the expansive force of the universe. But, in order for that to be so, the attractive force between all of those pairs would all have to be of just the proper magnitude to overcome the expansive force of the universe, obviously an impossible situation.
- Any cosmology that incorporates an ever expanding universe, beyond the distance I refer to as the c-barrier (Whitrow's paradox), requires relative speeds greater than that of light.
- BB expansion, said to be at the speed of light or greater, would have required infinities of energy.
- The nothingness of empty space can't have momentum as is said to cause the expansion of the space of the BB universe.

- The nothingness of empty space can't respond to gravity as is said to cause the deceleration of expansion of the space of the BB universe.
- If galaxies and galactic formations, that are held together by gravity, don't expand as time goes forward, they won't shrink as time is looked back on, and the universe couldn't be thought of shrinking back to a singularity as BBers like to recount.
- Any cosmology, such as BBT, that postulates the expansion of space is erroneous. Empty space is nothing: and "nothing" can't expand.
- Inconsistencies regarding the perceived velocities of quasars and their flares, that appear to be superluminal, can only be explained by a universe that, on the large scale, is not expanding.

If, on the large scale, portions of the universe were found to be expanding, it can only be at a low rate; and that expansion might only be due to the combined forces of matter and radiation departing from the galaxies in a manner similar to that of stellar winds exerting pressure on their surroundings.

Redshift in a Non-Expanding Universe.

As discussed in Chapter 21, it cannot be denied that the redshift of stars within our galaxy and of some nearby galaxies is the result of Doppler effect. However, in a universe that, on the large scale, is not expanding, the redshift of radiation from very distant bodies isn't primarily Doppler, and it certainly isn't cosmological, that is, due to expanding space. As far as known, the remaining possibilities leave only tired light, GRS, Halton Arp's new matter theory, the Wolf effect, or some combination of those.

An important consideration regarding tired light phenomena is that, if it does occur, it is the result of an "ether" in IGS. That ether may be due to some unknown matter, forces or fields, as some believe but, it more likely is the result of hydrogen that is known to permeate all of space.

Paul Marmet has suggested that, "the presence of large amounts of hard-to-detect molecular hydrogen in interstellar space could provide an alternate explanation to the Big Bang theory," that is, it could be the matter that causes the redshift of radiation from

~ 303 ~

distant bodies in the space of a non-expanding universe. He believes that inelastic collisions of light passing through hydrogen (H or H2) result in redshifts that are "indistinguishable from the phenomena caused by the Doppler effect." (He undoubtedly meant "intergalactic space" as well as "interstellar space"), and, based on his research and experimentation Paul Rowe has suggested that a "matrix of the protons and electrons" from which hydrogen is formed may be the ether that fills all of space.

Those ideas are supported by the discoveries of vast amounts of hydrogen in space that have been made in recent years. However, it is suggested here that tired light redshift can't account for the all of the redshift of radiation from distant massive bodies in space. There must be other causes of that redshift; and GRS must be an important contributor.

HEAT DEATH OF THE UNIVERSE

It is accepted by the establishment that the universe will ultimately succumb due to a high entropy death as believed to be demanded by the Second Law of Thermodynamics. Those cases where evidence is found of local decreases of entropy are explained similarly to the statement by physicists Menas Kafatos and Robert Nadeau in *The Conscious Universe*: "Even though the second law of thermodynamics is not violated globally and entropy increases overall, (there are) organic life forms, that end up being more ordered at the expense of the environment which acquires a higher entropy."

However there have been many scientists who have suggested that the heat death of a universal increase in entropy will not occur. Several examples of those that might suggest the possibility of a decrease of entropy in a recycling universe are presented here.

British physicist and engineer William Rankine, who, as early as 1852 speculated that, "the world, as now created, may possibly be provided within itself the means of reconcentrating its physical energies, and renewing its activity and life," and William MacMillan who said, "that there was no reason to assume that entropy would always increase and leave the universe as a dead soup of radiation."

Frederick Soddy believed that waste energy from one "cycle of evolution" is utilized to build new matter in another, "an equilibrium condition would result, and continue indefinitely," and

James Jeans suggested the creation of new generations of astronomical bodies "out of the radiation set free by the combustion of the old."

Paul Davies said that the "laws of physics bestow upon matter and energy an uncanny ability to organize themselves, a dispensation to arrange themselves and evolve...from simple to complex," and Barrow & Silk have told us that,"on small scales, entropy undoubtedly decreases as matter rearranges itself to form highly ordered living systems....[but] The net amount of disorder or entropy in the universe...does not increase significantly as stars form and die."

Helge Kragh has written regarding Hoyle's SST, "As in the earlier cosmologies of Nernst, MacMillan and physicist/cosmologist Robert A. Millikan, there was no heat death in Hoyle's model. He argued that although the entropy increases locally, the creation of matter prevents a global increase of entropy toward a maximum value," and that William Crookes also rejected the cosmic heat death of the universe.

Also according to Kragh, "Most likely, Nernst's interest in cosmology received inspiration from Svante Arrhenius, the great Swedish physical chemist (Nobel laureate in 1903)....Unwilling to accept the the universal heat death, Arrhenius searched...for mechanisms that would obliterate it. He believed he had found in radiation pressure a mechanism which allowed the possibility that 'the cosmic development can take place in a continuing cycle, where there is no trace of any beginning or end.'"

As mentioned above, Richard Tolman, stated that he saw "no evidence against the assumption that the material universe has always existed."

John Boslough has written in *Masters of Time* that Stephen Hawking believed that, "if the universe eventually collapsed...the dissipated energy lost during the entropy process would begin to gather itself together, then gradually work to reverse entropy. Disordered states would gradually become more ordered."

Roger Penrose clearly indicated his belief that, when the recycling BB universe re-explodes, its entropy would be at a very low value. Presumably, if that is acceptable to Penrose for a BB universe, it should also be acceptable for RUC. It would seem that all of those who had accepted a recycling BB universe must have believed that entropy must reset to zero or to a very low value.

Japanese physicist Yoichiro Nambu, famous as the originator of the idea of quarks and other advances in particle physics, "calculates that virus-size particles, when placed in a cusp-shaped container violate gravity and entropy. Perhaps they conceal a clue as to how life-forms defy entropy and become ever more organized," and Seth Fraden of Brandeis University is quoted (in *SCIENCE NEWS* in 1998) as having said, "Scientists, however, are discovering with apparent glee how often the road to disorder if paved with a little useful order. It's still not fully realized how general that phenomena is and how rich in potential."

James Paul Wesley has written in *Advanced Fundamental Physics* (in 1991) that, "Human bodies, themselves, constitute thermodynamic order created out of a sea of chaos: their bodies are a pool of low entropy compounds created out of an environment of high entropy compounds. Humans derive high utility mechanical energy or work from low utility disordered thermal energy which can create little order," and he asks, "What are the conditions that permit low entropy stars and planets to evolve out of high entropy clouds of gas and dust?...Astrophysicists, astronomers, and cosmologists have recognized the fact that stellar formation from gas and dust clouds constitutes an entropy reducing process; but no one seems to have here-to-fore appreciated the extremely important general significance of this fact."

He goes on to say that, "All of the thermodynamic ordering processes that we see in the universe, including life itself, arise from the fact that deep space is cold, a sink at 2.7° K into which high entropy waste radiation can be dumped. The validity of the primary law for ordering processes in nature depends upon the coldness of deep space."

Wesley may have gotten much of that correct. But, apparently because he has been taught that MBR photons throughout space are at that 2.7° K, he has accepted that to be its temperature. But of course, that isn't so. Those photons are not there, and, in any case, radiation passes through distant space without heating it. (Does the Sun's infrared radiation warm the empty space between it and Earth?) The true temperature of the empty space of the universe is zero K.

[It should be understood that only matter can be heated by EMR; not empty space. But it can't be any old matter. It's particles must have some "conductivity," and it must be "tuned" to the wavelength of the particular radiation. That is, like the elements of a radio antenna, it must be large enough to intercept some of the energy at that wavelength and reradiate some of it. If the particles are too small (compared to one quarter of that wavelength) they will not "receive" that "signal," that is, they will not be "heated," and they will not reradiate that energy.]

Although the ideas about exceptions to the Second Law of Thermodynamics may by correct, there is an alternate possibility for escape of the universe from heat death (which Wesley has touched upon) that doesn't require denial of that long tested and accepted law.

It is suggested here that matter may be regenerated and that galaxies are able to form as a result of energy that accumulates in space without violating that law. That energy includes all of the EMR that spews into IGS at the speed of light from all the stars that exist in all the galaxies in the universe, which includes all of the "dissipated" heat energy from all of those. It must be remembered the Second Law, that requires the nonreversibility of ever increasing entropy, was invented to deal with the lack of usefulness of heat (energy) at temperatures lower than ambient for the generation of mechanical energy in what are called "heat engines."

Here on Earth, and undoubtedly throughout the universe, when matter has a temperature that is above that of its surroundings (above ambient), that differential in heat "potential", if sufficiently great, can be utilized to produce mechanical energy. But when the differential temperature is at or below ambient, that is impossible. That idea has been extended to the belief that low energy heat, that is, long-wave EMR, can be of no use in the universe, and thus gradual cooling—heat dissipation—will eventually cause its death.

The Second Law had to do with the practical problem of power generation here on Earth, and the key to that is the idea of differential temperature. As one example of this, there have been experiments where the difference in sea water temperature from that of "quite cold" at depths to "somewhat warm" near the surface has been used to produce power.

In the same manner, long-wavelength heat energy that is radiated into space is not lost. It is available energy, although low compared to the temperature of some of the matter of galaxies, it is relatively high compared to the absolute zero temperature of empty space. Thus its energy might well be used in the processes of new galaxy formation; and the universe may not die the heat death. That reasoning does not deny the Second Law. Instead, because the temperature of empty space is zero, the difference between radiated energy and the coldness of space can be utilized in the generation of new galaxies.

The temperature of ice is 273 degrees C or K above absolute zero, and even the coldest temperature on the Earth of about -73 C (-100 F) is 200 degrees (C or K) above absolute zero. It would seem that nature should be able to utilize the energy available in those temperature differentials. Heat radiation, even at temperatures that low, is EMR, which (with the exception of a small percentage of redshift) like any other radiation, can travel vast distances through space without loss of energy; and that energy can be utilized in galaxy formation processes in IGS.

Nowadays EMR in the microwave range, at frequencies lower than infrared by a factor of about 100,000 (photons having energy that much lower) is regularly utilized to cook our food. For a whole century EMR in the low radio frequency range, at frequencies lower than infrared by a factor of about one billion has been used to produce detectable signal energy in antennas thousands of miles from their source. Those phenomena illustrates that energy in the infrared range, and well below it, might be utilized in space in other natural processes.

Some theorists have stated that the temperature of empty space is quite high. However, empty space is nothing, so that its temperature can only be considered to be absolute zero.

Some BBers have indicated their belief to be that the temperature of space is that of the MBR, 2.7 K. However, radio astronomer Adrian Webster has reported in a paper on the MBR in 1974 that the temperature of formaldehyde found in space is about one degree K. That raises the question of how the formaldehyde ever got that cold. If, according to BBT, the temperature of space is that of the MBR, it should have warmed the formaldehyde to 2.7 K. That bit of evidence tends to confirm two important ideas. One is that the equivalent temperature of empty space is below 2.7 K (undoubtedly zero); and the second is that, because it is not true that space is warmed to the temperature of the MBR as believed by BBers, they are denied a reason to believe in its presence.

(In support of that, recall the quotation in Chapter 6 from John

Gribbin that, "what Olbers is telling us is that the universe is not in thermodynamic equilibrium. Most of it is cold, in spite of the efforts of all the stars in the galaxies pouring out energy to warm it up.")

As mentioned above, EMR from the Sun can propagate through space without heating it. Certainly, that must apply to intergalactic space. Vacuum cannot be heated. Therefore, one might expect that the differential between the energy of low level radiation and the zero energy of empty space might be utilized.

As an alternative to the many suggestions of violation of the Second Law of Thermodynamics of the past, what is presented here might explain the ability for the formation of new galaxies without denying that law, and without condemning the universe to heat death.

DARK MATTER

The density of matter as it is being expelled from galaxies would be at its highest in the vicinity of its source galaxies, and should be decreasing in density at increasing distances from those sources. In fact, that is what has been observed.

As mentioned in Chapter 21, astrophysicist Anthony N. Aguirre reported, "diffuse halos of dust that extend hundreds of thousands of light-years from many of the universe's galaxies," and a team of astronomers including Douglas N. C. Lin of the University of California, Santa Cruz and his colleagues Burton F. Jones and Arnold R. Klemola has reported that, "this unseen material [dark matter] lies in a giant halo at least six times larger than the visible disk of [our] galaxy.

John Boslough wrote that Vera Rubin "has found all but irrefutable evidence that in spiral galaxies there was about five times as much mass as could be accounted for by the galaxy's visible stars. In groups of galaxies orbiting around each other....Rubin and Ford [coworker Kent Ford] analyzed over two hundred galaxies in the late 1970s and early 1980s...and in every galaxy they had examined...this hidden galactic stuff was at least ten times as massive as the luminous stars and the dust they could see with their telescopes. Somehow, over 90 percent of the matter in the universe had not been accounted for."

Vera Rubin herself has written that, "dark matter is not part of the overall background density of matter in the universe but rather is strongly clumped around galaxies. That is evident because the density of luminous matter decreases, albeit slowly, with distance from the galactic center, and the density even at large radial distances is between 100 and 1,000 times higher than the mean density of the universe."

That of course, is now explained as the matter that is expelled from the galaxies themselves.

Rowan-Robinson wrote (in 1977), in a discussion of dust grains, that "In fact, the dust concentration varies with distance from the galactic plain in a roughly inverse exponential way," Vera Rubin had reported (in 1982) that the density of dark matter around spiral galaxies decreases as the inverse square of the radius, and Peebles agreed (in 1993) that the "dark halo" of galaxies follows an inverse square law. However, because that matter doesn't depart from a single a point, but from bodies throughout a galaxy, and because of the non-spherical shape of galaxies, one might expect its distribution follows that law only as an approximation.

All of those reports support the belief that it is matter that is ejected from galaxies that causes their observed flat rotation curve rather than some strange unknown non-baryonic matter.

As discussed in Chapter 9, BB cosmologists have postulated all sorts of stuff as the missing matter of the universe, none of which have proved to be a reasonable alternative. The overwhelming favorite appears to have been BB neutrinos that are said to flood the universe.

It has been claimed that those neutrinos could have sufficient mass to solve their missing mass problem and "close" the universe. Unfortunately for BBT, neutrinos from Supernova 1987A were observed to have arrived on Earth at essentially the same time as light photons, indicating their mass to be insignificantly small, and the calculations of Appendix E, based on data by BB theorists, show the mass of those hypothetical neutrinos would be far too little to solve the BB missing mass problem.

It was reported in *SCIENCE NEWS* (in 1998) that Ostriker has suggested that "clouds of hydrogen" that "remain hidden from view because they radiate at wavelengths notoriously difficult to detect" are the missing matter of the universe.

However, that would require hydrogen to be concentrated around galaxies. But some galaxies, such as ellipticals, have been found to contain "little if any" dark matter, which would seem to deny that accumulation. On the other hand, if they are young as suggested above, they would be expected to eject less matter, that is, to have less dark matter in their vicinities. That lack would seem to support the concept of dark matter surrounding galaxies as the matter that is ejected in increasing amounts as galaxies reach middle age and in decreasing amounts as they age beyond that.

DISCOVER of June, 1997 reported on an amazing bit of work by astronomer Tony Tyson of Bell Labs who "made the first map of dark matter's distribution within a cluster of galaxies." Using the HST, he used the lensing of a cluster of galaxies thought to be some two billion light-years away to obtain images of a galaxy that is about 3 billion light-years behind the cluster. From images of the lensing cluster and the lensed galaxy he and associates were able to compute the mass distribution of the lensing galaxy cluster which showed peaks of dark matter around individual galaxies of the cluster, and combined to show a large swell of matter from the center of the cluster.

That configuration of matter rules out dark matter candidates that could not have provided it, such as BB neutrinos that are said to be evenly spread in space. But it is consistent with the distribution of matter that is ejected from galaxies as described above.

Margaret Geller, is quoted as having said, "When I hear about this dark matter, it sounds like the ether. What is it? Where is it, this stuff that explains everything?"

Her questions are now answered.

There may no longer be a need for speculation about which, of the variety of exotic stuff that has been postulated, might be the real dark matter. It is not some mysterious, unknown, non-baryonic matter, but the matter and radiation that is spewing from *dead and dying galaxies* and surrounds them in an approximate inverse square law pattern.

MICROWAVE BACKGROUND RADIATION

As would be expected due to the violence of the birth of new galaxies in space, and the center of older galaxies, radiation at wavelengths throughout the electromagnetic spectrum are received from space.

MBR Due to Thermalization.

As discussed in Chapter 13, in the past a number scientists, including Eddington, McKellar, Nernst and Regener, have made estimates of radiation temperature that were much closer to the actual measured value of 2.7 K than the values estimated by BB cosmologists. Those estimates, that were based on the astronomical data, that includes energy that might be received from processes of galactic formation in IGS, were presented as the cause of the MBR.

However, although their estimates were superior to BBer's estimates, the MBR can't merely be the average level of radiant energy from space as has been postulated by a number of theorists in the past. Unless it is thermalized, it couldn't have a black-body spectrum; and due to irregularities in the distribution of matter in IGS, it couldn't have the isotropy that the MBR is observed to possess.

The recycling universe described herein (and all others) require radiant energy from IGS to have been thermalized in the space that surrounds our galaxy in order to reach us as microwave radiation having a black-body spectrum.

Although some BBers have attempted to show that the thermalization of radiation from sources in space is impossible, others have disagreed. As mentioned in Chapter 13, statements of other BB cosmologists, including Barrow, Silk, Gott, Hawking, Sciama, and Pebbles et al. have agreed that radiation over a wide range of wavelengths might be expected from the creation of matter in space. Some of those cosmologists have denied the possibility of thermalization while their postulations would require it.

Some BB theorists have suggested that black-body radiation from the BB decoupling had been repeatedly absorbed and reradiated by matter in space, which would require thermalization. Among those are Barrow and Silk who (in 1980) suggested that radiation might have been rescattered and smoothed on its way to us, and Martin Rees who (in 1987) agreed that the energy from the explosions of massive stars would be absorbed by interstellar dust, which would then be emitted as MBR.

Other BB cosmologists have suggested schemes for the generation of radiation that results in the MBR that, although not acknowledged by them, would require thermalization to cause the MBR black-body spectrum that is observed. Those include American astrophysicist Richard Gott and Hawking, who suggested black holes throughout the universe as the source of that radiation.

In articles written by them, both Sciama and Peebles, et al., after agreeing that matter might be created in IGS, Sciama added that, "But why the observed spectrum should be that of a black-body over a wide range of wavelengths is totally obscure," and Peebles, et al, added, "but (it is) absurd to suppose the spectrum of the created radiation is just such that the integrated background...adds up to a thermal form" (that is, thermalized).

The obvious response to those comments is that, "the thermalization of matter in space would produce that result." It seems strange that cosmologists who deny thermalization can, when it suits their purpose, propose schemes that require it. It also seems strange that they can postulate that as much as 99 percent of the mass of the universe is of unknown dark matter while declaring that matter to be incapable of producing thermalization.

(Later on, in attempting to support photons from the BB decoupling as a the source of the MBR, Peebles, wrote in *Principles of Physical Cosmology* that, "when a hydrogen atom is ionized it produces two particles...[those] electrons exchange energy with the CBR; collisions among the particles keeps them all at the same temperature," which certainly sounds like thermalization.)

Matter from *dead and dying galaxies*, in addition to serving as the dark matter that surrounds galaxies, must also contain the thermalizing medium for the radiant energy from space. That should be especially convincing with the realization that astronomical evidence shows the integrated average level of radiation over much of the electromagnetic spectrum, from all directions of space, to be fairly even.

Whiskers and Grains.

There is both theoretical and observational evidence for the presence of graphite "whiskers" or "grains" throughout the space in and around our galaxy. Their size is such that they might absorb and reradiate energy in the band of wavelengths necessary to produce the thermalized MBR.

A number of references to such particles can be found in the literature. Those include:

Rowan-Robinson who wrote (in 1977), "The exact nature of these tiny (0.1 μm diameter) dust grains responsible for absorbing and scattering light within the galaxy is uncertain, but they probably consist of graphite cores surrounded by mantles of "dirty" ice [i.e., contaminated with metals] or silicates," and Martin Harwit who wrote that interstellar grains, "absorb or scatter light somewhat like a radio antenna." Those particles, which must be outside of interstellar space as well as inside, certainly could result in the thermalization of radiation at some frequencies.

As mentioned in Chapter 13, Ivan King has concluded that, "interstellar dust is a mixture of grains of different kinds." Again, if that is so, it must be outside of a galaxy as well as inside, and its particles, certainly can act like antennas to absorb and reradiate EMR, resulting in the thermalization of energy from space.

Peebles' (in 1993) stated that dust grains could not cause thermalization that results in MBR because its opacity would prevent the reception at other radio frequencies from space. However, if some of the particles of matter were of the proper size and material, that is, "tuned" to thermalize to certain bands of radiation to produced the MBR, they wouldn't prevent the reception of other frequencies.

Those particles of matter don't thermalize radiation in all bands of EMR, and they don't thermalize all of the energy in a particular band. They receive and reradiate just enough of the energy in a particular band or bands to produce the observed MBR blackbody spectrum at the energy level that is observed. After all, radiation arrives from space throughout almost the entire EMR spectrum in addition to that of the MBR. Only a tiny portion of that is thermalized.

OTHER BACKGROUND RADIATION

BBT fails to provide adequate rationale for radiation from space other than the MBR. But in the cosmology presented here, a background of all ranges of EMR, including radio, infrared, visible light, ultraviolet, X-ray and gamma rays, as well as gamma ray bursts and comic rays, might be expected from the violence occurring in the centers of galaxies, both mature galaxies and those in the process of formation. That, of course, agrees with observations.

An article in *SKY & TELESCOPE* (in 1999) reported, as is evident in observations of intergalactic clouds of matter and energy in which new galaxies are being formed, the star formation processes are violent, creating radiation throughout the electromagnetic spectrum, and undoubtably are the source of gamma ray bursts and cosmic rays. As previously noted, a number of BB cosmologists have agreed that the possibility of radiation from space over a wide range of wavelengths, might be expected from the creation of matter in space.

Astrophysicist Belinda J. Wilkes has agreed that, "quasars emit roughly equal amounts of energy across the electromagnetic spectrum, from infrared to X-ray and possibly gamma ray frequencies." (Those are really the violent centers of galaxies, new and old.)

Cosmic Rays.

As mentioned above, a number of scientists have indicated that cosmic rays might be responsible for the generation of some heavier elements within galaxies. If that is true, it might be expected that the source of cosmic rays that reach Earth's atmosphere are produced in the violent star-forming areas of galaxies; those in the early stages of formation and those young enough to still have violent star-forming centers. Ivan King has written that cosmic ray particles have energies in the range of 10^6 to 10^{20} eV, although most are around 10^9 eV. Most are protons and electrons, but some are heavier nuclei. One suggested source of these is supernovas, but there may be others.

SCIENTIFIC AMERICAN reported (in 1996) that "although theorists have long suspected supernova explosions could provide the jolt necessary to accelerate particles to cosmic ray energies....Many researchers have assumed that the high energy cosmic rays must originate in even greater shocks—those surrounding active, or exploding galaxies."

Although some astronomers suspect that cosmic rays are produced by supernovas (or hypernovas), others have suggested that they are produced in the violent centers of newly forming galaxies. For example, physicists Cronin, Gaisser and Swordy wrote (in SCIENTIFIC AMERICAN in 1997) that, "Somewhere in the universe...there are forces that can impart to a single proton 100 million times the energy achievable by the most powerful earthbound accelerators." They suggest that acceleration might be the result of supernova shock waves or "energetic and turbulent plasma of partially ionized gas in a state of violent activity" in space and, "Galactic space is therefore filled with an energetic turbulent plasma of partially ionized gas in a state of violent activity....Cosmic rays with energies above 10^{20} eV strike the earth's atmosphere at a rate of only about one per square kilometer a year." Although they wrote "galactic space," perhaps they should have written "galaxy forming areas of intergalactic space."

Astrophysicist L. H. Aller's discussion of cosmic rays in the *Encyclopedia of Physics* suggests that magnetic fields in the centers of "relatively normal" galaxies may accelerate charged particles to cosmic-ray energies. That would certainly apply to normal galaxies in the universe as described in this chapter, but would also apply to newly forming galaxies in space.

SKY & TELESCOPE reported (in 2000) that, "So far at least 25 extraterrestrial particles (probably protons) with energies exceeding 10^{20} eV have been recorded by cosmic ray detectors on Earth. Supernova explosions, which are thought to be the source of some cosmic rays, are not energetic enough to accelerate protons (hydrogen nuclei) to such energy, The cores of active galaxies might do the trick, but there's a problem; most of them are too far away."

According to *SCIENCE NEWS* (in 1998), BB theorists tell us that collisions of cosmic rays, while traveling through IGS, with MBR photons would "sap the cosmic ray's energies, limiting them to about about 50 million trillion electron volts (50 x 10^{18} eV) on arrival at terrestrial detectors," and *SKY & TELESCOPE* (in August, 2000) reported that astronomers Kenneth Greisen, Georgi Zatsepin, and Vader Kuzmin showed, in 1966, that, "protons with energies greater than 5 x 10^{19} eV must get slowed down during their cosmic trip by collisions with photons of the microwave background radiation."

But of course, the MBR didn't come from the BB decoupling myth. It isn't out there in IGS, so that cutoff doesn't occur. Cosmic rays having energies exceeding 10^{20} eV do reach the Earth's atmosphere, and it seems very likely that they come from distant galaxies, including the violent centers of newly forming galaxies of the universe.

The *Encyclopedia of Physics* says that, "Cosmic rays provide the only direct sample of extrasolar system material in the Universe," but that is far from the truth. In fact, except for the remnants from one or more older galaxies that formerly occupied the space of our galaxy, and except for the matter of our galaxy that was manufactured during its formation, the rest of its matter, is not just extra-solar material, but extragalactic material of older *dead and dying galaxies.*

Gamma Rays.

In addition to a general gamma ray background thought to be produced by electron-positron annihilation and radioactive decay occurring within the Milky Way, gamma rays from known sources such as pulsars, quasars, and Seyfert galaxies, and powerful bursts of gamma rays are detected from far distant sources in IGS.

Gamma ray bursts, that were first detected several decades ago by a nuclear surveillance spacecraft, are now detected at the rate of about one a day by satellites such as NASA's Compton Gamma Ray Observatory and the Italian-Dutch satellite Beppo-SAX. As in the case of cosmic rays, prevailing opinion is that their sources are supernovas in distant galaxies. However, it seems more reasonable to believe that many of them, and perhaps the majority of them, originate in the violent centers of galaxy forming areas in IGS.

Recent reports would seems to support that belief.

SCIENCE NEWS reported (in 1991) that, "gamma-ray bursters occur uniformly through the sky, not in any expected clustering either toward the center of the Milky Way or along its disk, scientists working with NASA's Gamma Ray Observatory revealed this week."

ASTRONOMY reported in (in 1997) that, "Now a recent discovery suggests that gamma-ray bursts lie at great distances." The Beppo-SAX telescope's high-resolution x-ray cameras were pointed in the direction of the burst and glimpsed an object that appeared to be a faint galaxy. "The optical counterpart to a gamma-ray burst? That's what astronomers think they have in the 26th magnitude dot at the center of this HST image."

On the same subject, as presented in *SCIENTIFIC AMERICAN*, that burst occurred on February 28, 1997. Within eight hours of the discovery of that burst, a source of X-rays was found within an arc-minute of where the burst was observed. and eight days later it had disappeared. That article reported that the Burst and Transient Source Experiment on the Compton Gamma Ray Observatory satellite has determined that, "The distribution of gamma-ray bursters does not trace out the Milky Way, nor were the bursts associated with nearby galaxies or clusters of galaxies....If originating at cosmological distances, the bursts must have energies of perhaps 10^{51} ergs," (equal to more than 10^{62} eV).

SCIENTIFIC AMERICAN reported a gamma ray burst (GRB) that was observed on May 8, 1997, the source of which was observed by an optical telescope on May 11. "The displacement of its absorption lines indicates a distance of more than seven billion light-years. If this interpretation holds up, it will establish once and for all that bursts occur at cosmological distances."

Regarding a gamma ray burst that was observed on December 14, 1997, *SCIENCE NEWS* reported (in May 1998) that the sequence of observations of its radiation, "suggests that the burst originated from a place containing lots of dust, which blocks visible light but is transparent to radio waves. Stellar nurseries are rich in dust, and previous studies had hinted that several other bursts originated in star-forming locales....[that] cosmic flash packed 100 times more energy than a supernova explosion."

As stated in *SCIENTIFIC AMERICAN* in August 1998, "astronomers now agree that the bursts [of gamma rays] are some kind of megaexplosions in distant galaxies....perhaps hypernovae—souped up supernovea." But, of course, for lack of a better explanation by those of the establishment, it has merely been assumed that the source of those bursts is supernovas or newly-invented "hypernovas."

ASTRONOMY reported a powerful gamma ray burst that occurred on January 23, 1999. Coordinate information was sent to astronomers around the world. A 12th magnitude object was found that brightened to 9th magnitude within 5 seconds. Eight minutes later it faded by factor of 1,000. Its redshift was 1.6, placing it 9 billion light-years away.

Undoubtedly that burster was very far away. However, the reader is reminded that such estimates of distance are based on questionable BB concepts (the usual erroneous *accepted interpretation of redshift data*). As reckoned in their accustomed manner, a redshift of 1.6 puts the ratio of velocity to that of light at about 0.72, and the corresponding age to be 9 billion light-years is apparently based on a hypothesized age of the BB universe of about 12.5 BYRs.

It is important to realize that, if gamma rays originated in that early BB universe, as determined in the usual manner, they might be redshifted by a factor of on the order of 1,000, resulting in unreasonably short wavelengths upon their origination. (If, for example a GRB is observed at a wavelength of 10^{-6} nanometer, and its redshift were 1,000, its wavelength at its origination would have been 10^{-9} nanometers. That wavelength is considerably far shorter than imagined for gamma radiation, providing yet another reason to question the *accepted interpretation of redshift data.*)

All of the articles cited above regarding gamma ray bursts, and many more in the recent literature, appear to confirm the RUC concept that violent events occur in galaxy-forming regions of IGS. The fact that they are detected in all directions of the sky confirms their extragalactic origin.

NASA scientist Gerald Fishman has said that gamma ray bursts are, "perhaps the least understood of all astronomical phenomena and one of the major mysteries in astronomy this century," but it would seem that RUC might have provided the solution to another mystery. Violent processes of galaxy formation in space would be expected to produce radiation over much, if not all, of the electromagnetic range, and to produce bursts of energy such as those observed in the gamma range.

X-Radiation.

In addition to individual sources such as active galaxies and pulsars, that produce regular pulses, x-rays are received fairly uniformly from every part of the sky. Background X-rays received at fairly equal intensity from all directions have been thought to come from a large number of quasars at great distance, each contributing a small fraction of the total. Other sources of X-ray may include black holes, neutron stars, supernova remnants, and hot interstellar gas.

That appears to be supported by an article by Ron Cowan (in *SCIENCE NEWS* in October, 2000) that stated, "For nearly 40 years, astronomers have tried to identify the origin of the faint glow of X-rays that bathes the sky. Chandra's sharp vision has resolved this glow into millions of individual sources. Many of them, Chandra reveals, as active galactic nuclei—galaxies whose cores contain massive black holes."

Except for the usual unsubstantiated assumption of radiation from black holes in the centers of galaxies (instead of merely radiation from their violent star-forming centers) that report provides some confirmation of RUC, at least in regard to X-radiation.

Other Ranges of EMR.

As in the case of gamma and X-rays, portions of other ranges of EMR, that is, ultra violet, light, infrared and radio, arrive at the Earth, or at its atmosphere, from space. The intensity of infrared, ultraviolet and X-radiation is severely attenuated by the Earth's atmosphere, but a "window" allows light in the visible range to pass relatively unattenuated.

As is well known, ultraviolet, visible and infrared radiation are produced by all stars and active galaxies throughout the universe.

As in the case of X-rays, in addition to its origination in discreet sources in space, a generally uniform background of infared radiation (heat) is observed. The COBE infrared background experiment has shown that infrared radiation permeates the sky.

It is known that stars and galaxies produce radiation in the radio range from the very short to very long radio wavelengths, and jets from active galaxies produce high levels of radio energy.

Radiation throughout those ranges of EMR is produced in ordinary stars and galaxies, but certainly it is also produced in the galaxy-forming areas of space.

SOME ODDS AND ENDS

The Great Attractor.

In addition to other considerations, the accumulation of matter and energy in various areas throughout IGS, that have not grown dense enough to be readily visible, might also offer an explanation for the mysterious Great Attractor that is a major factor in the otherwise unexplained motion of our galaxy, and others within the local group of galaxies, that speed toward it at several hundred kilometers per second.

Could it be that the Great Attractor is merely clusters of LSB galaxies like those that have gone undiscovered until fairly recently? Could it be groups of newly forming galaxies that are still a giant cloud or clouds of gas that haven't reached sufficient density for the fusion of stars to have commenced, and thus is not readily detectable?

As Goldsmith has written in a discussion regarding the clumping of dark matter in IGS, "the structure that we are able to observe may not be the densest clumps, and many other not-quite-so-dense ones may be sprinkled throughout the universe. Indeed, this seems quite reasonable if we assume that some minimal density of ordinary matter must be reached to 'trigger' the onset of star formation."

Relativity.

It is significant that RUC has little or no reliance on relativity, either special or general.

Time dilation, Einstein-Lorentz transformations, space expansion, curved space, both positive and negative, negative matter and energy, cosmic repulsion, and all that goes with those can be ignored. They are superfluous in the real world.

Although gravitational redshift and gravitational lensing were postulated by Einstein, those effects might simply be Newtonian rather than Einsteinian; and, although relativity indicates infinite energy would be required to accelerate matter to the speed of light, that is not necessarily a verification of relativity, but merely a fact of nature that Einstein was able to ascertain.

Quantum Theory.

It is also significant that RUC requires little reliance on quantum theory.

There seems little need for consideration of some the questionable features of quantum theory, such as particle-wave duality, observer participation, and the uncertainty principle. However, it may be that something like current quantum theory plays a role in the generation of new matter in space, but not as it is presently understood.

The process of new matter formation in space may be similar to that of the quantum theorists; that is, new elements come out of energy accumulation. But that energy is not of empty space, but from the accumulated energy from myriads of *dead and dying galaxies*, and the generation of matter is not on the ridiculously enormous scale of inflation theory (or other BB schemes), but on a particle-by-particle basis.

BB cosmologists are troubled that the amount of antimatter in the universe has not been found to equal that of matter as postulated by quantum theory. But, because that lack is likely to merely be a flaw in that theory, concern for it be unwarranted. In any case, there is little need for concern about that in a cosmology that is based on astronomical data and proven science.

RUC IN A NUTSHELL

It is clear that galaxies lose matter and radiated energy at enormous rates, thus they must eventually die. That matter and energy, combined with newly generated matter and hydrogen, accumulates in IGS to produce violent swirling clouds in which new galaxies are born. That process might take hundreds of billions of years. However, in a very large and very ancient, non-expanding universe, galaxies ever exist in various stages of their lives.

The Sun loses millions of tons of mass every second in the form of radiation and solar wind. The same is true of hundreds of billions of stars in other galaxies. Galactic matter and energy also is ejected by other phenomena. Although new stars continue to be born, older stars lose their matter and energy to space, and all of them gradually die. Thus galaxies, as well as their stars, gradually die.

Radiation leaves those galaxies at the speed of light, and much of their matter is ejected at above escape velocity of its source and speeds into IGS. There it accumulates, along with newly created matter, in "clouds" from which new galaxies form in a vast, non-expanding, recycling universe. Hydrogen, that is needed for the formation of new stars is largely absent in the matter from *dead and dying galaxies*, but abundant throughout space, also accumulates in those clouds.

The ejected matter that surrounds galaxies in an approximately inverse square distribution around them provides the dark matter that flattens the rotation curves of galaxies. Radiation throughout the spectrum is produced in the star-forming process, some of which is thermalized by that matter, resulting in the observed microwave spectrum.

Almost certainly the hydrogen or its components throughout IGS provide the ether that results in tired light redshift of radiation in space. That, combined with GRS, results in the observed redshifts of distant bodies in space.

As the Burbidges have been quoted as saying that, "the greatest shortcoming of all cosmological theories lies in their failure to provide a working model of the formation of galaxies." Until now that may have been true. But now that RUC has been discovered that hurdle has been leaped; and, as physicist William MacMillan told us in 1918, "It is not necessary to suppose that the universe as a whole has ever been or ever will be essentially different from what it is today."

TWENTY NINE

Conclusion

Overwhelming BB Problems.

Some of the well-known problems of BBT such as those of the singularity, smoothness, horizon, flatness, age, and galaxy formation were discussed in Chapters 7 through 12. Some less well-known or neglected BB problems including those regarding MBR, neutrinos, redshift, quasars, and its chronology, were discussed in Chapters 13 through 19. In addition to those, some new problems have been presented in this book. Among those are the impossibility of the accretion of matter for the formation of galaxies in a BB universe, discussed in Chapter 19, and the momentum, deceleration and the c-barrier problems (a second kind of horizon problem) that were presented in Chapter 21.

In Chapter 20, the dependence of BBT on General Relativity as the basis for closed curved space is questioned, especially negatively curved space; and such things as negative matter, density, energy and gravity that go with it. Those problems have to do with the empty space of the universe, which is nothing, and with negative matter, density, energy and gravity. "Nothing" can't be curved, either positively or negatively, and those negative things don't exist in the real world.

Also presented in Chapter 21, and reviewed in the previous chapter, are reasons to deny the postulated enormous rates of expansion of a BB universe (especially that of its space), and to deny similar rates of expansion postulated by other cosmologies.

Chapter 21 also introduced problems that result from the application of Lorentz transformations to the space of the BB universe, which is the basis for the *accepted interpretation of redshift data* that results in the erroneous determination of the distance and velocity of remote matter of the universe that has been accepted by all of the establishment. That fallacious scheme also results in the perception of the clumping of quasars and galaxies at great distances, in a universe that BBers insist must be homogeneous.

Additional problems regarding BBT, as discussed in Chapter 25, include such violations of logic as attributing closed universe features to other BB cases, faulty claims of successful predictions and tests of BBT, inept analogies to the BB, and the creation of a universe in a basement. That nonsense, and the violations of scientific method mentioned in Chapter 26, do nothing to substantiate BBT or to aid in the solution of its problems.

Ever since the invention of BBT, as its various problems have come to light, they have, one by one, been ignored or alternate schemes have been devised to circumvent them. None of those attempts have provided simple credible solutions to the problems. Regardless of those failures, the validity of the basic BB concept is rarely questioned by the establishment.

To outsiders, BB problems appear to be insurmountable, but the attitude of establishment is that those folks just don't understand advanced science.

Proofs of BBT.

As an example of that attitude, Peebles, Schramm, Turner & Kron wrote that, "At present, there are no fundamental challenges to the big bang theory, although there are certain unresolved issues within the theory itself. Astronomers are not sure, for example, how the galaxies were formed....but there is no reason to think that the process did not occur within the framework of the big bang. Indeed, the predictions of the theory have survived all tests to date."

The predictions were poor, many were really "retrodictions," that is, decided upon after the fact; and, as mentioned in Chapter 25, no such tests have been made. In fact, they would have been impossible to make. As Narlikar has asked, "How far has this theory been tested? To what extent can it be trusted in our extrapolation all the way to the big bang epoch?"

Marmet has written in *Absurdities in Modern Physics*, "Physicists believe that the most fundamental nature of physics is nothing but equations;" cosmologist Robert Oldershaw (in *New Scientist* in 1990) has written, "theory is far outracing experimental observations...a hypothesis can become to be regarded as being so convincing and elegant that it simply has to be right....A classic example is surely our relentless devotion to the traditional paradigm of the big bang in cosmology," and, as mentioned in Chapter 7, Ernan McMullan warned against such an enormous extrapolation of laboratory physics in his statement that there is "good historical reasons to distrust the applicability of standard theories to extreme conditions."

Nevertheless, throughout the history of BBT, attempts have been made to provide proofs of its validity. Those have included such items as the presence of MBR, an expanding universe, the abundance of light elements, an evolving universe, the three families of particles, gravitational lensing, and Olbers' paradox. However, careful examination of each of those shows them to be inadequate.

Inflation and Quantum Theory.

Throughout its history, BBT has run into technical difficulties. In each case attempts have been made to patch it up. But, as astronomer Brent Tully of the University of Hawaii is quoted as having said, "It's disturbing to see that there's a need for a new theory every time there's a new observation."

The most extensive of those patches has been inflation theory.

As discussed in Chapters 23 and 24, when that theory came along, it claimed to provide simple solutions to many of BBT's old problems. But that has not occurred. In fact, it has introduced some new problems. Among those are the postulation of a flat universe requiring sufficient missing matter to provide for a universe of critical density, and to provide the "seeds" for the formation of galaxies. However, efforts to find that matter have failed.

As discussed in Chapter 18, various aspects of quantum theory have been applied to BBT. Among those is the concept of symmetry breaking for the contrived orchestration of the creation of the various elementary particles at times when the postulated energy level of the BB agrees with that which is believed to be required for their creation.

But, as discussed in Chapter 23, quantum theory plays a much larger role in inflation theory.

According to quantum theory, virtual pairs of elementary particles might spontaneously appear in space due to quantum fluctuations of the energy of that space. Inflation theorists seized upon that idea to postulate a single enormous quantum fluctuation that resulted in the creation of the entire universe. That stretch of the imagination doesn't seem to provide a viable solution to the BB singularity problem; and inflation theory continues to represent a serious violation to the law of conservation of matter and energy.

Among other ideas that have grown out of "advanced" science and applied to BBT are such fantasies as magnetic monopoles, domains and domain walls, white holes, worm holes, cosmic strings, superstrings, textures and other concoctions of inventive minds.

Since the beginning of BBT, schemes of increasing complexity have been invented to overcome its problems. Despite that, simplicity has been claimed for the various versions of BBT. Carr had said that the Standard BB universe is "remarkably simple," and Linde told us in 1985 that, in five years, new inflation had "solved about 10 major cosmology problems in one simple model."

Although cosmologists have claimed simplicity and elegance for BBT, its complexity has become ever more troubling; and apparently, to modern theorists, what they consider to be elegance has become a preferred quality, superseding proven science and experimental data.

Cosmological Incest.

Because the majority of those involved in cosmology for the past half century have worked to provide theory and evidence in support of the favored theory, and their views are ever presented in the media, it's not surprising that the public has accepted BBT; and, based on faith in the skills and judgments of their predecessors and colleagues, virtually all establishment scientists have also fallen for it; hook, line and sinker.

In all of their work the flaws of BBT have been all but ignored. Those that are acknowledged are treated one at a time and dismissed one at a time, never gathered and examined for their overall impact as this book has attempted to do. A flaw occasionally makes its way into print, but it is immediately countered by minimizing its importance. Much of that unscientific endeavor is the result of the many personal ties among members of the establishment, including the "good old boys of cosmology."

Close associations are the norm among dozens of the best known names in cosmology, astronomy, astrophysics and theoretical physics who have taught each other, worked together, wrote books and papers together at the centers for the promulgation of BBT; schools such as Cambridge University, MIT, Princeton, Harvard, Cal Tech, University of California, and University of Chicago, and at institutions such as Fermilab, the Harvard-Smithsonian Center for Astrophysics, the Carnegie Institute's Department of Terrestrial Magnetism and various major telescope sites.

As a result, what I have called "cosmological incest" is rampant in those fields.

Although serious scientists attempt to maintain their objectivity, the combination of camaraderie, peer pressure, admiration and respect for each other, desire for acceptance and prestige, and economic considerations, has caused a close fraternity among those scientists. To them some form of BBT is the true cosmology. Criticism of it is offensive to them, and, as stated by Oldershaw, "Like religious zealots, big bang cosmologists have stubbornly refused to accept information that conflicts with their beliefs."

As Herbert Friedman wrote in *The Amazing Universe*, regarding his own profession, "Perhaps it is time for astronomers to pause and wonder whether they know too much and understand too little." That criticism doesn't apply to astronomers who are truly working scientists, but it certainly is appropriate for many cosmologists and other theorists of the establishment.

The Herd Instinct.

Young university scientists, who respect and honor their professors and mentors, are reluctant to present ideas that might conflict with what they have been taught. They are also concerned about their futures that are dependent on grants to maintain their positions. To their professors and to those who make study grants, BBT is all but a proven fact. Thus, funding of studies that might discredit it are not sought or not approved.

Regarding the education of young physicists Thomas Kuhn has said, "Of course it is a narrow and rigid education, probably more so than any other except perhaps in orthodox theology."

Geoffrey Burbidge has commented that, "Powerful mechanisms encourage this conformity. Scientific advances depend on the availability of funding, equipment and journals in which to publish. Access to these resources is granted by a peer review process....A few years back Halton C. Arp was denied telescope time at Mount Wilson and Palomar observatories because his observing program had found and continued to find evidence contrary to standard cosmology....The same attitude applies to academic positions. I would wager that no young researcher would be willing to jeopardize his or her scientific career by writing an essay such as this," meaning the one from which this quotation was taken.

In explaining of why so many misconceptions persist for so long in the human population, Marilyn Vos Savant once wrote in her syndicated newspaper article, "Science is rife with error. Because so many people are so thoroughly schooled in the common misconceptions, only the most brilliantly skeptical of them will ever discover a mistake. And even then, it will likely be denied for generations to come."

But it's not just young scientists who are reluctant to rebel.

Senior scientists educated in the environment of BBT can be overwhelmed by the preponderance of biased cosmological opinion, and they are also aware that their futures depend on the approval of their peers. Thus they continue to make biased investigation and write biased reports, the perpetrators apparently proud of their special efforts to support the favored theory. They insist that, like Dr. Pangloss, their's is the best of all possible worlds, and are confident that all the BB problems will ultimately be overcome by further pursuit of evidence in support of that theory.

The primary undesirable result of the fraternization of BBT cosmologists is that it has resulted in special efforts to support BBT at the expense of possible alternate cosmologies.

Others besides myself who have recognized those problems include Thomas Gold who, in an article in the 1993 issue of *OMNI* entitled *Heresy! Modern Galileos* referred to this as scientific herd instinct; when articles are reviewed by colleagues, decisions regarding grant applications are determined by this instinct, and newspaper columnist Christopher Hitchens has written about the "niche market of the intellectuals" once described by author Harold Rosenberg as 'the herd of independent minds.'"

That herd instinct has resulted in a great cost to the field of cosmology.

Dissenters.

When the problems of BB, the inadequacy of its proofs, misguided attempts to patch up its flaws, its lack of logic, violations of scientific method, and misrepresentation of facts, are taken into consideration, its vulnerability should be obvious. But, regardless of those failings, the BB is rarely questioned by the establishment.

To outsiders, BB problems appear to be insurmountable, but the attitude of establishment is that those folks just do not understand advanced science. Although Barry Parker, who doesn't believe that "there are any serious problems" with BBT, and that, "there will always be people 'howling in the dark'" against it, those who do the howling have some very good company.

Comments of a few of those who have howled are presented as follows:

Sir Arthur Eddington wrote (in 1928), "As a scientist I simply do not believe that the Universe began with a bang." and as Herbert Dingle said, mathematical physicists "have simply lost the power of understanding what they are doing" and "have substituted mathematics for reasoning."

Fred Hoyle (in 1982) wrote, "Over the past seventeen years astronomers and physicists the world over have made numerous investigations, with the outcome essentially nil. It has been a fruitless churning of mathematical symbols, exactly the hallmark of an incorrect theory," and as Rowan-Robertson admitted in *Cosmology*, "most of the models of the universe described in this [his] book are based on general relativity, which cannot be said to rest on a very solid experimental basis."

In defense of dissension, Dennis Overbye has written, "The reward for a new idea is not applause but argument from the people who take you seriously enough to try to destroy you. The glory and honor justly go to those who are willing to stand up for their ideas and commit themselves."

Over two thousand years ago Roman philosopher Lucretius warned against, "thrusting out reasoning from your mind because of its disconcerting novelty. Weigh it, rather, with a discerning judgment. Then, if it seems to you true, give in. If it is false, gird yourself to oppose it. For the mind wants to discover by reasoning what exists in the infinity of space."

As Richard Feynman has warned, "Learn from science that you must doubt the experts."

Revolution.

Jayant Narlikar, a former proponent of the discredited old SST—now involved in small bang ideas—has said that, "Astrophysicists of today who hold the view that the "ultimate cosmological problem" has been more or less solved may well be in for a few surprises before this century runs out," and astronomer and editor of *Star Date* magazine, Jeff Kanipe, has written, "The conflict between differing views of the universe presents a classic example of an established theory undergoing a revolution."

Max Planck is quoted as having said, "Important scientific innovation rarely makes its way by gradually winning over and converting its opponents. What does happen is that its opponents gradually die out and that the growing generation is familiar with the idea from the beginning."

According to physicist Thomas S. Kuhn in, *The Structure of Scientific Revolutions*, as reviewed in *SCIENTIFIC AMERICAN* in in 1991, "Scientists are deeply conservative. Once indoctrinated into a paradigm, they generally devote themselves to solving 'puzzles,' problems whose solutions reinforce and extend the scope of the paradigm, rather than challenging it. Kuhn calls this 'mopping up' But there are always anomalies, phenomena that the paradigm cannot account for or that directly contradict it. Anomalies are often ignored. But if they accumulate, they may trigger a revolution...in which scientists abandon the old paradigm for a new one.

"Denying the view of science as a continual building process, Kuhn asserts that a revolution is a destructive as well as a creative event. The proposer of a new paradigm stands on the shoulders of giants and bashes them over the head. He or she is often young or new to the field, that is, not fully indoctrinated."

That may describe the present status of cosmology. A revolution may be imminent.

BB cosmologist Paul Davies wrote, "The underlying order in Nature is therefore hidden from us and must be deduced by often elaborate procedures." The late American physicist Heinz Pagels expressed this hidden quality by referring to "the cosmic code." The laws of nature, he said, "are written in a sort of secret code, and therefore we do not perceive them directly. The job of scientists is to crack the cosmic code and read the message. Scientists do this by a careful combination of experiment and theory."

But science hasn't been as pure as that.

As previously mentioned, Kuhn suggested that science is a political rather than a rational process, and Ivers Peterson has suggested that some historians, philosophers and sociologists "argue that science has an undeserved reputation for objectivity. They maintain that social issues determine not only how science is done but also its content. Science itself is a matter of opinion—decided on the basis of personal or political beliefs....It is nothing but a social construction, perhaps even a group self delusion." Narlikar has quoted British astronomer Geoffrey Burbidge as having said that, "The views of cosmology in any epoch are largely determined by a few strong individuals, rather than by an objective appraisal of the information available."

Those opinions might be overly harsh regarding science in general, but they seem to be appropriate for the field of cosmology where scientific method often seems to be considered an unnecessary annoyance. If a fraction of the effort that has been spent in attempting to prove BBT had been used to investigate alternate ideas, there might now be a healthy competition between a number of viable cosmological choices; and BBT might not be among them.

Here's to the revolution!

Origins.

The difficulties that humans have gotten into regarding cosmology are the result of a powerful desire to find origins; of themselves and their world. The quest for ultimate answers to the origin of life and the universe is what drives men to religion, philosophy and science—including cosmology. So eager is man for answers about origins, that the BB answer to the question about the origin of the universe was eagerly accepted.

But there aren't any short-cuts. It must be realized that the question of the ultimate origin can't be answered. Unfortunately, neither BBT, nor RUC, nor any other cosmology can promise knowledge of the "first cause", and none probably ever will. As we learn new facts of nature, they merely bring to light the next generation of questions, which may be an even bigger and more difficult set. We are left, and probably always will be left, to ponder the ultimate origin of energy, matter, space, time and life.

John Wheeler once said, "We live in an island of knowledge surrounded by a sea of ignorance. As our island of knowledge grows, so does the shore of our ignorance," astronomer Herbert Friedman wrote in *The Amazing Universe*, "no matter how far we push back the veil of ignorance to reveal the existing universe, we shall always be stumped by the basic issue: What lies behind creation?" Bernard Lovell warned us that, the problem of creation "can tear the individual's mind asunder," and St. Augustine is said to have asked, "What was God doing before He created Heaven and Earth?" Which he answered with, "He was preparing Hell for those who inquire into such matters."

In the meantime, the BBT that seemed, for a while, to give the illusion of providing a description of the origin, must be abandoned. The quantity and magnitude of its flaws must be acknowledged, and the quest for alternative possibilities must continue.

It's not suggested here that humans stop striving for answers to their questions. What is suggested is that they try to discover a simpler less troubled cosmology, and, in the meantime, live with the ever troubling question of origin.

Dogs are pretty smart as animals go, but your dog will never be able to understand trigonometry or algebra. The process of evolution just hasn't equipped them to handle those concepts. Humans are somewhat smarter. They can handle that math, even calculus, and some ideas much more complicated than that. But, as in the case of "lower" animals, evolution hasn't equipped human brains to cope with complexities beyond a certain point. The fact should be faced that, no matter how great the desire and effort, there are some things that will never be understood.

Religion.

Some critics of BBT have called it The New Creationism.

That comment reveals an important element in the wide acceptance of BBT in the Judeo-Christian world: It is not terribly inconsistent with the creation of the universe as told in the Bible (and perhaps with creation stories of other religions as well). As mentioned in Chapter 26, Pope Pius IX endorsed BBT by saying that, "True science to an ever increasing degree discovers God as though God were waiting behind each door opened by science."

In his *NEW YORK TIMES* review of a book entitled *The First Squillion Years* by Fred Adams and Greg Laughlin, science writer Dick Teresi has written, "the universe generated by the big bang is a masterpiece of marketing. With its fiery explosion, worm holes, white dwarfs, red giants and black holes, the big-bang universe satisfies our Lucasfilm sensibilities. It also features an abrupt beginning to appease our Judeo-Christian creation myth."

Geoffrey Burbidge has written, "Big bang cosmology is probably as widely believed as has been any theory in the history of Western civilization. It rests, however, on many untested, and in some cases untestable, assumptions. Indeed the big bang cosmology has become a bandwagon of thought that reflects faith as much as objective truth....The big bang ultimately reflects some cosmologists' search for creation and for a beginning. That search properly lies in the realm of metaphysics, not physics."

Helge Kragh has quoted Richard Tolman as saying (in 1934) "We must be especially careful to keep our judgments uninfected by the demands of theology and unswerved by human hopes and fears," and, when asked her opinion of BBT, Marilyn Vos Savant responded to that (in 1996) by, "I think that if it had been a *religion* that first maintained the notion of all the matter in the entire universe had once been contained in an area smaller than the point of a pin, scientists probably would have laughed at the idea."

For those who have decided that the BB was God's method of creating of the universe, RUC doesn't deny God's responsibility for its creation. Instead it suggests that it may have happened very long ago—perhaps infinitely long ago—in a considerably different manner than that of BBT.

RUC as a Replacement.

It is suggested here that RUC is worthy of serious consideration as a replacement for BBT.

In the past, little thought has been given to the fate of matter and radiation from various sources within galaxies. But now it has been realized that, for hundreds of billions of years or more, matter and radiation has spewed into intergalactic space from all of the stars that have lived and died within all of the past and present galaxies. In that space matter and energy gather to form new galaxies.

Compared to BBT, the problems of RUC are minimal. Based on astronomical observations, long accepted science and logic, it avoids the many problems of BBT, it provides clear explanations for many of the mysteries of cosmology, and it requires none of the esoteric fantasies of modern theorists, just some tried-and-true science and logic.

A major consideration here should be that RUC solves a major problem of BBT that is seldom mentioned. As described by Geoffrey Burbidge in an article entitled *Why Only one Big Bang?*, "Within the frame work of the hot big bang, there is no satisfactory theory of how galaxies and large structures formed."

However, astronomical observations now provide for that theory. Matter and energy leaving galaxies provide evidence of the eventual death of stars and galaxies; and the accumulation of matter and energy from those in IGS, combined with the hydrogen that permeates all of space, provides evidence for the creation of new galaxies, stars and matter in an ancient and vast recycling universe.

The matter spewing from galaxies also provides explanations for the thermalization of radiation from space to produce the MBR and for the flat rotation curves of galaxies; and the hydrogen in space provides an explanation for the redshift of that radiation. The violent centers of newly forming and young galaxies provide the sources of radiation from space over the entire electromagnetic spectrum.

Why Not RUC Long Ago?

Considering recent evidence of matter leaving galaxies and evidence of clouds of matter in IGS where galaxy- and star-birth is

going on, it's amazing that some brilliant young astronomer or cosmologist hasn't hit upon the cosmology of the recycling universe
before now. But of course, they all have been too thoroughly
indoctrinated in BBT, and too thoroughly involved in searching
for evidence in support of that theory to step back, reexamine the
facts, and wake up to the possibility of a recycling universe.

Long ago, before there was any real evidence, some scientists
guessed that the universe was very old and some even suggested a
recycling universe.

One of those was Soviet astrophysicist Viktor Ambarzumian
who proposed (in 1957) that young galaxies were born from
material ejected from older, active galaxies. I have only recently
discovered mention of his work, predating my RUC by over 40
years, and apparently ignored by all until now.

Another of those was Grote Reber, who, having built the first
antenna for the reception of radio signals from space in 1936 qual-
ifies as the Father of Radio Astronomy. His opinion was that some
areas the universe having high temperature, density and pressure
(such as the interior of stars) are running down, while other areas
having low temperature, density and pressure (such as star-forming areas of space) are building up. Thus the universe, which
is unlimited in space and time, is constantly changing and
constantly renewing itself.

However the work of Ambarzumian, Reber and others
who made such suggestions was based largely on conjecture. They
lacked the astronomical evidence that has been reported in recent
years, so that nothing came of their efforts. But now that the
enormous loss of matter and energy from galaxies and the continuing formation of new galaxies in space has been recognized as the
process of the continuing life of the universe, BBT should die a
natural death.

Time for a Change.

The evidence against BBT is now so overwhelming that it is difficult to believe that anyone who is aware of the facts can continue
to support such a thoroughly discredited scheme. In the article
mentioned above Robert Oldershaw also wrote, "In the light of all
these problems, it is astounding that the big bang hypothesis is the
only cosmological model that physicists have taken seriously."

Of science and philosophy it is said that entities are not to be postulated beyond necessity. If ever a crop was ripe for reaping by William of Occam's razor, this is the time for harvest. It's totally unreasonable for scientists to continue to expend time, energy and expense to generate support for a complex and terribly flawed BBT. As Tom Van Flandern has written, "the big bang model of a universe with finite size and age may someday be viewed with the same quaint disdain as the original "stars painted inside a hollow sphere model;" but "may" should be "certainly will."

The establishment has been horsing around with BBT for half a century, adjusting, patching, brow-beating dissenters, and conducting anything but science. But all their efforts have failed, all their excursions have had dead ends, and all their fantasies have evaporated. The credibility of BBT has been annihilated. It's time to abandon that unworkable nonsense, face the facts, and look at some new possibilities.

BB must be replaced by something simple; something that is in accord with astronomical observations, proven laws of science, and our everyday experience. It is suggested that the recycling universe cosmology described in this book might provide hope that, sooner or later, the cosmological revolution will occur.

Appendices

APPENDIX A

Relativity

There was young lady named Bright
Who could travel faster than light.
She left home one day
In a relative way,
And returned on the previous night.
— Unknown

This appendix is presented, not only as an introduction to relativity that might be of value to the reader in relation to the subject of cosmology, but to illustrate that discrimination is required regarding what is presented in the media regarding scientific theory.

Both Special and General Relativity are first described as accepted by the establishment. Following that, some of the many problems related of those theories are briefly presented.

The Michelson-Morley Experiments.

In 1881 an experiment was conducted to measure the effect of the ether's relative velocity on the speed of light. That was done by the use of a large rotating mechanism that incorporated the use of a monochromatic light source, half silvered mirrors, and the observation of light interference patterns. To the amazement of all concerned, the effect was repeatedly found to be zero.

That experiment, by American physicists Albert A. Michelson and Edward W. Morley, was designed to compare the effect of the speed of the ether on the speed of light traveling with and traveling across the direction of the ether. Light traveling to and fro in the direction of the ether would be $1/(1-V^2/c^2)$ and the correction factor for light traveling to and fro across the ether would be the square root of that amount. (Travel across would take longer.) The difference between these factors would provide for the determination of the effect of the velocity of the ether.

The expected results were based on the known velocity of light and the expected velocity of the ether, which was thought to be as much as the velocity of the Earth through space. But the effects of the ether were judged to be absent. As a result of that experiment, the concept of the ether of space was abandoned, and thus there was no medium in which electromagnetic fields propagated and, even worse, there were no reference coordinates for the solar system, the galaxy or the universe. Physicists, previously convinced of ether as a medium for electromagnetism and a spatial reference, could make no sense of that.

Fitzgerald Contraction.

As a possible solution to the mystery of the missing ether, British/Irish physicist George F. Fitzgerald suggested what is known as the Fitzgerald contraction.

He proposed that matter moving through the ether shrinks by a factor of the square root of $(1-V^2/c^2)$ in the direction of motion of the ether. That amount of physical shrinkage in the Michelson-Morley device in the direction of the ether would correct for its apparent absence. Although that rationalization proved to be incorrect, this shrinkage factor was also later found to be significant.

Lorentz Transformations.

In 1895 Dutch physicist H. A. Lorentz, working on the solution to the mystery of the missing ether (independently of Fitzgerald) also proposed that the length of matter in the direction of its travel would be shortened by a factor of the square root of $(1-V^2/c^2)$, and he added that time would be slowed by a factor of the reciprocal of that expression.

Those conclusions resulted from his development of a set of empirically derived equations known as the Lorentz transformations, which were the result of the premise of a stationary ether and Newtonian physics. Unfortunately he ascribed no special physical significance to them, and merely considered them to be aids to calculations.

SPECIAL RELATIVITY

The Postulates of Special Relativity.

Albert Einstein published his work on the Special Theory of Relativity in 1905.

His results regarding length and time were the same as those of Lorentz, but, in addition to the absence of an ether in the space of the universe, his mathematics were based on the postulates that

- the motion of a body traveling at uniform velocity cannot be detected by observation on that body (only motion relative to it can be detected), and that
- light is propagated in empty space with a definite velocity c that is independent of the motion of the emitting body.

In other words, except for the speed of light, all motion is relative. Neither the concept of ether nor an absolute space reference were included.

Based on those postulates he was able to provide mathematical derivations for the Lorentz transformations. Those equations, previously thought to have no real physical significance gained importance.

To the factors given by Lorentz, that is, time slows and length shortens, he added that mass increases as the speed of light is approached.

The Einstein-Lorentz Transformations.

The Lorentz transformation was originally derived by Lorentz only up to the first order in velocity. In 1905 Einstein gave his own derivation of the full Lorentz transformations, accurate to all orders of velocity, and for length contraction and time dilation.

Those transformations, now commonly called the Einstein-Lorentz transformations, established the following relationships:

Relative to the time of a stationary body, the time of a moving body appears to slow by a factor of one divided the square root of $(1-V^2/c^2)$, where V is the relative speed of the moving body and c is the speed of light in a vacuum, which equals 300,000 kilometers per second. This is known as "time dilation."

The length of a moving body appears to shrink (in the direction of its motion) by a factor of the square root of $(1-V^2/c^2)$; and the mass of a moving body appears to increase by a factor of one divided by the square root of $(1-V^2/c^2)$.

As an example of these effects, as an object reaches a velocity of 80 percent of the speed of light (the square root of $(1-V^2/c^2) = 0.6$), to a stationary observer its time would appear to slow by a factor of 1-2/3, its length would appear to shrink by a factor of 0.6, and its mass would appear to increase by a factor of 1-2/3.

The Twin Paradox.

The Lorentz time transformation results in what is called the twin paradox.

If a space traveler left the Earth in a high speed (relativistic) spaceship for a number of years, due to his speed, his time would run slower than that of his ground crew. Therefore, when he returns to earth he will not have aged as much as they.

For example, if he and one of the ground crew were 30 years old at launch time and the spaceship had traveled at about 3/4 of the speed of light for 30 years, according to the Lorentz transformations, time dilation would be such that the spaceman's time in space was only about 20 years. Upon his return his age would be only about 50 instead of the 60 years of the ground crewman. (His age would be 30 times one plus the square root of $(1- (3/4c)^2/c^2)$ or 30 x $(1+ 0.66) = 49.8$ years.) If the spaceship traveled at 90% of the speed of light for 30 years the spaceman would return at age 43 as compared to the 60 years of the ground crewman.

At the low velocities normally encountered in our daily lives these equations of Special Relativity need not be considered. But when dealing with "relativistic" speeds such as those of distant galaxies, particle accelerators, or of future interplanetary rockets, for example, these effects could be important.

Velocity Greater Than c Not Possible.

According to the Lorentz velocity transformation, velocities greater than the speed of light (V greater than c), the square root of $((1-V^2/c^2))$ would equal some number multiplied by the square root of minus 1. The appearance of this "imaginary" number should make one uneasy about speeds greater than that of light, which is said to be impossible.

Also, the combination of two speeds in the same direction is no longer given by $V = V_1 + V_2$ but by $v = V_1 + V_2$ divided by $[1 + (V_1 + V_2)/c^2]$. For slow speeds this expression approaches the former equation, but at relativistic speeds it is important. If one of the speeds were c this equation becomes $V = c$.

It is claimed that, even if both of those speeds were equal to c, the result would be $V = c$.

Rotating Disk Example of Length Contraction.

In his explanation of Special Relativity Einstein provided an example of a large rotating disk in deep space (no gravitational field).

By use of a measuring rod it is thought that, because of tangential velocity at the edge of the disk, the measuring rod will shrink in that direction. But that it will retain its normal length in the radial direction.

Thus, if it is used to measure the circumference and the diameter of the disk, the ratio of the two measurements would be larger than 2π. That situation would occur regardless of the type of measuring device in use. For example, by driving an automobile around and across the disc (if fast enough), the same result would be obtained by means of odometer, speedometer and clock readings.

Equivalence of Mass and Energy.

Einstein was later (in 1907) able to determine that energy is equal to mass times c squared, or $E = Mc^2$. In addition to becoming the world's most famous theoretical physicist, his expression for energy's equivalence to the product of mass times c squared became the world's most famous equation. (In this equation energy is in ergs, mass is in grams, and c is 300 million meters per second.)

Upon rejection of the idea of the ether for its transport, it was necessary to explain the propagation of light, and other electromagnetic radiation, through empty space. Light rays might now be thought of as the flow of oscillating matter through space in accordance with Maxwell's equations.

Although Einstein's work presented a theoretical support for that idea, and he is given credit for it, it had been known that light exerts a pressure on a surface that intercepts it.

The existence of that pressure was first proven by the Russian physicist P. N. Lebedev and was shown to be equal to twice the amount of reflected energy divided by the velocity of light. The pressure of light on a mirror is analogous to that of a stream of water splashing off a wall. The rate of the mass of water (M) flowing at a velocity (V) results in a change in its momentum from +MV to -MV, or 2MV. For the mass of light reflecting from a mirror at velocity c its pressure must be 2Mc. Because that is equal to the empirically derived pressure of light of 2E/c, 2Mc = 2E/c and E = Mc^2.

Because c is an extremely large number it only requires a minute amount of mass to produce a prodigious amount of energy. An ordinary flashlight that produces a few watts of electromagnetic energy loses only on the order of a trillionth of a gram of mass per minute. On the other hand, the radiated energy of the Sun is enormous; its energy loss is equivalent to about 4 million tons per second.

The equivalence of mass and energy applies to all forms of mass and energy, including fire, explosion, and chemical and nuclear reactions. Even a glass of hot water weighs minutely more than when it loses some of its heat energy upon cooling.

GENERAL RELATIVITY

General Relativity is based on the postulates of Special Relativity. But Special Relativity had only to do with linear motion, that is, it was not concerned with acceleration or deceleration.

After publishing his work on Special Relativity, Einstein struggled for years to incorporate nonlinear motion into his ideas on relativity. He eventually accomplished his goal, producing a set of ten "field equations" that describe the four-dimensional space-time geometry of gravity.

Those equations, published in 1916, provided the basis for the General Theory of Relativity which treats time as a fourth "imaginary" dimension which, combined with the three dimensions of Euclidean space, produces a four-dimensional space-time construction or "continuum."

Unfortunately, four-dimensional space-time (based on a non-Euclidean form of geometry invented decades earlier by German mathematician Bernard Reimann cannot be clearly visualized by the human mind. It can be treated only as a mathematical construction whose four dimensions can, to a limited degree, be visualized as analogous to the surface of a three-dimensional sphere or other three-dimensional surface.

Curved Space.

An important consequence of General Relativity is that space is no longer impassive emptiness; it is distorted by gravity. The curvature of space results in the curved path of radiation or matter as it travels through a gravitational field.

As an example of the consequence of that idea, the appearance that space is positively curved within a gravitational field can be imagined by consideration of three observers each on a different planet of the solar system (that is, within the gravitational field of the Sun). If they were each to measure the angles of sighting to each other they would discover that the observed angles would add to more than 180 degrees; slightly more than they would for a flat surface. It is said that is the result of the Sun's gravity curving the space of its planets. The effect would be similar to measuring the angle between three points on the surface of a sphere (such as the Earth), which is considered to have positive curvature.

Only Positively Curved Space.

It should be emphasized that Einstein's interpretation of curved space included only positive curvature. His concept of curved space-time was analogous to a three-dimensional spherical or elliptical surface.

The absence of mass would result in zero curvature, the presence of some mass would result in some positive curvature, and greater mass would result in a greater degree of positive curvature.

The idea of a universe of negatively curved space was subsequently introduced by Russian mathematician Alexander Friedmann who is credited with finding a solution to Einstein's General Relativity equations.

Equivalence of Acceleration and Gravitation.

A second important consequence of General Relativity is that acceleration and gravity are said to be equivalent.

In attempting to explain that, an example of a person confined in an elevator-like box in outer space is often used. If that box is somehow continuously accelerated upward by an external force, it would be impossible for its occupant to distinguish between the effects of that acceleration or of a gravitational force, or some combination of those.

It is said that, if a ray of light were to travel through the box in such a way that its path could be observed (perhaps it grazes one of the walls), it would be parabolic. The path of that light beam would be "warped" equally by acceleration or gravitation. Thus Einstein concluded that gravity and acceleration not only produce similar results, but that they are equivalent.

Furthermore, he suggested that there is no force of gravity; only the geometry of curved space.

PROBLEMS OF SPECIAL RELATIVITY

Although relativity is thoroughly accepted by the establishment there are many reasons to question it. Most of its problems are well known to the establishment, but they are merely ignored: How could the greatest theoretical genius of all time be wrong about those things?

The Michelson-Morley Experiment.

Although generally ignored by the establishment, there have been a number of experiments in later years, beginning with that of French physicist Georges Sagnac in 1913, that provide convincing evidence that the conclusions from the M-M experiment were erroneous, and showing that the Earth is moving with respect to the rest of the universe.

Not only is the Earth orbiting around the Sun, and the solar system revolving around the galactic center, but in addition, unknown at the time of the M-M experiment (or the Sagnac experiment), the galaxy is moving toward the "Great Attractor." None of these speeds are trivial. Their combination is complex and adds to a varying net speed rising to as much as a few hundred kilometers per second. Any related experiment that is properly designed must not ignore those speeds.

Mutuality of Transformations.

It is important to note that, because, according to Special Relativity, there would be no universal frame of spatial reference; the situations described are mutual. That mutuality applies to all of the Lorentz transformations; those for time, length and mass, which seems to reduce them to nonsense.

For example, regarding two bodies departing from each other at relativistic speed, the relative times of each would be equally slowed, the relative masses of each would be equally increased, and the relative lengths of each would be equally decreased.

Einstein's Rotating Disk.

In a previous book I had suggested that the edge of Einstein's rotating disk discussed above would shrink by the same factor as his measuring rod, thus invalidating the result of his thought experiment. Why the disk would not shrink in proportion to the distance from its center, and how it might survive that shrinkage without severe distortion, were not explained.

(I had thought that my idea in regarding this was unique, but later learned that a similar idea, called the Ehrenfest paradox, had been presented by physicist Paul Ehrenfest in 1909.)

Lorentz Transformation as Applied to Space.

One aspect of Special Relativity relates to redshift, the lengthening of the wavelength of electromagnetic radiation (decreasing frequency) received from galaxies, quasars and other distant sources in the universe.

Redshift of radiation from relatively close sources, is directly proportional to the velocity (and thus to the distance) of the source: $V = cZ$ and $D = cZ/H_0$, where H_0 is an observationally determined quantity, the Hubble constant. But for distant sources, in order to accommodate the relativistic velocities of distant sources in an expanding universe, and in order to accommodate the closed curved space of a universe based on relativity, the Lorentz velocity transformations (as illustrated in Figure 4) have been applied to the empty space of the universe.

However, those transformations should be applied, (if at all) only to matter that is moving at relativistic speed. It is improper for it to be applied to the nothingness of empty space.

The Twin Paradox.

It is said that, as a result of time dilation, for a space traveler who left the Earth in a high speed (relativistic) spaceship, time runs slower for the spaceman as compared to the ground crew's time, when he returns he will not have aged as much as they who stay behind. However, due the mutuality of the transformation, both would age at the same rate.

The twin paradox is not only counter-intuitive, but it is improperly applied.

If it were merely the result of the time dilation of Special Relativity, the mutuality of time dilation would deny that effect. Furthermore, round-trip space-travel involves nonlinear motion, that is, acceleration and deceleration necessarily occurs. The Lorentz time transformation, as incorporated into Special Relativity, is concerned only with linear motion.

Therefore, that may be a proper subject of General Relativity, but not for Special Relativity.

Regardless of those matters, an atomic clock has been flown around the Earth (at speeds far lower than "relativistic") and has demonstrated a slowing, which has been claimed to provide proof of time dilation. But the fallacy in that is the confusion of the slowing of time with the slowing of a clock, which is a gravitational effect, having nothing to do with a Lorentz transformation.

Velocity of Light.

The idea that the observed velocity of light is at a fixed rate regardless of the relative speed of the observer defies all human understanding.

The related idea of the Doppler redshift (and blueshift) of light from "nearby" stars and galaxies that are moving relative to the observer, that is accepted by all concerned, should certainly lend support to the idea that the relative speed of the observer would add to or subtract from the speed of propagation of light in empty space.

As physics professor Andre K. T. Assis has written, "All velocities known to us are constant relative to the source (like bullets) or constant relative to the medium (like sound velocity which is constant relative to air, irrespective of the motion of the source).

But all of them vary according to the motion of the observer or detector."

Velocity Greater Than c.

It is well accepted that, although the Sun's light takes eight minutes to reach us, its gravitational effect is instantaneous or very close to that. A number of theorists have suggested that, in accordance with Mach's Principle, inertia is a reaction to the combined mass of the universe that, if not instantaneous, its reaction is considerably faster than the speed of light. (When the vehicle in which you are riding suddenly stops, there is no delay in your being thrown forward.)

As an example of that idea, Tom Van Flandern tells us that, "In the equations of motion of celestial mechanics, for example, each body in the solar system affects every other body from its true instantaneous position. By contrast, solar system bodies are not seen in their instantaneous true positions....In fact the Sun's gravity emanates from its instantaneous true position, as opposed to the direction from which its light seems to come. If gravity propagated at the speed of light it would act to accelerate the orbital speed of bodies....To be clear, we are arguing here that gravity acts faster than the speed of light, If the force of gravity is carried by entities called C-gravitons, these entities must move faster than light."

Black Hole Accretion.

According to Special Relativity, the speed of matter entering the event horizon of a black hole would slow to zero, (as its speed reaches infinity, its mass becomes infinite and its time stands still) so, as far as we are are concerned, it could never reach the black hole.

But according to theory, the particle itself would experience no unusual effects as it approached and crossed the black hole event horizon, what the particle might experience as a few seconds, an external observed might experience as billions of years.

Because we humans are the observers judging such matters, in accordance with our science and mathematics, even if black holes could somehow have formed in the first place, they could not continue to grow by the accretion of matter.

PROBLEMS OF GENERAL RELATIVITY

Einstein had suggested three tests of his theory of General Relativity: the gravitational redshift of spectral lines, the deflection of light by the Sun, and the perihelion advance of Mercury.

It has been claimed that all of those have been satisfactorily demonstrated. Those claims and other related matters are discussed in the following subparagraphs.

Closed Curved Space.

General Relativity says that the curvature of space results in the curved path of light as it travels through a gravitational field.

It is said that, due to the curvature of space, a high speed spacecraft, flying outward in any direction, or light from a laser might eventually return from the opposite direction. But for these stories to have any credence the space would have to have the positive curvature of a closed BB universe.

However, most members of the establishment don't accept that BB variety, but only the open or flat cases that have negatively curved or flat space. Regardless of that, they claim that such matter or radiation would eventually return from the opposite direction regardless of the type of BB universe they espouse.

Curved Nothing.

In causing the path of light to bend, it is quite possible that gravitational effects merely create the illusion of curved space. To those who believe that "empty space" means "nothing," "curved space" is an oxymoron; how can "nothing" be curved?

Although it may sound intellectual to discuss 4-dimensional space-time, space has but three Euclidian dimensions. Time may be considered to be an additional dimension, but that is an entirely separate matter that has nothing to do with the dimensions of space. The idea of time as an imaginary forth dimension that can result in closed curved space is a myth.

Gravitational Redshift.

Einstein predicted that gravitation would result in the redshift of radiation leaving massive bodies in space. That prediction has been confirmed by astronomical observations.

However, although it is sometimes billed as proof of General Relativity, it serves only as confirmation of Newtonian gravitational law.

(Although those of the establishment accept gravitational redshift in regard to the Sun and to some other stars in our galaxy, because it would fail to support their theory, BB cosmologists reject it as a significant cause of redshift of radiation from distant massive bodies.)

A Space Triangle.

The above example of three observers on different planets of the solar system, resulting in angles adding to more than 180 degrees, relativity indicates that to be due to curved space that in turn is due to the Sun's gravity.

But, if an experiment could be devised to measure those angles, and they add to more then 180 degrees, the correct reason is more likely to be that it was due to the Sun's gravity acting on the equivalent mass of the light in the paths between the planets.

Because photons of light have an equivalent mass, their path is merely "bent" by the gravity of a massive body, an effect that is related to gravitational redshift.

Bending a Light Beam by Gravity.

The curvature of space in the vicinity of a body such as our Sun is said to cause that path of light from a distant star to be "warped." Its effect was predicted to be twice that of the effect of gravity on the equivalent mass of photons, in accordance with Newtonian physics.

Eddington in 1919, using the occurrence of a solar eclipse to verify that prediction, found evidence of some warping, Regardless of the fact that Eddington's data was very poor, and far from providing support of relativity, it was subsequently hailed as proof of relativity's curved space.

Hailed as a marvelous scientific achievement, the results were highly questionable. The ability to measure the angular shift of the stars could under ideal conditions be no greater than about 1 arc-second but, if atmospheric turbulence and jungle temperature conditions were taken into consideration, it could not be as good as 2 to 3 arc-seconds. Although the resulting star data was essentially random, displacements as small as 0.01 arc second were claimed. Data favorable to Einstein's theory were reported to the public and that which was unfavorable was omitted.

Gravitational Lensing.

Einstein predicted that the curvature of light from more distant masses in space by the presence of closer masses in space could produce a lensing effect. If conditions were ideal, the radiation from the more distant mass might appear as a circle. If irregularities were involved, up to several disconnected images might be found in a roughly circular pattern.

Although evidence of that has been found, there is considerable doubt that it provides proof of curved space. Because the distances of both the source of the radiation and the lensing matter are subject to question, it is likely that the observed lensing is the effect of the gravity of the closer mass on the equivalent mass of photons from the more distant body.

Mercury's Perihelion.

Calculations based on General Relativity also provided for the determination of the small rotation of the axis of the elliptical orbit of the planet Mercury each time it passes close to the Sun. That was also acclaimed as proof of relativity.

Einstein thought they were fairly good, but there are reasons to question those results, which include:

- The Sun is not perfectly spherical.
- Its oscillations produce changes in its shape.
- There are tidal distortions of both the Sun and Mercury.
- The Sun's radiation pressure and solar wind could be significant.
- When bodies are close to each other, unless they are perfectly spherical, their centers of gravitational attraction are shifted; in this case, in an unknown manner.

Clifford Will wrote in *Was Einstein Right?* that the Sun is oblate, Ivan King wrote in *The Universe Unfolding* that, "Mercury has permanent tidal bulge," Heinz Pagels wrote in *Perfect Symmetry* that the Sun is, "vibrating in various modes like a shaking bowl off gelatin," and helioseismologist Jack Harvey has said that Sun is, "rocked with the equivalent of 400 billion Hiroshima bombs....It's like a pipe organ that 10 million tunes can be played on."

Equivalence of Acceleration and Gravitation.

In the elevator example discussed above, although sustained acceleration might feel the same as gravity, and although the light beam path may look like the same as might be produced by gravity, that provides no proof of the equivalence of acceleration and gravity, or that there is only acceleration instead of gravity. Although the mathematical equations for their effects might be quite similar, that doesn't prove that they are the same.

In fact, a careful examination of that situation, as described by Roger Penrose, a famed member of the establishment, shows in *The Emperor's New Mind* that acceleration and gravity are not identical.

However, most of the establishment not only accepts the equivalence of acceleration and gravitation, but they also accept the idea from quantum theory that gravitation is the result of particles they call gravitons. But, if acceleration and gravitation are equivalent, and the Einstein elevator is suddenly accelerated, gravitons must in some mysterious way be suddenly alerted to appear on the scene. Neither relativity or quantum theory can provide an explanation for that.

The Equivalence of Mass and Energy.

Science historian Helge Kragh has related that long before Einstein, others in addition to Lebedev, had suggested mass and energy equivalence. Those included William Crookes, who Kragh quoted as having said in 1986, "It is equally impossible to conceive of matter without energy, as of energy without matter, from one point of view the two are convertible terms," and that Soddy had suggested that equivalence in 1904. Kragh remarked that, "The suggestion of a mass-energy equivalence more than a year before Einstein's famous $E = Mc^2$ formula may seem astounding, but in fact such equivalence was well known before Einstein."

Mach's Principle.

Although Einstein initially accepted Mach's principle, and based his early work on it, he later denied its validity. As Kragh has written, "Originally Einstein believed that his relativistic theory of cosmology embodied Mach's principle, but in his later years he concluded that the principle could not be harmonized with the general theory of relativity."

Austrian mathematician, physicist and philosopher Ernst Mach (in 1893) had suggested that the inertial properties of matter are in some manner related to the rest of the matter of the universe, and thus are the cause of momentum. Michael Rowan-Robinson has stated that in one short sentence as, "Local inertial properties should be determined by the gravitational field of the rest of the matter of the universe."

As an illustration of that idea, if you were in outer space and you rotated your body, you would sense centrifugal force, as you would here on earth. If there were no other matter in the universe it would seem impossible for that to occur.

That simple example alone should provide sufficient evidence in support of Mach's principle. However, relativity supposes that effect to be the result of the properties of empty space that is not *really* empty, but contains some unknown, unproven physical content.

Black Holes.

If there are black holes, or if there had been a BB, both being singularities of infinite density, according to General Relativity their space would have infinite positive curvature, that is, infinite gravity, which presents some difficulties.

In the case of a black hole mentioned above, infalling matter would reach infinite mass and zero speed as it reaches its event horizon. As observed by an outsider, nothing would ever fall into it. In the case of a BB, nothing could have escaped such great gravity; or such great space curvature, as Einstein would have you believe.

Tests of General Relativity.

The results of tests that have been made regarding General Relativity have been far from conclusive. However, even if they had confirmed that theory, there is no reason to believe they would apply to the conditions of the BB singularity of infinite temperature, infinite density, and infinite gravity.

Regarding BB cosmology that is based on general relativity, Jayant Narlikar has written, "How far has this theory been tested?

To what extent is this theory to be trusted in our extrapolations all the way to the Big Bang epoch?"

EINSTEIN'S GENIUS

Albert Einstein has been publicized as the greatest genius that ever lived. He undoubtedly was very smart, but perhaps not the smartest ever.

His 4-dimentional space-time came from German mathematician Bernard Riemann and others, with the help of mathematician Marcel Grossman.

His photon particles of radiation came from German physicist Max Planck.

His transformations came directly from Lorentz.

Although later rejected by him, his early ideas regarding matter in space were based on Mach's Principle.

The equivalence of mass and energy was, based on the work of Lebedev and others.

He needed much help with his mathematics.*

He was unable to solve his own equations of General Relativity; later solved by Friedmann.

Of course, those sorts of statements might be made about many innovative scientists. What is incorrect is the label of "the greatest genius that ever lived." I submit that Isaac Newton, discoverer of the laws of gravity and inventor of calculus, for one, was a greater genius.

Both Special and General Relativity are far from proven scientific fact.

---

* See *Black Holes and Time Warps* by Kip S. Thorne: Einstein got advice from an old classmate, Marcel Grossman, a professor of mathematics, as to whether a set of equations had ever been developed that could help him figure out curved space. Grossman found that there was such mathematics that Bernard Riemann in the 1860s, and others over the the next 50 years (Italian Gregorio Riccio in the 1880s and Riccio's student Tullio Levi-Civita in the 1890s and 1900s) had developed that was called "absolute differential geometry." Einstein and Grossman struggled together with its equations (renamed "tensor analysis") to reconcile space-time curvature with the theory of relativity. In 1914 they eventually succeeded in writing a set of equations, now called the Einstein field equations, that were consistent with Einstein's theory.

APPENDIX B

Particle Physics

This appendix is intended to provide an introduction to the standard model of the fundamental particles of nature that might be of value to the reader in relation to the subject of cosmology, the Standard Model of Particle Physics.

The standard model is based on what is called "gauge theory," a unified theory of the electromagnetic, strong, and weak interactions of the elementary particles of nature. Characteristics of these particles are listed in Figure B, the Standard Model of Particle Physics.

Consideration of the hypothetical unit of gravitational force, the graviton, and the hypothetical unifying Higgs boson is also included. Although those particles have not been observed. they are included to provide a more complete picture of particle theory as envisioned by modern theorists.

Much of the details of the standard model are dependent upon what is called gauge symmetry, a theory concerned with mathematical transformations in space and time, and with the symmetries of the laws of nature and of the quantum particles of the standard model. Gauge theory is based on a complex branch of mathematics known as group theory that has to do with the effect of various sequences of transformations on an object or groups of objects in time and space.

It should be understood that the particles of nature are

called particles only as a matter of convenience.

According to modern theory they are forms of energy that exhibit the characteristics of both particles and waves. For example, photons appear as discrete increments of energy when causing a light sensing device such as a photomultiplier tube to emit single detectable electrons, but they also possess wave transmission characteristics over the entire electromagnetic spectrum, that includes radio, heat, light, ultraviolet, X-ray and gamma ray wavelengths.

This duality of characteristics provides a simple and well known example of the attributes of quantum theory which is believed to apply to all the elementary particles of nature. Although the duality of quantum phenomena is inconsistent with normal human experience and intuitive understanding, it has been demonstrated to apply to natural phenomena. Perhaps some future theory might be advanced that will reconcile quantum duality with everyday experience, but in the meantime it must be taken as correct.

There are at least five "layers" of the structure of the matter of the universe. These are molecules, atoms, nuclei, hadrons (protons and neutrons) and fermions (leptons and quarks). It is possible that a sixth, or even more, layers exist. Fermions may be made up of even smaller particles, but evidence of their existence has not been established.

The standard model is concerned with the structure of the atoms of the elements, but hasn't much to do with the molecules of compounds (molecular structure), which would take us into the field of chemistry. It is primarily concerned with the three lower layers of matter; especially the lowest two levels, fermions and hadrons, and with the forces that "mediate" the interactions between them.

The elementary particles called fermions are considered to be the building blocks of nature. Fermions are named after Italian-American physicist Enrico Fermi. They are divided into two general groups; leptons and quarks.

All fermions are spin 1/2 particles that have four possible polarizations (X, Y, Z or T), of which only two are available to electrons. (Spin 1/2 means that they have an angular momentum of 1/2 h, where h is Planck's constant, 10^{-27} erg-second.)

There are twelve fermions—six leptons and six quarks—each of which has a different rest mass. These occur in pairs; each of them has its antiparticle (not listed in Figure B) of opposite charge, but otherwise having the identical properties of the particle.

Leptons have electric charges of either one or zero, and quarks have electric charges of either plus 2/3 or minus 1/3.

The name "lepton" is the Greek word for "light" or "small", and the name "hadron" is from the Greek word for "thick." The word "quark" had no real meaning. It was adopted (from a passage in *Finnegan's Wake* by James Joyce that goes "three quarks for Muster Mark") for the name of particles first proposed (in 1963) by Murray Gell-Mann and independently by George Zweig (both of the California Institute of Technology) for the structure of hadrons.

Fermions are further divided into three families or generations.

Family one consists of the electron, its neutrino, and up and down quarks; family two of the muon, its neutrino, and charm and strange quarks; and family three of the tau, its neutrino, and top and bottom quarks (also called truth and beauty).

The ordinary matter of the universe is made up of the particles of family one. Second and third family particles (with the possible exception of neutrinos) are unstable, meaning that they are very short lived; they rapidly decay into more stable particles of lower mass. Their lifetimes are within the range of 10^{-25} to 10^{-6} seconds.

With the possible exception of the proton which has been shown to have a lifetime of at least 10^{31} seconds, far longer than the age of the universe as reckoned by BBT, all the fundamental particles have limited lifetimes.

Unless a neutron is in a stable nucleus, it decays (to a proton, electron and a neutrino) in about ten minutes, but more exotic particles have lifetimes between one millionth and one ten-trillionth of a second. As examples of short lived particles, muons (mu mesons) decay in about one millionth of a second to an electron, neutrino and an antineutrino; and pions (pi mesons), of which there are three kinds having plus, minus or no charge, decay much faster. Charged pions decay in 10^{-8} second and neutral pions decay in 10^{-16} second.

Scientists have for many years considered the possibility of the existence of more than three families of fundamental particles, but experiments at the Large Electron-Positron (LEP) collider at the

European Laboratory for Particle Physics (known as CERN) are believed to have demonstrated that the families are limited to three.

Each family of leptons and quarks is about one to two orders of magnitude more massive than the previous family. The more massive the particle, the more energy is required to produce it, and the minimum required energy is equal to its rest mass. That means that higher and higher accelerator energies are required to produce the more massive particles. For example, the Fermilab (for Fermi National Accelerator Laboratory) Tevatron near Chicago can produce proton-antiproton collisions as great as 1.8 trillion electron volts (TeV), sufficient to produce tau particles having a rest mass of 1.784 TeV.

It should be noted that, although these numbers are very large, one electron volt is only the energy needed to move an electron through a potential of one volt. Thus to move one electron, that has a rest mass of 9.11 times 10^{-28} grams, through a trillion volts (1 TeV)—or a trillion electrons through one volt—is only 1.6 ergs of work, about enough to lift a feather a few inches.

(An erg is the amount of work done by a force of one dyne moving through one centimeter, and a dyne is a force of only one gram-centimeter per second squared.)

Of the particles of the standard model, electrons, protons, neutrons and photons are the most familiar.

Electrons of course account for the flow of electricity in conductors, through the atmosphere as lightning, and as the beam of the cathode ray tubes of radar and television displays. They are spin 1/2 leptons having a rest mass of 0.511 MeV (0.511 million electron volts) and an electrical charge of minus one. Except for their greater mass and short life, muons (mu mesons) and taus (tau mesons) are similar to electrons. The antiparticle of the electron is the positron which has the same characteristics as the electron except for its unit positive charge.

Neutrinos are spin 1/2, zero electrical charge partners of the corresponding leptons of their family. They have very low mass as compared to their partners, or perhaps none at all. They are not involved in electromagnetic or strong interactions of the fundamental particles. Because of their low mass and lack of interactions, neutrinos can travel through other matter, including the entire diameter of the Earth.

There are six types or "flavors" of quarks; up, down, charm, strange, top and bottom. Up, charm and top quarks, one of each family, have electrical charges of plus 2/3 and rest masses of about 5 MeV, 1.5 GeV and about 175 GeV (175 billion electron volts) respectively. Down, strange and bottom quarks, the second of each family, have an electrical charge of minus 1/3 and rest masses of about 10 MeV, 150 MeV and 5 GeV respectively.

In addition to their electrical charge, each quark can be of three different "colors;" usually called red, green and blue. Quark's flavors and colors are purely artificial; they are arbitrarily chosen names for previously unknown characteristics of those particles. Color is to the strong force what charge is to the electric force.

Electric charge has only two states (positive and negative), whereas color has three states. The six corresponding antiquark colors (charges) are anti-red, anti-green and anti-blue.

Quarks are thought to be truly fundamental, having neither structure or spatial dimensions, but individual quarks have not been observed. However, accelerator experiments seem to verify that sets of three quarks exist within protons. Those particles, and their antiparticles, may still be considered hypothetical, but there is considerable evidence in support of their existence.

All particles made up of quarks are called hadrons, of which there are two classes: baryons (meaning "heavy ones"), made up of three quarks (also antibaryons made up of three antiquarks) that have 1/2 integer spin; and mesons, made up of a quark and an antiquark that have integer spin, i.e., they have a spin of zero or one.

Of the baryons, protons are made up of two up quarks and one down quark giving them an electrical charge of plus one, and neutrons are made up of one up quark and two down quarks giving them an electrical charge of zero. Neutrons and protons in turn adhere to form atomic nuclei. (Neutrons and protons are called nucleons.)

There are other hadrons called "strange" particles that result from accelerator collisions. Those include, for example, a relatively stable strange baryon called a "lambda" in which one of the up quarks is replaced by a strange quark. The proton, neutron and the lambda, among the lowest energy level hadrons, are relatively stable and readily observable. Others, of higher energy configurations, are very short lived, and rapidly decay into lower level hadrons.

Mesons, the second category of hadrons, are made up of a quark and an antiquark. They have integer spin and a charge of zero. As an example, B mesons are made up of a bottom quark and an anti-down or an antistrange quark. Pi mesons or pions, that have also been observed in accelerators, are short lived, light mass hadrons that are thought to be necessary to the structure of atomic nuclei, i.e., the force that binds proton and neutrons within atomic nuclei is thought to be due to the exchange of pions and other hadrons of this second type.

There are believed to be only four basic forces in our universe. Those are electromagnetism, the strong nuclear force, the weak nuclear force and gravity.

The electromagnetic force (EMF) binds nuclei and electrons, which are one kind of lepton, into atoms and the residual EMF binds atoms into molecules. The strong force binds quarks together to make protons and neutrons, the residual strong force binds protons and neutrons together into nuclei. The weak force is responsible for certain kinds of nuclear decay. The influence of the weak force and the strong force extends only over a short range, no larger that the radius of an atom nucleus.

Gravity and electromagnetism have unlimited range, and are therefore the most familiar of the forces.

Standard model gauge bosons (named after Indian physicist S. N. Bose) are believed to provide the four corresponding coupling forces that generate attraction and repulsion among the different types of fermions. The force between particles arises from the exchange of these "mediators" at finite speed, i.e., at speeds less than that of light.

The mediator of electromagnetism is the photon, of the strong force is the gluon, and of the weak force is the Z zero, the W minus and the W plus bosons. Those coupling forces have vector fields, meaning they have directional orientation and magnitude; and their carriers are spin 1. (Spin one bosons are "vector bosons.")

The hypothetical graviton (spin 2) is thought to be the mediator of gravitation, and the hypothetical Higgs boson (spin 0) is thought to be necessary for mathematical consistency of the entire standard model.

Photons (EMF vector bosons), the particles or quanta of electromagnetism, have zero rest mass, zero electric charge and infinite range, but a strength of only one one-hundredth of that of the strong nuclear force. They interact with all particles having electromagnetic charge. They bind electrons to nuclei to form atoms and thus play a major role in determining the chemistry of the universe. Quantum electromagnetic relationships are described by the mathematical theory called quantum electrodynamics or QED.

Gluons (strong force vector bosons), the mediators of the strong nuclear force, also have zero rest mass and zero electric charge, but their range is limited to about 10^{-13} centimeters. The strong force is responsible for the large amount of energy released by nuclear fusion. Gluons act within atomic nuclei to bind quarks together and to bind protons and neutrons. There are eight types of gluons, corresponding to eight combinations of the three colors of quarks, i.e., red-antigreen, red-antiblue, etc.

In addition to binding quarks to form protons and neutrons, gluons can bind to each other. For example, a red-antigreen gluon and a green-antiblue gluon can bind to form a red-antiblue gluon.

Quantum strong force interactions with quarks are described by the mathematical theory known as quantum chromodynamics or QCD ("chromo" for "color").

The weak nuclear force has a strength of about 10^{-13} times that of the strong nuclear force and a range of about 10^{-16} centimeters. The weak force acts on both leptons and hadrons and is responsible for radioactive decay of one particle to another of lesser mass. It is also responsible for nuclear reactions in the stars. Of its three related mediators, called intermediate vector bosons, Z zero has a rest mass of 91.2 GeV and an electrical charge of zero, W minus has a rest mass of 90 GeV and a charge of minus 1, and W plus has the same rest mass but the opposite electrical charge of plus one.

Intermediate vector bosons have lifetimes of only on the order of 10^{-25} seconds. Z zero, the most massive particle observed, weighs about 100 times as much as a proton. Individual Z zero particles differ slightly in mass; the spread of their mass is known as mass width. They decay in about 10^{-25} second to produce a pair of elementary particles such as an electron and a positron.

Theoretical physicists Steven Weinberg and Abdus Salam (in 1968) developed a unified quantum theory concerning the electromagnetic and the weak field phenomena that is known as electroweak theory.

In addition, attempts have been made by many others to extend this unification to include strong field theory into what is known as grand unified field theories or GUTs. Some variations of these theories appear to have some degree of merit.

Gravitons, the hypothetical mediating quanta of gravitation, are said to have a rest mass of zero, a spin of two, and no electrical charge. Gravitational force, which is believed to be a tensor field, has a strength of 10^{-38} times that of the strong force, but its range is infinite. (The definition of a tensor field, which involves the modulus—the parameters—of a quaternium, a set of four vectors, is beyond the scope of this book.)

Because of its extreme weakness, gravity has negligible impact on experimental verification of gauge theory. However, even though it is the weakest of the forces, its influence is effective at greater distance than the other three.

A major quest of theoretical physicists is to incorporate the force of gravity into an all-encompassing unified theory, which, although nonexistent, has been named the theory of everything or TOE. To date no satisfactory TOE has been developed.

The hypothetical Higgs boson has zero spin and zero electrical charge. Its rest mass is thought to be at least 90 GeV, and possibly as much as one TeV. It is the mediator of the hypothetical Higgs force, which is a scalar field, i.e., it has only magnitude; no directional orientation. Gauge theory predicts a Higgs field of infinite range that is needed for mathematical consistency of the standard model. It is thought to be necessary for the generation of the mass of other particles.

The Higgs boson is not considered to be a full fledged member of the standard model, but it is well accepted by physicists as essential to modern theory.

FERMIONS (All fermions are spin 1/2 particles)

Family	LEPTONS Particle Name	Symbol	Rest Mass	Electrical Charge	QUARKS Particle Name	Symbol	Rest Mass	Electrical Charge
1	Electron	e	0.511 MeV	- 1	UP	u	5 MeV	+ 2 / 3
1	Electron Neutrino	ν_e	< 10 eV	0	DOWN	d	10 MeV	- 1 / 3
2	Muon	$\mu-$	106.6 MeV	- 1	CHARM	c	1.5 GeV	+ 2 / 3
2	Muon Neutrino	ν_μ	< 0.25 eV	0	STRANGE	s	150 MeV	- 1 / 3
3	Tau (or Tauon)	$\tau-$	1,784 MeV	- 1	TOP or Truth	t	175 GeV	+ 2 / 3
3	Tau Teutrino	ν_τ	< 65 MeV	0	BOTTOM or Beauty	b	5 GeV	- 1 / 3

BOSONS

Force	Range	Strength*	Carrier	Rest Mass (Gev)	Spin	Electrical Charge
Electromagnetism (vector field)	Infinite	10^{-2}	Photon	0	1	0
Strong (vector field)	10^{-13} cm	1	Gluon	0	1	0
Weak (vector field)	10^{-15} cm	10^{-13}	Z°	91.2	1	0
			W-	90	1	-1
			W+	90	1	+1
Gravity (tensor field)	Infinite	10^{-38}	Graviton	0	2	0
Higgs (scaler field)	Infinite	?	Higgs Boson	>90	0	0

* Strength at 10^{-12} cm in comparison with the strong force

Various sources disagree on the values of ranges and strengths of some bosons.
The values given here cannot be considered to be exact.

FIGURE B. STANDARD MODEL OF PARTICLE PHYSICS

List of Characteristics

APPENDIX C

Quantum Theory

As indicated in Appendix B, the standard model of modern physics is based to a large extent on quantum theory. Various attempts to overcome faults that were found in Standard BBT have also been based on quantum theory. It may therefore be useful to review some ideas from quantum theory, and some of its history.

It was all started by German physics professor Max Planck in about 1900. His initial quantum ideas came out of his studies of black-body radiation from which his radiation law developed. (A black-body radiator is simply a material that has a very black rough surface that allows it to readily absorb or radiate heat energy.)

Planck found that he could derive the correct law of distribution of radiated energy if he made some assumptions, one of which was that energy is produced in discrete amounts; and another is that the amount of energy is equal to an integer multiplied by the frequency (the Greek letter nu), of the radiated energy and by Planck constant, h. ($E = Nh\nu$.)

It had been known for some time that light can cause electrons to be ejected from metals and that their velocity is not dependent on light intensity but on its frequency, and that the number ejected is not dependent on the frequency but on the intensity of the light. Based on that phenomenon, with knowledge of Planck's work, in 1905 Albert Einstein proposed that light acts as though it is transmitted in quanta, or units of energy, equal to hv, Planck's constant times frequency. (The constant N can be omitted if the proper units of h and v are used.)

In 1911 British physics professor Ernest Rutherford (born in New Zealand) proposed an atomic structure having electrons in orbit about the atomic nucleus, a brilliant idea, but according to classical physics it couldn't exist. Energy would be continuously radiated and electrons would spiral into the nucleus. Danish physicist Niels Bohr in 1913 modified Rutherford's model to incorporate the quantum ideas of Planck and Einstein. In his model electrons occupied only orbits of permitted energy levels. A quantum of energy is emitted when an electron "jumps" from one energy level to a lower one. This theory provided an explanation for discrete spectral emission lines from various elements.

However great the logic of quantum theory, until about 1920, it was still only an unverified theory.

At that time American theoretical physicist Arthur Compton, while studying the behavior of X-rays, found that when they were directed at matter they would be scattered, but the scattered radiation would be of longer wavelength. In 1923 he was able to explain this effect as the result of X-ray quantums on electrons. The X-ray quantum continues on its way but with lower energy, i.e., longer wavelength, and the electron absorbs the lost energy. Laboratory confirmation of this phenomenon, called the Compton effect, was a major factor in subsequent general acceptance of early quantum ideas and its further rapid development.

In 1925 Austrian physicist Wolfgang Pauli discovered his exclusion principle that further clarified atomic structure.

According to that principle, electrons in orbit about the atomic nucleus cannot be adjacent to each other due to their mutual repulsion; a kind of a quantum version of Archimedes' principle that no two bodies can occupy the same space at the same time. That repulsion is in addition to that of like negative charges. It was a newly discovered effect called exchange force that keeps electrons apart and prevents them from falling into the nucleus. It applies only to spin 1/2 particles, i.e., fermions (leptons and quarks); not to integer spin particles, the mediators of the fundamental forces. The Pauli exclusion principle showed, among other things, that in an atom there can be only a small number of energy states for an electron, and only a small number of electrons can occupy each state.

Also in 1925 German theoretical physicist Werner Heisenberg, with his colleagues at the Institute for Theoretical Physics at Copenhagen, using the mathematics of matrices, developed a mathematical description of the relationships of the frequency, the intensity and the polarization of atomic spectral emission lines. His mathematical method, called matrix mechanics, avoided the use of a mechanical model of the atom, and provided quantum theory with a sound mathematical basis.

In 1926 British theoretical physicist Paul Dirac presented an equivalent mathematical basis called non commutative algebra, and Austrian theoretical physicist Erwin Schrodinger presented his work on wave mechanics in which the state of a mechanical system is given by a "wave function."

Later, in collaboration with theoretical physicist Max Born (who was a teacher of Fermi, Heisenberg and American physicist J. Robert Oppenheimer) and Pascual Jordan, Heisenberg developed a more complete version of quantum theory, called quantum mechanics, that could be used to calculate the properties of atoms.

The simple picture of electrons as solid particles in orbit around a nucleus, like planets around the Sun, was no longer acceptable. The particles of physics appeared to have a dual nature, sometimes seeming to behave like particles and sometimes like waves. This new theory was able to explain their behavior in detail. It also applied to electromagnetism, i.e., it showed how Einstein's idea of particles of light (photons) could be mathematically described.

Much of the early work on the development of quantum theory was done at the Copenhagen Institute, where Niels Bohr was the undisputed leader and mentor of his disciples, that included Born, Heisenberg, Jordan and Pauli. That is where the Copenhagen or standard interpretation of quantum theory, which included the dual nature of quantum particle behavior and the concept of observer participation, originated. Bohr himself played a major role in these developments.

Basing his work on relativity, and the new quantum ideas, Sir Arthur Eddington (in 1926) published his work, *The Internal Constitution of the Stars*, in which he described the processes within the stars. He suggested that nuclear reactions provided their energy. Although those processes were not well understood until years later, his general concept and many of its details were later proven to be essentially correct.

In 1927 Heisenberg presented his famous uncertainty principle. According to that principle the position and the momentum (mass times velocity) of a particle cannot be measured simultaneously.

If those measurements of a single particle are repeated they will be found to fluctuate around an average value. Unlike measurements of classical mechanics, in quantum mechanics only a probability distribution of measurements can be determined. Classical physics is said to be a special case of quantum physics that applies to large-scale matter, but is not valid for fundamental microscopic particle behavior. A new way of thinking about particle physics had to be adopted.

(As Barrow and Silk wrote in *The Left Hand of Creation*, "Could we know exactly where the particle was in space? The uncertainty principle says no, and the reason is that when we try to measure its position, we inevitably move it in the process. By bouncing a photon off the particle into our microscope, we change its position. By the time we "see" it and record its position, it is no longer at that initial position The uncertainty principle tells us that the uncertainty that the act of measurement creates is at least as big as Planck's constant.")

In 1928 theoretical physicists Pascual Jordan, Eugene Wigner, and subsequently Heisenberg and Pauli, showed that each of the force fields of nature has an associated particle that is the quantized form of the field.

That was an entirely new idea. Fields have quantum attributes. Their particles, photons, gluons, Ws and Zs are included in the standard model. In modern field theory gravitation is thought to have its particle, the graviton, and even the hypothetical Higgs field is thought to have a Higgs particle.

By 1928 Paul Dirac had formulated what is known as the Dirac equation governing the behavior of electrons, but only for the very simplest system, that of the hydrogen atom, having only one proton and one electron. He found, however, that his equation also described a new particle having the same characteristics as the electron except that it had an opposite (positive) electrical charge. The existence of this antielectron, now known as the positron, was detected in 1932 by Carl Anderson, who was then a graduate student of physics at the California Institute of Technology.

Since that time antiparticles of many of the particles of the standard model have been observed in particle accelerators.

Dirac's work also showed that if a particle and its antiparticle should collide they would be annihilated, producing a shower of gamma rays, and, on the other hand, if enough energy is provided, a particle and its antiparticle could be created. The energy required would be equivalent to the rest masses of the particles, in accordance with Einstein's $E = Mc^2$.

Dirac's development of quantum electrodynamics (QED) in 1928, that utilized only one arbitrary constant, Planck's constant, provided the basis for many highly accurate predictions of elementary particle behavior.

The discovery of antiparticles drastically changed all of particle physics. Matter was previously thought to be permanent and unchangeable. Because it was demonstrated that particles and antiparticles can be created in the vacuum of high energy accelerators, it became possible to believe that might happen under natural circumstances.

Following that, several new particles were predicted and subsequently found.

Based on his previous work, and that of others, Wolfgang Pauli was able to predict the existence of an extremely low mass, charge-less particle that would therefore be difficult to detect.

Another of the architects of quantum theory, Enrico Fermi, named Pauli's particle the "neutrino" from the Italian word "bambino." The existence of this "baby" particle was confirmed in an accelerator in the 1950s. The neutrino was discovered by James Chadwick in 1932, and in 1934 a massive hadron, the pi meson, or pion, (200 times heavier than an electron) was predicted by Japanese physicist Hiedki Yukawa and was detected in 1938 in atomic nuclei.

Most of the new particles are extremely short lived—as short as 10^{-24} second—making them very difficult to detect.

In the 1940s several large particle accelerators were built to aid in the quest for more knowledge about particle physics.

It was known that the nucleus of atoms was made up of electrically neutral neutrons and positively charged protons. Much was known about the properties of electrons and photons, but little was known about the structure of neutrons and protons or other particles of the modern standard model.

In the late 1940s pi mesons were observed in accelerator laboratories. In the early 1950s many more such highly reactive particles were discovered. Those particles, called hadrons, created quite a problem. There was no understanding as to how they fit into the structure of matter.

It turned out that all hadrons, which includes protons and neutrons, are composed of a new variety of particles called quarks, held together by gluons. This elaborate theory, QCD, (See Appendix B) regarding the structure of hadrons is a truly remarkable result of the conceptual genius of its originators, physicists Murray Gell-Mann and George Zweig in 1963.

Since its discovery this structure has been confirmed beyond any doubt. Gell-Mann/Zweig theory provided an immense simplification to the understanding of the structure of the universe. Instead of the possibility of different neutrons and protons for each element, all of them are composed of combinations of a relatively small number of quarks; six "flavors" each of eight possible "colors" for a total of 48 possible varieties of quarks.

Individual quarks have not been observed, and that work wasn't taken very seriously until accelerator experiments in 1967 provided evidence of these point particles orbiting each other within protons and neutrons. Although there is no evidence of it as yet, quarks may someday be found to, in turn, consist of even smaller components, but there seems to be little doubt about the quark composition of hadrons.

Electrons, photons and quarks are said to be point particles, meaning they have no size, and therefore they are symmetrical. Like perfectly symmetrical spheres they have no orientation. An analogy to this may be water in the center of a tank whose molecules of H_2O are unaligned; they are oriented in random directions. But if that water should freeze its molecules become aligned, at least in local areas, and the symmetry is gone; symmetry has been "broken."

Prior to the 19th century a branch of mathematics called group theory, that had to do with "symmetrical operations" was invented by French mathematician Evariste Galois. As a simple example of that theory, when a sphere is subjected to two different series of rotations its appearance is unchanged. But when those operations are applied to nonsymmetrical objects

APPENDIX C • About Quantum Theory

the result of each series may be quite different.

Group theory describes symmetrical operations by a form of algebra that can be applied not only to three-dimensional space but to higher dimensional systems, including four-dimensional space-time, and to transformations of many kinds.

Hungarian-American physicist Eugene Wigner in 1939 was the first to consider group theory implications of the Lorentz transformations as related to quantum theory. From this he discovered that the mathematics of group theory can be used to classify each quantum particle according its rest mass and its spin.

If rest mass is zero, as it is for a photon, a particle can travel at the speed of light, and if greater than zero it can only travel at a lower speed. Quantum particles have spins of only zero and in increments of 1/2. If a particle has a spin of zero or a full integer it is a boson. If it has a spin of 1/2, 3/2, 5/2, etc., it is a fermion.

Wigner also showed that Heisenberg's uncertainty principle did not apply to the measurement of those characteristics of particles. Rest mass and spin can be precisely measured, thus providing a convenient means of classifying particles; especially so because it also applies to multiple particle configurations such as atomic nuclei.

Much of the standard model of fundamental particles is dependent upon gauge theory, or gauge symmetry, which relates geometrical transformations in space and time to particle symmetries in accordance with group theory and within the confines of the Special Theory of Relativity.

Some serious difficulties with quantum theory were encountered in the 1930s and 1940s. Some calculations persistently resulted in infinite masses, for which there is no place in the real world. These problems could be overcome by a mathematical trick called renormalization in which the infinite numbers were replaced by observed masses.

Renormalization has to do with the fact that calculations regarding a point particle, such as an electron, can result in an infinite mass at that point. But of course, the electron doesn't have infinite mass, so the actual mass is substituted for the infinity that arises, thus correcting the problem. This procedure provided correct solutions, but was still considered a trick.

In the late 1940s several theoretical physicists, including Freeman Dyson, Richard Feynman, Julian Schwinger and Sin-Itiro

Tomonaga working on quantum electrodynamics (QED), the study of the interactions of electrons and photons, showed that renormalization resulted in predictions of exactly the results of laboratory experiments regarding these particles.

(As described in *SCIENCE NEWS* (in 1990), "Absurdities had cropped up in the 1940s, when efforts to reconcile the theories of electromagnetism and quantum mechanics generated unacceptable, infinite values for properties such as charge and mass of an electron. [Feynman, Schwinger and Tomonaga] figured out a way to make the infinite values cancel out by means of a process called renormalization. In essence, the trio proposed that clouds of evanescent virtual particles obscured the properties of every real particle. They received the 1963 Nobel Prize in Physics for that achievement.")

Renormalization was no longer considered an "ad hoc" mathematical trick, but a necessary procedure of quantum theory. In the late 1960s mathematician Kenneth Wilson found a physical basis for the renormalization process in the strange scaling behavior of what are called "fractals" wherein the length of a crooked line (such as a coastline) may appear to vary greatly as the distance from which it is viewed is changed. This situation is analogous to that of quantum particles who's mass and coupling strength appears to change according to the distance at which they are examined.

According to current quantum thinking, all of the particles are manifestations of various fields. But the definition of a field is very difficult.

Before Einstein's paper on Special Relativity of 1905, the prevailing belief was that fields consisted of unknown matter that flowed through the aether of space, a concept that is believed to be discredited. Thus, the many fields of various kinds, that might best be visualized as forces that can occupy and travel through space, require no medium through which to travel.

Quantum theorists believe that space is not empty, but filled with those fields. Their energy fills the vacuum of space. Vacuum is not "nothing;" it is the lowest possible level of energy, and it is thought that fluctuations of this energy ("vacuum fluctuations") can cause particles to appear.

Some physicists believe that fields are all there are in the universe and that they are the simplest irreducible fundamental entities of physics. Perhaps all the particles of nature are fully defined by field equations that describe their properties and their interactions. According to quantum theorist Steven Weinberg, in *The First Three Minutes*, all of reality is a set of fields. Everything else can be derived from the dynamics of quantum fields.

Every field can be defined by its field equations and, if fields obey Einstein's Special Relativity and can be classified by Wigner's method, every field has a rest mass and a spin. Fields are further classified according to other characteristics such as electrical charge or color.

Some fields that correspond to massless quantum particles, such as electromagnetism and gravitation, have infinite range. Others correspond to the interactions of more massive particles, such as weak force bosons, that have very limited range.

Fields of the same type can of course combine to add or subtract in space in a straightforward manner to produce instantaneous net fields. Because fields are quantized, that is, they obey the laws of quantum theory, the intensity of a field at each point in space is a matter of probability. Just as the path and location of a quantum particle is subject to Heisenberg's uncertainty principle, that principle also applies to the fields of the quantum physics. Fields are thus probability waves for their quantum particles.

Although it seems far from obvious, some theoretical physicists claim that the universe is extremely simple: It consists only of space that is filled with nothing but quantum fields that can appear as quantum particles speeding in all directions as they interact with each other according to the rules of Special Relativity and quantum theory. The mathematics of quantum theory is said to overcome the duality of the fundamental particles and accurately describe their properties and their interactions in all respects throughout the entire universe and for all time.

[Scientist (chemist and science writer) Jim Baggot has written that, "A quantum particle is neither a wave or a particle. Instead we substitute the appropriate classical concept—wave or particle—as and when necessary," and goes on to say that according to Bohr, "There is no quantum world. There is only an abstract physical description."]

As mentioned in Appendix B, the standard model of particle physics is based on gauge theory, which in turn is based on group theory. This application of gauge theory is due to the work of physicists C. N. Yang and Robert Mills in 1968 which has become known as Yang-Mills field theory. The work of theoretical physicists has shown that Yang-Mills field quantities are not apparent until the symmetry of those fields are broken. (All particles were symmetrical until their symmetry was broken.) Thus all the matter of the universe is present because its original total symmetry once was broken.

Like supercooled water that suddenly freezes, symmetry was unstable, but broken symmetry, like the ice that forms, is stable. Apparently that symmetry breaking can be spontaneous, as was first suggested by Scottish physicist Peter Higgs of the University of Edinburgh in 1965.

Following that Steven Weinberg, Pakistani physicist Abdus Salam, Sheldon Glashow and other physicists used Higgs' idea in a Yang-Mills gauge theory model to unite the electromagnetic and the weak forces, thus developing the electroweak theory. This work was neglected until 1971 when it was shown that the Yang-Mills theories were renormalizable and could be used to calculate electromagnetic interactions in agreement with the results of quantum electrodynamics.

The Higgs boson was needed to make the electroweak theory renormalizable. Higgs' idea of a symmetry breaking field has tentatively been incorporated into the standard model. This hypothetical spinless but massive Higgs boson is used to mathematically investigate the symmetry breaking process. According to Yang-Mills theory all fields are massless and hidden, but when gauge symmetry breaks, some of them acquire mass.

The validity of electroweak theory, which was based on the Yang-Mills model and Higgs symmetry breaking was demonstrated by its prediction of the intermediate vector bosons, Z zero, W- and W+ particles. When they were experimentally discovered, Ws in 1982 and Zs in 1983, they had masses of almost the exact amounts predicted.

The detection of those extremely short-lived particles—the Zs have a life of 10^{-25} second—took until those late dates because of their great mass; about 90 GeV. The creation of detectable quantities of these particles required powerful accelerators that were not previously available. The Higgs boson, which may be considerably more massive than these particles, may require the use of even more powerful accelerators that are presently proposed or under construction.

Electromagnetic and weak field theories were thus unified to produce electroweak theory. The quest by theoretical physicists to add the strong field theory to that to produce what has been named grand unified theory, or GUT, has since continued but with only minor success. For a number of years physicists have felt confident that this will soon be accomplished. Perhaps it will be within a few more years.

That will leave the greatest quest of all, one that Einstein and other theorists have struggled with for decades, for a single unified theory of all the laws of the universe; the theory of everything, or TOE. In GUT, Einstein's Special Relativity is united with quantum theory by Wigner's work. If TOE is someday developed as hoped, it will unite his General Relativity with all of quantum theory.

Despite its several unsatisfactory aspects and difficult concepts, such as particle/wave duality, observer participation, the uncertainty principle, the wave function, particle pair creation, the Higgs particle, renormalization and symmetry breaking, the current gauge theory standard model represents the best information available on the fundamental particles of physics.

On the other hand, although both quantum theory and relativity have had successes, they are far from complete. Despite the efforts of theorists for most of the twentieth century, all attempts to unify gravity and quantum theory have failed. Undoubtedly there are flaws in both of those theories that must be attended to.

APPENDIX D

Flights of Fantasy

A few examples of the flights of fantasy of theoretical physicists during the past couple of decades are presented in this appendix. They are included in order to illustrate some of the wild ideas that been have proposed, and to provide some additional background related to Standard BBT and especially to inflation theory.

Vacuum Fluctuations.

The concept that the universe might consist of nothing but empty space filled with fields grew out of early quantum theory. From this came the idea that vacuum is not "nothing," but in "a state of least energy density."

Fluctuations of energy in vacuum can result in "false vacuum," in which it is said that gravity becomes a repulsive rather than an attractive force, and in which particles of matter can be spontaneously generated. (In inflation theory the repulsive force of false vacuum was later replaced by a cosmological constant: Einstein's cosmic repulsion.)

In 1973 Edward Tryon suggested that the entire universe originated as a vacuum fluctuation that "ran away with itself" generating highly curved space and producing an avalanche of particles that resulted in the BB. This was proposed as a means of circumventing the violation of the law of conservation of mass/energy of previous BBT, thus solving the singularity problem.

As mentioned in Chapter 23, Edward Tryon wrote that, although they are "utterly commonplace in quantum field theory...vacuum fluctuations on the scale of our Universe are probably quite rare," but as the result of one of those, "our Universe is simply one of these things which happen from time to time."

That flight of fantasy didn't make much impact until the 1980s when it provided the basis for inflation theory. A variation of that, suggested by Martin Rees in 1976, was that when the curvature of space had the extreme value of the early BB universe, particle pairs could have been created out of gravitational fields in a manner similar to the creation of electron-positron pairs in strong electromagnetic fields. Thus Rees suggested that the space somehow became extremely curved—perhaps infinitely curved—before any matter came into existence.

Grand Unified Theories.

Some quantum theorists have come to believe that all that exists in the universe are fields. If that is so, when the equations for those fields have been completely formulated all that needs to be known about physics, and probably metaphysics as well, will be known.

Einstein was able to produce his work without ever conducting an experiment. These theorists apparently have concluded that in like manner they might complete Einstein's quest for a unified theory by sitting and manipulating mathematical abstractions.

(Theorists shouldn't be misled by Einstein's lack of experimentation. He believed, as did Mach, that measurements are essential for the validation of theory, and he proposed at least three tests for General Relativity. Those included observations regarding the deflection of star light by the Sun, the precession of the perihelion of Mercury and gravitational red shift.)

Following the successes of theoretical physicists during the late 1970s and early 1980s in unifying electromagnetic theory with weak field theory to produce electroweak theory, many theorists have turned to the task of expanding that unification process to incorporate strong field theory to develop a grand unified theory, or GUT. Because it doesn't include gravity, GUT is not intended be a complete unification, but only the next giant step in that direction. Some theorists have felt that they were closing in on a credible GUT, but the extreme difficulty of incorporating gravity to produce the theory of everything, or TOE, may require many additional years of a effort.

The simplest of the GUT theories, known as the SU(5) theory, indicates that the strong, weak and electromagnetic forces were indistinguishable before 10^{-33} second after the BB, which, according to BBT, is equivalent to an energy level of 10^{15} GeV (billion electron volts) and a temperature of 10^{27} degrees K. As the universe, whose size at that time was only about 10^{-29} centimeter, cooled to about that temperature, symmetry was broken, producing quarks and gluons. (It wasn't until about 10^{-10} second that the symmetry of the electroweak forces were broken.) In this theory leptons might be thought of as quarks of a fourth color.

The SU(5) GUT scheme contains three subgroups called U(1), SU(2) and SU(3) and combinations of them. U(1) has to do with various quantum numbers such as baryon number and lepton number and with the gauge theory of electromagnetism (QED), SU(2) has to do with the gauge theory of weak interactions, and SU(3) has to do with hadrons and the gauge theory of strong interactions (QCD).

The SU(5) GUT has encountered several problems. One of these is that it predicts that protons decay in about 10^{30} years, which according to BBT is about 10^{20} (100 billion billion) times the age of the BB universe. One would therefore expect it to be rather difficult to measure that decay. But, by isolating many times more than 10^{20} protons (2 million gallons of water) and using detectors of the predicted products of proton decay (a positron and a neutral pion), it has been determined that, if protons do decay (they had previously been thought to be "immortal"), it takes considerably longer than 10^{30} years; at least 100 times longer.

Several proton decay experiments have been conducted (deep in salt and iron mines in the United States, in lead mines in Japan and in a tunnel between France and Italy), but no proton decays have been detected. (See footnote page 122.)

Another problem is that an SU(5) GUT appears to require an additional set of vector bosons which would in turn require an additional scalar field similar to the hypothetical Higgs field. The new bosons might have masses of hundreds of GeVs, many times greater than the weak vector bosons. Neither these bosons or the new Higgs-like field may ever be detectable.

A third problem encountered is that, if the new Higgs-type field exists, they would require the existence of large amounts of isolated north and south magnetic poles, or monopoles and anti monopoles.

GUT indicates that there may be as many magnetic monopoles in the universe as there are protons, which has been estimated to be about 10^{80}. Although their abundance, their huge mass and their strong field should make them readily detectable, attempts to find them have been unsuccessful. (Of course, BB theorists have also suggested that they might prove to be the missing matter of the universe.)

The chance for acceptance of an unmodified SU(5) GUT is obviously quite poor. As a result, a number of variations have been proposed. One such variation involves additional sets of particles of greater mass called technicolor quarks (techniquarks) mediated by technicolor gluons and reacting in technicolor fields. Theorists may be looking for these in the products of more powerful accelerators of the future.

Magnetic Monopoles.

The idea of magnetic monopoles goes all the way back to 1931 when Dirac, while working on electromagnetic field theory, found that the mathematics indicated the possibility of their existence. If so, they would have a magnetic charge analogous to the electrical charge of an electron.

The idea of magnetic monopoles was brought up to date by Dutch physicist Gerard t'Hooft and Russian physicist A. M. Polyakof in 1974 when they showed (theoretically) that when symmetries of some of the gauge field theories are broken, magnetic monopoles (for some reason, also called "hedgehogs") would be produced, and that their properties could be calculated.

It also has been proposed that magnetic monopoles are "solitons" of energy in space. Solitons were first discovered as surges of channel water; solitary waves of energy that travel at relatively high speed. The mathematics of the soliton has been known for a century. It has been applied in other fields such as plasma physics, and more recently to magnetic monopoles that are said to remain intact and propagate in a manner similar to water solitons. Of course, as with other quantum particle pairs, if a monopole and an anti monopole were to meet they would annihilate with an enormous release of energy.

According to GUTs, magnetic monopoles are estimated to be about 10^{-14} centimeter in diameter and to be extremely massive, about 10^{16} times more massive than a proton. Assuming BBT to be correct, they were created in the first 10^{-35} second after the BB, traveled ever since, and now roam the universe. They are extremely abundant, absolutely stable, and are said to possess some additional exotic characteristics.

As mentioned, there may be as many as 10^{80} of them in the universe, and because of their powerful magnetic field they should be easy to detect. Immense accelerators would not be required for that purpose. In fact, devices have been designed to detect GUT monopoles by electromagnetic induction. However, except for one presumably false indication that has never been repeated, none have been detected.

If magnetic monopoles were as massive and abundant as supposed, they would undoubtedly have caused the collapse of the early BB universe. That possibility alone provided doubts about either GUT or BBT, or both. That doubt is said to have provided the motivation for the development of inflation theory by its originator, MIT physics professor Alan Guth.

Multiple Worlds and Domains.

One of the first to relate quantum theory to cosmology was renowned American physicist John Archibald Wheeler.

In regard to the cycling BB case, which he apparently accepted at that time, he suggested in 1970 that the probability amplitude concept of quantum theory as applied to the collapse of the universe might provide some answers concerning the outcome of that event. According to Wheeler the universe is "squeezed through a knot hole" and what comes out is anybody's guess. Each collapse could result in a whole new set of properties but, as in quantum electrodynamics, the outcome is subject to the participation of the observer. (Perhaps he thought there were observers of those events.)

Wheeler introduced to BB cosmology a many-worlds concept that was proposed in 1957 by his student Hugh Everett in his Ph.D. thesis. In this many-worlds interpretation of quantum mechanics a system is not well defined until it has been measured or "observed" in some manner. A measurement can not be made with certainty, only the probability of the outcome of a measurement can be predicted. This concept is especially strange when applied on the macroscopic level. Everett decided that the universe splits into parallel branches when observed, each branch corresponding to a different possible outcome, which could result in an infinite number of universes, each one having its own space and time.

This many-worlds concept sounds rather bizarre but, as we will see, Russian physicist Andrei Linde apparently thought enough of it to integrate it into his theory of chaotic new inflation. In his version of BBT, as the early universe cooled, separate domains developed in various regions of the universe that had totally different sets of physical laws. They were separated by massive domain walls, and observers in one domain, such as ourselves, have no means of establishing contact with other domains. Because of vast inflation of the universe, the domain walls are beyond the range of telescopes, and for the same reason the problematic magnetic monopoles are so far away that they don't disturb the evolution of our domain.

The generation of domain walls has also been described in another manner. It has been suggested that, as the extremely early BB universe cooled, the Higgs field came into being. If the cooling was not uniform the Higgs field would have different properties in different regions of space. This would result in some strong interactions at the boundaries of regions, generating massive domain walls.

Peebles, who presents domain walls as proven fact, suggests that, "in conventional physics domain walls gravitationally repel both matter and antimatter." Presumably, some domains are of matter and others of antimatter, thereby explaining the absence of anti-matter in our surroundings. Apparently his idea of "conventional physics" is quite different than those of us who live and work in the world of productive enterprise.

The Theory of Everything.

As with their previous attempts to produce lesser unifications, when physicists have attempted to integrate gravity with quantum theory to produce a TOE, infinities show up. But in this case equations for the graviton's interactions were found to be nonrenormalizable; infinities appeared that could not be disposed of.

As suggested in Appendix A, there may be another problem related to quantum theory's gravitons and relativity's equivalence of gravity and acceleration that could present an obstacle in the development of a TOE. As in the example of Einstein's thought experiment of Appendix A regarding an elevator in space, the sudden appearance of gravitons upon the acceleration of an object seems impossible to explain.

Although theoretical physicists have worked for many years to reconcile gravity and quantum theory, the above mentioned problems, and several others, have prevented any real progress. Some degree of success might be claimed for GUT theories in unifying electromagnetic, weak and strong forces, but until gravity is integrated with quantum theory there can be no single integrated TOE.

Although Stephen Hawking had suggested that the end may be in sight of theoretical physics, 20 years have passed since he made that comment, and no significant progress has been made toward its demise.

Supersymmetry and Beyond.

The flights of fantasy of theoretical physicists seem almost limitless. Perhaps just a few more should be mentioned as examples of their extreme ideas.

Among those is the reportedly renormalizable supersymmetry grand unified theory, known as SUSY-GUT, that involves the proposal of five dimensions and in which the spin of particles can change. The desirable result of this is that all particles can be viewed as a single Yang-Mills superfield. This theory results in the proposal of new particles that are mirror images of the particles of the standard model. Newly proposed particles necessary to super-symmetry theory are hypothetical light supersymmetric particles or LSPs (which, as might be supposed, are produced, not by ordinary symmetry breaking, but by supersymmetry breaking).

Supersymmetry theory proposed the existence of mirror image particles that have been given such names as photinos, leptinos, quarkinos, gluinos, winos, higginos and gravitinos.

Further modifications of supersymmetry have resulted in a

theory called supergravity that incorporates gravity as a gauge field. Einstein's theory of gravity can thus be considered as a description of the hypothetical spin 2 boson called the graviton, as discussed in Appendix B. This variation is alleged to be at least partially renormalizable.

Superstring theory, which was developed in the 1980s, is an attempt at achieving a TOE.

It postulates that all the matter and forces of nature, including electromagnetism, gravity, the strong, and the weak forces, are the result of vibrations of minutely small strings of extremely high energy that form loops throughout space. (These strings are not the same as the giant, massive cosmic strings of earlier GUT theory.)

In what appears to be an attempt to surpass Einstein in the count of dimensions of the universe, more advanced theories have been presented that incorporate as many as 10 or 11 dimensions, and one with as many as 26 dimensions. It is of some comfort to note that those dimensions beyond the fourth, as in the case of the fifth dimension of supersymmetry, are all "small dimensions," perhaps only the size of the Planck length (10^{-33} centimeters), that do not conflict with our everyday experience.

Some physicists have advanced the idea of "worm holes" of space. Perhaps when the matter of one domain (or universe) collapses into a black hole it can leave that domain by means of a four-dimensional tunnel. Its mass/energy can reappear in another domain at another time and space. Also, new energy, perhaps in the form of massive brilliant quasars (quasistellar radio sources), can arrive in our domain by squeezing through worm holes from other domains. In this scheme, quasars are thought to be white holes, that function in a manner the opposite to that of black holes.

Some say whole new universes can be generated by worm holes in space-time. Perhaps the energy for the BB at the start of our own space-time arrived through a worm hole, thus solving the mass/energy conservation problem of BBT. It has also been suggested that worm holes provide a rationale for the vast expansion of the early universe as postulated under inflation theory.

Based on what has gone on in the past there will undoubtedly be more flights of fantasy as time goes on. If the same pattern is followed, each of these will be more grand and complex and make greater claims in support of BBT. As mentioned in Chapter 26, Paul Dirac once said, "It is more important to have beauty in one's equations than to have them fit experiment." Theoretical physicists seem to have taken those words to heart and are carrying them to extremes in their quest for beauty in support of their ideas.

Harvard physicist Sheldon Glashow, one of the originators of electroweak theory, ridiculed superstring theorists, saying that in ignoring experimentation they had deserted science for theoretical "elegance". Regarding scientists working on TOE, Murray Gell-Mann, a Nobel Prize winner for his work in quantum chromodynamics, is quoted as saying, "Most of them don't know what they are doing. They're just using various mathematical tricks." Hopefully the direction of cosmological endeavor will soon change toward a broader goal than merely to provide more and more elaborate theoretical schemes in support of BBT.

Black Holes.

Because the possibility of the existence of black holes is almost universally accepted, it may seem that they shouldn't be excluded as a flight of fantasy.

But there is a lot more to black hole lore than commonly known. For example, contrary to popular belief, energy may be able to escape their enormous gravitational force, and some who believe there was a BB also believe that a large number of relatively small black holes may exist throughout the universe.

The idea of black holes has been in the literature of a couple of centuries. The earliest known reference to such an idea is that of British astronomer and philosopher John Mitchell, who in 1784 who wrote, "all light emitted from such a body would be made to return to it by its own power of gravity." However, it wasn't until many years later that General Relativity provided a theoretical basis for that idea.

When stars the size of the Sun die, i.e., use up their nuclear fuel, gravitation causes them to collapse into what is called white dwarfs, dim stars that are about the size of the earth that have very high density.

Stars that are about one half again as large, but less than about 3-1/2 times as large as the Sun, collapse into neutron stars that are on the order of 10 miles in diameter and have enormous densities.

Stars that are more than about 3-1/2 times the size of the Sun are believed to collapse into black holes that are so compact that their escape velocity is greater than the speed of light. That means that, regardless of how hot and luminous they might be, no light, heat or other radiation or matter can escape from them. Thus they cannot be seen or directly sensed by any type of radiation detector.

Black holes, that were given that name by John Wheeler, are enclosed within an area that is called their event horizon, also called the Schwarzschild radius after German professor of astronomy Karl Schwarzschild who originated the idea in 1916 (and died that same year). External matter or radiation that nears the event horizon is more and more subject to the attraction of the gravitational force of the black hole. But when it falls within the invisible event horizon it is gone. It cannot escape, and its energy equivalent becomes part of the black hole. We are told that, regardless of what matter falls into a a black hole, all that is retained is mass, charge and angular momentum.

If another star should be nearby its matter might gradually be pulled into the black hole. That might happen if the black hole and a star are members of a binary pair, which, because of the abundance of binary stars in the universe, may not be a rare occurrence. The abundance of binary stars also results in the rather common occurrence of star-neutron star binaries.

The observation of star-hole binaries also appears to provide the best evidence of the existence of black holes. Because the pair orbit about their common center of gravity, the wobbling motion of the normal star of the pair can be analyzed to detect the presence of its invisible partner. It turns out that that kind of observation provides rather convincing evidence of the existence of black holes, without one ever having been directly observed.

Cal Tech astronomer theorist Kip Thorne is 80% certain that Cygnus X-1 is a binary pair in which the invisible member of the pair is a black hole. Most astronomers would agree with him.

Even though neither matter nor radiation can directly escape black holes, it is believed that they can lose mass by a process that is explained by quantum theory. At the very edge of the event horizon, where gravitational field energy levels may be sufficiently high, particle pairs might form. Instead of rejoining in mutual annihilation, before that can happen, one particle of a pair might fall through the event horizon. Either a particle or an antiparticle might then be free to escape the clutches of the black hole. Thus matter, or its energy equivalent, effectively leaves the area and the black hole slowly loses mass. This process is named Hawking radiation after its originator, who is responsible for development of much of current theory regarding black holes.

Hawking, who is a proponent of BBT, also tells us that at the time of the BB conditions (within the first 10^{-20} second) were right for the birth of a very large number of much smaller black holes. Huge forces occurring an instant after the start of the BB could produce sufficient pressure to compress irregular areas of matter into billions of small black holes that now populate the universe. Because they cannot be seen, they may provide the dark matter of the universe that is sought by cosmologists who have been attempting to determine whether the universe is open, flat or closed.

(The fact that the BB explosion was said to result in expansion at many times the speed of light and was said to have no irregular areas of matter, denying the possibility of the formation of small black holes, apparently didn't concern Hawking.)

In contrast to large black holes resulting from collapsing stars, that might take far longer than the age of the BB universe to evaporate by Hawking radiation, these small black holes might have lives short enough to regularly meet their death in violent explosions; perhaps as many as two per century per cubic light year in our neighborhood. (No reason for such explosions has been given, but, because one light-year is about 6 trillion miles, perhaps they aren't too serious a threat to us anyway.)

Hawking theorized that when small black holes, which may be about the size of a proton and may weigh about a billion tons, are near the end of their existence their gravitational field can no longer hold them together, and they explode in a powerful burst of gamma rays. If that were so, those might be a source of the gamma ray bursts that are so much in the news of late.

APPENDIX E

Calculations

Appendix E Contents.

E-1. REFERENCE DATA

Calculations in this appendix are based on the following data:

Conversion Factors and Constants:

The speed of light equals 3×10^8 meters per/sec = 3×10^5 km per/sec = 3×10^{10} cm/sec.

One electron volt equals (1 eV) = 1.602×10^{-12} erg.
(One erg = 6.242×10^{11} eV.)

One Joule equals 10^7 ergs. (One erg equals 10^{-7} Joule.)

One eV = 1.602×10^{-19} Joule.

[$(1.602 \times 10^{-12}$ erg/eV) x (10^{-7} Joule/erg) = 1.602×10^{-19} Joule/eV]

One gram = 9×10^{20} ergs. (From E=Mc^2; E in ergs, M in grams, and C = 3×10^{10} cm/sec.)

One ton equals 9.07185×10^5 grams or 907.185 kilograms.

One liter equals 10^3 cubic centimeters.

One kilogram per cubic kilometer equals 10^{-12} gram per cubic centimeter.

[10^3 grams ÷ (10^5 cm)^3 = 10^{-12} gm/cm^3]

One mile equals 1.609344 kilometers.

One kilometer = 0.621371 mile.

One day = 86,400 seconds, one week = 6.048 seconds x 10^5

One year equals 3.1558 x 10^7 seconds.

One light-day equals 2.592 x 10^{10} kilometers or 2.592 x 10^{15} centimeters.

[(8.64 x 10^4 sec) x (3 x 10^5 km/sec) = 2.592 x 10^{10} km/lt-day).]

One light-week equals 1.8144 x 10^{11} kilometers or 1.8144 x 10^{16} centimeters.

[(6.048 x 10^5 sec) x (3 x 10^5 km/sec) = 1.8144 x 10^{11} km/lt-wk).]

One light-year equals 9.46728 x 10^{12} kilometers or 9.46728 x 10^{17} centimeters.

[(3.1558 x 10^7 sec) x (3 x 10^5 km/sec) = 9.4674 x 10^{12} km/lt-yr).]

One light-year equals 5.8827 x 10^{12} miles.

[(9.46728 x 10^{12} km/ lt-yr) x (0.621371 mi/Km) = 5.8827 x 10^{12} miles.]

One parsec equals 3.26 light-years.

The tangent of one arc-minute equals 0.00029. Because that relationship is linear for very small angles, the tangent of one arc-second is 0.00029 ÷ 60 = 4.8333 x 10^{-6}.

The Gravitational Constant, G, equals 6.672 x 10^{-8} cm^3/gram-sec^2.

Gravitational redshift equals (approximately) GM/Rc^2 (mass in grams and radius in centimeters).

Escape velocity equals the square root of $2GM/R$ (mass in grams and radius in centimeters).

Earth Data.

The Earth's average radius is about 6,350 kilometers (Equatorial 6,378 km, polar 6,332 km, or about 6.35 x 10^8 centimeters.)

Its mass is 5.9763 x 10^{24} kilograms or about 5.9763 x 10^{27} grams.

Its volume is $4/3\pi$ x $(0.635 \times 10^4)^3 = 4.1888 \times 0.25605$ x $10^{12} = 1.07253 \times 10^{12}$ cubic kilometers.

Its average density is about $5.9763 \times 10^{24} \div 1.07253 \times 10^{12} = 5.5721 \times 10^{12}$ kilograms per kilometer, or 5.5721 grams per cubic centimeter.

Sun Data.

The Sun's radius is 695,090 km, or 6.9509×10^{10} cm.

Its mass is about 2×10^{30} kilograms, or 2×10^{33} grams, or 2.2046×10^{27} tons.

(2×10^{30} kg $\div 907.185$ kg/ton $= 2.2046 \times 10^{27}$ tons.)

Its volume is $4/3\pi$ x $(0.69509 \times 10^6)^3 = 4.1888 \times 0.35583$ x $10^{18} = 1.40674 \times 10^{18}$ cubic kilometers.

Its average density is $2 \times 10^{30} \div 1.40674 \times 10^{18} = 1.42173$ x 10^{12} kilograms per cubic kilometer, or 1.42173 grams per cubic centimeter.

Solar System Data.

The radius of the solar system is assumed here to equal the distance of Pluto from the Sun, which is about 5.9×10^9 kilometers.

Its diameter is 1.18×10^{10} km, or 0.455 light-day.

(1.18×10^{10} km $\div 2.592 \times 10^{10}$ km/lt-day $= 0.45525$ lt-day.)

Its mass is essentially that of the Sun, 2×10^{30} kilograms, or 2×10^{33} grams. (The Sun's mass is 99.86 percent of the mass of the solar system.)

Milky Way Data.

Assuming a radius of 50,000 light-years and a thickness of 2,000 light years, the Milky Way radius is $(0.5 \times 10^5$ light years) x $(9.46728 \times 10^{12}$ km per light-year) $= 4.7336 \times 10^{17}$ km.

Its thickness is $(0.2 \times 10^4$ light-years) x $(9.46728 \times 10^{12}$ km per lt-yr) $= 1.8935 \times 10^{16}$ km.

Its volume is 2π x $(4.73364 \times 10^{17}$ kilometers)^2 x $(1.89356 \times 10^{16}$ kilometers) $= 2\pi \times 22.407 \times 10^{34}$ x 1.89356×10^{16} cubic kilometers $= 2.6659 \times 10^{52}$ cubic kilometers.

Assuming its mass equal to that of 100 billion Sun-like stars, its average density would be 10^{11} x 2 x 10^{30} ÷ 2.6659 x 10^{52} = 0.7502 x 10^{-11} kilograms per cubic kilometer, or 7.502 x 10^{-24} grams per cubic centimeter.

Observable Universe Data.

Based on the *accepted interpretation of redshift data*, the radius of the observable universe is about 10 billion light years, which equals (10^{10} light years) x (9.46728 x 10^{17} centimeters per light-year), or 9.46728 x 10^{27} centimeters.

Its volume is $4/3\pi$ x $(0.946728$ x $10^{28})^3$ = 4.1888 x $(0.84855$ x $10^{84})$ = 3.5544 x 10^{84} cubic centimeters, or 3.5544 x 10^{81} liters.

It is estimated that are 10^{22} average (Sun-sized) stars in the observable universe, each having a mass of 2 x 10^{33} grams (10^{11} average galaxies each having 10^{11} average stars). Therefore the mass of the observable universe is estimated to be 2 x 10^{55} grams (2 x 10^{52} kilograms).

Its average density is about 2 x 10^{55} grams ÷ 3.5544 x 10^{84} cubic centimeters = 5.6268 x 10^{-30} grams per cubic centimeter.

The total equivalent energy of the observable universe has been estimated to be about 10^{68} Joules.

[My calculations show that to be 18 times greater. (2 x 10^{55} grams) x (9 x 10^{20} ergs/ gram) x (10^{-7} Joules/erg) = 1.8 x 10^{69} Joules.]

Stefan-Boltzmann Law.

According to the Stefan-Boltzmann law, energy is proportional to the 4th power of temperature, and black body temperature of 1K is equivalent to 4.72 eV per liter.

Therefore the MBR photon temperature, said to be at about 2.7 K, is equivalent to an energy density of 250.84 eV per liter, or 4.0184 x 10^{-17} Joule per liter.

(4.72 eV x $(2.7)^4$ per liter = 250.84 eV per liter, and that times 1.602 x 10^{-12} erg per eV times 10^{-7} Joule per erg = 4.0184 x 10^{-17} Joule per liter.)

The BB neutrino temperature, said to be at about 2K, is equivalent to an energy density of 75.52 eV per liter, or 1.2098 x 10^{-17} Joule per liter.

(4.72 eV x 16 per liter = 75.52 eV per liter, and 75.52 eV per liter x 1.602 x 10^{-12} erg per eV times 10^{-7} Joule per erg = 1.2098 x 10^{-17} Joule per liter.)

E-2. MBR AND NEUTRINO ENERGY
MBR Photon Energy.

From the reference data above, the BB photon temperature, said to be at 2.7 K, is equivalent to an energy density of 250.84 eV per liter, or 4.0184 x 10^{-17} Joule per liter, and the volume of the observable universe is 3.5544 x 10^{81} Liters.

Therefore, the total BB photon energy in the observable universe is 1.4283 x 10^{65} Joules.

[(3.5544 x 10^{81} liters) x (4.0184 x 10^{-17} Joule per liter), or 1.4283 x 10^{65} Joules.]

The ratio of total BB photon energy in the observable universe to the total equivalent energy of the observable universe is 1.4283 x 10^{-3}, or 0.14283 percent.

(1.4283 x 10^{65} Joules ÷ 10^{68} Joules = 1.4283 x 10^{-3}.)

The average density of MBR photons throughout the space of the present observable universe has been estimated to be about 400 per cubic centimeter, or 400,000 per liter, resulting in a photon energy of about 6.271 x 10^{-4} eV or about 0.000627 eV.

(250.84 eV per liter ÷ 400,000 = 6.271 x 10^{-4} eV.)

(Steven Weinberg has estimated the present energy of MBR photons in the universe to be 0.0007 eV, very close to the value calculated here.)

If the total energy of the observable universe is 10^{68} Joules as has been estimated, the loss of energy of MBR photons since the decoupling has been about 1.4 times the present total equivalent energy of the observable universe.

[1.4238 x 10^{68} Joules) ÷ (10^{68} Joules) = 1.4238.]

Because the MBR photons are said to have cooled by a factor of about 1,000 (from 3,000 K to 3 K—a redshift of 1,000) since the decoupling, they have lost 99.9 percent of their original energy.

Calculated Another Way.

As a check on those figures, the average energy of MBR photons is proportional to their temperature, but the number of photons per unit volume is proportional to the cube of temperature.

The energy density of MBR photons at a temperature of 2.7 K is equal to 280.84 ev per liter, but at the time of the decoupling they are claimed to have been at a temperature of abour 3,000 K. According to the Stefan-Boltzman law, their energy density would then have been at $(3,000/1)^4$ x 4.72 eV/ Liter = 81 x 10^{12} x 4.72 = 3.8232 x 10^{14} eV per liter.

Because of the radius of the BB universe, according to Figure 1, has increased linearly with time, the volume of that universe has increassed as the cube of time.

Since the time of the decoupling, time is said to have increased from about 10^{13} seconds to 4.7337 x 10^{17} seconds (15 billion years), and thus has increased by a factor of 4.7337 x 10^4. The volume of the universe has therefore increased by a factor of $(4.7337 \times 10^4)^3$, or 1.0607 x 10^{14}.

The total energy of MBR photons at the time of the decoupling would have been (3.8232 x 10^{14} eV per liter) x (the present volume of the observable universe of 3.5544 x 10^{81} liters) ÷ (1.0607 x 10^{14}) = 1.2811 x 10^{82} eV, and (1.2811 x 10^{82} eV) x (1.602 x 10^{-14} Joules per eV) equals 2.0524 x 10^{68} Joules.

Thus the energy loss of the MBR photons since the decoupling, as compared to the an estimate of the equivalent energy of the present observable universe of 10^{68} Joules, is equal to about 2, serving as a good check of the above estimate of 1.4.

BB Neutrino Energy.

From the reference data above, the BB neutrino temperature, said to be at 2K, is equivalent to an energy density of 75.52 eV per liter, or 1.2098 x 10^{-17} Joule per Liter, and the volume of the

observable universe is 3.5544×10^{81} liters.
  [$(75.52$ eV/liter) x $(1.602 \times 10^{-12}$ erg/eV) x 10^{-7}
  Joule/erg) = 1.2098×10^{-17} Joule/liter.]

The total BB neutrino energy in the observable universe is
4.3×10^{64} Joules.
  [$(3.5544 \times 10^{81}$ liters) x $(1.2098 \times 10^{-17}$ Joule/liter)
  = 4.3×10^{64} Joules.]

The ratio of total BB neutrino energy in the observable
universe to the total equivalent energy of the observable universe
would be 4.3×10^{-4}, or 0.00043 percent.
  [$(4.3 \times 10^{64}$ Joules) $\div$ $(10^{68}$ Joules) = 4.3×10^{-4}.]

The average density of BB neutrinos throughout the space of
the present universe has been estimated to be about 113 per
cubic centimeter, or 113,000 per liter, results in a neutrino
energy of about 0.00067 eV.

  (75.52 eV per liter $\div$ 113,000 neutrinos per liter =
  6.6832×10^{-4} eV.)

According to Figure 1, the BB neutrino decoupling occurred at
at redshift of one billion and a temperature of about 10^9 K. If so,
the time of its decoupling the total neutrino energy would be
about 10^9 times greater than at the present, or about 4.3×10^{73}
Joules.

From the time of their decoupling to the present they would
have lost all but a tiny fraction of that energy, a total loss of
about 4.3×10^{73} Joules.

Therefore, if the total energy of the observable universe is 10^{68}
Joules as has been estimated, that loss of energy is equal to
430,000 times the total equivalent energy of the present observable universe.

  (4.3×10^{73} Joules $\div$ 10^{68} Joules = 4.3×10^5.)

E-3. QUASARS
The Ability to View a Distant Quasar.

For a quasar having a redshift of about 2, and thought to
be about 10 billion light-years distant (based on the *accepted
interpretation of redshift data*) and one light-week in diameter, the
tangent of its observed angle would be $(7/365.25) \div 10^{10}$ =
1.9165×10^{-12}.

Its angle would therefore appear to be $1.9165 \times 10^{-12} \div 4.8333 \times 10^{-6} = 3.9652 \times 10^{-7}$ arc-second, which is far beyond the ability of resolution of any existing telescope. That quasar can only be seen as a point of light.

If that quasar was in the center of a galaxy the size of the Milky Way, 100,000 light-years across, the tangent of its observed angle of that galaxy would be $10^5 \div 10^{10} = 10^{-5}$.

The observed angle of that galaxy would therefore be $10^{-5} \div 4.8333 \times 10^{-6} = 2.069$ arc-second, which is within the resolving ability of existing telescopes.

Its diameter would appear about to be 20 times larger than the 0.1 resolution that has reported for the Hubble Space Telescope. Thus, some features of normal sized galaxy might be seen, but that would not include a central quasar.

If a quasar in its center was only one light day in diameter, as some are thought to be, it would appear to be 1/7 as large (if it could be seen), or 5.665×10^{-8} arc-second, even further beyond the ability of resolution of any existing telescope.

Quasar Density.

It has been estimated that the amount of light from a quasar is 100 billion to as much as a trillion times that of the Sun, possibly requiring a mass of as much 100 million times the mass of the Sun.

Assuming a quasar of that mass, 2×10^{38} kilograms (100 million times the Sun's mass), and a diameter of one light-day, which equals 2.592×10^{10} kilometers:

Its volume would be $4/3\pi \times (2.592 \times 10^{10})^3 = 4.1888 \times 1.7414 \times 10^{31} = 7.2945 \times 10^{31}$ cubic kilometers.

Its average density would be $2 \times 10^{38} \div 7.2945 \times 10^{31} = 0.27418 \times 10^7$ kilograms per cubic kilometer, or 0.27418×10^{-5} grams per cubic centimeter, or about 2×10^{-6} times the Sun's average density.

$(0.27429 \times 10^{-5} \div 1.42174 = 0.1929 \times 10^{-5})$

Its average density compared to that of the Milky Way is about $0.27418 \times 10^{-5} \div 7.502 \times 10^{-24} = 3.6\ 55 \times 10^{17}$ times greater.

A Quasar One Billion Light-Years Distant.

Regarding an article in *SKY & TELESCOPE* of 1998 showing a photograph of an image 17 arc-seconds wide, that is said to be of a "quasar host" galaxy one BLYs distant, the tangent of the image of that angle is 17 x (4.8333 x 10^{-6}) or 82.166 x 10^{-6}.

The diameter of that galaxy is therefore 82,166 light-years.
[Its diameter equals its distance times the tangent of that angle, 10^9 lt-yrs x (82.166 x 10^{-6}) = 82,166 lt-yrs.]

The tangent of the observed angle of a quasar in that galaxy having a diameter of one light-week would equal 1.923 x 10^{-11}.
[The tangent of that angle equals its diameter divided by its distance: (1 lt-wk) ÷ (10^9 lt-yrs x 52 lt-wks/lt-yr) = 1.923 x 10^{-11}.]

The observed angle of a quasar of that size and at that distance would be about 4 x 10^{-6} arc-second, far smaller than could be seen by any existing telescope. (The Hubble Space Telescope resolution is reported to be about 0.1 arc-second.)
[The tangent of 1,923 x 10^{-11} divided by the tangent of one arc-sec (4.8333 x 10^{-6}) = 3.9788 x 10^{-6} arc-sec.]

At a distance of one BLYs, a quasar would have to be at least 25,000 times larger than one-light week in diameter in order to be seen by the Hubble Space Telescope.
(0.1 ÷ 4 x 10^{-6} = 25,000.)

E-4. GRAVITATIONAL REDSHIFT

Gravitational redshift (GRS) is equal to G M/R c^2, mass in grams and radius in centimeters.

GRS of the Sun.

The Sun's radius is 695,090 km, or 6.9509 x 10^{10} cm.

Its mass is 2 x 10^{30} kilograms or 2 x 10^{33} grams.

Its GRS = G M/R c^2 = (6.672 x 10^{-8} cm^3/gram-sec^2) x (2 x 10^{33} grams) ÷ (6.9509 x 10^{10} cm) x (9 x 10^{20} cm^2/sec^2) = 2.133 x 10^{-6} = 0.000002133.

GRS of White Dwarf Sirius B.

Sirius B's mass is said to be 1.05 times that of the Sun or 2.1×10^{33} grams.

Its diameter is said to 31,000 km, or 3.1×10^9 cm.

Its radius is 1.55×10^9 cm.

The ratio of its radius to the Sun's equals 1.55×10^9 cm ÷ 6.9509×10^{10} cm = 0.0223.

Because GRS is proportional to mass and inversely proportional to radius, it equals $(1.05 \div 0.0223) \times (0.2133 \times 10^{-5}) = 1.0043 \times 10^{-4}$, or about 0.0001, which is about 50 times greater than the redshift of the Sun.

GRS of a Neutron Star.

A mass of a typical neutron star is said to be about that of the Sun, or 2×10^{33} grams.

Its diameter is said to 10 miles, or 16.09 Km.

Its radius is 8.045×10^5 km.

The ratio of its radius to the Sun's radius equals $8.045 \times 10^5 \div 6.9509 \times 10^{10} = 1.1574 \times 10^{-5}$.

Its GRS = (mass ratio ÷ radius ratio) × Sun's redshift = $[1 \div (1.1574 \times 10^{-5}) \times (0.2133 \times 10^{-5})] = 0.1843$, about 86,400 times greater than the redshift of the Sun.

GRS of the Earth.

The Earth's average radius is about 6,350 kilometers.

Its mass is 5.9763×10^{24} kilograms or about 5.9763×10^{27} grams.

Its GRS = G M/R c^2 = $(6.672 \times 10^{-8}$ cm^3/gram-sec$^2)$ × $(5.9763 \times 10^{27}$ grams$) \div (6.35 \times 10^8$ cm$) \times (9 \times 10^{20}$ cm^2/sec$^2)$ = 6.977×10^{-10}, or about 7 parts in 10 billion, about 3.5 ten thousandths of the redshift of the Sun.

$(7 \times 10^{-10} \div 2 \times 10^{-6} = 3.5 \times 10^{-4}.)$

GRS of a Quasar.

Consider a hypothetical quasar having a mass of 10^8 (100 million) times that of the Sun or 2×10^{38} kilograms, and a diameter of one light-day, which equals 2.592×10^{10} kilometers.

Its GRS = GM/Rc^2 = $(6.672 \times 10^{-8}\ cm^3/gram\text{-}sec^2) \times$ $(2 \times 10^{41}\ grams) \div (2.592 \times 10^{15}\ cm) \times (9 \times 10^{20})\ cm^2/sec^2$ = 0.00572, about 2,682 times the redshift of the Sun.

If the mass of that quasar was just a few times greater, and its size just a few times smaller, its GRS might be in the range of 0.1 to 0.2, similar to that of a neutron star, and a major fraction of the highest redshift ever determined for a quasar.

E-5. MASS LOSS
Star Mass Loss.

The radiant energy escaping from a typical star like our Sun is estimated to be equivalent to 4 million tons per second, equal to 1.26×10^{14} tons per year or about 1.145×10^{17} kilograms per year. Escaping at the speed of light, most of that undoubtedly continues on out of its galaxy.

$(4 \times 10^6\ tons/sec \times 3.15576 \times 10^7\ sec/yr = 1.2623 \times$ $10^{14}\ tons/yr.\ 1.2623 \times 10^{14}\ tons/yr \times 907.185\ kg/ton =$ $1.145 \times 10^{17}\ kg/yr.)$

The mass loss of stars in the form of stellar wind has been estimated to be much greater than the loss due to radiation.

According to Heinz Pagels, "the solar wind dumps hundreds of million of tons of solar material into outer space each second." If the mass loss due to solar wind were just 100 times that of the loss due to radiation the Sun would lose about 10^{19} kilograms of mass per year.

The mass of a typical star like the Sun has been estimated to be about to 2×10^{30} kilograms. At that rate of mass loss, the Sun might last 200 billion years. But, of course, it is scheduled to blow up as a red giant long before that; when its nuclear fuel runs out.

$(2 \times 10^{30} \div 10^{19} = 2 \times 10^{11}.)$

Galaxy Mass Loss.

If Pagels' estimate is correct, and the mass loss due to solar wind were 100 times that of the loss due to radiation, and if that all of that radiation and mass (including solar flares, superflares, powerful winds, jets of black holes and quasars, etc.) were to leave the star's galaxy, the mass leaving a typical galaxy would be about 10^{30} kilograms per year.

(10^{11} stars x 10^{19} kg/year/star equals 10^{30} kg/year.)

If a typical galaxy like the Milky Way were to continue to have an average of about 100 billion average stars of 2×10^{30} kilograms of mass (a total of 2×10^{41} kilograms) during its lifetime, and it lost about 10^{30} kilograms of mass per year, it might live about 200 billion years. (A typical galaxy might start with many more stars, and end with many less, but the average might be like that of the middle-aged Milky Way.)

Universe Mass Turn-Over.

If there are about 100 billion such galaxies in the observable universe, their total mass would be about 10^{52} kilograms per year. If the the average loss of mass per galaxy were 10^{30} kilograms of mass per year, the average loss of all those galaxies would be 10^{41} kilograms per year. Thus, on average, the total mass of the observable universe would be "recycled" during a period equal to he the 200 billion year age of a typical galaxy.

If the universe were larger, and regardless of how large it really is, the rate of mass "turn-over" would be at that amount.

E-6. ESCAPE VELOCITY

Escape velocity (Ve) is equal to the square root of (2 GM/R), mass in grams and radius in centimeters.

Escape Velocity of the Earth.

From the reference data above, the Earth's radius is 6.350×10^{8} centimeters and its mass is 5.9763×10^{27} grams.

Ve = 2 x (6.672×10^{-8}) x (5.9763×10^{27}) ÷ $(6.350 \times 10^{8})^{1/2}$
= $(125.587 \times 10^{10})^{1/2}$ = 11.2×10^{5} cm/sec = 11.2 km/sec
($\approx$ 7 miles per sec $\approx$ 25,200 mph).

Escape Velocity of the Sun.

From the reference data above, the Sun's radius is
6.9509×10^{10} centimeters and its mass is 2×10^{33} grams.

$Ve = [2 \times (6.672 \times 10^{-8}) \times (2 \times 10^{33}) \div (6.9509 \times 10^{10})]^{1/2} = (38.395 \times 10^{14})^{1/2} = 6.1964 \times 10^7$ cm/sec $= 619.64$ km/sec
(≈ 385 miles per sec $\approx 1,386,000$ mph).

E-7. STELLAR SYSTEMS FROM SUPERNOVAS

Mass of SN1987A is about 20 times that of the Sun, or
4×10^{31} kilograms, and its size is about 170,000 times the size of
the Sun.

Its radius is therefore about 695,090 kilometers $\times 170,000 = 1.18165 \times 10^{11}$ kilometers, or 4.5588 light-days.
$\quad (1.18165 \times 10^{11}$ km $\div 2.592 \times 10^{10}$ km/lt-day $=$
$\quad 4.5588$ lt-days.)

SN1987A Matter Spread in a Spherical Solar System.

Assuming the space in which a solar system forms has a radius
equal to that of the distance of Pluto from the Sun, that space has
a radius of 5.9×10^9 kilometers, or about 0.2275 light days (and
its diameter about 0.445 light-day. (5.9×10^9 km $\div 2.592 \times 10^{10}$
km/lt-day $= 0.2275$ lt-days.)

The volume of that sphere $= 4/3\pi \times (0.59 \times 10^{10})^3 = 4.1888 \times 0.20538 \times 10^{30} = 0.86029 \times 10^{30}$ cubic kilometers, or 0.86029×10^{25} cubic centimeters.

The average density of that volume, based on the Sun's mass $=$
2×10^{33} grams $\div 0.86029 \times 10^{45}$ cm$^3 = 2.3248 \times 10^{-12}$ gram per
cm^3. (Essentially all of the mass of the solar system is that of the
Sun.)

The average density of the matter of SN1987A, if spread
through that volume, would be 4×10^{31} Kilograms $\div 0.86029 \times 10^{30}$ cubic kilometers $= 4.6496 \times 10^1$ kilogram per cubic kilometer, or 4.6496×10^{-11} gram per cubic centimeter.

The ratio of the average density of SN1987A matter in that
volume compared to that of the Sun $= 4.6496 \times 10^{-11}$ gram per
cubic centimeter $\div 1.42173$ grams per cubic centimeter $= 3.2704$
$\times 10^{-11}$, or about 3.27 parts per 100 billion.

SN1987A Matter Spread in the Milky Way.

The average density of the matter of SN1987A if spread through the volume of the Milky Way would equal 4×10^{31} kilograms $\div$ 2.6659×10^{52} cubic kilometers = 1.5004×10^{-21} kilogram per cubic kilometer, or 1.5004×10^{-33} gram per cubic centimeter.

The ratio of the average density of SN1987A matter in the volume of the Milky Way compared to the Sun's average density would be 1.5004×10^{-33} gram per cubic centimeter $\div$ 1.42173 grams per cubic centimeter = 1.0553×10^{-33}.

BIBLIOGRAPHY

Abell, George O., David Morrison and Sidney Wolf, *Realm of the Universe* (1980)

Abbott, Larry, *The Mystery of the Cosmological Constant* in *SCIENTIFIC AMERICAN,* May 1988

Albert, David Z., *Bohm's Alternative to Quantum Mechanics* in *SCIENTIFIC AMERICAN,* May 1994

Albert, David Z., *Quantum Mechanics and Experience* (1994)

Allen, Harold W. G., *Cosmic Perspective* on Internet, www. webservr.com/science, Aug. 2000

Appenzeller, Tim, *Latest Quarry in Quasar Quest,* in *SCIENCE* Vol. 236 Sept. 6, 1991

Arp, Halton C., *Quasars, Redshifts and Controversies* (1987)

Arp, Halton C., *Fitting Theory to Observation in Progress in New Cosmologies* edited by Halton C. Arp, C. Roy Keys and Konrad Rudnicki (1993)

Arp, Halton. C, *Seeing Red - Redshifts, Cosmology and Academic Science* (1998)

Arp H. C., G. Burbidge, F. Hoyle, J. V. Narlikar and N. C. Wickramasinghe, *The extragalactic Universe:* an alternative viewpoint in *NATURE* Aug. 30, 1990

Assis, A. K. T., *The Redshift Revisited* in *Plasma Astrophysics and Cosmology* edited by A. L. Peratt (1995)

Assis, A. K. T., *A Steady State Cosmology - Beyond the Big Bang* in *Progress in New Cosmologies* edited by Halton C. Arp, C. Roy Keys and Konrad Rudnicki (1993)

Assis, A. K. T. and M.C.D. Neves, *History of the 2.7K Temperature Prior to Penzias and Wilson* in *APEIRON* July 1995

Baggot, Jim, *The Meaning of Quantum Theory* (1993)

Barrow, John and Joseph Silk, *The Left Hand of Creation* (1993)

Barrow, John and Joseph Silk *The Structure of the Early Universe* in *SCIENTIFIC AMERICAN* April, 1980

Bartusiak, Marcia, *Cosmic Jekyll Hyde* in *ASTRONOMY* May 1998

Bartusiak, Marcia, *Doubtful Elements,* in *DISCOVER* Aug. 1992

Bartusiak, Marcia, *Giving Birth to Galaxies* in *DISCOVER* Feb. 1997

Bartusiak, Marcia, *Outsmarting the Early Universe* in *ASTRONOMY* Oct. 1998

Bartusiak, Marcia, *The Texture of the Universe* in *DISCOVER* Nov. 1991

Beardsley, Tim, *Quantum Dissidents* in *SCIENTIFIC AMERICAN,* Dec. 1992

Beck, Sara, *Dwarf Galaxies and Star Bursts* in *SCIENTIFIC AMERICAN* June 2000

Bergamini, David and the Editors of LIFE, *The Universe* (1962)

Bernstein, Max P., Scott A. Sandford and Louis J. Allamandola, *Life's Far-Flung Raw Materials* in *SCIENTIFIC AMERICAN* July 1999

Blandford, Roger D., Mitchell C. Begelman and Martin J. Rees, *Cosmic Jets* in *SCIENTIFIC AMERICAN* May 1982

Bondi, H. and W. B. Bonnor, *Rival Theories of Cosmology* (1960)

Bonnor, W. B., *Relativistic Theories of Cosmology* in *Rival Theories of Cosmology* by H. Bondi et al. (1960)

Boslough, John, *Stephen Hawking's Universe* (1985)

Boslough, John, *Masters of Time* (1992)

Bowyer, Stuart, *Extreme Ultraviolet Astronomy* in *SCIENTIFIC AMERICAN* Aug. 1994

Bothun, Gregory D., *The Ghostliest Galaxies* in *SCIENTIFIC AMERICAN* Feb. 1997

Brown, Malcolm, *Ether Re-emerges as the Je Ne Sais Quoi of Physics* in *The New York Times* Feb. 4, 1999

Brush, Stephen G., *How Cosmology Became a Science,* in *SCIENTIFIC AMERICAN* Aug.1992

Burbidge, Geoffrey, *Why Only One Big Bang?* in *SCIENTIFIC AMERICAN* Feb. 1992

Burch, James I., *The Fury of Space Storms* in *SCIENTIFIC AMERICAN* April 2001

Calder, Nigel, *Einstein's Universe* (1979)

Carr, Bernard J., *On the Origin, Evolution and Purpose of the Physical Universe* in *The Irish, Astronomical Journal* March 1982

Carter, Brandon, *Large Number Coincidences and the Anthropic Principle in Cosmology* in *Confrontation of Cosmological Theories with Observational Data* edited by M.S. Longair (1974)

Chaikin, Andrew, *Great Wall of the Cosmos* in *OMNI* Aug. 1991

Chaisson, Eric J., *Early Results from the Hubble Space Telescope* in *SCIENTIFIC AMERICAN* June 1992

Chupp, Edward L., *The Gamma Ray Cosmos* in *SCIENCE* Dec. 1992

Coleman. R. V., *Whiskers* in *Encyclopedia of Physics* (1991)

Coles, Peter, and George Ellis, *The Cased for an Open Universe* in *NATURE* Aug. 25, 1994

Cornell, James, Editor, *Bubbles, voids and bumps in time: the new cosmology* (1989)

Courvoisier, Thierry and E. Ian Robson, *The Quasar 3C 273,* in *SCIENTIFIC AMERICAN* June 1991

Cowen, Ron, *ASCA sheds light on galaxy formation* in *SCIENCE NEWS* July 22, 1995

Cowen, Ron, *Big, Bigger...Biggest* in *SCIENCE NEWS* Aug. 12, 2000

Cowen, Ron, *A Cool View Of the Heavens* in *SCIENCE NEWS* Mar. 16, 1996

Cowen, Ron, *Found: Primordial Water - A meteorite's salty tale* in *SCIENCE NEWS* Oct. 30, 1999

Cowen, Ron, *Hubble Captures a Violent Universe* in *SCIENCE NEWS* Jan. 1992

Cowen, Ron, *Stormy Weather* in *SCIENCE NEWS* Jan. 13, 2001

Cowen, Ron, *Tracking a black hole eruption* in *SCIENCE NEWS* Dec. 6, 1997

Cronin, James W., Thomas K. Gaisser and Simon P. Swardy, *Cosmic Rays at the Energy Frontier* in *SCIENTIFIC AMERICAN* Jan. 1997

Davies, Paul, *Other Worlds* (1980)

Davies, Paul, *The Edge of Infinity* (1981)

Davies, Paul, *Superforce* (1984)

Davies, Paul and John Gribbin, *The Matter Myth* (1992)

Davidson, Arthur F., *Far-Ultraviolet Astronomy on the Astro-1 Space Shuttle Mission* in *SCIENCE* Jan. 15, 1993

Dawson, Jim, *Exciting... Star Gazing* in *Sacramento Union* Oct. 20, 1991

Dermer, Charles and Reinhard Schlickeiser, *Quasars, Blazers and Gamma Rays* in *SCIENCE* Vol. 257 Sept. 18, 1992

Dicke, R. H., *Dirac's Cosmology and Mach's Principle,* in *NATURE* Nov. 1961

Dicus, Duane A., John R. Letaw, Doris C. Teplitz and Vidor L. Teplitz, *The Future of the Universe* in *SCIENTIFIC AMERICAN* March 1983

Disney, Michael, *A New Look at Quasars* in *SCIENTIFIC AMERICAN* June 1998

Dressler, Alan, *The Large-Scale Streaming of Galaxies* in *SCIENTIFIC AMERICAN* Sept. 1987

Eicher, David J., *Galactic Genesis* in *ASTRONOMY* May 1999

Einstein, Albert, *The Meaning of Relativity* (1956)

Einstein, Albert, *Relativity—The Special and General Theories* (1961)

Einstein, Albert, *On the Generalized Theory of Relativity* in *Laureate Anthology* Scientific American, Inc. (1990)

Ellis, G. F. R., *Cosmology and Verifiability* in *Quarterly Journal of The Royal Astronomical Society* No. 3, 1975

Feynman, Richard, *The Character of Physical Law* (1965)

Fisher, Arthur, *Searching for the Beginning of Time - The Cosmic Connection* in *POPULAR SCIENCE* April 1991

Fishman, Gerald J. and Dieter H. Hartmann, *Gamma Ray Bursts* in *SCIENTIFIC AMERICAN* July 1997

Flam, Faye, *Physicists Ponder a New Neutrino Problem* in *SCIENCE* Vol. 257, Aug. 21, 1992

Flam, Faye, *In Search of a New Cosmic Blueprint* in *SCIENCE* Nov. 22, 1991

Flam, Faye, *Giving Galaxies a History* in *SCIENCE* Feb. 28, 1992

Frank, Adam, *Blowin' in the Solar Wind* in *ASTRONOMY* Oct. 1998

Frank, Adam, *In the Nursery of the Stars* in *DISCOVER* Feb. 1996

Flamsteed, Sam, *Crisis in the Cosmos* in *DISCOVER* March 1995

Flamsteed, Sam, *The Young and the Globular* in *DISCOVER* June 1992

Freedman, David H., *The Theory of Everything* in *DISCOVER* Aug. 1991

Freedman, David H., *Particle Hunters* in *DISCOVER* Dec. 1992

Freedman, Wendy L. et al., *Distance to the Virgo cluster galaxy M100 from Hubble Space Telescope observations on Cepheids* in *NATURE* Oct. 27, 1994

Fowler, W, A., G. R. Burbidge and E. M. Burbidge, *Stellar evolution and the synthesis of the elements* in *The Astrophysical Journal* 122:271-85, 1953

Freedman, Wendy L., *The Expansion Rate and Size of the Universe* in *SCIENTIFIC AMERICAN* Nov. 1992

Friedman, Herbert, *The Amazing Universe* (1985)

Frieman, Joshua A. and Ben-Ami Gradwohl, *Dark Matter and the Equivalence Principle* in *SCIENCE* June 4, 1993

Frye, Brenda and Tom Broadhurst, *Tiny Primeval Galaxies Packed Wallop* in *ASTRONOMY* April 1999

Gale, George, *The Anthropic Principle* in *SCIENTIFIC AMERICAN* Nov. 1981

Gale, George, *Cosmological Fecundity: Theories of Multiple Universes* (1989)

Gamow, George, *Biography of Physics* (1961)

Gamow, George, *Creation of the Universe* (1961)

Gamow, George, *The Evolutionary Universe* in *SCIENTIFIC AMERICAN* Sept. 1956

Gamow, George, *Modern Cosmology* in *SCIENTIFIC AMERICAN* Mar. 1954

Gehrels, Neil et al., *The Compton Gamma Ray Observatory* in *SCIENTIFIC AMERICAN* Dec. 1993

Giovanelli, Riccardo and Martha Haynes, *Protogalaxy* in *POPULAR SCIENCE* Dec. 1989

Gibbons, Ann, *In the Beginning, Let There Be Beryllium* in *SCIENCE* Jan. 10, 1992

Glanz, James, *Accelerating the Cosmos* in *ASTRONOMY* in Oct. 1999

Goldberg, Stanley, *Understanding Relativity* (1984)

Goldsmith, Donald, *The Astronomers* (1991)

Goldsmith, Donald, *Einstein's Greatest Blunder?* (1995)

Goldsmith, Donald, *Fingerprint of Creation* in *DISCOVER* Oct. 1992

Goldsmith, Donald, *Supernova! The Exploding Star of 1987* (1989)

Gott, J. Richard III, James E. Gunn, David N. Schramm & Beatrice M. Tinsley, *Will the Universe Expand Forever?* in *SCIENTIFIC AMERICAN* March 1976

Graham, David, Clusters in Collision in *ASTRONOMY* May, 1999

Gregory, Stephen A. and Laird A. Thompson, *Superclusters and Voids in the Distribution of Galaxies* in *SCIENTIFIC AMERICAN* March 1982

Gribbin, John, *Space Warps* (1983)

Groth, Edward J., P. James E. Peebles, Michael Seldner and Raymond M. Soneira, *The Clustering of Galaxies* in *SCIENTIFIC AMERICAN* Nov. 1977

Grunbaum, Adolf, *The Psuedo-Problem of Creation in Physical Cosmology* in *Philosophy of Science* Vol. 56 No. 3, Sept. 1989

Gulkis, Samuel, Philip M. Lubin, Stephan S. Meyer and Robert F. Silverberg, *The Cosmic Background Explorer* in *SCIENTIFIC AMERICAN* Jan. 1990

Guth, Alan H. and Paul J. Steinhardt, *The Inflationary Universe* in *SCIENTIFIC AMERICAN* May 1984

Halliwell, Jonathan J., *Quantum Cosmology and the Creation of the Universe* in *SCIENTIFIC AMERICAN* Dec. 1991

Hart, Michael H. and Ben Zuckerman, Editors, *Extraterrestrials; Where Are They?* (1982)

Harwit, Martin, *Astrophysical Concepts*, Springer-Verlag, 2nd Edition (1991)

Hawking, Stephen W., *A Brief History of Time* (1982)

Hawking, Stephen W., *The Quantum Mechanics of Black Holes* in *SCIENTIFIC AMERICAN* Jan. 1977

Hawking, Stephen W. and Roger Penrose, *The Nature of Space and Time* in *SCIENTIFIC AMERICAN* July 1996

Martha Haynes, *Protogalaxy* in *POPULAR SCIENCE* Dec. 1998

Hegyi, Dennis, *Interstellar Medium* in *Encyclopedia of Physics* (1991)

Henry, J. Patrick, Ulrich G. Briel and Hans Bohringer, *The Evolution of Galaxy Clusters* in *SCIENTIFIC AMERICAN* Dec. 1998

Hewitt, Jacqueline N., *Gravitational Lenses* in *Encyclopedia of Physics* (1991)

Hilgevoord, Jan, Editor, *Physics and Our View of the World* (1995)

Hogan, Craig J., *Primordial Deuterium and the Big Bang* in *SCIENTIFIC AMERICAN* Dec. 1996

Hogan, Craig J., Robert P. Kirshner and Nicholas B. Suntzeff, *Revolutions in Cosmology* in *SCIENTIFIC AMERICAN* Jan. 1999

Horgan, John, *Culture Clash* in *SCIENTIFIC AMERICAN* Aug. 1993

Horgan, John, *The End of Clumpiness* in *SCIENTIFIC AMERICAN* Feb. 1992

Horgan, John, *Universal Truths* in *SCIENTIFIC AMERICAN* Oct. 1990

Hoyle, Fred, *ASTRONOMY* (1962)

Hoyle, Fred, *The Nature of the Universe* (1960)

Hoyle, F., G. Burbidge and J.V. Narlikar, *A Quasi-Steady State Cosmological Model with Creation of Matter* in *The Astrophysical Journal*, June 20, 1993

Hubble, Edwin, *Observational Approach to Cosmology* 1937

Hubble, Edwin, *The Problem of the Expanding Universe* in *AMERICAN SCIENTIST* Vol. 30 No. 2, April 1942

Hubble, Edwin, *The Realm of the Universe* (1925)

Huchra, John P., *The Hubble Constant* in *SCIENCE* April 17, 1992

Human, Katy, *Solar Wind Blows* in *ASTRONOMY* Jan. 2000

Iben, Icko Jr. and Alexander V. Tutukov, *The Lives of Binary Stars: From Birth to Death and Beyond* in *SKY & TELESCOPE* Dec. 1997

Islam, J. N., *An Introduction to Mathematical Cosmology* (1992)

Jayawardhana, Ray, *The Age Paradox* in *ASTRONOMY* June 1993

Jayawardhana, Ray, *Micro-Quasars Found in Our Galaxy* in *SCIENCE* Sept. 1994

Johnson, George, *Once Upon a Time There Was a Big Bang Theory* in *The New York Times* March 8, 1998

Kahabka, Peter, Edward P. J. van den Heuvel and Saul A. Rappaport, *Supersoft X-Ray Stars and Supernovae* in *SCIENTIFIC AMERICAN* Feb. 1999

Kafatos, Menas and Robert Nadeau, *The Conscious Universe* (1990)

Kaler, James, *Ask Astro* in *ASTRONOMY* July 1999

Kanipe, Jeff, *Beyond the Big Bang* in *ASTRONOMY* April 1992

Kanipe, Jeff, *Infrared Camera Goes the Distance* in *SCIENCE NEWS* Oct. 1999

Kanipe, Jeff, *The Pillars of Cosmology: A Short History and Assessment* (1993)

Kaufmann, William J., III, *Relativity and Cosmology* (1973)

Keel, William, *Before Galaxies Were Galaxies* in *ASTRONOMY* July 1997

Kearns, Edward, Takaaki Kajita and Toji Totsuka, *Detecting Massive Neutrinos* in *SCIENTIFIC AMERICAN* Aug. 1999

Kennicutt, Robert C., Wendy L. Freedman and Jeremy R. Mould, *Measuring the Hubble Constant with the Hubble Space Telescope* in *The Astronomical Journal* Vol. 110 No. 4 Oct. 1995

Kierein, John, *Implications of the Compton effect interpretation of the redshift* in *IEEE Transaction on Plasma Physics* Vol. 18, No. 1, Feb. 1990

King, Ivan R., *The Universe Unfolding* W. H. Freeman and Co. (1976)

King, Ivan R., *Globular Clusters* in *SCIENTIFIC AMERICAN* June 1985

Kinney, Anne L., *When Galaxies Were Young* in *ASTRONOMY* May 1998

Kirshner, Robert P., *Supernova 1987A - The First Ten Years* in *SKY & TELESCOPE* Feb. 1997

Krauss, Lawrence M., *Cosmological Antigravity* in *SCIENTIFIC AMERICAN* Jan. 1999

Kolb, Edward W., *Physics of the Early Universe* in *SCIENCE* Vol. 235 Jan. 1987

Kragh, Helge, *Cosmology and Controversy* (1996)

Kraan-Korteweg, Renee C. and Ofer Lahav, *Galaxies behind the Milky Way* in *SCIENTIFIC AMERICAN* Oct. 1998

Knapp, Gillian, *The Stuff Between the Stars* in *SKY & TELESCOPE* May 1995

Krauss, Lawrence M., *Dark Matter in the Universe* in *SCIENTIFIC AMERICAN* Dec. 1986

Krauss, Lawrence M., *The Fate of Life in the Universe* in *SCIENTIFIC AMERICAN* Nov.1999

Kunzig, Robert, *Lone Star in Virgo* in *DISCOVER* Feb. 1999

Kunzig, Robert, *The Wolf Effect* in *DISCOVER* Aug. 1988

Kuhn, Thomas S., *The Structure of Scientific Revolutions* (1996)

Lada, Charles, J., *Energetic Outflows from Young Stars* in *SCIENTIFIC AMERICAN* July 1982

Landy, Stephen D., *Mapping the Universe* in *SCIENTIFIC AMERICAN* June 1999

Laughlin, Gregory, Peter Bodenheimer and Fred C. Adams, *The End of the Main Sequence* in *The Astrophysical Journal* June 10, 1997

Lerner, Eric, *The Big Bang Never Happened* (1991)

Lerner, Eric, *The Big Bang Never Happened* in *DISCOVER* June 1988

Leslie, John, *Physical Cosmology and Philosophy* (1990)

Linde, Andrei, *The Self-Reproducing Inflationary Universe* in *SCIENTIFIC AMERICAN* Nov. 1994

Linde, Andrei, *The Universe: Inflation Out of Chaos* in *NEW SCIENTIST* March 1985

Liversidge, Anthony, *Heresy! Modern Galileos* in *OMNI* June 1993

Love, Thomas R., Cosmological *Implications of a Massive Neutrino* in *IEEE Transaction on Plasma Physics* Dec. 1992

Macchetto, F. Duccio and Mark Dickinson, *Galaxies in the Young Universe* in *SCIENTIFIC AMERICAN* May 1997

Malin, David, *A Universal Color* in *SCIENTIFIC AMERICAN* Aug. 1993

Malphrus, Benjamin K., *The History of Radio Astronomy and The National Radio Astronomy Observatory* (1996)

Mann, Alfred K., *Shadow of a Star* (1997)

Margon, Bruce, *The Origin of the Cosmic X-Ray Background* in *SCIENTIFIC AMERICAN* Jan. 1983

Marmet, Paul, *Absurdities in Modern Physics: A Solution* (1993)

Marmet, Paul, *Einstein's Theory of Special Relativity versus Classical Mechanics* (1997)

Marmet, Paul, *Non-Doppler Redshift of Some Galactic Objects* in *IEEE Transactions on Plasma Physics* Feb. 1990

Marmet, Paul, *Red Shift of Spectral Lines in the Sun's Chromosphere* in *IEEE Transactions on Plasma Science* April 1989

Marmet, Paul and Grote Reber, *Cosmic Matter and the Non-Expanding Universe* in *IEEE Transaction on Plasma Physics* April 1989

McMullin, Ernan, *Is Philosophy Relevant to Cosmology?* in *American Philosophical Quarterly* July 1981

Menas Kafatos and Robert Nadeau, *The Conscious Universe* (1990)

Mirabel, I. F. and L. F. Rodriquez, *A superluminal source found in the Galaxy* in *NATURE* Sept. 1, 1996

Mitchell, William C., *The Cult of the Big Bang* (1995)

Moore, Katz, Lake, Dressler and Oemler, *Galaxy harassment and the evolution of clusters of galaxies* in *NATURE* Feb. 15, 1996

Mukerjee, Madhusree, *Explaining Everything* in *SCIENTIFIC AMERICAN* Jan. 1996

Mukerjee, Madhusree, *Strings and Gluons—The Seer Saw Them All* in *SCIENTIFIC AMERICAN* Feb. 1995

Muller, Richard A., *The Cosmic Background Radiation and the New Aether Drift* in *SCIENTIFIC AMERICAN* May 1978

Mussser, George, *Skewing the Cosmic Bell Curve* in *SCIENTIFIC AMERICAN* Sept. 1999

Mussser, George, *Galactic Archaeology* in *SCIENTIFIC AMERICAN* June 2001

Nadis, Steve, *Here, There, and Everywhere?* in *ASTRONOMY* Feb. 2001

Narlikar, Jayant V., *Was There a Big Bang?* in *NEW SCIENTIST* July 1981

Naeye, Robert, *Dim Lights Everywhere* in *DISCOVER* May 1994

Naeye, Robert, *Kaboom! How Stars Explode* in *ASTRONOMY* July 1997

Naeye, Robert, *Stars on the Brink* in *ASTRONOMY* Jan 1997

Naeye, Robert, *White Dwarfs by the Trillions?* in *ASTRONOMY* April 2000

Oldershaw, Robert, *What's wrong with the new physics* in *NEW SCIENTIST* Dec. 22, 1990

Olson, Steve, *Black Hole Hunters* in *ASTRONOMY* May 1999

Ortega, Tony, *The Quaking Sun* in *ASTRONOMY* Jan. 2000

Osmer, Patrick, *Quasars as Probes of the Distant and Early Universe* in *SCIENTIFIC AMERICAN* Feb. 1982

Osterbrook, Guin and Brashear, *Hubble and the Expanding Universe* in *SCIENTIFIC AMERICAN,* July 1993

Osterwald, Stan and Richard Feinberg, *Galaxy Redshift Reconsidered* in *SKY & TELESCOPE* Feb. 1993

Overbye, Dennis, *Lonely Hearts of the Cosmos* (1992)

Pagels, Heinz R., *A Cozy Cosmology* in *THE SCIENCES* March 1985

Pagels, Heinz R., *Perfect Symmetry* (1985)

Parker, Barry, *The Vindication of the Big Bang* (1993)

Peebles, P. J. E., *Principles of Physical Cosmology* (1993)

Peebles, P. J. E. and David T. Wilkinson, *The Primeval Fireball* in *SCIENTIFIC AMERICAN* June 1967

Peebles, Schramm, Turner and Kron, *The case for the relativistic hot Big Bang cosmology* in *NATURE* Aug. 29, 1991

Peebles, Schramm, Turner and Kron, *The Evolution of the Universe* in *SCIENTIFIC AMERICAN* Oct. 1994

Penrose, Roger, *The Emperor's New Mind* (1989)

Peratt, Anthony L., *Evolution of the Plasma Universe, Parts I and II* in *IEEE Transactions on Plasma Science* Dec. 1986

Peratt, Anthony L., *Introduction to*

Plasma Astrophysics and Cosmology in *Plasma Astrophysics and Cosmology* edited by A. L. Peratt (1995)

Peratt, Anthony L., *Not With A Bang* in *THE SCIENCES* Jan./Feb. 1990

Perryman, Michael, *Hipparcos: The Stars in Three Dimensions* in *SKY & TELESCOPE* June 1999

Peterson, Ivars, *Particles of History* in *SCIENCE NEWS* Sept. 12, 1992

Peterson, Ivars, *State of the Universe: If Not a Big Bang, Then What?* in *SCIENCE NEWS* April 13, 1991

Phipps, Thomas E., Jr., *Heretical Verities* (1986)

Picard, Alan, *Large Scale Structures in the Universe* in *The Astronomical Journal,* Aug. 1991

Powell, Corey, *Astronomers in the Dark* in *SCIENTIFIC AMERICAN* April 1993

Powell, Corey, *Born Yesterday* in *SCIENTIFIC AMERICAN* May 1992

Powell, Corey, *The Golden Age of Cosmology* in *SCIENTIFIC AMERICAN* July 1992

Powell, Corey, *A Second Glance* in *SCIENTIFIC AMERICAN* April 1992

Powell, Corey, *Tuning in to Deep Space* in *DISCOVER* Dec. 1999

Reber, Grote, *A New Non-Doppler Redshift* in *PHYSICS ESSAYS* Vol. No. 1 1988

Reber, Grote, *Endless, boundless, stable universe* in *Univ. of Tasmania Occasional Papers* No. 9, 1977

Rees, Martin, *The 13,000,000,000 Year Bang* in *NEW SCIENTIST* Dec. 1976

Rees, Martin, *Exploring Our Universe and Others* in *SCIENTIFIC AMERICAN* Dec. 1999

Rees, Martin and Joseph Silk, *The Origin of Galaxies* in *SCIENTIFIC AMERICAN* June 1970

Richer, Harvey B., *Have Milky Way MACHOs Been Found?* in *SCIENCE NEWS* Sept. 18, 1999

Roth, Joshua, *Gamma-Ray Bursts: A Growing Enigma* in *SKY & TELE-SCOPE* Sept. 1996

Roth, Joshua and Joel R. Primack, *Cosmology: All Sewn Up or Coming Apart at the Seams?* in *SKY & TELE-SCOPE* Jan. 1996

Rowe, Paul E., *Hydrogen gas from vacuum, Parts I & II* in *Journal of New Energy* Vol, 1 No. 2

Rowe, Paul E., *Hydrogen gas from vacuum, Part III* in *Infinite Energy* Vol 4 No. 20

Ruthen Russell, *Puzzling Powerhouse* in *SCIENTIFIC AMERICAN* Dec. 1992

Rowan-Robinson, Michael, *Cosmology* (1977)

Rubin, Vera C., *Dark Matter in Spiral Galaxies* in *SCIENTIFIC AMERICAN* June 1983

Ryback, Carol, *Star Burst Galaxies Can Become Superwinds* in *ASTRONOMY* Feb. 2000

Sagan, Carl and Frank Drake, *The Search for Extraterrestrial Intelligence* in *SCIENTIFIC AMERICAN* May 1975

Sandage, Allen R., *The Red Shift* in *SCIENTIFIC AMERICAN* Sept. 1956

Sawyer, Kathy, *Unveiling the Universe* in *National Geographic* Oct. 1999

Schmidt, Maarten and Francis Bello, *The Evolution of Quasars* in *SCIENTIFIC AMERICAN* May 1971

Schramm, David N. and Gary Steigman, *Particle Accelerators Test Cosmological Theory* in *SCIENTIFIC AMERICAN* June 1988

Sciama, Dennis, *Cosmology before and after Quasars* in *SCIENTIFIC AMERICAN* Sept. 1967

Semeniuk, Ivan, *Catching Cosmic Ghosts* in *ASTRONOMY* June 1999

Semeniuk, Ivan, *Showered in Mystery* in *ASTRONOMY* Jan. 2001

Shapley, Harlow, Editor, *The Source Book on Astronomy* (1960)

Shapiro, Robert and Gerald Feinberg, *Life Beyond Earth* (1980)

Sheldon, Eric, *Faster than Light* in *SKY & TELESCOPE* Jan. 1990

Silk, Joseph, *The Big Bang* (1980, revised 1989)

Sobel, Dava, *George Smoot Interview* in *OMNI* March 1994

Suess, H. E. and H. C. Urey, *Abundance of Elements in Review of Modern Physics* 28:53-75, 1956

Swinburne, Richard, *Argument from the Fine-Tuning of the Universe* in *Physical Cosmology and Philosophy* (1990)

Talcot, Richard, *Gamma Ray Bursters: Near of Far?* in *ASTRONOMY* Dec. 1995

Teresi, Dick, *The First Squillion Years*, book review in *The New York Times* April 1999

Thorne, Kip S., *Black Holes and Time Warps* (1994)

Thorne, Kip S., *The Search for Black Holes* in *SCIENTIFIC AMERICAN* Dec. 1974

t'Hooft, Gerard, *Gauge Theories of the Forces between Elementary Particles* in *SCIENTIFIC AMERICAN*, June 1980

Tifft, William G., *Redshift Quantization - A Review* in *Plasma Astrophysics and Cosmology* edited by A. L. Peratt (1995)

Trautman, Rachael, Brendin J. Griffin and David Scharf, *Microdiamonds* in *SCIENTIFIC AMERICAN*, Aug. 1998

Trefil, James, *Discovering Cosmic Rays* in *ASTRONOMY* Jan. 2001

Trefil, James, *The Moment of Creation* (1983)

Trefil, James, *Putting Stars in their Place* in *ASTRONOMY* Jan. 2000

Trimble, Virginia, *A Year of Discovery* in *SKY & TELESCOPE* Feb. 2000

Tryon, Edward P., *Is the Universe a Vacuum Fluctuation?* in *NATURE* Dec. 14, 1973

Turner, Edwin L., *Gravitational Lenses* in *SCIENTIFIC AMERICAN,* July 1988

van den Bergh, Sidney, *The Age and Size of the Universe* in *SCIENCE* Oct. 16, 1992

van den Bergh, Sidney and James E. Hesser, *How the Milky Way Formed* in *SCIENTIFIC AMERICAN* Jan. 1993

Van Flandern, Tom, *Dark Matter, Missing Planets and New Comets* (1993)

Veltman, Martinus J. G., *The Higgs Boson* in *SCIENTIFIC AMERICAN* Nov. 1986

Veilleux, Sylvain, Gerald Cecil and Jonathan Bland-Hawthorne, *Colossal Galactic Explosions* in *SCIENTIFIC AMERICAN* Feb. 1996

Verschuur, Gerrit L., *In the Beginning* in *ASTRONOMY* Oct. 1993

Webster, Adrian, *The Cosmic Background Radiation* in *SCIENTIFIC AMERICAN* Aug. 1974

Weinberg, Steven, *The First Three Minutes* (1977)

Weiss, Peter, *Another Face of Entropy* in *SCIENCE NEWS* Aug. 15, 1998

Wesley, J. P., *Advanced Fundamental Physics* (1991)

Wheeler, John Archibald, *Beyond the End of Time* in *Gravitation* edited by Charles W. Misner et al. (1971)

White, Simon D. M. et al., *The baryon content of galaxy clusters: a challenge to cosmological orthodoxy* in *NATURE* Dec. 2, 1993

Whitt, Kelly Kozer, *The Universe According to Arp* in *ASTRONOMY* Nov. 1999

Wilczek, Frank, *The Cosmic Asymmetry between Matter and Antimatter* in *SCIENTIFIC AMERICAN* Dec. 1980

Wilkes, Belinda, *The Emerging Picture of Quasars* in *ASTRONOMY* Dec. 1991

Will, Clifford, *Was Einstein Right?* (1986)

Yam, Philip, *Stardust Memories* in *SCIENTIFIC AMERICAN* Oct. 1990

Yilmaz, Huseyin, *Theory of Relativity and The Principles of Modern Physics* (1965)

Zimmerman, Robert, *Scoping Out the Monster Star* in *ASTRONOMY* Feb. 2000

Zimmerman, Robert, *Seeing with X-Ray Eyes* in *ASTRONOMY* May 2000

Zombeck, Martin V., *Handbook of Space, Astronomy and Astrophysics* (1990)

Zwicky, Fritz, *On the Possibilities of a Gravitational Drag of Light* in *Physics Review, Letters to the Editor* Vol. 34 Dec. 23, 1929

Zwicky, Fritz, *On the Red Shift of Spectral Lines through Interstellar Space* in Proc. N.A.S. Vol. 15, 1929

Zwicky, Fritz, *Remarks on the Red Shift from Nebulae* in *Physical Review* Vol. 18., Nov. 13, 1938

NAME INDEX

A

Abell, George O., 90, 145
Abbott, Larry, 92
Adams, C. Fred, 90, 268, 335
Aguirre, Anthony N., 202, 309
Alfvén, Hannes, 13, 232, 258, 285
Allamandola, Louis J., 281, 297
Allen, Harold, 165
Aller, L. H., 88, 284, 316
Alpher, Ralph, 16, 104-106, 113, 237
Ambarzumian, Viktor, 337
Ander, Edward, 281
Anderson, Carl, 372
Appenzeller, Tim, 247
Arp, Halton C., viii, 112, 127, 130-132, 145, 146, 150, 155, 161, 172, 255, 260, 287, 289, 303, 330
Arrhenius, Svante, 305
Aristotle, 202
Assis, Andre K.T., 262, 286, 350

B

Baade, Walter, 75, 301
Baggot, Jim, 255, 375
Bahcall, John N., 146
Barrow, John D., 41, 45, 57, 110, 115, 155, 168, 203, 227, 237, 244, 247, 305, 312, 372
Bartusiak, Marcia, 86, 95, 280, 286, 300
Beck, Sara, 271, 288
Bergson, Henri, 277
Bernstein, Max, P., 281, 297
Berrschinger, Edmond, 99
Bland-Hawthorne, Jonathan, 271, 199
Bodenheimer, Peter, 90, 268
Bohm, David, 207
Bohr, Niels, 207, 370, 371, 177

Bohringer, Hans, 42, 46, 98, 280
Bok, Bart J., 195, 275
Bondi, Herman, 16, 52, 177, 257
Bonner, W. B., 21, 33, 51, 254
Born, Max, 207, 371
Bose, S. N., 364
Boslough, John, 55, 98, 168, 253, 305, 309
Bothun, Gregory, 288
Bowyer, Stuart, 173
Boyd, Richard, 176
Brecher, Kenneth, 158, 159, 160
Briel, Ulrich G., 42, 46, 98, 280
Broadhurst, Tom, 265
Brush, Stephen G., 104
Burbidge, Geoffrey, 93, 100, 131, 177, 230, 254, 259, 270, 322, 330, 333, 335, 336
Burbidge, Margaret, 100, 177, 270, 322
Burch, James L., 271
Burleigh, Matt, 290
Burns, Jack, 290
Burrows, Adam, 298
Buseck, Peter, 281

C

Campbell, David, 90
Cardelli, Jason, 279
Carr, Bernard J., 35, 45, 52, 62, 100, 107, 172, 183, 204, 213, 249, 250, 328
Carter, Brandon, 250
Cecil, Gerald, 271, 299
Chadwick, James, 373
Chaikin, Andrew, 62
Chappell, John, viii
Charlier, C. V. L., 50
Chen, B., 301
Ciardillo, Robin, 296
Civita, Tullio, 357
Clayton, Robert, 282
Cohen, Andrew G., 205
Collins, Barry, 43, 283
Comins, Neil F., 151, 292

Glashow, Sheldon, 205, 378, 389

Gold, Thomas, 16, 52, 257, 330

Goldberg, Stanley, 181

Goldsmith, Donald, 68, 108, 109, 112, 145, 151, 185, 225, 291, 320

Gott, J. Richard, 20, 34, 61, 84, 116, 312, 313

Graham, David, 280

Greisen, Kenneth, 316

Gribbin, John, 50, 57, 142, 156, 197, 212, 221, 308

Grossman, Marcel, 357

Gulkis, Samuel, 88, 177

Gunn, James E., 20, 34, 61, 84, 87, 177, 240

Guth, Alan H., 16, 17, 62, 68, 213-218, 220, 223, 229, 238, 246, 247, 385

Guthrie, Bruce, 131

H

Harvey, Jack, 354

Harwit, Martin, 89, 114, 123, 273, 278, 314

Hawking, Stephen W., 35, 43, 116, 117, 205, 208, 244, 283, 305, 312, 313, 387, 391

Haynes, Martha, 287

Heisenberg, Werner, 207, 371, 372, 375, 377

Henry, J. Patrick, 42, 46, 98, 280

Herman, Robert, 16, 104-106, 113, 237

Hesser, James E., 45, 284

Higgs, Peter, 378

Hilgevoord, Jan, 240

Hitchens, Christopher, 331

Holberg, Erik B., 278

Holt, Steve, 150

Holtzman, John A., 287

Hogan, Craig J., 174

Hoyle, Fred, 14-16, 52, 105, 156, 172, 177, 253, 254, 257, 259, 270, 305, 331

Hubble, Edwin, 14, 36, 73-78, 91, 127, 184, 262

Huchra, John, 59, 76, 92

Humason, Milton, 15, 73, 74, 91, 184

Hu, Esther, 150

I

Ibata, Rodrigo, 290

Iben, Iceo, Jr., 178, 265

Impey, Chris, 44, 281, 288

Irwin, Michael, 155

J

Jacoby, George, 296

Jakobsen, Peter, 275

Jauncey, David F., 154

Jeans, Sir James, 269, 277, 305

Johnson, George, 202

Jones, Burton, F., 309

Jordan, Pascual, 371, 372

Joyce, James, 361

K

Kajita, Takaaki, 125

Kaler, James, 178

Kafatos, Menas, 304

Kanipe, Jeff, 100, 173, 332

Katz, Neal, 160

Kaufman, William, 155, 156

Kearns, Edward, 125

Kedziora-Chudczer, Lucyna, 154

Keel, William, 148

Kierein, John, 132, 261

King, Ivan R., 68, 87, 90, 107, 114, 144, 147, 186, 268, 282, 299, 314, 315, 354

Kinney, Anne L., 42, 97

Kirshner, Robert, 293

Klemola, Arnold, 309

Knox, Wayne, 134

Kolb, Edward W., 169, 230

Kormendy, John, 284, 293, 296, 297

Kragh, Helge, viii, 91, 104, 182, 186, 187, 198, 277, 278, 305, 335, 355

Kraan-Korteweg, Renee C., 99, 194, 283

SUBJECT INDEX

A

B

F

H

T

About the Author

WILLIAM C. MITCHELL was born in Connecticut, on December 28, 1925, attended elementary and high schools also in that state.

As a teenager, he spent over 3 years in the U. S. Navy as a radar technician. After receiving additional instruction at the Naval Research Labs on top secret radar countermeasures equipment (the birth of what is now called electronic warfare) and taught that subject for a year at the Pacific Fleet Schools in Hawaii.

He graduated from the University of Connecticut, with a B. S. in Engineering in 1950, elected to honorary engineering societies Eta Kappa Nu and Tau Beta Pi. (By age 24 he had graduated from high school, spent over 3 years in the Navy, graduated from college, was married, had an engineering position, and a son.)

He worked as a radar design engineer at Bendix Radio Corporation in Towson, Maryland and at Gilfillan Brothers and Litton Industries in the Los Angeles area for about 10 years. Later he was Chief Engineer of a small company specializing in digitally controlled industrial processing, that is, computerization of processes such as digitially controlled automatic blending of gasoline products at refineries and loading of exotic liquid missile fuel and oxidizer at Edwards Air Force Base, as early as 1960.

The last 19 years of his full-time employment as Sub-Project Engineer and later as Project Engineer at TRW Systems in Redondo Beach, California was primarily on NASA scientific spacecraft programs. But he also worked (in 1975) on such projects as the establishment of technical requirements for a new Pacific Fleet Commander In Chief headquarters (CINCPAC) in

Hawaii, and (in 1979 to 1981) on the installation of the NASA Data Tracking and Relay Satellite System (TDRSS) ground station at White Sands, New Mexico.

Following retirement from TRW (in 1981), he worked as a consultant engineer on several spacecraft programs, but also on such projects as the computerization of FBI Identification Division data information storage and retrieval in Washington, DC.

Although never fulfilling requirements for an advanced degree, Mitchell completed a number of graduate courses in mathematics, science and engineering during his years of employment.

He has in the past been an airplane pilot, with commercial license, instrument rating, and aerobatics training; and a Cessna owner for a number of years. Other interests have included, music, swimming, boating, fishing and skiing. Of special interest has been family; including Holly, his wife of 56 years, son, daughter, and grandchildren.

He became heavily involved in cosmology in the mid-1980s and, after considerable study, became disenchanted with Big Bang Theory. Since then he has worked full-time on cosmology, and wrote a number of papers on that topic. In the mid-1980s, he wrote *The Cult of the Big Bang* (now out of print) and, for the past 3 years, devoted his efforts to the preparation of this book, *Bye Bye Big Bang - Hello Reality*.

BYE BYE BIG BANG